This is the first book to use all the Aramaic Dead Sea scrolls to reconstruct original Aramaic sources from parts of Mark's Gospel. The scrolls have enabled the author to revolutionise the methodology of such work, and to reconstruct whole passages which he interprets in their original cultural context. The passages from which sources are reconstructed are Mark 9.11–13; 2.23–3.6; 10.35–45; and 14.12–26. A detailed discussion of each passage is offered, demonstrating that these sources are completely accurate accounts from the ministry of Jesus, from early sabbath disputes to his final Passover. An account of the translation process is given, showing how problems in Mark's text arose from the difficulty of translating some Aramaic expressions into Greek, including the notoriously difficult 'son of man'. A very early date for these sources is proposed, implying a date c. 40 CE for Mark's Gospel.

MAURICE CASEY is Reader in Early Jewish and Christian Studies in the Department of Theology at the University of Nottingham, where he has been since 1979. He has written three previous books: *Son of Man: The Interpretation and Influence of Daniel 7* (1980); *From Jewish Prophet to Gentile God: The Origins and Development of New Testament Christology* (1991); and *Is John's Gospel True?* (1996).

SOCIETY FOR NEW TESTAMENT STUDIES

MONOGRAPH SERIES

General editor: Richard Bauckham

102

ARAMAIC SOURCES OF MARK'S GOSPEL

Aramaic Sources of Mark's Gospel

MAURICE CASEY

CAMBRIDGE
UNIVERSITY PRESS

PUBLISHED BY THE PRESS SYNDICATE OF THE UNIVERSITY OF CAMBRIDGE
The Pitt Building, Trumpington Street, Cambridge CB2 1RP, United Kingdom

CAMBRIDGE UNIVERSITY PRESS
The Edinburgh Building, Cambridge CB2 2RU, United Kingdom
40 West 20th Street, New York, NY 10011–4211, USA
10 Stamford Road, Oakleigh, Melbourne 3166, Australia

First published 1998

Printed in the United Kingdom at the University Press, Cambridge

Typeset in Times 10/12pt [CE]

A catalogue record for this book is available from the British Library

Library of Congress Cataloguing in Publication data
Casey, Maurice.
Aramaic sources of Mark's Gospel / Maurice Casey.
    p.   cm. – (Society for New Testament Studies Monograph series 102)
Includes bibliographical references and index.
ISBN 0 521 63314 1 (hardback)
1. Bible. N.T. Mark – Sources.
2. Dead Sea scrolls – Relation to the New Testament.
3. Aramaic literature – Relation to the New Testament.
4. Jesus Christ – Language.
I. Title.   II. Series: Monograph series (Society for New Testament Studies); 102.
BS2585.2.C35   1998
226.3′042–dc21   98–13839   CIP

ISBN 0 521 63314 1 hardback

CONTENTS

PREFACE

This book was written in 1994–6, when I held a British Academy Research Readership awarded for the purpose. I am extremely grateful to the Academy for this award, which enabled me to complete a major piece of research.

I am also grateful to all those who have discussed with me the problems of method and of detail which this work has entailed. I effectively began this research while reading for a doctorate at Durham University under Professor C. K. Barrett, whose extraordinary combination of learning and helpfulness with lack of bureaucracy or interference remains a model to which one can only aspire. I should particularly like to thank also the late Professor M. Black, Dr G. J. Brooke, Professor B. D. Chilton, Professor J. A. Fitzmyer, Professor R. Kearns, the late Professor B. Lindars, Professor M. Müller, and Professor M. Wilcox. I should also like to thank members of the Aramaic Background and Historical Jesus seminars at the Society for New Testament Studies, the Jesus seminar at meetings of British New Testament scholars, and an annual seminar on the use of the Old Testament in the New now generally held at Hawarden, for what I have learnt from them. I alone am responsible for what I have said.

I should also like to thank Professor A. C. Thiselton, Head of the Department of Theology at the University of Nottingham since 1991, for his impartial and unfailing support of work; my Nottingham colleague Dr R. H. Bell for many hours spent sorting out problems with the word processor on which this book was written; and the libraries of Durham University, St Andrews University, the School of Oriental and African Studies and the British Library for the facilities necessary for advanced scholarly work.

Finally, I should like to thank Professor R. Bauckham, Ms R. Parr and an anonymous Aramaist for their favourable comments and acceptance of this work for publication in very mildly revised form.

ABBREVIATIONS

Most abbreviations are standard. Those for biblical books follow the recommendations of Cambridge University Press; those for periodicals and series of monographs follow S. Schwertner, *International Glossary of Abbreviations for Theology and Related Subjects* (Berlin/New York, 1974); most others follow the recommendations for contributors to *Biblica*. Others are as follows:

ABRL   Anchor Bible Reference Library
ANRW   H. Temporini and W. Haase (eds.), *Aufstieg und Niedergang der Römischen Welt*, many vols. (Berlin, 1972–)
BN   *Biblische Notizen*
IJSL   *International Journal for the Sociology of Language*
JSP   *Journal for the Study of the Pseudepigrapha*
JSS.S   Journal of Semitic Studies, Supplements
MPIL   Monographs of the Peshitta Institute, Leiden
TWNT   G. Kittel and G. Friedrich (eds.), *Theologisches Wörterbuch zum Neuen Testament*, 10 vols. (Stuttgart, 1933–79)

1

THE STATE OF PLAY

The Gospel of Mark is written in Greek, though Jesus spoke Aramaic. Moreover, Jesus' ministry was exercised among Jews, whereas, by the time Mark's Gospel was written, many of Jesus' followers were Gentiles, and this Gospel shows traces of Gentile self-identification. It follows that the change in language from Aramaic to Greek was part of a cultural shift from a Jewish to a Gentile environment. If therefore we wish to recover the Jesus of history, we must see whether we can reconstruct his sayings, and the earliest accounts of his doings, in their original Aramaic. This should help us to understand him within his own cultural background.

For this purpose, we must establish a clear methodology, not least because some people are still repeating every mistake with which the history of scholarship is littered. I therefore begin with a critical Forschungsberichte. This is not a comprehensive catalogue of previous work, but a selective discussion of what advances have been made, what significant mistakes have been made, and the reasons for both of these.

The early fathers give us very little reliable information about the transmission of Jesus' words in Aramaic before the writing of the Gospels. Eusebius has the apostles speak ἡ Σύρων φωνή (*Dem. Ev.* III.4.44; 7.10), his name for the Aramaic dialects contemporary with him, but he gives us no significant help in getting behind the Gospel traditions. He quotes Papias early in the second century, Ματθαῖος μὲν οὖν Ἑβραΐδι διαλέκτῳ τὰ λόγια συνετάξατο, ἡρμήνευσεν δ'αὐτὰ ὡς ἦν δυνατὸς ἕκαστος (*HE* III.39.16). This is not true of Matthew's Gospel as a whole, but it may reflect the transmission of Gospel traditions in Aramaic.

There are plausible reports of lost Gospels written in a Hebrew language, probably Aramaic rather than Hebrew. Jerome, understandably stuck on ἐπιούσιον in the Lord's prayer, looked in a

Gospel called 'according to the Hebrews', and found 'maar', with the sense 'crastinum', 'to-morrow's', and hence a future reference.[1] This is very likely to be right, a preservation of the Lord's prayer from the Aramaic-speaking church.[2] מחר really does mean 'tomorrow's', and the reference is likely to have been eschatological. Those Gospels which survive, however, all of them in the dialects of Aramaic generally known as Syriac, are translations from our present Greek Gospels *into* Aramaic. The process of translating the Greek Gospels into Aramaic is significantly different from trying to reconstruct original sources. Nowhere is this better illustrated than with the term 'son of man'. This was originally the Aramaic בר (א)נש(א), a normal term for 'man'. By the processes of translation and Christological development, this became a Christological title in Greek, ὁ υἱὸς τοῦ ἀνθρώπου.[3] Since it had become a Christological title, it could not be translated *into* Syriac with בר (א)נש(א). Hence Tatian produced the expression ברה ראנשא, and later translators produced also ברה דגברא and ברה דברנשא. These expressions naturally lent themselves to interpretation remote from the original בר (א)נש(א). Philoxenus of Mabbug commented:

עלהדא לם אתקרי ברה דאנשא, מטל דהוא ברה דאנשא
חדתא דקמם עבר פוקדנא.

'For this reason, then, he was called "the (lit. his) son of (the) man", because he became the (lit. "his") son of the new man who preceded the transgression of the commandment.'[4] Here the term has been interpreted as 'the son of *the* man', and the man in question has been identified as Adam, so that in effect the term is held to mean 'son of Adam'. This is quite remote from the meaning of the original בר (א)נש(א). Once ברה דאנשא was established as the term which Jesus used to refer to himself, Syriac fathers could use בר (א)נש(א) of him in its original sense, apparently unaware that he had done so, and in ways remote from his view of himself. An anonymous poem on faith has this:

---

[1] D. Hurst and M. Adriaen (eds.), *S. Hieronymi Presbyteri Opera*. Pars I, 7. *Commentariorum in Matheum Libri IV* (CCSL LXXVII. Turnholti, 1969), ad loc.
[2] J. Jeremias, *New Testament Theology*, vol. I (London, 1971), pp. 196, 199–201; see p. 51 below.
[3] See pp. 111–21, 130–2 below.
[4] J. W. Watt (ed.), *Philoxenus of Mabbug: Fragments of the Commentary on Matthew and Luke* (CSCO 392, SS 171. Leuven, 1978), frag. 23.

לא הוא לבר אנשא בתולתא טעינא הות

It was not (a/the) son of man that the virgin was carrying.[5]

What this means is that Mary gave birth to Jesus as both God and man, not only to a man as a normal human mother does. Thus the Syriac versions and fathers alike, though helpful in some matters if used carefully, are no simple guide to what was said and meant by Aramaic sources of the Gospels.

The next significant development took place as independent scholarship emerged slowly from the Reformation and the Enlightenment. A few learned men noticed Semitic features in the Greek of the Gospels, and sought to explain them with reference to the actual Semitic terms which lay behind them. As scripturally orientated scholars, however, they tended to resort to Hebrew rather than Aramaic, because their primary resource was the Old Testament. Sometimes, this did not matter in itself. For example, in 1557 Theodore Beza commented on the idiomatic use of πρόσωπον at Matt. 16.3, 'Hebraicè פנים'.[6] This points to a correct understanding of this idiomatic usage.

Such an approach, however, will inevitably come to grief when Aramaic and Hebrew are seriously different. The term 'son of man' is again the best example of this. Commenting on Matt. 12.8 in 1641, Grotius gave several reasons why ὁ υἱὸς τοῦ ἀνθρώπου could not be a simple reference to Christ, including that 'בן אדם [*filium hominis*]' meant 'hominem quemvis', 'any man'.[7] This comes close to a reason why ὁ υἱὸς τοῦ ἀνθρώπου could not be a Christological title on the lips of Jesus, but it leaves insoluble problems behind it. If we know only this, we cannot explain why Jesus used the Aramaic term (א)בר (א)נש, or how it came to be transmuted into a Christological title. The Bible-centred nature of this limitation is especially obvious in Grotius, for he could read Aramaic and Syriac.

During this period, scholars also edited texts and wrote works of reference. The first edition of the Syriac New Testament caused a great stir in 1555, on account of its claim to be written in the

[5] S. P. Brock, 'An Anonymous Madrasha on Faith', *OrChr* 64, 1980, 48–64, p. 50, stanza 4, line 1.

[6] T. Beza, *Novum d n Jesu Christi testamentum* (Geneva, 1557), ad loc. I had access to *JESU CHRISTI D. N. Novum Testamentum* (Geneva, 1565).

[7] H. Grotius, *Annotationes in libros evangeliorum* (Amsterdam/Paris, 1641), ad loc. I had access to this as *Annotationes in quatuor Evangelia & Acta Apostolorum* in *H. Grotii Opera Omnia Theologica* (Amsterdam, 1679), book II, vol. I.

language of Jesus.[8] In 1596 the Maronite George Michael Amira made a similar claim in the introduction to his Syriac grammar, giving this as a reason for its usefulness. He proceeded to illustrate this, commenting for example on ταλιθα κουμι (Mk 5.41): ܛܠܺܝܬܳܐ ܩܽܘܡܝ . . . id est, puella surge, "girl, get up"'. He inferred from this that Christ used the Syriac language.[9]

One of the most impressive text editions was the Walton polyglott, published in 1655–7.[10] The title page declares its contents, including the text of the Bible, with the Samaritan Pentateuch, the Targums, the LXX, the Syriac and other versions, with Latin translations of the oriental texts and versions. While paying tribute to his predecessors, Walton noted his improvements, including more extensive presentation of Aramaic and Syriac versions. Two pieces of prolegomena are also especially relevant. Proleg. XII *De Lingua Chaldaica & Targumim*, 'On the Chaldaean Language and the Targums', was a very sound introduction for its day. Correct information includes sorting out the different names for this language: 'appellata est Syriaca à regione Syriae, Aramaea ab Aram, & ab Assyria Assyriaca: aliquando etiam dicta est Hebraea . . . quod populus Hebraeus post captivitatem Babylonicam hac usus sit pro vernacula'.[11] It is not surprising that Walton found the Targums difficult to date. One of his errors of method is still found among New Testament scholars: he used New Testament parallels in arguing for an early date for whole Targums.[12] In the mid seventeenth century that was a reasonable thing to do. We have now noticed, however, that it is some traditions which are thus shown to be early, and these may be incorporated in Targums which did not reach their present form until centuries later. Another useful prolegomenon was XIII, *De Lingua Syriaca, et Scripturae Versionibus Syriacis*, 'On the Syriac Language, and the Syriac Versions of Scripture'. This contains a very learned and coherent discussion of the dialect spoken by Christ and the apostles. Taking up claims that Jesus spoke Syriac, Walton concludes that this is the right language, but not the right dialect.

[8] J. A. Widmanstadius and M. Merdenas (eds.), *Liber Sacrosancti Evangelii de Jesu Christo Domino et Deo nostro* (Vienna, 1555).

[9] *GRAMMATICA SYRIACA, SIVE CHALDAICA*, Georgij Michaelis Amirae Edeniensis è Libano, Philosophi, ac Theologi, Collegij Maronitarum Alumni (Rome, 1596), (unnumbered) p. 7.

[10] B. Waltonus et al. (eds.), *Biblia Sacra Polyglotta* (6 vols., London, 1655–7).

[11] *Ibid.*, vol. I, p. 81.

[12] *Ibid.*, vol. I, p. 85.

Throughout this period, the publication of texts, commentaries and works of reference formed an important contribution to knowledge. Significant analytical developments had to await the massive explosion of knowledge which took place in the Victorian era. New discoveries included two hitherto unknown Syriac versions of most of the canonical Gospels, the Old Syriac and the Christian Palestinian Syriac lectionary. They too caused excitement because they were in the right language. Cureton, who discovered the first part of the Old Syriac, declared, 'this Syriac text of the Gospel of St. Matthew which I now publish has, to a great extent, retained the identical terms and expressions which the Apostle himself employed; and . . . we have here, in our Lord's discourses, to a great extent the very same words as the Divine Author of our holy religion himself uttered in proclaiming the glad tidings of salvation in the Hebrew dialect to those who were listening to him, and through them, to all the world'.[13] The Palestinian Syriac lectionary of the Gospels was from the right area, as well as in the right language. The first codex came to light in the eighteenth century, and the discovery of two further codices in 1892–3 led to the publication of the standard edition.[14]

Others scholars turned to Jewish Aramaic. In 1894, Dalman published his *Grammatik des jüdisch-palästinischen Aramäisch*.[15] This was a valuable study of the Aramaic which it investigated. At the same time, some obvious problems were looming, if this Aramaic was taken as the major source for reconstructing sayings of Jesus. Dalman used sources which were much later in date than the Gospels, and he made extensive use of selected Targums. If we used this Aramaic to 'reconstruct' Gospel narratives and sayings of Jesus, we might end up with the wrong dialect, and with translation Aramaic rather than the natural language.

The Victorian era also saw the production of the major rabbinical dictionaries of Levy and Jastrow.[16] These were fine pieces of

---

[13] W. Cureton (ed.), *Remains of a Very Antient Recension of the Four Gospels in Syriac, hitherto unknown in Europe* (London, 1858), p. xciii.

[14] A. S. Lewis and M. D. Gibson (eds.), *The Palestinian Syriac Lectionary of the Gospels, Re-edited from two Sinai MSS. and from P. de Lagarde's Edition of the 'Evangeliarium Hierosolymitanum'* (London, 1899).

[15] G. Dalman, *Grammatik des jüdisch-palästinischen Aramäisch nach den Idiomen des palästinischen Talmud und Midrasch, des Onkelostargum (Cod. Socini 84) und der jerusalemischen Targume zum Pentateuch* (Leipzig, 1894. ²1905).

[16] J. Levy, *Chaldäisches Wörterbuch über die Targumim und einem grossen Theil des rabbinischer Schriftthums* (2 vols., Leipzig, 1867–8; ³1881); J. Levy, *Neuhebräisches und chaldäisches Wörterbuch über die Talmudim und Midraschim* (4 vols.,

work, and in their own right significant contributions to knowledge, which greatly facilitated the study of rabbinical literature. More than a century later, they remain indispensable for serious research workers. Problems have arisen in the work of scholars who have used them to reconstruct sayings of Jesus, but who have not always had first-hand acquaintance with rabbinical texts. Such faults are not those of the compilers.

While these major developments were in train, a number of detailed suggestions were made, which brought both progress and problems of method. For example, Nestle suggested that Luke's 'cities' in his version of the parable of the talents (Matt. 25.14–30// Luke 19.11–27) was due to the misunderstanding of כּכְּרִין, 'talents', which had been read as כּרכִין, 'cities'.[17] At one level, this was a bright idea. Matthew and Luke have parallel passages with many variations: alternative translations of Aramaic sources were a possibility worth exploring, and misunderstandings and mistakes might seem to be a good way of verifying that something has gone wrong. This example has, however, all the problems which have attended such attempts. In the first place, the Lukan version makes sense on its own. Jesus might have said both parables, for they are very different, or the Lukan version might have been told and retold by people who liked it better in the Lukan form. Secondly, כּרכִין is not the only Aramaic word for 'cities': the choice of this word is especially arbitrary when the Lukan version is sensible.

A number of suggestions were made in a long series of articles by J. T. Marshall.[18] Some of his points were perfectly sound, though not necessarily new. He explained that Ἑβραϊστί at John 5.2; 19. 13, 17 must mean 'in Aramaic' rather than 'in Hebrew' because of the Aramaic endings of Βηθεσδά, Γαββαθα and Γολγοθα. He

Leipzig, 1876–89. 2nd edn, Berlin/Vienna, 1924); M. Jastrow, *A Dictionary of the Targumim, the Talmud Babli and Yerushalmi, and the Midrashic Literature* (2 vols. London, 1886–1903. Rep. New York, 1950).

[17] An almost off-hand comment in a book review, *TLZ* 20, 1895, 565.

[18] J. T. Marshall, 'The Aramaic Gospel', *Expositor*, 4th series, 3, 1891, 1–17, 109–24, 205–20, 275–91, 375–90, 452–67; 4, 1891, 208–23, 373–88, 435–48; 6, 1892, 81–97; cf. W. C. Allen, 'The Aramaic Gospel', *Expositor*, 4th series, 7, 1893, 386–400, 454–70; S. R. Driver, 'Professor Marshall's Aramaic Gospel', *Expositor*, 4th series, 8, 1893, 388–400, 419–31; J. T. Marshall, 'The Aramaic Gospel', *ExpT* 4, 1892–3, 260–7; C. Campbell, 'Professor Marshall's Theory of an Aramaic Gospel', *ExpT* 4, 1892–3, 468–70; J. T. Marshall, 'The Aramaic Gospel: Reply to Dr. Driver and Mr Allen', *Expositor*, 4th series, 8, 1893, 176–92; E. Nestle, 'The Semitic and the Greek Gospels', *ExpT* 8, 1896–7, 42–3, 138–9; J. T. Marshall, 'The Semitic and the Greek Gospels', *ExpT* 8, 1896–7, 90–1.

correctly explained ταλιθα κουμι (Mark 5.41) and ἀββα (Mark 14.36), and he associated σαβαχθανι (Mark 15.34) with the Aramaic form of Ps. 22.1. He consulted the Targums in passages where the LXX has words found in the Gospels. He also has a good account of problems which arise when material is translated from one language to another.[19] His work has, however, a number of problems which proved difficult to resolve. One was over vocabulary. Allen accused him of coining for words meanings which they did not possess. His examples included ארבעה, 'bed', which Allen argued was used only of cattle, with the meaning 'act of lying down'. Marshall correctly pointed out that רבע does mean 'recline' of human beings, but it is only with the discovery of 4Q Tobit that we have early evidence of this, and Driver responded rightly by commenting that this did not justify the production of a noun, ארבעה or מרבעא, 'bed'.[20] The underlying problem was the absence of Aramaic from the right period. Creative Aramaists responded somewhat like native speakers, extending the semantic areas of words to provide whatever meanings they needed: accurate critics pointed out that they had gone beyond the evidence of extant texts.

Another problem was the reconstruction of Jesus' dialect: Marshall proposed to use Talmudic evidence fleshed out with the Samaritan Targum.[21] All this evidence is late, and the available text of the Samaritan Targum was hopelessly corrupted by mediaeval scribes. Marshall's model of the synoptic problem was also difficult: he interpreted variants as translation variants without proper consideration of whether one might be due to secondary editing. For example, he interpreted ὀφειλήματα (Matt. 6.12) and ἁμαρτίας (Luke 11.4) as alternative translations of one Aramaic original, without considering whether ἁμαρτίας may be a Greek revision of the Semitising ὀφειλήματα. Allen properly pointed out that the rare word ἐπιούσιον (Matt. 6.11//Luke 11.3) implies a single Greek translation.[22] Some of Marshall's points depend on misreadings which are at best very hypothetical. For example, he suggested that the difference between ἀπολέσωσιν (Mark 3.6) and ποιήσαιεν

---

[19] Marshall, 'Aramaic Gospel', *Expositor*, 4th series, 3, 1891, 10, 11, 276–8, 116ff.

[20] Allen, 'Aramaic Gospel', 388, 395–6; Marshall, 'Reply to Dr. Driver and Mr Allen', 183; Driver, 'Professor Marshall's Aramaic Gospel', 392–3.

[21] Marshall, 'Aramaic Gospel', *Expositor*, 4th series, 4, 1891, 208ff.

[22] Marshall, 'Aramaic Gospel', *Expositor*, 4th series, 3, 1891, 124; Allen, 'Aramaic Gospel', 468–9.

(Luke 6.11) was due to a confusion between אבד and עבד. Equally, however, Luke may have editcd Mark. This is the preferable hypothesis because it makes sense both of passages where verbal identity is too great for us to posit separate translations and of Lukan editing. It is also a disadvantage that Marshall is dealing with single words. Driver correctly demanded whole sentences before the method could be seen clearly enough for a final judgement to be passed on it.[23]

It follows that Marshall's work could not take this set of problems to an acceptable conclusion. At least, however, Marshall, Driver and Allen worked with the correct view that Jesus spoke Aramaic. This was not clear to everyone. A few scholars argued that Jesus taught in Hebrew. At the end of the nineteenth century, Resch argued this in some detail, and he sought to reconstruct דִּבְרֵי יֵשׁוּעַ in Hebrew.[24] This work has a number of faults of method which still recur in scholarship. One is Resch's basic failure to distinguish between an edited translation *into* Hebrew, which he offers, and serious reconstruction. So, for example, he follows Matthew and Luke in omitting Mark 2.27, and puts what is effectively a translation of Luke 6.5 (//Matt. 12.8//Mark 2.27–8) as his verse 29, *after* Mark 3.5//Matt. 12.13// Luke 6.10, its position in Codex Bezae:

וַיֹּאמֶר אֲלֵיהֶם בֶּן־הָאָדָם גַּם אֲדוֹן הַשַּׁבָּת

This does not permit an explanation of *why* Jesus used בן־האדם, a traditional translation of ὁ υἱὸς τοῦ ἀνθρώπου *into* Hebrew, or of why Mark added 2.27 and put ὥστε at the beginning of 2.28, or of why anyone moved what has become a statement of Jesus' sole authority over the sabbath away from the end of the two pericopes in which sabbath halakhah is disputed. Ironically, Resch has made it more rather than less difficult to explain Jesus' teaching in its original cultural context.

Another major fault is to suppose that synoptic parallels are to be explained from misreadings of a Hebrew underlay. For example, at Matt. 10.10//Luke 10.7 Resch suggests that the original reading was מִחְיָה, correctly translated as τροφῆς (Matt. 10.10). This was

[23] Marshall, 'Aramaic Gospel', *Expositor*, 4th series, 3, 1891, 465–6; Driver, 'Professor Marshall's Aramaic Gospel', 430–1.

[24] A. Resch, *Aussercanonische Paralleltexte zu den Evangelien* (TU X. 5 vols., Leipzig, 1893–7); A. Resch, *Die Logia Jesu* (Leipzig, 1898); A. Resch, ספרי תלדות ישוע המשיח (Leipzig, 1898).

corrupted to מחיתו, so the other translator decided to read מחירו and translated τοῦ μισθοῦ αὐτοῦ (Luke 10.7).[25] But it is difficult to see why the original text should have had מחיה rather than שׂכר, conjectured misreadings are not enough to solve the synoptic problem, and in this case Matthew had good contextual reason to alter μισθοῦ to τροφῆς.

Thirdly, Resch could not explain Aramaic evidence. At Mark 15.34//Matt. 27.46, he follows Codex Bezae in supposing that Jesus said Ps. 22.1 in Hebrew, and he suggests that the Aramaic version in most manuscripts was produced when Hebrew was no longer understood.[26] This argument cannot cope with the weight of attestation in favour of the Aramaic version, nor is it a convincing explanation of change in Greek Gospels. The Greek translations also supplied at Mark 15.34//Matt. 27.46 make it unnecessary for everyone to understand the Aramaic, and it is very doubtful whether Aramaic was better understood by Greek-speaking congregations than Hebrew was. The variant reading of Bezae, however, is readily explained as assimilation to the canonical text of Ps. 22.1. Resch was not helped by supposing that ἐλωî = אֱלֹהִי and לְמָא must both be Hebrew, which led him to describe the Gospel evidence as a *Mischtext*. This should not be accepted. Any source is most unlikely to have been vocalised, so the ω is the decision of a transliterator who was not very good at transliteration, may have suffered from interference from the Hebrew אֱלֹהִים, and may have pronounced the Aramaic ā as ọ̄, for this shift is attested elsewhere (for example אֱנוֹשׁ for אֱנָשׁ, 1QapGen XXI.13).[27] The word למה is perfectly good Hebrew. Resch should have known that it was Aramaic too from Ezra 4.22 (cf. 7.23), and from later evidence: early attestation is more abundant now (for example 1QapGen XXII.32). Resch's description of the quotation of Ps. 22.1 as a *Mischtext* is accordingly the kind of mistake which was understandable a century ago, and which we should no longer make.

While a few scholars argued that Jesus taught in Hebrew, some argued that he taught in Greek. In 1767, Diodatus argued this, primarily on the basis of the hellenisation of Judaism.[28] Having surveyed the evidence down to 1 Maccabees, noting towards the

---

[25] Resch, *Aussercanonische Paralleltexte* III, pp. 182–4.
[26] *Ibid.*, pp. 355–61.
[27] K. Beyer, *Die aramäischen Texte vom Toten Meer* (Göttingen, 1984), p. 137.
[28] D. Diodati, *DE CHRISTO GRAECE LOQUENTE EXERCITATIO* (Naples, 1767; rep. London, 1843).

end the evidence of extreme hellenisation at 1 Macc. 1.14–17, he inferred that Greek was widely spoken in Judaea. He argued that at this stage Jewish people were bilingual, but he supposed that Aramaic died out in the succeeding years. As evidence he noted documents such as the Wisdom of Solomon written in Greek, and the need for Ecclesiasticus to be translated into Greek. He also noted evidence such as the inscriptions on Herod's coins being in Greek.[29] He added the evidence of the New Testament being written in Greek. He then made a crucial point, commenting that if we consider Judaea at the time of Christ, we find no document written in Chaldaean or Syriac.[30] This was true when Diodatus wrote it, and made his view a great deal more reasonable then than it has been since the discovery of the Dead Sea scrolls. His presentation had, however, three serious weaknesses which could be seen at the time. His presentation of the hellenisation of Judaism is undifferentiated by identity: the hellenisation of people like Herod and those mentioned in 1 Macc. 1.14–17 does not entail the hellenisation of faithful Jews. Secondly, his detailed arguments from Gospel evidence assume the literal truth of its surface narrative. In Luke 4, for example, the LXX is quoted when Jesus reads from the Bible,[31] but the story may not be literally true, or it may use the Bible of Greek-speaking Christians to communicate with them, even though Jesus read from a Hebrew scroll. Thirdly, Diodatus could not cope with Gospel evidence that Jesus spoke Aramaic. He suggests that the Aramaic words in the Gospels show occasional use of Aramaic words, not that Aramaic was the vernacular,[32] but he was quite unable to explain this occasional use.

In 1888, Roberts attempted a more thorough and extensive presentation of the same view.[33] He suffers from the same problems as Diodatus. The assumption that the surface level of the Gospels is literally true is worse than ever. For example, at John 12.20ff., some Greeks come to see Jesus. However, the result of this is not that Jesus sees the Greeks, but that he comments on his death, which had to take place before Greeks could enter the churches. We should infer that Jesus did not see them. Roberts, however,

---

[29] *Ibid.*, pp. 37, 76, 85ff.

[30] *Ibid.*, p. 153.

[31] *Ibid.*, pp. 123–5.

[32] *Ibid.*, p. 163.

[33] A. Roberts, *Greek: The Language of Christ and his Apostles* (London, 1888); similarly T. K. Abbott, *Essays, Chiefly on the Original Texts of the Old and New Testaments* (London, 1891), pp. 129–82.

imagines that they must have been present for this speech, so Jesus did see them, and must have spoken Greek so that they could understand him.[34] This is not a convincing interpretation of the text, and ignores the fact that most of the fourth Gospel is not historically true. This was also easier to do in 1888 than it is now. Roberts also generalises Diodatus' argument from the LXX. He notes correctly that Jesus is represented as relying on written scriptures. He suggests that Hebrew was a dead language, and declares that there were no written Targums (that shown to Gamaliel, t. Shab 13.2; y. Shab 15c. 5–7; b. Shab 115a, being unofficial and not accepted). This leaves the LXX as the only version which Jesus could have used.[35] Here too we must note that in 1888 the opinion that Hebrew was a dead language was reasonable, given the prevailing views of Daniel and of Mishnah, and the fact that the Hebrew documents from the Dead Sea had not been discovered. Equally, the view that there were no written Targums was reasonable when the Dead Sea Targums had not been found.

It follows that Roberts gets into his most obvious tangles in trying to explain the Gospel evidence that Jesus spoke Aramaic. He follows Diodatus in supposing that the Aramaic words mean that Jesus used Aramaic occasionally. At once, he has to admit that there is no evident reason for Jesus to have used Aramaic when the Gospels attribute Aramaic words to him.[36] This is an important weakness, mitigated in 1888 by the fact that no one understood translators well enough to explain why they retained some few words and not more. On Mark 5.41, Roberts suggests that the girl to whom Jesus spoke in Aramaic was the daughter of a strictly Jewish family and therefore not familiar with Greek.[37] This is reasonable in itself, but Roberts does not seem to have realised that it is reasonable only if we undermine his reasons for thinking that everyone spoke Greek. At Mark 15.34 he is in such a quandary that he argues that Jesus said Ps. 22.1 in Hebrew, repeating his distinguished type (David),[38] but the evidence is clearly Aramaic and there is no typology in the text.

These weaknesses are sufficiently severe for the view that Jesus

---

[34] Roberts, *Greek*, pp. 157–9.
[35] *Ibid.*, *Greek*, ch. V.
[36] *Ibid.*, *Greek*, pp. 96–8.
[37] *Ibid.*, *Greek*, pp. 105–6.
[38] *Ibid.*, *Greek*, pp. 108–9.

taught in Greek to have remained that of a small minority. It is none the less significant that such views were more reasonable when they were first put forward than they are now, following the discovery of the Dead Sea scrolls.

The view that Jesus spoke and taught in Aramaic was accordingly the prevailing view in 1896, the first watershed in the study of our subject. This year saw the publication of the first major monograph which attempted to see behind the Greek Gospels to the Aramaic sayings of Jesus: Meyer, *Jesu Muttersprache*.[39] Meyer assembled the main evidence for believing that Jesus spoke Aramaic, and supplied a sensible discussion of what Aramaic sources should be used. He tried to go for Galilean Aramaic, since this was Jesus' dialect. For this purpose he used both the Jewish Aramaic of the Palestinian Talmud and Christian Palestinian Syriac. He stated openly that these sources were too late in date, but since earlier ones were not available, he used them all the same. The great advance which he made was to offer reconstructions of whole Aramaic sentences, which he located in their original cultural context. For example, he suggested this for Mark 2.27–8:[40]

שבתא בגין ברנשא איתעבידת ולא ברנשא בגין שבתא:
בגלל כן מריה הוא דשבתא ברנשא.

The great advantage of this is that it enables the final example of ברנשא to appear as it must appear in Aramaic, as a normal term for man. Only a whole sentence can do this, and whole sentences cannot fail to do it. For this reason, the procedure as a whole was an essential step forward. This is a particularly good example, because the son of man statement of Mark 2.28 is closely tied to the unambiguously general statement of 2.27. At the same time, the proposed reconstruction has problems. One is positing ברנשא behind both examples of ὁ ἄνθρωπος in 2.27. This made it difficult to understand the translator, and Meyer made no serious attempt to do so. The use of the late expression בגלל כן behind the difficult ὥστε is also problematical: it would surely have been more likely to have given rise to διὰ τοῦτο.

---

[39] A. Meyer, *Jesu Muttersprache: Das galiläische Aramäisch in seiner Bedeutung für die Erklärung der Reden Jesu und der Evangelien überhaupt* (Freiburg i. B. / Leipzig, 1896).
[40] *Ibid.*, p. 93.

Meyer's reconstruction of Matt. 12.32 further illustrates these points:[41]

כל דיימר מלא על ברנש ישתביק לה וכל דיימר על
רוחא דקודשא לא ישתביק לה.

Here too, it is a great advantage that the complete sentence ensures that ברנש emerges as a normal term for man. It is also good that there are no problems with the late date of the Aramaic used. Moreover, this is a Q saying, and the proposed reconstruction permits the understanding of Luke 12.10 as an alternative under-standing of the same Aramaic. This might have led to important advances in our understanding of Q. Also helpful was Meyer's reference to Mark 3.28, πάντα ἀφεθήσεται τοῖς υἱοῖς τῶν ἀνθρώπων, where he saw a clear echo of ברנשא in the original saying. None the less, he had insufficient appreciation of the need to understand the translator. The use of ברנש in the indefinite state, which is entirely reasonable on Aramaic grounds, requires an explanation of the consistent use of the articles in ὁ υἱὸς τοῦ ἀνθρώπου. Meyer compared the use of בר נשא with ההוא גברא,[42] but this is a different expression, and he was not able to show that the one was used like the other.

As we consider Meyer's work a century afterwards, his great advance is his attempt to produce complete reconstructions of some sayings. At the same time, however, his work left five definable problems which continue to require attention.

1. Much of the Aramaic which he used was from sources which were too late in date. Meyer knew this perfectly well, but there was nothing that he could do about it. One consequence was simply that a lot of his work could not be verified. A second result has remained concealed ever since: no one could see how far his ability to produce puns and the like really resulted from his use of a wider range of Aramaic than was ever available to Jesus.

2. It follows that his work contains too many puns. For example, at Matt. 3.9//Luke 3.8, Meyer suggests a *Gleichklang* between אבניא for λίθων and בניא for τέκνα. That is not unreason-able, but it does involve the selection of בניא, which might well have been translated υἵους, rather than ינקין, which was bound to be rendered τέκνα. He then suggests that the difference between δόξητε at Matt. 3.9 and ἄρξησθε at Luke 3.8 is due to the

difference between תִּשְׁרוּן and תְּשַׁרוּן, and that this is evidence of an Aramaic *Grundlage*.[43] There are two things wrong with this. One is that the case for this difference in Aramaic cannot be confirmed for Aramaic of the right period. The other is that it does not permit a plausible model for the behaviour of the translator(s). The whole of the surrounding context is verbally identical in Greek. This does not make sense of having two translators. If, however, there was only one translator, it is more plausible to suppose that this part of Q reached the evangelists in Greek, and that one of them altered it for stylistic reasons, as both of them altered Mark. It follows that what particularly impressed Meyer as evidence of an Aramaic *Grundlage* cannot function as such.

3. This is part of the larger problem that Meyer could not see how translators worked. His treatments of both ὁ υἱὸς τοῦ ἀνθρώπου and of δόξητε//ἄρξησθε are examples of this. It is still a serious problem. We shall see that recent research in Translation Studies in general and the LXX in particular can be fruitfully applied here.

4. Several suggestions for a common underlay for more than one passage of Greek form bright suggestions which have never been worked through thoroughly enough to show that there ever was such an underlay. For example, at Matt. 21.31–2//Luke 7.29–30, Meyer suggests that Matthew's βασιλείαν τοῦ θεοῦ represents מַלְכוּתָא דיהוה, while Luke's βουλὴν τοῦ θεοῦ represents מִילְכְתָא דיהוה. He further suggests that Matthew's προάγουσιν represents זְכִי (Peal), whereas Luke's ἐδικαίωσαν represents זַכִּי (Pael). From this, Meyer concludes that Jesus said either קוֹמֵיכוֹן) יְזַכּוּן קוֹמִיכוּן מילכתא דיי' (יִזְכּוּן מינכון למילכתא דיי', or galil. für קָדָמְכוֹן)'.[44] Here there are two major problems. One is the massive difference between either proposed pronunciation and the Lukan passage, in which ἐδικαίωσαν is positioned a very long way from βουλὴν τοῦ θεοῦ. This underlines the second major problem, that a complete reconstruction would be required for this hypothesis to be confirmed, together with a proper account of the processes of translation and editing which led to the two passages which we now read. In short, we have not been given reason to believe that these two passages derive from one Aramaic underlay. It has been a perpetual illusion of Aramaists working on the Gospels that when two meanings of the same or similar Aramaic

[43] *Ibid.*, p. 79.
[44] *Ibid.*, pp. 86–7.

words are proposed, differences between Gospel passages have been explained. This example demonstrates that this is not sufficient. It is also regrettably typical that the two meanings of זכי cannot be validated for Aramaic of the right period, that the plausible-looking Galilean form may also be too late in date, and that יהוה is not likely to have been written for אדני, but אלהא is much more probable for θεοῦ.

5. With such loose methods, examples can be posited in the Gospel attributed to John, which consists largely of secondary rewriting in Greek.[45] For example, at John 8.34 a proposed wordplay fuels Meyer's reconstruction: כָּל עָבְדִי (דְּעָבֵיד) עוּיא עַבְדָּא הוּא דַעוּיא.[46] Suggestions like this have the potential to damage the quest for the historical Jesus by making the latest and most unreliable of the Gospels appear early and authentic. Scholars have not realised how easy it is to produce supposed wordplays from mildly Semitic Greek.

These five problems have dogged the most learned and serious scholarship ever since. From an historical perspective, however, they must not be allowed to detract from the brilliance of Meyer's achievement. His work is very learned, and extremely ingenious, and it is not to be expected that creative pioneering scholarship should get everything right first time. Meyer had no proper models as a basis for his innovations. He advanced knowledge by reconstructing whole sentences, and by a variety of suggestions which required further critical assessment, and which should have led to increasingly refined work. It is a measure of his achievement that it was fifty years before it was seriously improved upon, and that scholarship still suffers from the problems which he left behind.

In the same year, Lietzmann surveyed the use of בר (א)נש(א) in the Targums of Onkelos and Jonathan, the Palestinian Syriac Gospels, and several tractates of the Palestinian Talmud.[47] This massive survey of Aramaic source material convinced him correctly that בר נש was a straightforward term for a person, but he went on to conclude that ὁ υἱὸς τοῦ ἀνθρώπου was a technical term of Hellenistic theology. This was hardly a satisfactory conclusion for a

[45] P. M. Casey, *Is John's Gospel True?* (London, 1996).

[46] Meyer, *Muttersprache*, p. 79, using the wordplay suggested by A. Smith Lewis, *A Translation of the Four Gospels from the Syriac of the Sinaitic Palimpsest* (London, 1894), p. xv.

[47] H. Lietzmann, *Der Menschensohn: Ein Beitrag zur neutestamentlichen Theologie* (Freiburg i. B. /Leipzig, 1896).

term absent from Acts (except 7.56) and from the Epistles. Where he did believe that בר נשא was original in a son of man saying, Lictzmann did not offer reconstructions, and his simple comments on the inappropriateness of ὁ υἱὸς τοῦ ἀνθρώπου rather than ὁ ἄνθρωπος as a translation show that he belonged to a period of scholarship when translators could not be fully understood.

The next major work was that of Dalman, *Die Worte Jesu*.[48] This was a less helpful contribution than has sometimes been thought. A useful introduction sets out reasons why we should suppose that Jesus spoke Aramaic, and should use this knowledge to illuminate his words. It has, however, significant problems of method. For example, Dalman argued that ἀποκριθεὶς εἶπεν must go back to *Hebrew*, not Aramaic. He concluded that it was not genuine Aramaic, so that the evangelists will have known it from the Hebrew Bible, whether directly or through the LXX.[49] Yet Dalman knew perfectly well that ענה ואמר was used in biblical Aramaic (for example Dan. 3.24). Dalman could not have known texts such as 4Q550 V.8, but the fundamental problem is his concept of genuineness. Nothing should be excluded from first-century Aramaic because it was originally Hebrew.

Dalman has a number of criticisms of other scholars, many of which are valuable. For example, criticising Resch in particular, he makes the point that, where different Gospel writers have synonyms, merely pointing out that one Hebrew word could lie behind both does not provide sufficient evidence of a Hebrew original.[50] When, however, he has to tackle the serious question of whether there is sufficient evidence in Q passages of an Aramaic original, all he can do is point out where others have made mistakes. For example, he comments on Nestle's suggestion that at Matt. 23.23 ἔλεος represents רחמין, which was confounded with רחמתא to give ἀγάπη at Luke 11.42, to which τοῦ θεοῦ was appended. Dalman points out that it is at least equally credible that the synonyms ἔλεος and ἀγάπη were interchanged and τοῦ θεοῦ added when this editing had been done in Greek.[51] This gets us nowhere. What was needed was the reconstruction of whole passages, to see

[48] G. H. Dalman, *Die Worte Jesu*, vol. I, *Einleitung und wichtige Begriffe* (Leipzig, 1898. There was no second volume); ET *The Words of Jesus. I. Introduction and Fundamental Ideas* (Edinburgh, 1902; [2]1930).

[49] Dalman, *Worte*, p. 20; ET p. 25.

[50] Dalman, *Worte*, pp. 34–5; ET pp. 44–5.

[51] Dalman, *Worte*, p. 54; ET p. 68.

if a decision could then be taken as to whether an Aramaic underlay
was probable, or whether we should adopt an alternative theory of
some kind of Q which was transmitted in Greek and edited twice.
From this point of view, the absence of Luke 11.40 from Matthew
is just as important as the plausibility of רחמיא being misread as
רחמתא, and the main point is that all such bits of evidence need to
be discussed together. Dalman, like those whom he criticised, took
only one small piece of evidence at a time, a process which never
could lead to the uncovering of written Aramaic sources.

The main section of Dalman's book is organised around 'Begriffe', which are hardly what Jesus had. They are culturally
German, and barely at home in first-century Judaism. The nearest
thing to a 'Begriff' in Jesus' teaching is the kingdom of God, and in
discussing this Dalman made an extraordinary and extraordinarily
influential mistake: he attributed to Jesus the use of מלכותא דשמיא
rather than מלכותא דאלהא on the ground that he was avoiding
the divine name.[52] But אלהא is not the divine name! It was the
ordinary Aramaic term for 'God'. It was not the only term
for 'God', and some texts do use other expressions (for example
מלך שמיא, Dan. 4.34), but it continued in use, whereas the
Tetragrammaton could be lawfully used only by the high priest on
Yom Kippur. Dalman's section on 'Son of Man' is equally disastrous, not least because (א)נש(א) בר is not a 'Begriff'.[53] He
begins with the Hebrew בן אדם, which is in the wrong language.
He then infers that the singular בר (א)נש(א) was not in use in
Jewish Palestinian Aramaic of the earlier period. It was not his
fault that neither the Sefire inscriptions nor the Dead Sea scrolls
had been discovered, but errors of method must still be attributed
to him. He could have followed other scholars in taking more
notice of the mundane nature of בר (א)נש(א) in thousands of
examples in later sources, especially as the plural was already
extant, in the definite state and with mundane meaning, at Dan.
2.38; 5.21.

Dalman was so impressed by the difficulty of doing adequate
reconstructions of whole sentences that he could hardly see the
point of this work. In the foreword to *Jesus-Jeshua*, he deliberately
prescinds from making an Aramaic translation of Jesus' discourses,
seeing no point in another Targum of the Gospels when there were

[52] Dalman, *Worte*, pp. 75–7, ET pp. 91–4, and the same mistake at pp. 75–9,
159–62, 223; ET pp. 91–4, 194–7, 272.
[53] Dalman, *Worte*, pp. 191–219; ET pp. 234–67.

Aramaic and Hebrew translations already.[54] There were, and another was not required. Dalman failed to distinguish between translating material *into* Aramaic and the more difficult task of reconstructing what Gospel writers translated *from* Aramaic into Greek. It was accordingly rather inconsistent of him to offer Aramaic versions of several sentences. They are remarkably un-illuminating. For example, he offers this version of Matt. 5.19:

> *ūman dimebaṭṭēl ḥadā min hālen miṣwātā ze'ēraiyā umeal-*
> *lēph ken libnē nāshā (biryātā) hū 'atīd lmitkerāyā ze'ērā*
> *bemalkhūtā dishemaiyā. Ūman dimekaiyēm yāthēn*
> *umeallēph ken hū 'atīd lemitkerāyā rabbā bemalkhūta*
> *dishemaiyā.*[55]

The idea of doing the whole verse is a potentially fundamental advance, as we have seen in discussing Meyer. Apart from being difficult to read because it is in the wrong script, however, Dalman's version is unhelpful because it is most unlikely to have existed before he made it up. This saying is attested by Matthew only, and has an excellent Sitz im Leben in the early church, where it accepts assimilation in the Gentile mission, but criticises metaphorically those who were not observant. It is difficult to see that it has any Sitz im Leben in the ministry of Jesus, where this was not an issue. The vocabulary is largely Matthean, and the most probable view of its origin is that Matthew composed it in Greek as part of his introduction to the Sermon on the Mount, which he constructed from traditional material which he vigorously edited.[56]

Without proper criteria for distinguishing the authenticity of Aramaic versions of Gospel sayings, there is nothing to stop us from producing versions of material in the fourth Gospel. Dalman preferred Matthew and Luke, but Johannine efforts include *mushlam* for Τετέλεσται (John 19.30). As far as any understanding of the historical Jesus goes, this is irrelevant, because the Johannine material is secondary and was produced in Greek.[57] Dalman knew that it might have been, and it follows that his detailed discussion

[54] G. Dalman, *Jesus-Jeschua: Die drei Sprachen Jesu* (Leipzig, 1922), p. III; ET *Jesus-Jeshua: Studies in the Gospels* (London, 1929), p. xi.

[55] Dalman, *Jesus-Jeschua*, p. 58; ET p. 62. The transliteration given here follows the English version.

[56] Cf., e.g., W. D. Davies and D. C. Allison, *A Critical and Exegetical Commentary on the Gospel according to Saint Matthew* (3 vols., ICC. Edinburgh, 1988–97), vol. I, pp. 495–8.

[57] Casey, *Is John's Gospel True?*

of Aramaic and of other Jewish sources does not bear properly on the questions which should be at issue in the discussion of such a verse.[58]

We must conclude that Dalman's major contribution to knowledge lay in the Jewish background to the New Testament, rather than in understanding sayings of Jesus.

The next major attempts to contribute to this work were those of Burney and Torrey.[59] Both showed learning and ingenuity, but were so unsound of method that very few of their suggestions have survived criticism. Burney pointed out a number of features of Semitic writing in the Gospels. For example, he pointed out how common parataxis is, and noted that it is characteristic of Semitic style, whereas Greek has many particles and subordinating participles.[60] Again, he devoted a whole chapter to 'The Use of Parallelism by Our Lord'.[61] Having first noted this as a formal characteristic of Hebrew poetry,[62] he set out many Gospel sayings in such a way as to draw attention to this feature of them. Burney also offered complete Aramaic reconstructions of several passages, including, for example, the whole Johannine prologue, and Matt. 8.20//Luke 9.58.[63] He also distinguished carefully between Semitisms, Aramaisms and Hebraisms.[64]

How promising this sounds! Yet the whole exercise was vitiated by errors of method – even the case for the Gospels being translation Greek was not properly made. For example, parataxis is also found in Greek papyri, so it can hardly function on its own as evidence of translation Greek. Moreover, Johannine Greek, with its relatively restricted vocabulary, repetitive mode of expression, and lack of distinctively Greek particles, is very well adapted for communication between people who had several different first languages, and Greek as their second language.[65] This might have been just as important as Hebrew and Aramaic in the emergence of

[58] Dalman, *Jesus-Jeschua*, pp. 190–6; ET pp. 211–18.

[59] C. F. Burney, *The Aramaic Origin of the Fourth Gospel* (Oxford, 1922); C. C. Torrey, 'The Aramaic Origin of the Gospel of John', *HThR* 16, 1923, 305–44; C. F. Burney, *The Poetry of Our Lord* (Oxford, 1925); C. C. Torrey, *The Four Gospels: A New Translation* (London, 1933); C. C. Torrey, *Our Translated Gospels* (London, 1937).

[60] Burney, *Aramaic Origin*, pp. 5–7, 56–8.

[61] Burney, *Poetry*, ch. 2.

[62] *Ibid.*, *Poetry*, pp. 15–22.

[63] Burney, *Aramaic Origin*, ch. 1; *Poetry*, pp. 132, 169.

[64] Burney, *Aramaic Origin*, introduction.

[65] Casey, *Is John's Gospel True?*, p. 94.

Johannine Greek. Parataxis in the fourth Gospel is therefore different from parataxis in Mark, where there are other reasons to believe in Aramaic sources.

Parallelism is an equally unsatisfactory criterion. Burney set out most of his evidence in English, which underlines the fact that anyone familiar with Hebrew poetry can write in parallel lines in other languages, Greek included. Johannine examples may be entirely of this kind. Some of Burney's examples are also very dubious examples of parallelism. He comments on Mark 3.4//Luke 6.9, 'Instances of synonymous distichs or tristichs occurring singly or in groups of two or three are frequent.' He then sets it out:

> Is it lawful on the sabbath to do good or to do harm?
> To save a life or to kill?[66]

I shall argue that this verse was indeed taken from an Aramaic source. It is, however, most unlikely that Jesus, Mark's source or anyone else thought that this was poetry.

This is even more marked with rhyme, which should not be regarded as a feature of ancient Semitic verse at all. Burney brought forward no evidence that rhyme was a feature of Aramaic verse. He discussed Hebrew poetry instead, and commented that 'the few occurrences which can be collected seem for the most part to be rather accidental than designed'.[67] His examples are indeed all produced at random by the fact that Hebrew words have a limited number of endings, with the result that similar ones occasionally occur together in groups. Burney produced the same effect with Aramaic versions of selected sayings of Jesus. For example, Burney translated John 10.1ff. into what he called 'rhymed quatrains, with the exception of the second stanza, which on account of its weight stands as a distich'.[68] He set out the first verse like this:

> man dᵉlḗt ‘ālḗl bᵉtar‘ấ
> lᵉdīrấ dᵉ‘ānấ
> wᵉsālḗḵ bᵉ’áḥᵃrāyấ
> hū́ gannā́b ūlīsṭā’ấ

In the first place, it is difficult to see that this rhymes in any reasonable sense. In so far as it does so, this is because so many Aramaic words have similar endings. Moreover, Burney writes

---

[66] Burney, *Poetry*, p. 64.
[67] *Ibid.*, p. 147.
[68] *Ibid.*, pp. 174–5.

ūlīsṭā'ā for 'robber', using the fourth Gospel's Greek word, ληστής, as an Aramaic loanword and putting it in the definite state. While the Greek ληστής was eventually borrowed into Aramaic, it is not probable that this had already happened, and the native Aramaic גזל is surely more probable. We must conclude that Burney's attempt to write rhyming Aramaic verse is entirely spurious.

Burney's versions also contain mistakes. For example, in Matt. 8.20// Luke 9.58, he has *ḳinnīn* for Q's κατασκηνώσεις. This is the wrong word. The Aramaic קנין means 'nests', so any reasonable translator would have translated it as νοσσιάς, using the straightforward Greek word for 'nests'. Accordingly, the Aramaic must have been a word such as משכנין, a general term meaning somewhere to stay, and reasonably used for the many trees round Capernaum in which native and migrating birds roost in large numbers. Other possibilities are מטללין and מדרין.[69] Burney's mistake was not, however, a random one. His tradition told him that the term 'nest' occurred in this saying (so, for example, the text of the RV in both places). He therefore translated this *into* Aramaic. This is the central fault at the basis of his reconstructions: they are not really *reconstructions* at all; they are *translations* of the kind that Dalman warned us against.

This is the fault at the basis of Burney's discussion of supposed mistranslations. They are for the most part not mistranslations of Aramaic sources, but creative work by Burney. For example, Burney argued that the frequency in John of the Greek particle ἵνα was due to the influence of the Aramaic relative particle ד, and that in some cases it had been mistranslated. His examples include John 6.50: 'This is the bread which comes down from heaven, so that one may eat of it and not die.'[70] Burney supposed that this originally meant '*which* a man shall eat thereof and shall not die'. This is quite arbitrary. The evangelist's purpose clause makes excellent sense. In his view, Jesus did become incarnate in order to bring salvation, and as the metaphor of bread is carried through, it becomes clear that the Christian Eucharist is essential for salvation.[71] This is the misplaced creativity which runs through the whole of Burney's discussion. Secondly, Burney's judgement that John uses ἵνα so

---

[69] P. M. Casey, 'The Jackals and the Son of Man (Matt. 8. 20//Luke 9. 58)', *JSNT* 23, 1985, 3–22, at 8, 20–1; cf. pp. 69–71 below.

[70] Burney, *Aramaic Origin*, pp. 69–78, at 76.

[71] Cf. Casey, *Is John's Gospel True?*, pp. 42–51.

frequently that his usage requires this kind of explanation is based on comparing the fourth Gospel with three other documents, the Gospels of Matthew, Mark and Luke. Some Greek documents use the particle ἵνα more frequently than they do, so that a more thorough comparison would be needed before we could regard Johannine usage as non-Greek.[72]

Once we are prepared to assert mistranslations like this, the way is clear for us to read all sorts of things into an imagined Aramaic substratum. Burney found the virgin birth behind John 1.13.[73] Burney notes that the plural of the verb, אִתְיְלִידוּ, 'were born', is the same as the singular אִתְיְלִיד, 'was born', with the addition of the one letter ו, which on its own is the word for 'and', the first word of John 1.14. So Burney suggests an accidental doubling of this letter ו, which mistakenly caused the verb to be taken as a plural. He reconstructs the Aramaic source like this:

$$\text{..לִמְהֵימְנִין בִּשְׁמֵיהּ. דְּלָא מִן דְּמָא (or) דְּמִין(?) וְלָא מִן}$$
$$\text{צְבוּת בִּסְרָא וְלָא מִן צְבוּת גַּבְרָא אִילָהֵן מִן אֱלָהָא}$$
$$\text{אִתְיְלִיד.}$$
$$\text{וּמֵימְרָא בִּסְרָא אִתְעֲבֵיד...}$$

> ... to those that believe in His name; because He was born, not of blood, nor of the will of the flesh, nor of the will of man, but of God.
> 8. And the Word was made flesh ...'

Thus he presents the author 'drawing out the mystical import of the Virgin-Birth for believers'. The supposed corruption, misreading and consequently erroneous translation are an entirely spurious part of this argument, the function of which is to find Christian doctrine in a document from which a Christian scholar believed it should not be absent.

Torrey recognised that Burney's proposed mistranslations were not satisfactory, which is very ironical, for Torrey proceeded to major on mistranslations as his central criterion for believing that the Gospels were translated from Aramaic. He had one or two good ideas. At Luke 12.49, he noted that the Greek text (τί θέλω εἰ) must mean 'what do I desire if'. He reconstructed this

---

[72] Cf. E. C. Colwell, *The Greek of the Fourth Gospel: A Study of its Aramaisms in the Light of Hellenistic Greek* (Chicago, 1931), pp. 92–3.

[73] Burney, *Aramaic Origin*, pp. 34–5, 41–2, followed by Torrey, *Translated Gospels*, pp. 151–3.

מָה צָבֵא אֲנָא הֵן, and translated it 'how I wish that'.[74] Torrey did
not fully understand the translator, who was not only rendering
word for word, but also suffering from interference. His Aramaic is
perfectly correct, however, and should be accepted as an explanation of the Lukan expression. Torrey also commented plausibly on
Luke 1.39, εἰς πόλιν Ἰούδα. Noting correctly that Judah was not a
city, Torrey reconstructed מדינת יהודה, meaning 'to the province
of Judah'.[75] At the same time, however, Torrey was very dogmatic
and not altogether convincing about the behaviour of the translator. He was quite sure that מדינא in Hebrew and Jewish Aramaic
always meant 'province', and that in Gentile usage it always meant
'city'. He thought that the trouble was simply caused by Luke's
being Gentile. It is not, however, obvious that Luke was the
translator, and Torrey had insufficient grounds for his assertion
about Gentile usage. Moreover, we should add the problem of
interference. A bilingual who was used to the first of the two nouns
being in the construct, and the second not having case, might have
read the expression in what has become the traditional way, 'to a
city of Judah'.

Despite a small number of gains of this kind, Torrey's work
suffers from serious defects. It is very badly set out. Aramaic usage
is often authoritatively declared without supporting evidence.
Torrey also deals often with only one or two words, which greatly
facilitates playing tricks. Some suggestions are plausible, but
doubtful because we do not have sufficient reason to believe that
there ever was an Aramaic original to the passage discussed. For
example, he describes the single word εἰσῆλθον at Luke 7.45 as 'An
especially clear case of false rendering'.[76] He reconstructs the word
as עלת. He supposes that the source meant עָלַת, 'she came in', but
was misread in an unvocalised text as if it were עַלֵת, 'I came in',
partly because the translator rendered עלת correctly with εἰσῆλθον
in the previous verse. This explanation is plausible, and gives a
better account of the translator than Torrey usually does. Doubts
remain because this piece is in Luke only, and is fluently written in
Greek. It may be therefore that the author was not quite as sure as
Torrey that the woman came in after Jesus, and really meant 'since
I came in, she has not stopped kissing my feet', which is very
entertainingly put.

[74] Torrey, *Translated Gospels*, pp. 31, 34.
[75] *Ibid.*, pp. 82–6.
[76] *Ibid.*, pp. 98–100.

More serious are cases where Torrey has creatively rewritten the text with Aramaic backing. For example, for μετ᾽ ὀργῆς at Mark 3.5 Torrey reconstructs ברגז. This is not an unreasonable version of the two words taken in isolation: viewing the sentence as a whole, I shall use the same word for ὀργή in a complete reconstruction of the verse, beginning ופנה עליהון לרגז. Torrey, however, was quite sure that Jesus was not angry. He argues that the word signifies 'distress, deep sorrow', citing *Tg*. Ps. 6.8; Job 17.7, both of which are too late in date, together with 2 Sam. 19.1, which is in the wrong language.[77] Torrey's argument is thus a mixture of good and bad method. It was right to find the underlay of ὀργῆς, and wrong to take it in isolation from the rest of the sentence. It would have been entirely right to offer a careful outline of the semantic area of רגז, and not to be hidebound by the translator in considering what Mark's source really meant and what Jesus really felt. It was wrong to have such a conviction that Jesus could not have been angry, and to rummage around texts in either Hebrew or Aramaic, written centuries before and afterwards, to find a meaning which fits a conviction that Jesus was not angry.

With such method, the rewriting can go much further astray, especially in dealing with texts which were first written in Greek. I have noted the Johannine prologue, where Torrey accepted Burney's use of a supposed Aramaic substratum to introduce the virgin birth where they felt that it should not have been left out.[78] Torrey was equally sure that the imperfect ἦν at 1.15, and the participle ὤν at 1.18, could not be right. So he suggested that ἦν at 1.15 was due to the misrendering of הוא, which should have been rendered 'is', but which the translator interpreted as הֲוָא, 'was': while at 1.18, הֲוָא, which should have been rendered 'was', was read as הוא, and misrendered 'is'.[79] Both suggestions arise from Torrey's lack of sympathy for the Johannine way of putting things. Here the author looks back on the ministry of Jesus from the perspective of the church, seen through the rewritten witness of John the Baptist. This is the reason for the past tense. Similarly at 1.18, Jesus is in the bosom of the Father, for that is where he has been since the time of the ministry, the narrative of which begins at 1.19. Torrey's comment on 1.15 is classic: 'The fact that the Grk. translator of the Gospel erred here is placed beyond doubt by the

[77] *Ibid.*, p. 68.
[78] See p. 22 above.
[79] Torrey, *Translated Gospels*, pp. 117–18.

subsequent examples of the same mistake.' What this really means
is that Torrey was very good at naughty tricks and played this one
elsewhere too. At this stage, a supposed Aramaic stratum has
become an excuse for altering difficult texts to something more
convenient.

Torrey's suggestions also involved some poor work by translators, and at times this goes beyond the reality of this world, in
which some poor translating is indeed done, into the realms of
lunacy. For example, at John 7.38 he suggests that מִן גַּוַּהּ, 'out of
the midst of her', was misread as מִן גַּוֵּהּ, 'out of his belly'.[80] This
gives us a sensible original meaning, and enables us to find
scriptures which refer to the flowing of water out of Jerusalem.
However, Torrey's account of the translator is an account of an
extraordinary blunderer. That cannot be excluded *a priori*, and we
would have to believe it on the basis of good evidence, but on the
basis of conjectures of this sort it is hardly convincing.

Not only did Torrey fail to give proper details of the attestation
of difficult Aramaic, but in some cases he got it wrong. For
example, at Mark 7.3 he suggested that πυγμῃ was a translation of
לִגְמֹד, 'with the fist', whereas the translator should have read לְגַמְד,
and should have translated this 'at all'.[81] It is not, however, clear
that these were Aramaic words. Neither occurs in Aramaic of
anything like the right period, and as far as I know there is no
Aramaic word גמד = 'fist'. Finally, some suggestions are not
properly worked through. For example, he makes the claim that
'Lk. 16:18, last clause, gives an exact verbal rendering of the Aram.
here conjectured for Mk.!'[82] He does not, however, explain this.

We must therefore conclude that, like Burney, Torrey took work
on the Aramaic substratum of the Gospels backwards rather than
forwards. He had learning and ingenuity, but no serious controls,
and he understood neither texts nor translators. Some of the
contemporary discussion of his work was equally poor. Goodspeed
argued that there could not have been any Aramaic Gospels,
because there was no Aramaic literature at that time.[83] His wild

[80] *Ibid.*, pp. 108–11.
[81] *Ibid.*, pp. 93–4.
[82] *Ibid.*, p. 95.
[83] E. J. Goodspeed, *New Chapters in New Testament Study* (New York, 1937),
pp. 127–68. Cf., e.g., D. W. Riddle, 'The Logic of the Theory of Translation Greek',
JBL 51, 1932, 127–38; D. W. Riddle, 'The Aramaic Gospels and the Synoptic
Problem', *JBL* 54, 1935, 127–38; E. J. Goodspeed, 'The Possible Aramaic Gospel',
JNES 1, 1942, 315–40.

polemic failed to come to terms with indications that there was such Aramaic literature, and his second-rate analysis of Gospel evidence shows that he had not taken seriously, and perhaps had not read, the work of Meyer. From this grim retrospect, we can see the more clearly what a shining light Meyer had been, and Black was to be. Before offering an assessment of Black, we must draw attention to some features of the work done in the intervening period by scholars who did not write whole books about the Aramaic substratum of the Gospels.

Firstly, some scholars whose prime purpose was to illuminate the Gospels and their accounts of the historical Jesus used their knowledge of Aramaic to do so. One of the most helpful was Wellhausen, some of whose suggestions have withstood subsequent criticism. For example, at Mark 3.4 he argued for *achi* behind σώζειν, a suggestion which I have adopted.[84] After more than one attempt, he suggested that at Matt. 23.26 κάθαρισον correctly represents the Aramaic *dakkau* (*reinigt*), whereas at Luke 11.41 τά ἐνόντα δότε ἐλεημοσύνην represents a misreading of the same word as *zakkau* (*gebt Almosen*).[85] This is also plausible, and a useful contribution to the whole question of the relationship between the different forms of Q material. At the same time, however, the fact that Wellhausen normally confined himself to single words meant that this was a very conjectural process, which could never lead either to a complete understanding of Gospel sources or to a proper understanding of translators. Wellhausen also noted that Codex Bezae had a greater claim to preserve the original text of the Gospels in various passages, more so than Westcott and Hort had bargained for.[86] This work was carried further by Wensinck, who argued that Bezae and its allies represent more faithfully the original form of the text of Luke, and that a corrected edition was issued by him.[87] While Wensinck's theory should not be accepted, his comprehensive collection of Semitisms was useful, and the realisation that the more Semitic readings in the western text might be more original is important in permitting the reconstruction of some passages.

If specialists Dalman, Burney and Torrey could be as un-

[84] J. Wellhausen, *Das Evangelium Marci* (Berlin, 1903), p. 23.
[85] J. Wellhausen, *Einleitung in die drei ersten Evangelien* (Berlin, [2]1911), p. 27.
[86] *Ibid.*, p. 9.
[87] A.J. Wensinck, 'The Semitisms of Codex Bezae and their Relation to the non-Western Text of the Gospel of Saint Luke', *Bulletin of the Bezan Club* 12 (Leiden, 1937), 11–48.

successful as the account above has indicated, it is not surprising that other New Testament scholars could also make some unconvincing suggestions. One of the most famous was by C. H. Dodd. In the wake of the work of Schweitzer and Weiss, some good Christian people would rather that Jesus had not expected that the kingdom would come at once, and had not been mistaken, for this is a mistake with severe consequences for orthodox Christology. Some texts are problematical from this point of view, including Mark 1.15, where Jesus says ἤγγικεν ἡ βασιλεία τοῦ θεοῦ, which means that the kingdom of God is at hand, about to come. Dodd suggested that the word behind ἤγγικεν was *m'ta*, and that it meant the same as ἔφθασεν at Matt. 12.28//Luke 11.20, so we should translate 'The Kingdom of God has come.'[88] Here we see the same flaws of method as in the work of Burney and Torrey. The text is inconvenient, the Aramaic substratum is not extant. A single word is therefore suggested to clear up the problem. The translator is not properly explained, though Dodd went to the LXX in an effort to do this. He noted, for example, the rendering of מטא with ἐγγίζω at LXX Dan. 4.9, 19.[89] The translator of LXX Daniel is not a good model, and in these two passages he has rendered interpretatively, so that the tree reached up to heaven but didn't quite get there. In this, as in much else, the LXX was corrected by Theodotion. Examples like this should never be used to equate the semantic areas of different words in the same or in different languages. Moreover, by using one word Dodd avoided the main questions. Have we sufficient reason to believe in an Aramaic version which meant something different from the text which we have got? When we reconstruct a whole sentence, can we see how and why the translator changed the meaning of the text when he translated it? The second question is especially important in this case, since Dodd proposed to attribute to Jesus a theory of realised eschatology supposedly of central importance, and have the translator fail to transmit it by means of the obvious rendering of מטא with φθάνω.

All the suggestions made during this period can hardly be said to amount to a significant contribution to scholarship. The basic reason for this was the methodological flaws common to all this work. The standard of verification was too low, and some scholars

---

[88] C. H. Dodd, *The Parables of the Kingdom* (London 1935, [2]1961), pp. 36–7.
[89] C. H. Dodd, '"The Kingdom of God has Come"', *ExpT* 48, 1936–7, 138–42, at 140–1.

were only too happy to make up stories about Aramaic originals which had convenient results.

A fundamental achievement of scholarship in the first half of this century was the discovery and editing of important texts. Aramaic papyri were discovered at Elephantine and elsewhere, including letters, a copy of the Bisitun inscription of Darius I and the proverbs of Ahiqar. Sachau published major finds in 1911, and the standard edition of many of these documents was published with English translation and notes by Cowley in 1923.[90] This formed an important contribution to our knowledge of Aramaic vocabulary and grammar. The discovery of the Sefire inscriptions was also important, though it was some time before the standard editions were produced.[91]

Many texts which were known only to specialists in Syriac were also published, and so were made available to New Testament scholars who learn Syriac. Of particular importance were the two major series, *Patrologia Orientalis* and *Corpus Scriptorum Christianorum Orientalium: Series Syriaca*. Another significant part of the advancement of relevant knowledge was the compilation of works of reference, especially dictionaries and grammars. These included F. Schulthess, *Lexicon Syropalaestinum* (1903) and *Grammatik des christlich-palästinischen Aramäisch* (1924).

There were also continuing attempts to carry forward the task of dating texts and understanding the development of Aramaic, including the relationship of its several dialects. Of particular importance was the work of Kahle, though his dating of Targumic materials has not survived criticism.[92] Segal contributed an important essay on Mishnaic Hebrew as a living language.[93] We have seen that it was often regarded as a dead language: what Segal did was to demolish all attempts to support this by means of analysing the language itself. Unfortunately, he later went on to declare that Hebrew was the lingua franca of Judaea and spoken in Galilee, at

---

[90] E. Sachau, *Aramäische Papyrus und Ostraka aus einer jüdischen Militär-kolonie zu Elephantine* (Leipzig, 1911); A. Cowley, *Aramaic Papyri of the Fifth Century B. C.* (Oxford, 1923).

[91] The best is J. A. Fitzmyer, *The Aramaic Inscriptions of Sefire* (BibOr 19, 1967. Rev. edn, BibOr 19A, 1995).

[92] P. Kahle, *Masoreten des Westens II* (Stuttgart, 1930); *The Cairo Genizah* (Schweich Lectures, 1941. London, 1947), esp. pp. 117–32; 2nd edn (Oxford, 1959), esp. pp. 191–208.

[93] M. H. Segal, 'Mišnaic Hebrew and its Relation to Biblical Hebrew and to Aramaic', *JQR* 20, 1908, pp. 647–737.

least by the educated classes.[94] This is a classic case of a scholar
beginning with careful and innovative analysis of the available
evidence, and then going on to conjecture authoritatively in a gap.
At the same time, Segal did not make the errors of method which
we shall find in later work which made similar claims:[95] he suffered
from the absence of Aramaic documents which were subsequently
discovered.

One other feature of New Testament scholarship in this period
must be briefly noted. Most scholars writing on Jesus and the
Gospels left Aramaic out. For example, C. H. Turner omitted it
from most of his studies of Markan style, including, for example,
his discussion of some twenty-six occurrences of ἄρχομαι, an
obvious translation of שׁרי. Zerwick almost omitted Aramaic from
a whole book on Markan style.[96] Streeter virtually omitted the
Aramaic dimension from his discussions of the priority of Mark
and the nature of Q: a most inadequate treatment is just squeezed
into the discussion of the 'minor agreements'.[97] Bultmann and
Dibelius gave only a very occasional mention to an occasional item
in their pioneering works of Formgeschichte, in which they bred
unnecessary scepticism about the historical worth of sayings and
narratives which they failed to see in their cultural context.[98]
Aramaic receives only the briefest mention in Headlam's Life of
Jesus.[99] This omission of Aramaic drastically inhibited the task of
seeing Jesus against the background of his own culture.

We must now consider the work of Matthew Black, *An Aramaic
Approach to the Gospels and Acts* (Oxford, 1946). In this book,
Black gathered together the best of previous work, and added
many points of his own. In his review of previous work, Black laid
down a number of correct principles. For proposed mistranslations,

[94] M. H. Segal, *A Grammar of Mishnaic Hebrew* (Oxford, 1927), pp. 5–20.

[95] See pp. 57–63 below.

[96] C. H. Turner, 'Markan Usage: Notes, Critical and Exegetical, on the Second
Gospel. VIII. Auxiliary and Quasi-auxiliary Verbs', *JThS* 28, 1927, 349–62,
reprinted with other studies in J. K. Elliott (ed.), *The Language and Style of the
Gospel of Mark* (NT. S LXXI, 1993); M. Zerwick, *Untersuchungen zum Markus-Stil*
(Rome, 1937).

[97] B. H. Streeter, *The Four Gospels: A Study of Origins* (London, 1924),
pp. 296–8.

[98] M. Dibelius, *Die Formgeschichte des Evangeliums* (Tübingen, 1919. ²1933). ET
From Tradition to Gospel (New York, 1965); R. K. Bultmann, *Die Geschichte der
synoptischen Tradition* (FRLANT 29, NF 12. Göttingen, 1921). ET *The History of
the Synoptic Tradition* (Oxford, 1963).

[99] A. C. Headlam, *The Life and Teaching of Jesus the Christ* (London, 1923).

he laid down that 'the mistranslation must at least be credible; and the conjectured Aramaic must be possible'. This excludes a high proportion of suggestions, and in this matter Black unfailingly observed his own principles. He also followed Driver in calling for the presentation of whole sentences.[100] We have seen Meyer do this, and the faults of not doing so: this was a necessary principle, which, however, Black did not keep to all the time. Black also offered a sound overall summary of the range of available Aramaic sources, of Aramaic dialects, and of the languages which Jesus is likely to have known. He concluded that Jesus will have taught almost entirely in Aramaic, and that his task was to determine the extent of Aramaic influence in the Gospels.[101] He discussed whole features of the Aramaic language as well as detailed reconstructions. For example, he has a whole section on asyndeton.[102] This includes discussion of whether the extent of asyndeton in John's Gospel might be due to Jewish or Syrian Greek, rather than actual translation. Black's separation out of these possibilities was much more careful than the work of his predecessors.

Helpful reconstructions attempted by Black include Mark 4.31b: *di kadh* **z^{e}ri^c** *b$^{e\text{'}}$***ar'a** **z$^{e\text{'}}$er** *hu' min kullhon* **zar'in** *dib$^{e\text{'}}$***r'a**.[103] Here the choice of script is regrettable, because it makes the sentence so difficult to read, and the vocalisation is for the most part seriously uncertain, as Black noted.[104] The main point, however, is that a play on words between the words for 'sowing', 'seeds' and 'earth' is inevitable. It is also easier to appreciate for being part of a completely reconstructed line. Useful comments on passages which are not reconstructed include Luke 14.5, where there must indeed be wordplay on 'son' (*b^{e}ra*) and 'ox' (*b$^{e\text{'}}$ira*), and the proposed word for 'pit' (*bēra*) is also perfectly plausible.[105] Helpful discussions of linguistic features include aorists such as ἐβάπτισα at Mark 1.8, which must represent a Semitic perfect.[106] Thus, in addition to sound principles, Black contributed the largest number of sound examples of Aramaic influence in New Testament Greek so far collected.

Black also contributed helpful criticisms of previous work. For

[100] M. Black, *An Aramaic Approach to the Gospels and Acts* (1946), pp. 7, 12.
[101] *Ibid.*, ch. 2.
[102] *Ibid.*, pp. 38–43.
[103] *Ibid.*, p. 123.
[104] *Ibid.*, p. v.
[105] *Ibid.*, p. 126.
[106] *Ibid.*, p. 93.

example, he did not continue Burney's spurious efforts to find rhyme in Aramaic poetry. He also criticised Torrey's Aramaic, noting that some of his supposed words are not attested.[107]

The extensive and sober discussions of all these features, with ample examples, are the major points which make this book the best so far published on this subject. It still left serious problems, however, mostly the same ones as were bequeathed by Meyer.

1. There is first of all the perennial problem of the meagre remains of Aramaic from the time of Jesus. We can see some of the effects of this in the light of subsequent discoveries. For example, Black declared that 'the construct has largely fallen into abeyance in all Aramaic dialects'.[108] There are now too many examples of it from documents near the time of Jesus for us to agree with this: for example אנש 1QapGen XX.16; בית 1 En. 22.4. Again, in assessing Wellhausen's suggestion that an ambiguous *'shkah* might lie behind variant readings at Luke 13.24, Black very cautiously points out that שכח was not known in Palestinian Aramaic: it is now extant at 1QapGen XXI.13, where it represents יוכל of MT Gen. 13.16.[109] The small amount of extant Aramaic made documents even more difficult to date than they are now. This is one reason why Black accepted faulty early dates for the Palestinian Pentateuch Targum and the Targum to the Hagiographa.[110]

2. Even though Black largely saw through Burney and Torrey, he still has too much stress on wordplay. For example, he still has the doubtful pun on אבניא for λίθων and בניא for τέκνα at Matt. 3.9//Luke 3.8.[111] More seriously, he has several unconvincing arguments involving Johannine passages, and variant readings in all the Gospels. For example, he suggests that at John 3.33 the Aramaic שדריה, 'sent him', has been misread as שרירא, ἀληθής, and he approves of the parallelism which he thinks he has restored.[112] The trouble with this is that the text of the fourth Gospel makes sense as it is, and we have no reason to believe these conjectures. The textual variants, though often fascinating, are also dubious. For example, Black retails Cureton's suggestion that at Matt. 20.21 the Sinaitic and Curetonian Syriac have מרי, 'My

[107] *Ibid.*, pp. 105, 8–9.
[108] *Ibid.*, p. 68.
[109] *Ibid.*, p. 96.
[110] *Ibid.*, pp. 20–2.
[111] *Ibid.*, p. 107; see pp. 13–14 above.
[112] *Ibid.*, pp. 110–11.

Lord', in place of the Greek εἰπέ, because they read an Aramaic text in which אמר, correctly rendered εἰπέ, had been corrupted to מרי.[113] The trouble with this is that we have no reason to believe that they read an Aramaic text at all, and an alternative explanation is readily available: the Syriac translator felt both that Zebedee's wife was bound to address Jesus respectfully, and so put מרי and that his Syriac sentence flowed better without a literal equivalent of εἰπέ. All this comes partly from not realising how easy it is to create wordplays in Aramaic.

3. While Black's attempts to understand translators were an improvement on his predecessors', severe problems remained. For example, Black argued that at Mark 14.25 'πίνω καινόν is impossible in Aramaic and can scarcely have been original'.[114] What is impossible is to translate πίνω καινόν literally *into* Aramaic, which is what we are tempted to do if we can only envisage a translator translating absolutely literally from Aramaic into Greek. I shall suggest that Mark's source read אשתינה והוא חדת דדת, and that Mark's text is a solution to the problem of translating this into decent Greek.[115]

4. Some suggestions are still not fully worked through. For example, Black suggests that the difference in Aramaic between two phrases in Mark 8.38 and Luke 9.26 is slight, and is due to differing interpretations of an Aramaic proleptic pronoun.[116] He does not, however, offer proper reconstructions of either, so does not get involved in how בר (א)נש(א) could have functioned in either saying, or in the (surely improbable) model of the synoptic problem which is implied.

5. Despite his greatly improved methods, Black was still left with many examples of Semitic phenomena in the Gospel attributed to John. I have noted his treatment of John 3.33. Proper explanation of this would not be possible until scholars realised the ease with which wordplays can be produced and the limited significance of features such as parallelism, and came to terms with Johannine Greek as either a form of Jewish Greek or an adaptation of Greek for speakers of several different first languages.

As in the case of Meyer, the problems outstanding must not be allowed to obscure the brilliance of Black's achievement. This was

---

[113] *Ibid.*, p. 186.
[114] *Ibid.*, p. 171.
[115] See p. 243 below.
[116] Black, *Aramaic Approach*, p. 73.

the most learned and ingenious book on this subject, the only good one for fifty years and still the best fifty-two years later. It was so because Black carefully gathered together all that was known, saw through most of what could be seen to be false, ingeniously added much, and wrote it all up with great care.

The most important feature of work since Black has been the discovery, editing, examination and use of the Dead Sea scrolls. Several scrolls and fragments are written in Aramaic. They have provided many examples of words which were only known from later documents in other dialects. They have permitted extensive grammatical analysis, as a result of which it has become possible to date other Aramaic documents with greater precision. They have fuelled the question of exactly which sort of Aramaic should be used to reconstruct sayings of Jesus, a question which I hope to resolve with this book.

The first major document to be made available was the Genesis Apocryphon, the most legible columns of which were first published in 1956, and studied over the following years.[117] The next was the Targum of Job, published in 1971.[118] With most documents being in Hebrew, it was especially important to have these two major ones in Aramaic, to reinforce the established view that this was the language spoken by most people in Israel, in which Jesus will therefore have taught. The Genesis Apocryphon is a Haggadic piece of a relatively popular kind, whereas most of the Hebrew documents are relatively learned. The Job Targum is a quite literal translation. Its existence is pointless unless there were Jews who wanted to know what the book of Job said, and who could

---

[117] N. Avigad and Y. Yadin, *A Genesis Apocryphon: A Scroll from the Wilderness of Judaea. Description and Contents of the Scroll, Facsimiles, Transcriptions and Translation of Columns II, XIX–XXII* (Jerusalem, 1956); E. Y. Kutscher, 'The Language of the Genesis Apocryphon: A Preliminary Study', *Scripta Hierosolymitana IV, Aspects of the Dead Sea Scrolls*, ed. Ch. Rabin and Y. Yadin (Jerusalem, 1957), pp. 1–35; J. A. Fitzmyer, *The Genesis Apocryphon of Qumran Cave I: A Commentary* (BibOr 18. Rome, 1966; BibOr 18A. ²1971); T. Muraoka, 'Notes on the Aramaic of the Genesis Apocryphon', *RQ* 8, 1972, 7–51.

[118] J. P. M. van der Ploeg and A. S. van der Woude (eds.), *Le Targum de Job de la Grotte 11 de Qumrân* (Leiden, 1971); M. Delcor, 'Le Targum de Job et l'Araméen du temps de Jésus', *RevSR* 47, 1973, 232–61; M. Sokoloff, *The Targum to Job from Qumran Cave XI* (Ramat Gan, 1974); J. A. Fitzmyer, 'Some Observations on the Targum of Job from Qumran Cave 11', *CBQ* 36, 1974, 503–24, rep. in J. A. Fitzmyer, *A Wandering Aramean* (SBLMS 25. Missoula, 1979), pp. 161–82; T. Muraoka, 'The Aramaic of the Old Targum of Job from Qumran Cave XI', *JJS* 25, 1974, 425–43; T. Muraoka, 'Notes on the Old Targum of Job from Qumran Cave XI', *RQ* 9, 1977, 117–25.

understand an Aramaic translation but not the Hebrew text. We have to infer that, whereas learned Essenes could read and write in Hebrew, most Jews spoke Aramaic.

The other major single find was the fragments of the books of Enoch, including the related book of Giants, but not the Similitudes. The extant fragments belong to a document partly extant also in Greek, and the most extensive text of what we call 1 Enoch survives in Ge'ez. This find therefore increased the amount of material available for us to study the techniques of people who translated from Aramaic into other relevant languages. A proper edition was produced by J. T. Milik, but not until 1976.[119]

A large number of works survived only in fragments. The amount of this literature further strengthens the argument that Aramaic was the language primarily spoken by most Jews at the time of Jesus. It is also especially important that there is one, perhaps two, further Targums. The most important is 4Q156, a fragment containing what survives of an Aramaic translation of Lev. 16.12–21.[120] This is too small for us to be sure that it is from a complete Targum, but this is the most likely possibility. Accordingly, this piece demonstrates that there were Jews who were so observant that they wanted to know what Leviticus said, but who could not read or understand Hebrew. This is natural, since the reading of the Torah in the synagogue would require an Aramaic version unless everyone spoke Hebrew or Greek. It would therefore make very little difference if this piece should have been from some kind of lectionary, or other composite work: it is unambiguous evidence of faithful Jews who needed the text of the Torah in Aramaic because they could not cope with the instructions for Yom Kippur in Hebrew. There is also an Aramaic version of Tobit, which requires further study to determine whether it is an original text or a Targum.[121] Our

---

[119] J. T. Milik, *The Books of Enoch: Aramaic Fragments of Qumrân Cave 4* (Oxford, 1976); cf. L. T. Stuckenbruck, 'Revision of Aramaic–Greek and Greek–Aramaic Glossaries in *The Books of Enoch: Aramaic Fragments of Qumrân Cave 4*, by J. T. Milik', *JJS* 41, 1990, 13–48.

[120] J. T. Milik and R. de Vaux (eds.), *Qumrân Grotte 4. II. I. Archéologie II. Tefillin, Mezuzot et Targums (4Q128–4Q157)* (DJD VI. Oxford, 1977), pp. 86–9, 92–3; J. A. Fitzmyer, 'The Targum of Leviticus from Qumran Cave 4', *Maarav* 1, 1978, 5–23; A. Angerstorfer, 'Ist 4Q Tg Lev das Menetekel der neueren Targumforschung?', *BN* 15, 1981, 55–75; Beyer, *Die aramäischen Texte*, pp. 278–80; A. Angerstorfer, 'Überlegungen zu Sprache und Sitz im Leben des Toratargums 4Q Tg Lev (4Q 156), sein Verhältnis zu Targum Onkelos', *BN* 55, 1990, 18–35.

[121] Cf. J. A. Fitzmyer, 'The Aramaic and Hebrew Fragments of Tobit from Qumran Cave 4', *CBQ* 57, 1995, 655–75.

appreciation of these pieces was inhibited by the scandalous delay in publishing them, so that it has only recently become possible to utilise them fully in the reconstruction of sayings of Jesus.

Taken together, the scrolls have massively increased the number of Aramaic words known to have existed before the time of Jesus. For example, אבר, 'limb', was previously known from later Jewish Aramaic, Samaritan Aramaic and Christian Palestinian Aramaic: it is now found in 4Q561. בטן, 'to be pregnant', was known from later Jewish Aramaic, Samaritan Aramaic, Christian Palestinian Aramaic and Syriac: it is now found in 4QEn[a] (1 En. 7.2). דול, 'to quiver, shake', was known with certainty only in Syriac: it is now found in 4Q560 (cf. 1Q20). חרז, 'to string', was known from later Hebrew and Aramaic, especially Syriac: it is now found at 11QtgJob XXXV.4.

Some words which we knew in biblical Hebrew and later Aramaic are now extant also in the Aramaic in the scrolls. Perhaps the most important is the noun מכאב, now extant at 4QTLevi VIII.1; VIII.3, with . . .]מכאבן at VII.3, so there should be no doubt that the verb כאב could also be used in the Aramaic of our period. It was previously known with certainty only in Hebrew and later Aramaic, Syriac being the only sort of Aramaic in which it was common. This clears up the previously insoluble problem of which word Jesus could have used to say that a/the son of man suffers (cf. Mark 8.31; 9.12). Other words include אבל, 'to mourn', previously known in biblical and later Hebrew, and later Jewish Aramaic, Samaritan Aramaic, Christian Palestinian Aramaic and Syriac: it is now found at 4QTLevi V.2 and 4QGiants 428. בזז, 'to rob, plunder', was known from biblical as well as later Hebrew, later Jewish Aramaic, Samaritan Aramaic, Christian Palestinian Aramaic and Syriac: examples from our period now include 1QapGen XXII.11 and 4Q318.III. 8. Taken all together, this group of words show that the Aramaic of our period was more influenced by Hebrew than we had previously realised, a natural result of a much longer period of diglossia than we previously knew about.

Some words already known from before the time of Jesus are now extant in a sense previously known only from a later date. For example, we knew the word רבע meaning 'lie down' in general, and used of reclining at table in Christian Palestinian Aramaic and in Syriac, long after the time of Jesus. It is now extant at 4Q196 (Tobit 2.1) of Tobit reclining at table, so I have used it

for ἀνακειμένων in my reconstruction of Mark 14.18. The word
זהר was known in several dialects meaning 'take care', but with the
quite different meaning 'shine' only in Syriac: it is now found
meaning 'shine' at 11QtgJob XXX.4.

Of particular importance are the examples of בר אנ(ו)ש in the
ordinary sense of 'man', 'person'. This occurs as a rendering of the
Hebrew בן אדם at 11QtgJob IX.9; XXVI.3. At 1QapGen XXI.13
בר אנוש corresponds to the Hebrew איש at Gen. 13.16, so its
occurrence is not due to mechanical translation, and with כול and
the negative לא it means 'no one', in a general statement. It has
therefore been chosen deliberately in as mundane a sense as
possible. It also occurs in the plural at 1 En. 7.3; 22.3; 77.3 [4Q
Enastr[b] 23]; 1QapGen XIX.15; 4QGiants 426; 11QtgJob XXVIII.2.
Not only does it not occur as a title, but it is not possible to see how
it could be used as a title at the same time as it was in normal usage
in this mundane sense.

The overall effect of these discoveries has been to make it
possible to rely primarily on Aramaic from approximately the time
of Jesus to reconstruct his sayings. Moreover, they have made
dialectal differences less important than they were. When we had
only early and late evidence available, the differences between
Galilean and other Aramaic appeared great, and it seemed important that we did not have direct access to Jesus' dialect. Now it
seems clear that the differences were small, not remotely com-
parable with the common habit of New Testament scholars of
dealing with his sayings, and Gospel sources, in the wrong language
altogether. The degree of interpenetration from Hebrew, emerging
from centuries of diglossia, is also important: we can no longer
assume that evidence of a Hebraism in a text such as Mark 14.25
means that it was not originally in Aramaic – rather, we must note
the idiomatically Hebrew use of the Aramaic and Hebrew word
יסף at 4Q198 (Tobit 14.2); 11QtgJob XXV.8, and infer that this
usage had penetrated Aramaic.[122]

The Dead Sea scrolls were not the only discovery to be made
during this period. The most famous of the other texts made
available was Codex *Neofiti I*, a Targum to the Pentateuch. While
this was at first thought to be earlier in date than now seems
reasonable, careful studies have slowly enabled us to date documents more accurately. The work of York and Kaufman has made

---

[122] Cf. pp. 86, 242–3 below.

it clear that rabbinical Targums cannot be dated as early as the time of Jesus.[123] Work on the Dead Sea scrolls has proceeded slowly, and its effects have been gradually combined with work showing that these Targums must be dated later. When I reconstructed Mark 2.23–8 for publication in 1988,[124] I made use of as much of the Qumran material as was available, and could not imagine how Mark 9.11–13 could possibly be done: more Qumran material has been available for writing this book, together with a gradually clearer idea of the dating of other sources. The overall effect of all this work is to reduce our dependence on later source material, and to make the reconstruction of Gospel sources more possible.

A number of other texts which were previously known only in manuscript were made available for the first time, including Narsai's homily on the Ascension of Elijah and Enoch.[125] Some texts previously known in old and unreliable editions were published by modern critical scholars on the basis of a much wider range of manuscripts. Such works included the *Testament of Mar Ephraem*, previously known only from Assemani's 1740 edition, now made available in a critical text edited by Beck, who has contributed a number of fine editions.[126] This contains three examples of the idiomatic use of בר (א)נש(א) in a general statement used by the author with particular reference to himself. It is also an unusual work in that a Greek translation is extant. So, for example, we know that at line 124 the Greek translator rendered ברנשא with ἄνδρα, and for כל ברנש at T. Ephraem 944 he put τῆς τοῦ θεοῦ ἐκκλησίας. The interest of these renderings underlines the desirability of a modern critical edition of the Greek translation. Other

[123] A. D. York, 'The Dating of Targumic Literature', *JSJ* 5, 1974, 49–62; S. A. Kaufman, 'On Methodology in the Study of the Targums and their Chronology', *JSNT* 23, 1985, 117–24; S. A. Kaufman, 'Dating the Language of the Palestinian Targums and their Use in the Study of First Century CE Texts', in D. R. G. Beattie and M. J. McNamara (eds.), *The Aramaic Bible: Targums in their Historical Context* (JSOT. SS 166. Sheffield, 1994), pp. 118–41. Cf. further, e.g., T. Muraoka, 'A Study in Palestinian Jewish Aramaic', *Sefarad* 45, 1985, 3–21.
[124] P. M. Casey, 'Culture and Historicity: The Plucking of the Grain (Mark 2. 23–28)', *NTS* 34, 1988, 1–23.
[125] J. Frishman, 'The Ways and Means of the Divine Economy: An Edition, Translation and Study of Six Biblical Homilies by Narsai', Ph. D. thesis, Rijksuniversiteit, Leiden (1992).
[126] E. Beck (ed.), *Des Heiligen Ephraem des Syrers Sermones IV* (CSCO 334–5, SS 148–9. Louvain, 1973).

works which have been produced in proper critical editions for the first time include the Samaritan Targum.[127]

A number of texts already published in critical editions have been produced in better ones. These include Porten and Yardeni's edition of Aramaic documents from Egypt.[128] The Sinaitic and Curetonian versions of the Gospels have been republished in a synoptic edition with the Peshitta, with a much-needed critical edition of the Harklean version.[129] A large number of texts in Syriac were made available, either for the first time or in better editions than previously, in two important series already noted from previous years: *Patrologia Orientalis* and *Corpus Scriptorum Christianorum Orientalium: Series Syriaca.*

A number of texts were also made available together with tools of study. The work of W. Strothmann was especially notable, in publishing concordances together with texts. This made it much easier to see, for example, that בר (א)נש(א) does not occur in long stretches of Syriac, and then does occur in a very mundane and straightforward way. For instance, in Jacob of Serug's *Three Poems on the Apostle Thomas in India*, בר(א)נשא does not occur until line 671, and only four times in over 2,500 lines: this may be compared with בנישא 11 times, אנש(א) 27, גברא/ה 26, and with common words such as אזל 110, אמר 134, חזא 166.[130] This highlights the unsatisfactory standard of judgement unthinkingly employed by scholars who suppose that it is 'rare' in the literature of our period.

A significant number of tools of study were also published separately. These included a concordance to the Babylonian Talmud and to Targum Ps.-Jonathan. A start was also made to a concordance to the Palestinian Talmud and to a grammar of Christian Palestinian Aramaic. Fitzmyer and Kaufman produced a comprehensive bibliography to the older Aramaic. Macuch produced the first modern critical grammar of Samaritan Aramaic,

[127] A. Tal (ed.), התרגום השומרוני לתורה *The Samaritan Targum of the Penta-teuch* (3 vols., Tel-Aviv, 1980–3).

[128] B. Porten and A. Yardeni, *Textbook of Aramaic Documents from Ancient Egypt, Newly Copied, Edited and Translated into Hebrew and English* (4 vols. Jerusalem, 1986–).

[129] G. A. Kiraz (ed.), *Comparative Edition of the Syriac Gospels, Aligning the Sinaiticus, Curetonianus, Peshîttâ and Harklean Versions* (4 vols. NTTS XXI. Leiden, 1996).

[130] W. Strothmann (ed.), *Jakob von Sarug: Drei Gedichte über den Apostel Thomas in Indien* (Göttinger Orientforschungen, 1 Reihe: Syriaca, vol. 12. Wiesbaden, 1976).

and Sokoloff edited a new dictionary of Jewish Aramaic in the periods of the Talmuds and Midrashim.[131]

The majority of these text editions and tools of study are unproblematic. They form straightforward contributions to knowledge. Taken together, they have enabled us to see more clearly the nature and development of the Aramaic language over a period of many centuries. Consequently, they have made the task of reconstructing sayings of Jesus, and interpreting these reconstructions, more possible.

Two problems were not satisfactorily resolved. One was the nature of Galilean Aramaic. In a significant series of studies, Kutscher pointed out various difficulties in reconstructing Galilean Aramaic at all, especially those provided by corrupt non-Galilean texts.[132] Reinforcing the first of these points with a devastating review of the state of relevant text editions, Sokoloff pointed out that even what is Galilean at a late date is not necessarily *specific* to Galilee.[133] The real consequence of these observations is that texts conventionally regarded as witnesses to Galilean Aramaic do not provide us with the sort of Aramaic spoken by Jesus in first-century Galilee, let alone with what was written in Mark's sources, which may have been in Judaean Aramaic for all we know. A related problem is that of oral as opposed to written Aramaic. The secondary literature is full of scattered comments which propose to privilege some documents, especially Targums, but nothing solid has ever been demonstrated.[134] It therefore remains doubtful whether there were any significant differences between oral and

[131] Ch. J. and B. Kasowsky (eds.), *Thesaurus Talmudis Concordantiae Verborum Quae in Talmude Babylonico Reperiuntur* (42 vols., Jerusalem, 1954–89); E. G. Clarke, with W. E. Aufrecht, J. C. Hurd and F. Spitzer (eds.), *Targum Pseudo-Jonathan of the Pentateuch: Text and Concordance* (Hoboken, 1984); M. Kosovsky (ed.), *Concordance to the Talmud Yerushalmi* (Jerusalem, 1979–); Ch. Müller-Kessler, *Grammatik des Christlich-Palästinisch-Aramäischen*, part I, *Schriftlehre, Lautlehre, Formenlehre* (Hildesheim, 1991); R. Macuch, *Grammatik des Samaritanischen Aramäisch* (Berlin, 1982); J. A. Fitzmyer and S. A. Kaufman, *An Aramaic Bibliography. Part I: Old, Official, and Biblical Aramaic* (Baltimore/London, 1992); M. Sokoloff, *A Dictionary of Jewish Palestinian Aramaic of the Byzantine Period* (Ramat-Gan, 1990).

[132] E. Y. Kutscher, *Studies in Galilean Aramaic* (Hebrew, Jerusalem, 1952. ET Jerusalem, 1976).

[133] M. Sokoloff, 'The Current State of Research on Galilean Aramaic', *JNES* 37, 1978, 161–7.

[134] For a recent survey, see L. T. Stuckenbruck, 'An Approach to the New Testament through Aramaic Sources: The Recent Methodological Debate', *JSP* 8, 1994 (*sic*!), 3–29, esp. 17–28.

written Aramaic during our period, beyond those which are so inherent in the ways people communicate that they are found in written texts, including the Gospels and, for example, the sayings of rabbis in the Palestinian Talmud.

Three scholarly books[135] on the Aramaic substratum of the teaching of Jesus have been published in the last fifty years, including the third edition of M. Black, *An Aramaic Approach to the Gospels and Acts* (1967).[136] This contained some significant changes from the 1946 edition. It made use of the work of Wilcox on the Semitisms of Acts, which do not fall for discussion here.[137] Black also gave clear recognition to the importance of the Qumran material.[138] Unfortunately, however, very little of it was available for him to study, so there was no point in trying to reorganise the whole book around it. This edition is accordingly an updated 1946 work, not a new book. The use of *Tg. Neofiti* was equally problematic. It was not published, so the portions which Black had seen, together with the small quantity of material from the Dead Sea, did not give him reason to reject the early dating fed to him. This was particularly the case as he already believed in too early a date for other Palestinian Pentateuch Targums. Thus he followed Kahle in supposing that the non-Mishnaic interpretation of Exod. 22.5–6 must date from before the time when the oral Law codified in Mishnah had any validity, and hence that a written Targum must have existed in very ancient times.[139] The assumption that what is non-Mishnaic must be that old is no longer accepted, and in any case what is dated early is an interpretative tradition of a passage, not a whole written Targum.

This edition had additional appendices. Appendix C, on the unpublished work of A. J. Wensinck, has some good examples of the valid use of Aramaic from long after the time of Jesus to illuminate Gospel expressions. For example, Wensinck noted two Targumic occurrences of יליד אתתא in the debate between Moses

---

[135] I do not discuss G. R. Selby, *Jesus, Aramaic and Greek* (Doncaster, 1990), which is too ignorant to be taken seriously; or B. Fletcher, *The Aramaic Sayings of Jesus* (London, 1967), an overtly amateur work.

[136] M. Black, *An Aramaic Approach to the Gospels and Acts* (Oxford, ³1967). I do not treat separately the second edition of 1954, which had relatively few alterations.

[137] M. Wilcox, *The Semitisms of Acts* (Oxford, 1965).

[138] Black, *Aramaic Approach* (³1967), pp. 39–41.

[139] *Ibid.*, pp. 38–9. See further M. Black, 'Aramaic Studies and the Language of Jesus', in M. Black and G. Fohrer (eds.), *In Memoriam Paul Kahle* (BZAW 103. Berlin, 1968), pp. 17–28, rep. in S. E. Porter (ed.), *The Language of the New Testament: Classic Essays* (JSNT. SS 60. Sheffield, 1991), pp. 112–25.

and the Red Sea, at Exod. 14.29. This provides a genuine parallel to
the Q expression γεννητοὶ γυναικῶν at Matt. 11.11//Luke 7.28.[140]
This is not a natural Greek expression, and the parallel is so close
that, taking account also of the Hebrew אשה יליד (Job 14.1; 15.14;
25.4; Sir. 10.18; 1QS XI.21; 1QH XIII.7; XVIII.12–13), we must
infer the use of this expression by Jesus, long before an example is
extant in our meagre Aramaic texts.

In appendix E, Black published a seminal paper by G. Vermes on
the use of the term בר (א)נש(א) in Jewish Aramaic.[141] After a brief
critical review of previous work, Vermes laid out the basic uses of
בר (א)נש(א) as a normal term for 'man'. He then proceeded to the
most important part of the paper, its use as a circumlocution for 'I',
which enabled him to produce a solution to the son of man
problem. It is the evidence collected under this heading which made
this paper a seminal one, for several scholars who did not
altogether agree with Vermes' interpretation were none the less
impressed by the evidence which he brought forward. In 1976, I
proposed that the idiom was the application of a general statement
by a speaker to himself, a theory which I have developed and
refined in subsequent publications.[142] Vermes' mistake stemmed
partly from the fact that Pragmatics had still not got off the
ground. For example, he commented on GenR VII.2, where Jacob
of Nibburaya is threatened with a flogging for his incorrect
halakhic judgement that fish should be ritually slaughtered, and
asks:

א״ל בר איניש דאמר מילא מן אורייתא לקי.

Vermes translates, 'Should בר נש be scourged who proclaims the
word of Scripture?' He comments: 'Theoretically, of course, *bar
nāsh* may be rendered here as "one", but the context hardly
suggests that at this particular juncture Jacob intends to voice a
general principle.'[143] This presupposes that we have to choose
between a general statement and a reference to the speaker, but we
should not do this. On the contrary, it is precisely because the
statement remains a general one that it is so well adapted to

[140] Black, *Aramaic Approach* (^{3}1967), p. 298.
[141] G. Vermes, 'The Use of בר נשא/בר נש in Jewish Aramaic', appendix E in
Black, *Aramaic Approach* (^{3}1967), pp. 310–28; reprinted in G. Vermes, *Post-Biblical
Jewish Studies* (Leiden, 1975), pp. 147–65.
[142] P. M. Casey, 'The Son of Man Problem', *ZNW* 67, 1976, 147–65; see
pp. 111–21 below.
[143] Vermes, 'Use of בר נש', p. 321.

functioning in the circumstances which Vermes correctly outlined; 'In most instances the sentence contains an allusion to humiliation, danger, or death, but there are also examples where reference to the self in the third person is dictated by humility or modesty.'[144] In such circumstances, people use general statements to influence others. Jacob of Nibburaya was trying to avoid being flogged precisely by hoping that the general principle that a person who expounded the Torah should not be flogged would be accepted and applied to him.

The next book on this subject was F. Zimmermann, *The Aramaic Origin of the Four Gospels* (1979). Zimmermann presented himself as carrying forward the work of Torrey, and his work is full of methodological errors. The majority of his examples are changes in single words, supposedly mistranslations of an Aramaic substratum. For the Aramaic behind the Gospels, he selects what he calls 'proto-Syriac', but for his examples he uses ordinary Syriac, and later Jewish Aramaic too. This gives him a larger vocabulary than any Aramaic speaker ever had, with which to play tricks. He omits the Dead Sea scrolls and all earlier Aramaic sources, which is methodologically unsound, because the words in the scrolls were in existence in Aramaic within a relatively short time of the ministry of Jesus and the writing of the Gospels. At no point does he justify his assumptions about the content of 'proto-Syriac'.

With so much Aramaic to play with, Zimmermann does get one or two examples almost right. He notes the peculiarity of Mark 3.3, ἔγειρε εἰς τὸ μέσον, and sees this as a misinterpretation of קום.[145] He does not, however, explain what the translator should have put. I shall suggest that קום בגוא has been translated literally by a bilingual suffering from interference.[146] Zimmermann correctly notes the peculiarity of ἀπὸ μιᾶς at Luke 14.18, and that the Syriac *meḥada'*, 'at once', explains it. He claims, however, that it is found only in Syriac and that it is evidence that 'The Aramaic written Gospels are a product of the Diaspora of Syria.'[147] He does not tell us where in Wellhausen he found this, nor does he answer Black's point: '*min ḥªdha, mēḥda*, appears in Palestinian Syriac too

---

[144] *Ibid.*, p. 327.
[145] Zimmermann, *The Aramaic Origin of the Four Godpels* (New York, 1979) p. 83.
[146] See pp. 180–1 below.
[147] Zimmermann, *Aramaic Origin*, p. 20.

frequently to be dismissed as a borrowing from Syriac'.[148] Zimmermann's argument in any case falters on the meagre quantity of extant Aramaic. There is virtually no Galilean Aramaic of the right period for this or any other expression to be absent from, nor is there sufficient Aramaic of any dialect in the right period. Luke's ἀπὸ μιᾶς is so un-Greek, and corresponds so precisely to מן חדא, that we must accept that it is a bilingual's mistake, but we may not deduce anything as precise as Zimmermann does.

The majority of Zimmermann's examples are not to be accepted. For example, at Matt. 18.24 Zimmermann thinks that the servant could not have owed his master 10,000 talents, the equivalent of 10 million dollars. He therefore suggests that 'The translator misvocalised the form רבו, det. רבותא. . . . rendering "10,000" instead of רבותא *rabbutha* . . . meaning in this context "large amount, considerable sum." The passage now carries the meaning that the servant owed the master *much money*.'[149] Here, as so often, Zimmermann has rewritten a text which he does not like, at the hand of an Aramaic excuse. Matthew's 10,000 talents makes perfect sense as a deliberately ridiculous sum, and hyperbole was part of Jesus' teaching technique (cf., for example, Mark 10.25; Matt. 23.24). Matthew's text is therefore perfectly in order.

With methods like this, many texts can be rewritten, not least from the fourth Gospel. Zimmermann does not like Jesus' statement at John 8.28, Ὅταν ὑψώσητε τὸν υἱὸν τοῦ ἀνθρώπου, τότε γνώσεσθε ὅτι ἐγώ εἰμι. He gives as his ground for this that the expression 'lifting up' with reference to the crucifixion 'is incongruous', that 'lifting up' in this sense was done by the Romans, and that it is difficult to have Jesus forecasting his own crucifixion.[150] None of this is satisfactory. The fourth Gospel has Jesus predict his crucifixion and be in charge of it when it happens, it holds the Jews responsible, and considers Jesus' identity revealed in it. Zimmermann may not like this, but that is no excuse for rewriting the text. Zimmermann offers כד מתרים לכון בר נשא . . . אנא אתי: this was supposed to mean 'When I will no longer be with you, you will know who I was/am.' The first part of this is entirely spurious. Secondly, Zimmermann does not discuss בר נשא, which cannot

---

[148] Black, *Aramaic Approach* (^{3}1967), p. 113, properly citing Wellhausen, *Einleitung* (^{2}1911), p. 26.
[149] Zimmermann, *Aramaic Origin*, p. 34.
[150] *Ibid.*, p. 146.

function as a simple substitute for the first person like this. Nor does Zimmermann explain the behaviour of the translator. Moreover, his אנא את׳ merely shows that he does not have any sympathy for Johannine 'I am' statements either. His discussion does nothing to show that his supposed original ever existed before he made it up.

We have seen Torrey and Burney use such methods to write the virgin birth into the Johannine prologue.[151] There is, however, nothing particularly orthodox or Christian about this arbitrariness, and Zimmermann uses his method to remove the λόγος![152] His criticism of this, that it is not used in the rest of the Gospel and appealed to later Christian philosophers, is not sufficient foundation for supposing that it is not really there. The fourth Gospel uses λόγος until the incarnation, and other terms thereafter, beginning with Ἰησοῦ Χριστοῦ (John 1.17), which is not difficult to understand. Zimmermann supposes that the original was אמרא, which was intended to mean 'lamb'. He notes correctly the importance of the Lamb of God in John 1, and at the crucifixion, but that does nothing to justify his creative rewriting of the text, nor does he provide a reasonable account of Johannine theology about a pre-existent Lamb.

We must conclude that Zimmermann's methods are not satisfactory. Like Torrey and Burney, he would have taken scholarship backwards, if enough scholars had followed him.

The remaining monograph on this area as a whole is that of G. Schwarz, *'Und Jesus sprach'*.[153] This is a very learned book. Schwarz provides a list of the Aramaic words in the Gospels, with explanations of their use. He presents Aramaic reconstructions of numerous passages. These are accompanied by detailed evidence of the attestation of words in primary source material. Schwarz's reconstructions are also ingenious. For example, Schwarz offers a basically reasonable discussion of the difficult passage Matt. 8.22// Luke 9.60. Using an earlier suggestion of Perles, he explores the possibility that the most difficult part of this verse might be reconstructed שבוק מיתיא למקברי מיתיא. This originally meant 'Leave the dead to the gravediggers', which is a reasonable thing

---

[151] See pp. 22, 24 above.

[152] Zimmermann, *Aramaic Origin*, pp. 167–70.

[153] G. Schwarz, *'Und Jesus sprach': Untersuchungen zur aramäischen Urgestalt der Worte Jesu* (BWANT 118 = VI, 18. Stuttgart, 1985, ²1987).

for Jesus to have said. It was misread by the translator, a misreading no more far gone than many in the LXX.[154]

It would therefore be good if we could hail this as an important contribution to knowledge, but its weaknesses of method are too great for us to do so. One major problem is the choice of Aramaic source material. This is frequently late in date. Nor is it always particularly Galilean, the justification occasionally offered for preferring one form to another.[155] For example, in discussing Matt. 6.2–3, Schwarz cites 2 Chr. 5.12 מחצצרין for חצצר; what he calls Tg. Jer, and should call Tg. Ps-Jonathan, at Lev. 19.13 for סוטרא; and Tg. Neof. Exod. 10.2, with Tg. Onq. Gen. 44.1, for שוי.[156] All these sources date from long after the time of Jesus, none of them is particularly Galilean, and it is a further disadvantage of method that they are all translation Aramaic too. סוטרא is particularly unlikely for these reasons, for it is not attested in earlier Aramaic at all. אגר is attested in earlier and later Aramaic, and we now have it with the right meaning at 4QTobit 12.1. We should surely infer that אגר was the word which Jesus used, where Matthew has μισθόν. שוי, though abundantly attested, is the wrong word because it has the wrong meaning! Its semantic area includes that of English words such as 'put', 'place', and it is used to render the Hebrew שׂים at Tg. Neof. Exod. 10.2 because of its semantic overlap with שׂים. Hence Onqelos has שׁוית, whereas the Peshitta alters to עבדת. This illustrates the perils of using translation Aramaic: Tg. Neofiti and Tg. Onqelos have suffered interference from שׂים, and consequently cannot provide evidence that שׁוי normally means 'do'. At Gen. 44.1, שׁוי is used by Tg. Onqelos to render שׂים with the meaning 'put'. Hence Tg. Neofiti and the Samaritan Targum have it too, and the Peshitta retains שׂים, which is common in Syriac as well as in Hebrew. Schwarz more or less notices this with the second example, and suggests an original meaning *einlegen*, 'put in', the use of ποιεῖ (Matt. 6.3) being a mistranslation. We shall see that this sort of conjectural alteration is Schwarz's second major fault. In this case, we must rather treat the translator's use of ποιεῖ as the most straightforward possible evidence that Jesus said עבד, a word which is widely attested in all

---

[154] *Ibid.*, pp. 91–7, using R. Perles, 'Zwei Übersetzungsfehler im Text der Evangelien, 1. Mt 8, 22 (= Lk 9, 60)', *ZNW* 19, 1919–20, 96.

[155] Schwarz, *'Und Jesus sprach'*, e.g., p. 50, preferring the Galilean מוספה to the Babylonian אוסופי.

[156] *Ibid.*, p. 202.

periods of Aramaic and properly corresponds to the semantic area of ποιεῖ.

Sometimes Schwarz's suggestions can be improved by means of additional references to earlier primary sources, which indicates how his methods are a matter of deliberate choice. For example, he suggests מסגרא for φυλακήν at Matt. 5.25//Luke 12.58.[157] As evidence for this, however, he quotes only one passage of *Tg. Psalms* (142.8), which is sufficient to show only that this word was known to some people who spoke Aramaic more than half a century later than the time of Jesus. We might at once prefer בית עגן from 1 En. 22.4. We must, however, consider also early Aramaic evidence of the use of the root סגר in the sense of 'confine', 'restrain'. It is used at Dan. 6.23 of God's angel who 'shut', 'closed', the mouths of the lions, so it is right to take account of the many examples of סגר used in biblical Hebrew with a similar semantic area, and with it the use of the Hebrew מסגר of a dungeon (Isa. 24.22, cf. Isa. 42.7; Ps. 142.8). Its existence in Aramaic is confirmed by 1QapGen XXII.17, and Dupont-Sommer is probably right to restore the actual word [מ]סגרא on an ostrakon from Elephantine.[158] Late examples of סגר in both Jewish Aramaic and in Syriac may then reasonably be used to confirm that the word became Aramaic by the time of Jesus, that it was not just a rare loanword in the cited texts. We should infer that מסגרא was used for 'prison' in Aramaic at the time of Jesus, and follow Schwarz in this particular reconstruction.

Schwarz's second major fault of method is the arbitrariness of his alterations to the text, both in ferreting out supposed mistakes and variants in translation, and in deliberate emendation. For example, in his discussion of Matt. 5.20,[159] Schwarz first seeks to establish that צמקתא may signify 'almsgiving', which is not exactly wrong, but which is not sufficient to justify Schwarz's view that the translator should have put ἐλεημοσύνη because צדקתכון really meant 'euer Almosen'. He then proceeds to the centrally arbitrary notion that τῶν γραμματέων καὶ Φαρισαίων is a gloss. He offers two points in justification of this. Firstly, he would follow Schlatter in expecting τῆς before τῶν. This is not a proper criterion, because a

[157] *Ibid.*, p. 190.
[158] A. Dupont-Sommer, 'Un ostracon araméen inédit d'Eléphantine (Collection Clermont-Ganneau n° 44)', in D. Winton Thomas and W. D. McHardy (eds.), *Hebrew and Semitic Studies Presented to G. R. Driver* (Oxford, 1963), pp. 53–8.
[159] Schwarz, *'Und Jesus sprach'*, pp. 79–85.

glossator is not more likely to produce our text than a translator, a possibility which Schwarz does not explore. Nor does he discuss the proposed parallel at Maxim. Tyr. 15.8d. We might suggest the following reconstruction of the whole phrase:

הן לא ישׂגא צדקתכון יתיר מן דספרין ודפרושין

The translator's πλεῖον for יתיר is as straightforward as possible. He will have been used to the genitive of comparison as an equivalent of מן in expressions like this, and he will have been accustomed to putting nouns in the genitive as an equivalent of ד. This is how he came to put simply γραμματέων and Φαρισαίων in the genitive, adding one τῶν because he felt that the expression needed to be made more definite. This is mildly conjectural in detail but entirely plausible, whereas Schwarz is certainly wrong about a main point.

Schwarz's second argument is to repeat Grundmann's dissatisfaction with the text: Grundmann declared that in the time of Jesus there were different groups in Judaism, whereas this expression reflects the situation after the 'Jewish' war of 66–70 CE. This is not satisfactory. 'Scribes and Pharisees' is not an expression characteristic of sources after 70 CE, whereas Mark provides clear evidence of opposition to Jesus from Pharisees (Mark 2.24; 3.6) and from 'scribes who came down from Jerusalem' (3.22). This opposition was early and important enough to give rise to polemical sayings of this kind.

By this means Schwarz obtains a supposed original:

אמין אמד אנא לכון
דאין לא ספיק צדקתכון סגי
לא תיעלון למלכותא דאלהא.

> Amen, ich sage euch:
> Wenn euer Almosen nicht sehr reichlich ist,
> dürft ihr nicht eingehen in die Königsherrschaft Gottes.

One might render this in English: 'Amen I say to you: if your almsgiving is not munificent, you will not enter the kingdom of God.' This is a saying of Schwarz, which has no Sitz im Leben in the teaching of Jesus. Schwarz repeatedly alters texts in this way, and this repeated mistake is sufficient to ensure that most of his results are not valid.

Schwarz also makes too much of structural neatness, alliteration and what he regards as other signs of Aramaic poetry. For example, at Matt. 5.3, Schwarz replaces αὐτῶν ἐστιν ἡ βασιλεία τῶν οὐρανῶν with αὐτοὶ πλουτισθήσονται. Among his reasons is that this is precisely antithetic to οἱ πτωχοί.[160] This is not a sufficient reason for making this drastic change to Matthew's text. Again, for ὁμοία ἐστὶν at Matt. 11.16 (//Luke 7.31), Schwarz has מתילא. While a stronger case can be made for this than the single passage quoted from *Tg. Psalms* (101.8), דמא is at least as likely. Schwarz's case is surely not helped by observing that he gets twenty-five examples of ל in five lines.[161] It is not just that the use of genuine synonyms, and the employment of a wider range of Aramaic than was ever available to any one speaker, permits one to increase the number of לs in a piece. It is that large amounts of the same letter do not necessarily give us a more original text. The use of criteria like this produces neat patterns, not original sources.

With methods like this, we can once more find examples in the Gospel attributed to John. For example, Schwarz does not like ἀληθῶς with Ἰσραηλίτης at John 1.47. He would prefer the author to have written ἀληθινὸς Ἰσραηλίτης. This does not justify his description of ἀληθῶς as *attributiv*, or his consequent classification of it as different from 4.42; 6.14; 7.40; 8.31. Still less does it mean that there was once an original Aramaic which read ישר.[162]

These faults of method permeate Schwarz's work. We must therefore conclude that most of his results are wrong. Similar comments apply to his 1986 monograph on the son of man problem.[163] Schwarz follows Meyer and Vermes in arguing that בר (א)נש(א) simply = *ich*,[164] which is unfortunate because it biasses the whole discussion. He attaches particular importance to a Geniza fragment of a Targum to Gen. 4.14, comparing it with the MT and *Tg. Neofiti*. The Targumic passages are as follows:

1.   *Tg. Neof.* Gen. 4.14

הא טרדת יתי יומא דין מעילוי אפי דארעא ומן קדמ[י]ך
לית אפשר לי למטמרה.

Look! You have banished me this day from upon the face

---

[160] *Ibid.*, pp. 159–64.
[161] *Ibid.*, pp. 260–6.
[162] *Ibid.*, pp. 112–14.
[163] G. Schwarz, *Jesus 'der Menschensohn': Aramaistische Untersuchungen zu den synoptischen Menschensohnworten Jesu* (BWANT 119 = VI, 19. Stuttgart, 1986).
[164] *Ibid.*, pp. 73–7.

of the earth, and from before you it is not possible for me
to hide.

2. Leningrad, Saltykov-Schedrin, MS Antonin Ebr III B
   739v, at Gen. 4.14 (Klein, p. 9).

הא טרדת יתי יומה הדן מן עלוי אפי ארעא ומן קדמיך
אדני לית אפשר לברנש למטמרה.

Look! You have banished me this day from upon the face
of the earth, and from before you, Lord, it is not possible
for a son of man to hide.

Here the meaning of the Hebrew text was not acceptable to some
Aramaic translators, for they believed that Cain could not be
hidden from God because no one can be hidden from God.[165] *Tg.
Neofiti* simply has Cain say that he cannot hide from God, but the
Geniza fragment has generalised. It gives us a general statement
which refers particularly to Cain. The main point is that the Geniza
fragment is *different* from the MT and *Tg. Neofiti*, and it should
not be interpreted as if it were the same. ברנש was so well
established as a general term for 'man' that the only way to remove
the general level of meaning would have been to say what *Tg.
Neofiti* says instead. Both versions are perfectly straightforward.
We must infer that the Geniza piece has made Cain use a general
statement which has particular reference to himself. It follows that
Schwarz's central point is wrong. He must miss the general level of
meaning in those sayings which have one, and he cannot use its
presence or absence as a criterion of authenticity.

In other respects, Schwarz's book suffers from the same defects
as his more general monograph. Once again, he emends the text on
the basis of unsatisfactory criteria. For example, he shortens Mark
10.45, on the ground that each *Stichos* is differently constructed, so
that the verse has a rhythm unknown in Semitic poetry.[166] But
Mark 10.45 is written in Greek prose, we have no reason to think
that its source was in Semitic verse rather than Aramaic prose, and
Schwarz has never demonstrated the fruitfulness of his analysis of
Semitic verse. By these means[167] he deletes οὐκ . . . διακονηθῆναι
ἀλλὰ διακονῆσαι, which removes the connection of this saying

[165] On translations which contradict the text, see M. L. Klein, 'Converse Translation: A Targumic Technique', *Bib* 57, 1976, 515–37.
[166] Schwarz, *Menschensohn*, p. 89.
[167] For the complete discussion, see Schwarz, *Menschensohn*, pp. 89–94, 171–6.

with the immediately preceding context, and ἀντὶ πολλῶν, which reduces the clarity of the saying. This leads to the following 'reconstruction':

אתא בר נשא למיתן נפשיה פורקן

Ich kam, um *mich* selbst als Lösegeld zu geben.

This interpretation of בר נשא removes the connection of the saying with Jesus' answer to Jacob and John earlier in the passage. This is not reconstruction of an original saying in its cultural context: it is the destructive removal of it from reality.

As in his more general monograph, Schwarz does not give early attestation of Aramaic words. For example, he suggests למשבוק behind ἀφιέναι at Mark 2.10, citing only *Tg. Onqelos* Num. 14.19; Deut. 29.19.[168] He should have noted that there are abundant early occurrences of this word, including 4QPrNab and 11QtgJob XXXVIII.2, in both of which it is used with reference to sins. He should also have discussed the semantic area of שבק, which over-laps with ἀφίημι and is seriously different from 'forgive' and *vergeben*. In some cases, Schwarz uses words which are attested only in Aramaic too late for the time of Jesus, though this is not as extensive a problem as in some of his other work. There are also places where Schwarz has the wrong word. For example, he puts the traditional קינין behind κατασκηνώσεις at Matt. 8.20//Luke 9.58, and translates 'Nester'.[169] As we have seen, however, the Aramaic קנין really does mean 'nests', so much so that any reason-able translator would have translated it as νοσσιάς. Schwarz's mistake facilitates the interpretation of the saying of Jesus alone, for nature does not provide birds with nests, so the general level of meaning has been lost.[170]

We must therefore conclude that Schwarz's methods are not satisfactory. Despite his learning and ingenuity, therefore, we cannot accept many of his results.[171]

A few other scholars used Aramaic words to assist with their interpretation of Gospel passages when they were writing mono-

---

[168] *Ibid.*, p. 111.

[169] *Ibid.*, pp. 191–2.

[170] See p. 21 above and pp. 69–71 below; Casey, 'Jackals'.

[171] I therefore do not discuss his other work, which includes many learned articles, and G. Schwarz, *Jesus und Judas: Aramaistische Untersuchungen zur Jesus-Judas-Überlieferung der Evangelien und der Apostelgeschichte* (BWANT 123. Stuttgart, 1988).

graphs on aspects of the life and teaching of Jesus. Jeremias is perhaps the most famous, and some of the work which he did is new and right. For example, it was often suggested that the Greek ἄρτος could not designate unleavened bread.[172] Since Mark has ἄρτος at the Last Supper, it seemed to follow that the Last Supper was not a Passover meal. In a fine scholarly discussion, securely based in primary source material retailed in its original languages, Jeremias showed that both ἄρτος and the Aramaic and Hebrew לחם were normal terms for referring to the unleavened bread at passover.[173]

Jeremias also made use of the work on Aramaic done by his predecessors. For example, he improved on Burney's reconstruction of the Lord's prayer.[174] Though regrettably printed in English letters, this formed a sound basis for exegesis:

> 'Abbā
> yithqaddásh sh^{e}mákh / tethé malkhuthákh
> laḥmán d^{e}limḥár / habh lán yoma dhén
> ush^{e}bhoq lán ḥobhaín / k^{e}dhish^{e}bháqnan l^{e}ḥayyabhaín
> w^{e}la tha'elínnan l^{e}nisyón.

Among the advantages of seeing this in Aramaic are the possibility of expounding למחר, an improvement on Burney's d^{e}yōmá, whereas ἐπιούσιον, when treated only in Greek, was effectively an insoluble problem; and the Aramaising Greek for 'sins' and 'sinners', which opens a window onto the Aramaic tradition, and illustrates the fact that Luke is more inclined to remove such evidence than Matthew. It is also a great advantage that the whole passage can be seen.

At the same time, Jeremias suffered from the faults of his generation. He did not have the Dead Sea scrolls to work with, so he used Aramaic of all periods, including translations *into* Aramaic, and he did not offer complete discussions of the translation process. For example, in discussing Luke 14.8–10, he alleges that Luke's γάμους and Matthew's δειπνῆσαι (Matt. 20.28 D it sy) both go back to an original Aramaic *mištutha*.[175] He does not, however,

---

[172] E.g. by J. Wellhausen, "Ἄρτον ἔκλασεν, Mc 14, 22', *ZNW* 7, 1906, 182.

[173] J. Jeremias, *The Eucharistic Words of Jesus* (2nd ET London, 1966), pp. 62–6.

[174] J. Jeremias, *The Prayers of Jesus* (ET London, 1967), p. 94, with extensive discussion; *New Testament Theology*, vol. I, p. 196.

[175] J. Jeremias, *The Parables of Jesus* (ET London, ²1963), pp. 25–6.

give any attestation for this word, nor does he discuss *how* two independent translators could have arrived at such different forms, nor does he seek to explain the place of the passage in the manuscript tradition of Matthew. He does not offer a complete reconstruction, and comments only on words which fit his model of two translations from Aramaic. He suggests that the Syriac and Christian-Palestinian versions be used as 'an additional means of controlling the process of retranslation', which illustrates beautifully his failure to distinguish between reconstructing an original and translating the Gospels *into* Aramaic. Consequently, he could not handle passages where a translator had made changes to a more Greek idiom, leaving the Semitic underlay not apparent to someone translating literally into Aramaic. So at Mark 14.22 he regards the genitive absolute ἐσθιόντων αὐτῶν as a 'graecism' which is 'unknown in Semitic', and he regards that as supporting the common view that it is a redactional link.[176]

These serious problems should not be allowed to conceal the value of Jeremias's work. He showed, albeit intermittently, that normal exegetes of the Gospels can gain further insights into the life and teaching of Jesus by careful consideration of the Aramaic level of the tradition.

Another scholar who has made important contributions to this work is J. A. Fitzmyer. Perhaps his most permanent contributions have been to the Aramaic background to the New Testament. He has produced important editions of texts, including the Sefire inscriptions and the Genesis Apocryphon.[177] These editions are meticulously presented, and include discussions of Aramaic grammar and syntax which form genuine contributions to knowledge in their own right. Other learned articles have made a similar contribution, for example to the analysis of 11QtgJob, and the interpretation of 4Q246.[178] Fitzmyer is also responsible for two standard working tools, an edition of Qumran texts and a comprehensive bibliography to older Aramaic.[179] His article on the languages of Palestine at the time of Jesus is a model of learning,

---

[176] Jeremias, *Eucharistic Words*, p. 184.

[177] Fitzmyer, *Aramaic Inscriptions of Sefire*; *Genesis Apocryphon*.

[178] J. A. Fitzmyer, *Essays on the Semitic Background of the New Testament* (London, 1971, rep. Missoula, 1974); *Wandering Aramean*; '4Q246: The "Son of God" Document from Qumran', *Bib* 74, 1993, 153–74.

[179] J. A. Fitzmyer and D. J. Harrington, *A Manual of Palestinian Aramaic Texts* (BibOr 34. Rome, 1978); Fitzmyer and Kaufman, *Aramaic Bibliography*.

clarity and sound judgement.[180] He has also made significant contributions to the study of individual NT words and expressions, as, for example, κορβαν (Mark 7.11), the Aramaic קרבן now extant on an ossuary.[181] As far as Aramaic reconstructions of sayings of Jesus are concerned, Fitzmyer has reaffirmed the earlier principle that whole sayings should be reconstructed.[182]

Fitzmyer has also attempted a potentially fruitful yet hazardous classification of Aramaic into different phases.[183] His five phases are (1) Old Aramaic, from roughly 925 BCE to 700 BCE, which includes the Sefire inscriptions: (2) Official Aramaic, from roughly 700 BCE to 200 BCE, which includes the Elephantine papyri and the Aramaic of Ezra: (3) Middle Aramaic, from roughly 200 BCE to 200 CE, which includes the Dead Sea scrolls and the documents from Muraba'at: (4) Late Aramaic, from roughly 200 CE to 700 CE, which includes the Talmuds, Samaritan Aramaic and a large amount of Syriac, both biblical versions and church fathers: (5) Modern Aramaic. The advantage of this classification is that it enables us to focus clearly on the changes which took place, as we seek to decide which Aramaic can legitimately be used to reconstruct sayings of Jesus.

Equally, however, this classification can be very problematic if it is interpreted too strictly. This is most obvious with the Aramaic of Daniel. From a technical point of view, Fitzmyer's classification of it in Official Aramaic is reasonable, but its date is too late, c. 166–5 BCE. This highlights the lack of any clear moment when people passed from one phase of Aramaic to another: 200 BCE was not a watershed. The second problem arises from Fitzmyer's attempt to exclude Late Aramaic from work on the substratum of the teaching of Jesus. There is still too little Aramaic extant from the Second Temple period for this to be satisfactory. For example, at Luke

---

[180] J. A. Fitzmyer, 'The Languages of Palestine in the First Century A. D. ', *CBQ* 32, 1970, 501–31, rev. *Wandering Aramean*, pp. 29–56. A more up-to-date account, 'The Languages that Jesus Spoke', was discussed by the Historical Jesus seminar at the SNTS meeting in Chicago, August 1994. See further J. A. Fitzmyer, 'Problems of the Semitic Background of the New Testament', in J. M. O'Brien and F. L. Horton (eds.), *The Yahweh/Baal Confrontation and Other Studies in Biblical Literature and Archaeology: Essays in Honour of E. W. Harrick* (New York, 1995), pp. 80–93.

[181] J. A. Fitzmyer, 'The Aramaic *qorbān* Inscription from Jebel Ḥallet et Ṭûri and Mk 7:11/Matt 15:5', *JBL* 78, 1959, 60–5, rev. edn *Semitic Background*, pp. 93–100.

[182] E. g. J. A. Fitzmyer, *The Gospel According to Luke* (AB 28–28A. 2 vols., New York, 1981–5), vol. II, p. 947.

[183] Fitzmyer, *Wandering Aramean*, pp. 57–84.

14.18 we have the expression ἀπὸ μιᾶς. We have seen that this is a literal translation of the idiomatic Syriac expression מן חדא, which means 'all at once'. We must infer that מן חדא was in use in the Aramaic of our period, a possibility which Fitzmyer himself takes seriously.[184] The most serious example of this problem was Fitzmyer's argument that examples of the idiomatic use of בר (א)נש(א) collected by Vermes should not be accepted because they do not have the prosthetic א. Subsequent work has shown that the semantic area of בר (א)נש(א) is not affected by whether it has the prosthetic א, and it is in any case entirely possible that the prosthetic א was not pronounced by Galileans.[185] If we do not use Late Aramaic at all, we shall also find that we cannot fulfil Fitzmyer's perfectly sound requirement that we always reconstruct whole sentences. It follows that we must take positive advantage from Fitzmyer's excellent work on the Aramaic background of the Gospels. We must not, however, adopt a literal interpretation of some of his principles, but must rather seek a more nuanced understanding of how to move forward.

Towards the end of this period, Wilcox provided useful summaries of the status quaestionis, together with learned and incisive comments of his own.[186] Three points of method are especially worthy of note. Faced with evidence that some apparent Semitisms have parallels in Greek papyri, Wilcox reiterated a more nuanced view of the position of Wellhausen: the mere fact that a locution is found in papyri does not show that it is not a Semitism, when it occurs in a source which we have other reasons to believe was a translation from Aramaic. Secondly, faced with Fitzmyer's view that only Aramaic from the time of Jesus and earlier should be used in reconstructions of his sayings, Wilcox accepted the importance of Aramaic of early date, but also brought forward specific examples to justify careful use of later source material. These

[184] Fitzmyer, *Luke*, p. 1055; see pp. 42–3 above.

[185] Cf. G. Vermes, *Jesus the Jew* (London, 1973), pp. 188–91; G. Vermes, 'The Present State of the "Son of Man" Debate', *JJS* 29, 1978, 123–34, at 127–30; G. Vermes, 'The "Son of Man" Debate' *JSNT* 1, 1978, 19–32, at 23–5; J. A. Fitzmyer, 'The New Testament Title "Son of Man" Philologically Considered', in *Wandering Aramaean*, pp. 143–60, at 149–53; J. A. Fitzmyer, 'Another View of the "Son of Man" Debate', *JSNT* 4, 1979, 58–68, esp. 61–4; Schwarz, *Menschensohn*, pp. 71–3, 84; P. M. Casey, 'The Use of the Term בר (א)נש(א) in the Aramaic Translations of the Hebrew Bible', *JSNT* 54, 1994, 87–118.

[186] M. Wilcox, 'Semitisms in the New Testament', *ANRW* II. 25. 2 (1984), pp. 978–1029; M. Wilcox, 'The Aramaic Background of the New Testament', in Beattie and McNamara, *Aramaic Bible*, pp. 362–78.

included אפתח in Vat. Ebr. 440 of Genesis 49.1, a clearly Aramaic text with the same assimilation of the ת to the ס as presupposed in ἐφφαθα of Mark 7.34; and שכח in the sense of 'be able' in the Targumic Tosefta of Genesis 4.7, found in Oxf. Ms. Heb. c. 74(P), as well as at 1QapGen XXI.13, a document in which it also means 'find' (for example 1QapGen XXI.19).[187] Most fundamentally, noting my article on Mark 2.23–8, he properly related Aramaisms to Jewish culture: 'the whole approach to the Aramaic and Hebrew background of the New Testament must be linked in with as full an historical, social and midrashic perspective as possible, and that the atomistic "spot the Aramaism" endeavours of the past, whatever their merits, must give way to that new approach'.[188]

Many people working in other fields of study have made contributions to knowledge which are important in their own right, and essential for progress in the reconstruction of sayings of Jesus. Since the late 1960s, there has been a massive explosion of knowledge in the fields of Bilingualism and Translation Studies. In 1989, Heidi Schmidt gathered together a collection of essays on the phenomenon of interference.[189] A correct understanding of interference is essential if we are to understand our Gospel translators, and consequently essential if we are to have any confidence in our Aramaic reconstructions. Švejcer discussed one particular problem which is especially important for understanding the production of the translation ὁ υἱὸς τοῦ ἀνθρώπου: 'Literal Translation as a Product of Interference'.[190] This is only one example of the way in which scholars in other fields have contributed knowledge which is essential for us.

There has also been a massive increase in our understanding of the early translations of the Hebrew Bible. For the LXX, we now have the programmatic essays of Barr, Brock and Tov.[191] Among

---

[187] Wilcox, 'Semitisms', pp. 998–9, 1011–12.

[188] Wilcox, 'Aramaic Background', pp. 376–7, noting Casey, 'Plucking of the Grain'.

[189] H. Schmidt (ed.), *Interferenz in der Translation* (Übersetzungswissenschaftliche Beiträge 12. Leipzig, 1989).

[190] A. D. Švejcer, 'Literal Translation as a Product of Interference', in Schmidt, *Interferenz*, pp. 39–44.

[191] J. Barr, *The Typology of Literalism in Ancient Bible Translation* (NAWG 11. Göttingen, 1979); S. P. Brock, 'Aspects of Translation Technique in Antiquity', *GRBS* 20, 1979, 69–87; S. P. Brock, 'Towards a History of Syriac Translation Technique', in R. Lavenant (ed.), *IIIe Symposium Syriacum* (OCA 221, 1983), pp. 1–14, reprinted in S. P. Brock, *Studies in Syriac Christianity: History, Literature and Theology* (London, 1992); E. Tov, 'Die griechischen Bibelübersetzungen',

other things, these essays make clear the differing degrees of literalness which may be found within the work of a single translator. There have also been a number of detailed studies of particular translators and of particular words and constructions. For example, in a detailed study of the translation of כי with ὅτι, Aejmelaeus showed that it is often used incorrectly by the standards of monoglot Greek speakers precisely *because* it is so often used correctly.[192] This set up too close an association between the two words in the minds of translators who were suffering the double level of interference which is inevitable when translators translate texts.

There have also been detailed studies of other biblical versions. The most important for our purposes are the Peshitta and the Targums. For example, Taylor wrote a monograph on the Peshitta of Daniel.[193] This is not just a compendium of information about this translation, but a careful analysis which pays proper attention to translation technique. I contributed a detailed study of the translation of the words for 'man' in the Peshitta and in several different Targums.[194] This comparison of the reactions of several different translators to the same problems illuminated some false assumptions in the conventional secondary literature to the Son of man problem.

The study of these versions is especially interesting from our point of view because the same languages are being used. At the same time, we have to be very careful because these translators were not working in the same direction. Similar comments apply to the Syriac versions of the New Testament. For example, Joosten's study of Syriac versions of Matthew shows careful analysis of translation technique, going *from* Greek *into* Syriac.[195]

ANRW II. 20. 1 (1987), 121–89; S. P. Brock, 'Translating the Old Testament', in D. A. Carson and H. G. M. Williamson (eds.), *It is Written: Scripture Citing Scripture, Essays in Honour of Barnabas Lindars* (Cambridge, 1988), pp. 87–98; E. Tov, 'The Septuagint', in M. J. Mulder and H. Sysling (eds.), *Mikra* (CRINT II, 1. Assen/Maastricht/Philadelphia, 1988), pp. 161–88.

[192] A. Aejmelaeus, 'OTI *causale* in Septuagintal Greek', in N. Fernández Marcos (ed.), *La Septuaginta en la investigación contemporanea (V Congreso de la IOSCS)* (Madrid, 1985), pp. 115–32 = A. Aejmelaeus, *On the Trail of the Septuagint Translators: Collected Essays* (Kampen, 1993), pp. 17–36.

[193] R. A. Taylor, *The Peshitta of Daniel* (MPI. VII. Leiden, 1994).

[194] Casey, 'Use of the Term בר (א)נש(א)'.

[195] J. Joosten, *The Syriac Language of the Peshitta and Old Syriac Versions of Matthew: Syntactic Structure, Inner-Syriac Developments and Translation Technique* (Leiden, 1996).

The general standard of recent research into Bilingualism, Translation Studies and the ancient versions of the Bible has been very high. Most studies have made a genuine contribution to knowledge. Consequently, this work puts us in a position to make a much more informed study of the Aramaic sources of the Gospels.

For this purpose, we must of course be right about what language the sources were in! There have been periodic attempts to argue that Jesus taught in Hebrew or Greek rather than Aramaic, and these have continued even since the discovery of the Dead Sea scrolls. We must briefly examine some of them, to uncover their faults of method.

The two most significant attempts to argue that Jesus taught in Hebrew are those of Birkeland and Carmignac. Birkeland begins by discounting literary remains as evidence of a popular tongue.[196] This is methodologically unsound. There is no doubt that scribes wrote in Hebrew: they did not have reason to use Aramaic unless it was a popular tongue. Birkeland also ignores the evidence of inscriptions, such as the Aramaic inscriptions on the shekel trumpets in the Temple (m. Sheq 6.5). Birkeland turns to expressions such as Ἑβραΐδι διαλέκτῳ (for example Papias, at Eus. *HE* III.39.16).[197] He pours scorn on the normal view that terms such as Ἑβραΐδι in expressions like this could refer to the use of Aramaic: he insists Hebrew must be referred to. This argument has a classic fault of method, that of proceeding logically in the wrong language. In English, 'Hebrew' means 'Hebrew' and not 'Aramaic'. This is not, however, true of Greek expressions such as Ἑβραΐδι διαλέκτῳ. Greek speakers continued to use words such as Ἑβραῖος to refer to Jews (for example Phil. 3.5): it was therefore natural for them to use such expressions as Ἑβραΐδι διαλέκτῳ to refer to the native tongue of most Jews, which was Aramaic. It is therefore expressions of this kind which need examining, without an assumption derived from the wrong language.[198]

For example, Josephus tells us that σάββατα means 'rest' κατὰ τὴν Ἑβραίων διαλέκτον (*AJ* I, 33). The form σάββατα is distinc-

[196] H. Birkeland, *The Language of Jesus* (Avhandlinger utgitt av Det Norske Videnskaps-Akademi i Oslo II. Hist. Filos. Klasse. 1954. No. I. Oslo, 1954). For criticism, J. A. Emerton, 'Did Jesus Speak Hebrew?', *JThS* NS 12, 1961, 189–202.
[197] Birkeland, *Language of Jesus*, 13. See p. 1 above.
[198] The same mistake is made, e.g., by J. M. Grintz, 'Hebrew as the Spoken and Written Language in the Last Days of the Second Temple', *JBL* 79, 1960, 32–47, at 32–3, 42; P. Lapide, 'Insights from Qumran into the Languages of Jesus', *RQ* 8, 1975, 483–501, at 488–90.

tively Aramaic because of the ending, so it follows that Josephus was happy with the description of Aramaic as τὴν Ἑβραίων διαλέκτον. Birkeland takes such examples to be a confusion arising from the Aramaisation of the vocabulary of the spoken Hebrew of that time. This is another error of method, that of explaining away the evidence of our primary sources instead of explaining it. Birkeland has done so because he has taken an incorrect frame of reference from his logically abstracted use of the English word 'Hebrew'. Birkeland also notes *talita kumi* attributed to Jesus at Mark 5.41, and he agrees that this is Aramaic. He suggests that this is quoted in Aramaic *because* Jesus normally spoke Hebrew.[199] This is extraordinarily contorted. If Jesus normally spoke Hebrew, he would not have reason to change at this point, and the translator's means of conveying this information is equally odd. On the normal view, however, the translator has simply decided to quote his actual healing words, which is an intelligible thing to do. Birkeland also finds himself unable to explain the need for Targums, and never discusses any details of a possible Hebrew substratum of Greek Gospels.

It follows that Birkeland's methods are too weak to demonstrate anything.

The work of Carmignac was more learned and ingenious, but still unsatisfactory of method.[200] Carmignac begins by telling us how easy he found it to translate the synoptic Gospels *into* Hebrew. This reflects his ability as a Hebraist, and the fact that these Gospels arose from a Semitic substratum. It does not, however, mean that Gospel sources were in Hebrew rather than Aramaic. Nor is it sufficient to show that the Gospels are wholly translations. Moreover, all existing attempts at translation into Hebrew have problems with some expressions. Carmignac would have to discuss and justify his proposed Hebrew source for expressions such as πάσχα (for example Mark 14.12), ἐπιβαλών (Mark 14.72) and ὁ υἱὸς τοῦ ἀνθρώπου. He would also have to explain how Jesus could use Hebrew in a culture where Aramaic was pervasive enough to require the existence of Targums.

Carmignac's proposed Hebraisms in the Gospels have three major problems. The first is the difficulty of distinguishing some of

---

[199] Birkeland, *Language of Jesus*, pp. 24–5.

[200] J. Carmignac, *La Naissance des Evangiles synoptiques* (Paris, 1984). For criticism, P. Grelot, *L'Origine des Evangiles: Controverse avec J. Carmignac* (Paris, 1986).

them from Septuagintalisms. For example, he discusses ἐγένετο ἐν τῷ . . . καὶ. Carmignac's figures for this are Mark two, Matthew six, Luke thirty-two, and he says correctly that this can be a translation of the Hebrew ויהי ב.[201] Equally, however, he notes that this translation is used many times in the LXX, which opens up the possibility that Gospel examples are due to familiarity with the LXX, not to direct translation. Carmignac argues that this cannot be the case because in the New Testament this locution is confined to the synoptic Gospels. This is an unsatisfactory basis of comparison, because the New Testament is of composite authorship. It is entirely intelligible that some authors should use any given Hebraism or Septuagintalism, and that others should not. In this case, moreover, we have a locution which is obviously more suitable for narrative than for anything else, so only the four Gospels and Acts really provide a comparative base. We should infer that Mark and Matthew needed something to make them use this locution, that Luke liked it very much but reconsidered his decision when he came to write Acts, and that the authors of the fourth Gospel did not like it.

Carmignac considers Luke 9.28, and raises the crucial question of whether it comes from Luke himself or from his supposed Hebrew source. The answer is surely that it comes from Lukan editing, because Luke is so clearly editing Mark in the context. At 9.27, his wording is very close to that of Mark until he drops the words ἐληλυθυῖαν ἐν δυνάμει. This is part of the process of altering Jesus' inaccurate prophecy of the coming of the kingdom, and it is carried further at 9.28, where the use of ἐγένετο is part of Luke's means of dating the Transfiguration eight days after Jesus' prediction, to present it as a fulfilment of that prediction. This editing has such an excellent Sitz im Leben in Luke's life situation that we must attribute it to him, not to a Hebrew source. This is the second major problem with Carmignac's suggestions: they are often given as explanations of independent translations made by the synoptic evangelists, when editing of Mark by Matthew or Luke is a more probable explanation.

The third major problem with Carmignac's Hebraisms is that he or his predecessors have created the occurrence of many of them, using tricks now familiar to us from scholarly discussion. For example, he proposes that in the Lord's prayer *acquitter* = נסא,

---

[201] Carmignac, *Evangiles synoptiques*, p. 35.

dettes and *débiteurs* = נשׁה, which is not so in Aramaic, and *tentation* = נסה.[202] We have, however, no reason to believe that this series of puns existed before mediaeval scholars made it up. Only Carmignac's conviction that similar words are of central importance justifies his selection of נשׁא/עסא rather than the common סלח for 'forgive'.[203] There are no problems in the way of an Aramaic reconstruction of Matt. 6.12–13a//Luke 11.4:

ושבק לנא חובינא   כאף אנחנא שבקנא חיבינא,

ואל תאעלנא לניסיון.

It is not an advantage of Carmignac's theory that he increases the number of puns, because we have no reason to believe that Jesus used more puns than this.

These problems are so serious that Carmignac's hypothesis cannot be accepted. Nor should we accept two recent attempts to illuminate a Gospel from translation *into* Hebrew. When he translated Mark into Hebrew, Lindsey declared that it was easier to do this to Luke. He regarded this as a serious argument for the priority of Luke, and a group of scholars periodically repeat his comments.[204] His arguments have never been presented with sufficient scholarly rigour. Inadequate comments include the declaration of 'the Hebraic perfection' of Luke 12.10, without offering any reconstruction of it.[205] This verse includes the term ὁ υἱὸς τοῦ ἀνθρώπου: a ridiculously brief discussion assures us that Jesus used the Aramaic בר אנשׁ when speaking Hebrew, but there is no proper discussion of Aramaic usage, either here or when it is declared a 'deity-laden' expression.[206] Uncritical comments include the bare declaration that the Aramaic version of Ps. 22.1 at Mark 15.34 is a replacement of Jesus' saying at Luke 23.46, without any explanation of why Mark should do anything so peculiar.[207]

Howard has argued that pre-Matthean material can be recovered from the sections of translation of the Gospel of Matthew into

[202] *Ibid.*, p. 38.
[203] Carmignac's full discussion, with a complete reconstruction, is given in J. Carmignac, *Recherches sur le 'Notre Père'* (Paris, 1969).
[204] R. L. Lindsey, *A Hebrew Translation of the Gospel of Mark* (Jerusalem, 1969). Cf., e.g., R. L. Lindsey, *Jesus Rabbi and Lord: The Hebrew Story of Jesus Behind Our Gospels* (Oak Creek, 1990); D. Bivin, 'A New Solution to the Synoptic Problem', *Jerusalem Perspective* 4, 1991, 3–5; B. H. Young, *Jesus the Jewish Theologian* (Peabody, 1995).
[205] Lindsey, *Hebrew Translation*, p. 37.
[206] *Ibid.*, pp. 71–2; *Rabbi and Lord*, pp. 51–2.
[207] Lindsey, *Hebrew Translation*, p. 63.

Hebrew found in the *Evan Bohan*, a fourteenth-century Jewish anti-Christian treatise by Shem-Tob ben-Isaac ben-Shaprut.[208] Howard's only points of substance are that some of the translation is older than the treatise of Shem-Tob, and that his work incorporates genuinely old tradition. The work in its present form, however, has many late features and a rather wild text. For example, for ὁ υἱὸς τοῦ ἀνθρώπου at Matt. 8.20, Shem-Tob has בן אדם בן הבתולה, and for κατασκηνώσεις the interpretative rendering קנים. The expression בן אדם is not a possible underlay for ὁ υἱὸς τοῦ ἀνθρώπου, but a rather inadequate translation *into* Hebrew which would have to be explained to Hebrew-speaking Christians whose natural language did not contain it. In this example, it is turned into a specific description of Jesus by the expression בן הבתולה, 'the son of the virgin', which must be older than Shem-Tob because he would have no motivation to add it, but which remains a secondary Christian addition which may not be *much* older. קנים, 'nests', is an interpretative rendering of κατασκηνώσεις already found, as קנא, in the Sinaitic Syriac at Luke 9.58 (but not at Matt. 8.20), and, as קנין, in the Palestinian Syriac lectionary of both passages. Howard does argue that the *Evan Bohan* contains late revisions and explanatory additions, but there is no evidence in the text that they are later than the production of the Hebrew translation. At Matt. 4.23, τὸ εὐαγγέλιον τῆς βασιλείας is rendered זבד טוב לעז מאוונ̇ג̇''יילייו ממלכות שמים, which is another obvious attempt to translate Matthew's Greek text *into* Hebrew. Howard regards this as early because זבד forms a word connection with זבדיאל at 4.21 in Hebrew but not in Greek.[209] The whole expression, however, is an obvious attempt at explicitation, so we must rather infer that Howard's criteria are unsatisfactory.

Howard draws attention to textual variants which are also found in older sources. For example, he notes the addition of המלך at Matt. 2.19, where sin cur pesh read מלכא.[210] All that evidence of this kind shows is that the late wild text of the *Evan Bohan* collected some readings which are found earlier. This particular reading could have arisen twice. Herod is called 'king' at Matt. 2.1, 3, 9, and by the *Evan Bohan* at Matt. 2.7, and by sin cur at Matt. 2.15. It

---

[208] G. Howard, *The Gospel of Matthew according to a Primitive Hebrew Text* (Macon, 1987); rev. edn, *Hebrew Gospel of Matthew* (Macon, 1995).

[209] Howard, *Hebrew Gospel*, pp. 184–90, esp. p. 185.

[210] *Ibid.*, pp. 194–6.

may be a copyist's addition more than once at 2.19, especially as Howard records its omission at 2.19 by manuscripts ABDEFG of the *Evan Bohan*. Howard's most dramatic suggestion is that the ending of the Gospel in the *Evan Bohan* supports a shorter ending known to Eusebius.[211] This should not be accepted either. All our Greek manuscripts have the longer ending, which authorises the Gentile mission in accordance with the needs of the early church, but after the resurrection of Jesus when it took place, not before, when everyone knew that there was no Gentile mission. Unlike the *Evan Bohan*, the shorter early text includes the Gentile mission. The short text of the *Evan Bohan* has a Sitz im Leben among Jews who were not happy about Gentile Christianity, so it has a perfectly good Sitz im Leben in the mediaeval period.

Howard also draws attention to old traditions which are found in the *Evan Bohan*. For example, he notes the use of תלה with regard to Jesus' death at b. San 43a and in the *Tol'doth Yeshu*, and he argues that this word refers to hanging rather than crucifixion.[212] Points of this kind show that Shem-Tob used older Jewish tradition, but they do nothing to show that his Hebrew text of Matthew is older than the fourteenth century.

Accordingly, Howard's most crucial arguments are those which purport to show that the quotations of Matthew in the *Evan Bohan* are not an edited translation, but an original composition. His first argument is from the language of the *Evan Bohan*. This is a mixture of biblical Hebrew, Mishnaic Hebrew and later rabbinical and even mediaeval Hebrew. Howard asserts that biblical Hebrew would be dominant if this were a late composition, on the ground that it is dominant in other works. This is an arbitrary assertion: Howard fails to show that there was a standard habit which this author was bound to follow. Howard proceeds to argue from puns, wordplays and alliteration.[213] He thinks they go far beyond what a translator would have created, and that they enhance the text of Matthew in a way that an anti-Christian author like Shem-Tob would not have done. There is some truth in the second point, but this only shows that parts of the text were inherited rather than done by Shem-Tob himself. Howard completely fails to demonstrate the first point. We have seen an example of word connection by the translator at 4.23. A different sort of example is found at 4.21, where Shem-Tob has

[211] *Ibid.*, pp. 192–4.
[212] *Ibid.*, pp. 207–8.
[213] *Ibid.*, pp. 184–90.

שְׁנֵי אַחִים אֲחֵרִים for ἄλλους δύο ἀδελφούς: Howard does not explain what else he could have put. The Syriac versions are similar: for example, sin cur have תרין אחין אחרין. At 7.6, Shem-Tob has חזיר for τῶν χοίρων and, later in the verse, יחזרו for στραφέντες. One cannot see why we should suppose that the translator noticed, let alone why this is more likely to have been done by an author than a translator. All such evidence is explicable as the work of translators.

We must therefore conclude that Howard's hypothesis is completely unsatisfactory. He did not take seriously the gross improbability of arguing that pre-Matthean material is to be found in a mediaeval anti-Christian tractate, nor did he test the inadequate methodology of his argumentation.

Some scholars, notably Turner and Porter, have continued to argue that Jesus taught in Greek. Both omitted major pieces of evidence which show that Jesus preached in Aramaic. Turner proposed that Jesus spoke Jewish Greek, or biblical Greek.[214] Some of the time, he calls this 'a distinguishable dialect of spoken and written Jewish Greek',[215] and he has been heavily criticised for not bringing forward enough evidence to justify its being a separate dialect.[216] This is a valid criticism, but it is not the main point. The study of Jewish languages has uncovered a wide range of phenomena, including variant forms of languages which are not extensive enough for conventional classification as separate dialects.[217] What we need to know, therefore, is whether the Gospel evidence is satisfied by supposing that Jesus spoke such a form of Jewish Greek, so it is important that Turner's arguments do not show this. Against the possibility that Matthew was written in Aramaic, Turner puts up its use of μέν . . . δέ and the genitive absolute. Both are specifically Greek constructions much commoner in the Gospels than in the translation Greek of the LXX, and Turner uses this as an argument against an Aramaic or Hebrew

[214] N. Turner, 'The Language of Jesus and his Disciples', in *Grammatical Insights into the New Testament* (Edinburgh, 1965), pp. 174–88, rep. in S. E. Porter (ed.), *The Language of the New Testament: Classic Essays* (JSNT. SS 60. Sheffield, 1991), pp. 174–90.
[215] Turner, *Grammatical Insights*, p. 183.
[216] G. H. R. Horsley, 'The Fiction of "Jewish Greek"', in G. H. R. Horsley, *New Documents Illustrating Early Christianity*, vol. 5, *Linguistic Essays* (Marrickville, 1989), pp. 5–40.
[217] J. A. Fishman (ed.), *The Sociology of Jewish Languages*, IJSL 3, 1981; J. A. Fishman (ed.), *Readings in the Sociology of Jewish Languages* (Leiden, 1985); J. A. Fishman (ed.), *The Sociology of Jewish Languages*, IJSL 67, 1987.

Q, and, by implication, any of the synoptic tradition.[218] But this argument is valid *only* against an Aramaic Matthew, which we should not indeed believe in. It cannot be an argument against Aramaic sources, for these could be revised. For example, we find Matthew using μέν when revising his Markan source at Matt. 13.8 (cf. Mark 4.8), and a genitive absolute at Matt. 9.10, revising Mark 2.15. Turner's argument from statistics comparing Gospel with LXX usage presupposes that Gospel translators could not differ from LXX translators. In fact they could: they might have noticed that the LXX has too few occurrences of such Greek features because literary monoglot Greeks told them so, and they might therefore have made increasing use of them, a process evidently carried further by Gospel editors.

Turner also repeats Abbott's argument that we cannot explain Mark's supposedly 'peculiar' practice of reproducing a few Aramaic words. He suggests that Jesus spoke Aramaic on these occasions, contrary to his usual practice.[219] But it is difficult to see why he should do so, and Turner's suggestion that he may have been addressing individuals whose sole language was Aramaic is ridiculous for Jesus addressing God (Mark 14.36; 15.34), and difficult to reconcile with Turner's general reasons for thinking that Jesus spoke Greek, since these imply that everyone else did. It is much more likely that we have one of the many translators who leave occasional words in the original language for dramatic effect, and it is coherent that Matthew and Luke tend to omit them (Matt. 9.25 and Luke 8.54 omit ταλιθα κουμ; Matt. 15.5 omits κορβαν, and Matthew omits Mark 7.34, while Luke omits the whole of Mark 7; Matt. 26.39 and Luke 22.42 omit ἀββα; Luke omits the cry from the cross at Mark 15.34–5, while Matthew re-edits the Aramaic just this once). This is surely because the translators were in direct touch with the source material, whereas the editors felt free to edit because they were not suffering from the degree of interference unavoidable in translators.

Turner then looks for evidence of composition in Greek. All he demonstrates, however, is that parts of Matthew, Luke and John were written or edited in Greek. For example, he notes the expression ἐν καρδίᾳ καλῇ καὶ ἀγαθῇ at Luke 8.15.[220] This has a

---

[218] Turner, *Grammatical Insights*, pp. 176–9.
[219] *Ibid.*, p. 181, repeating Abbott, *Essays*, without precise reference to Abbott, and without any reference to Diodatus or Roberts: see pp. 10, 11.
[220] *Ibid.*, p. 181.

traditional Greek phrase with no direct Aramaic equivalent, and there is alliteration in the Greek. However, we already knew that Luke was editing Mark 4.20, from which this phrase is absent. Evidence of this kind demonstrates only that all the synoptics are not literal translations of Aramaic Gospels: it does nothing to show that they were written without Aramaic sources. Again, Turner comments on John 3.3, 7.[221] These verses were indeed written in Greek, and fundamentalist assumptions are required for us to imagine that they could possibly contain words of Jesus.

It follows that Turner failed to show that Jesus taught in Greek. The arguments of Porter are no more convincing.[222] Porter suggests that Jesus is not recorded as using Aramaic apart from quotations. He notes that these are often taken as evidence that Jesus spoke Aramaic, but he suggests the contrary: 'By this reasoning it is more plausible to argue that Jesus did most of his teaching in Greek, since the Gospels are all Greek documents.'[223] This is a quite unsatisfactory attempt to sidestep one of the central pieces of evidence. The Gospels were written to communicate the good news about Jesus to Greek-speaking Christians. It follows that the language in which they are written does not tell us which language Jesus spoke. Mark's use of Aramaic words suggests that everyone knew that Jesus spoke Aramaic, not Greek, for these Aramaic words must be explained. That can be done by supposing that Jesus spoke the lingua franca of Jews in Israel during his ministry, and that some words were left in the original tongue by the translators. This is supported by peculiarities such as ὁ υἱὸς τοῦ ἀνθρώπου, which is not normal Greek, and is intelligible as a translation of בר (א)נש(א). This explanation cannot be upset by counting the extent of the use of each language in documents written for people who spoke Greek. This is why it is so important that Porter does not provide a satisfactory explanation of the presence of these Aramaic words, or any explanation of other features of Aramaic.

Porter lays great stress on general facts about the broad use of Greek in Israel, but he does not differentiate this material properly, either by identity or by date. For example, he has Galilee 'com-

---

[221] *Ibid.*, p. 182.
[222] S. E. Porter, 'Did Jesus Ever Teach in Greek?', *TynBull* 44, 1993, 199–235; revised as 'Jesus and the Use of Greek in Galilee', in B. Chilton and C. A. Evans (eds.), *Studying the Historical Jesus: Evaluations of the State of Current Research* (NTTS XIX. Leiden, 1994), pp. 123–54. See further P. M. Casey, 'In Which Language Did Jesus Teach?', *ExpT* 108, 1997, 326–8.
[223] Porter, 'Jesus and the Use of Greek', p. 125, n. 9.

pletely surrounded by hellenistic culture'.[224] This Hellenistic culture was, however, Gentile, and its presence in cities such as Tyre and Scythopolis is entirely consistent with its rejection by Aramaic-speaking Jews. Again, Porter refers to the Greek names of the musical instruments at Dan. 3.5.[225] These are, however, the instruments of Nebuchadnezzar, and represent in real life the favourite instruments of the Hellenistic persecutor Antiochus IV Epiphanes. They are the only Greek words in the text of Daniel precisely because they represent Hellenistic persecution, so they reveal very little knowledge of Greek and absolute rejection of it. Among genuine evidence for Jews using Greek, Porter cites the funerary inscriptions from Beth She'arim.[226] While he notes that they date from the first *to the sixth* century CE, he does not draw from this the necessary conclusion: they do not tell us how many Jews in first-century Capernaum used Greek. Jews who lived in Israel after the time of Jesus gradually spoke more and more Greek, and it is this which these inscriptions reflect.

This is supported by two inaccurate generalisations. Correctly noting that in a multilingual situation, one language may carry more prestige than another, Porter announces that 'In Palestine, the prestige language was Greek.'[227] In whose view? We may imagine this view being held at the court of Herod Antipas, and in a technical sense among Aramaic-speaking Jews who used Greek for business purposes. Porter gives us no reason to believe that this was the view of chief priests, scribes, Jewish peasants or the Jesus movement. In a sense, the prestige language was Hebrew, since this was the language of the Torah, which provided the halakhah on the basis of which the whole of daily life was run. From another perspective, instruction in the halakhah was given to most Jews in Aramaic, into which the Torah was translated. This could be perceived as being the central factor, and peasants and craftsmen might decide to operate only among Aramaic-speaking Jews. From this perspective, politics, education and economics were run in Aramaic. Fundamentally, therefore, Jewish people could take a different view of what a prestige language was from that represented in the multicultural research on which Porter depends.

Porter discusses Jewish literature which survives in Greek.

[224] *Ibid.*, p. 135.
[225] *Ibid.*, p. 139.
[226] *Ibid.*, pp. 146–7.
[227] *Ibid.*, p. 133.

Noting that 2 Esdras and Judith survive largely in Greek, he comments 'quite possibly reflecting Jewish linguistic priorities for preservation of religious texts'.[228] As a commentary on a culture which produced the Hebrew Bible and the Dead Sea scrolls, this is quite surreal. Some texts were written, and others preserved, in Greek because so many Jews spoke Greek, the lingua franca of the eastern half of the Roman empire, including the massive diaspora communities of Greece, Asia Minor and Egypt. In our period the Hebrew Bible was completed, and most of the Dead Sea scrolls were written, in Hebrew and Aramaic, because these were the sacred tongue and the lingua franca of the vast majority of Jews in Israel. Mishnah was written in Hebrew, and the Palestinian Talmud in a mixture of Aramaic and Hebrew, because this situation continued later. This would be inexplicable if Porter were right.

Porter also misinterprets important pieces of detailed evidence. For example, he notes that Josephus acted as interpreter for Titus so that he could communicate with Jerusalem Jews. Porter suggests that Titus spoke Greek which his listeners did not understand sufficiently well, and comments that 'it is not known whether the deficiency in this situation was with his listeners or with Titus'.[229] It is perfectly well known: Titus was fluent in Greek (Suet. *Div. Tit.* III.2). He told Josephus to negotiate with the Jews τῇ πατρίῳ γλώσσῃ (*BJ* V.360–1), which was obviously not Greek, and was in fact Aramaic rather than Hebrew. Thus the lingua franca of Jerusalem Jews was Aramaic, a fact which fits all our evidence but not Porter's frame of reference.

In the final section of his article, Porter's not-too-hidden agenda emerges: 'there is a possibility if not a likelihood that we have some of the actual words of Jesus recorded in the Gospels'.[230] This is a fundamentalist's dream, and uncritical assumptions are required to carry it through. One of Porter's passages is John 12.20–8, already used like this by Roberts in 1888. We have seen that it is completely secondary.[231] Porter also discusses Jesus' trial before Pilate. Porter concludes from the fact that interpreters are not mentioned in the scriptural accounts that there were none there, another inference already made by Roberts.[232] This requires the text to be quite

---

[228] *Ibid.*, p. 140.
[229] *Ibid.*, p. 141.
[230] *Ibid.*, p. 148.
[231] See pp. 10–11 above.
[232] Roberts, *Greek*, p. 165.

stunningly sacred. Is it not enough that what scripture *does* say be thought true, without having to suppose further that what it does *not* say be taken so literally?

These attempts to show that Jesus taught in Greek are accordingly to be regarded as quite spurious.

Equal trouble can still be caused by omitting the Aramaic level of the tradition. This has been much less common in scholarship since the work of Black, but it is still found, especially in American scholarship which is heavily influenced by selected literary theories. For example, Robbins has the 'imprint of the hand of Mark' visible in his use of καί to join sentences in the passion narrative, with reference to earlier scholarship and without considering a possible source which used ן.[233] He suggests that complex editing produced Mark 14.21, without considering the Aramaisms in this verse.[234] Kelber virtually omitted consideration of Aramaic from *The Oral and Written Gospel*, thereby omitting evidence that Mark depends partly on written sources.[235] It is mentioned only to tell us that even if features such as the third-person plural narrative and the historic present might be traceable to Aramaisms or Semitisms, 'this does not preclude their oral propensity'.[236] The literary trends of scholarship reached a logical peak in the work of Burton Mack, for they are basically founded on literary approaches to fiction, and fiction is what Mack asserts Mark's Gospel is.[237] So he tells us that it is 'impossible to regard the Son of Man sayings as early', and that 'very late' stories include Mark 2.23–8, without any discussion of בר (א)נש(א) or other Aramaic aspects of these passages.[238] On the Last Supper, 'the Pauline texts must be given priority',[239] but there is no discussion of the Aramaisms in the Markan account.

Aramaic has been very little used in some discussions of the synoptic problem. For example, it plays a very small role in

---

[233] V. K. Robbins, 'Last Meal: Preparation, Betrayal and Absence (Mark 14:12–25)', in W. H. Kelber (ed.), *The Passion in Mark: Studies on Mark 14–16* (Philadelphia, 1976), pp. 21–40, at 23–4, with n. 6.

[234] Robbins, 'Last Meal', pp. 31–4.

[235] W. H. Kelber, *The Oral and the Written Gospel* (Philadelphia, 1983). For criticism, J. Halverson, 'Oral and Written Gospel: A Critique of Werner Kelber', *NTS* 40, 1994, 180–95.

[236] Kelber, *Oral and Written Gospel*, p. 66.

[237] B. L. Mack, *A Myth of Innocence: Mark and Christian Origins* (Philadelphia, 1988). For criticism, L. W. Hurtado, 'The Gospel of Mark: Evolutionary or Revolutionary Document?', *JSNT* 40, 1990, 15–32.

[238] Mack, *Myth of Innocence*, pp. 102, 197, cf. 242.

[239] *Ibid.*, p. 298.

Farmer's recreation of the Griesbach hypothesis, apart from a quite unconvincing discussion of the Aramaic words in the text of Mark, all of which would have to be secondary if Farmer were right. Aramaic is omitted, for example, from Farmer's discussion of Mark 1.41. Thus the supposed omission of σπλαγχνισθείς by both Matthew and Luke forms a minor agreement which is very difficult to explain on the hypothesis of Markan priority, whereas the independent omission of ὀργισθείς, which should be read as a translation of רגז, is quite easy to explain.[240] Perhaps because of its omission by Farmer and others, Aramaic plays very little part in Tuckett's otherwise devastating critique of the Griesbach hypothesis: it might have been especially helpful in the discussion of Mark 3.28–9, Matt. 12.31–2 and Luke 12.10, but the main point is that Aramaic reconstructions have a potential which this discussion did not exploit.[241] Further work on the Semitisms of Codex Bezae and other manuscripts could also be fruitful.[242]

If, however, Aramaic is omitted, at least we can all see that it is omitted. One of the most remarkable features of some recent contributions to the Son of man problem is that they purport to discuss a major Aramaism, whereas the logic of their argument is entirely dependent on its being conducted in English. An extensive example is provided by Burkett.[243] His article was written to refute a solution to the Son of man problem put forward by a series of scholars, including myself. After a number of objections which I discuss elsewhere,[244] Burkett declares that the most serious objection is exegetical. In presenting this objection, however, Burkett does not even interact with the theory which I have proposed. I proposed *Aramaic* reconstructions of sayings of Jesus because Aramaic is the language which Jesus spoke: Burkett's criticisms are, however, entirely directed at *English* translations, and the distortions which this involves are horrendous. Burkett criticises my interpretation of Matt. 8.20, but he neither quotes nor discusses the

[240] W. R. Farmer, *The Synoptic Problem: A Critical Analysis* (London/New York, 1964), esp. pp. 172–4, 145.

[241] C. M. Tuckett, *The Revival of the Griesbach Hypothesis* (MSSNTS 44. Cambridge, 1983), esp. pp. 87–9.

[242] Cf. p. 26 above. There is a very brief treatment in D. C. Parker, *Codex Bezae: An Early Christian Manuscript and its Text* (Cambridge, 1992), pp. 188–9, 253–6. It is virtually omitted from D. C. Parker and C.-B. Amphoux (eds.), *Codex Bezae: Studies from the Lunel Colloquium June 1994* (NTTS XXII. Leiden, 1996).

[243] D. Burkett, 'The Nontitular Son of Man: A History and Critique', *NTS* 40, 1994, pp. 504–21.

[244] See pp. 118–21 below.

Aramaic reconstruction of Matt. 8.20//Luke 9.58, which I offered
and translated as follows:

לתעליא איתי להון חורין ולצפרי שמיא משכנין
ולבר אנש לא איתי לה אן דיסמוך רישה בה.

> The jackals have holes, and the birds of the air have roosts,
> and a son of man has nowhere to lay his head.

Burkett also quotes one of my exegetical comments on this
Aramaic reconstruction: 'the divine provision of resting-places for
jackals and birds is contrasted with the lack of such provision for
men, who have to build houses to have anywhere to stay'.[245] He
then suggests, 'Casey subtly changes the verb of the saying from
"have" to "be provided".' This is untrue. The Greek verb ἔχω does
not have a literal equivalent in Aramaic. However, it sometimes
functions in the same way as the Aramaic expression איתי ל, which
is not a verb. It may therefore be used to translate it (cf. Dan. 3.15;
1 En. 23.3). Accordingly, what I offered is not a subtle change, but
the most straightforward reconstruction imaginable of idiomatic
Aramaic which Jesus could have spoken, and straightforward
behaviour by the translator. I used the term 'provision' in my
explanation of the general level of meaning in English, which has
no more precise equivalent of איתי ל either. Thus Burkett's
criticism ignores the proposed reconstruction altogether. Where the
Aramaic uses an idiom not found in English, he has merely found
that my translation and my description do not use the same word.
They should not do so because it is essential that we bring out the
meaning of these sayings by describing their cultural assumptions
and their implications, and we cannot do this if we confine
ourselves to repeating one translation of them.

Burkett then suggests that the proposed generalisation is not
true, 'since birds have to build their nests no less than humans have
to build their homes'. Here Burkett uses the traditional translation
'nests', the inaccuracy of which I pointed out.[246] This is a serious
misrepresentation, because nature provides birds with roosts, and
jackals with holes, and truly does *not* provide birds with nests. I
gave all the necessary information about the behaviour of these

---

[245] Burkett, 'Nontitular Son of Man', 517, quoting P. M. Casey, 'General,
Generic and Indefinite: The Use of the Term "Son of Man" in Aramaic Sources and
in the Teaching of Jesus', *JSNT* 29, 1987, 21–56, at 37.
[246] Cf. p. 21 above.

creatures for the general level of meaning of my Aramaic re-construction to be plausible. I particularly noted the position of Palestine on a route for migratory birds, which need roosts and do not build nests when migrating, and I mentioned the native Lesser Kestrel roosting in hundreds in the trees round Capernaum.[247] Finally, I noted that the saying applies particularly to Jesus and his disciples. Burkett alleges that for this interpretation, 'The indefinite "a son of man" would have to be qualified.' There are two things wrong with this. In the first place, it is again in the wrong language. Whatever state it was in, (א)שׁ(א) בר was not 'The indefinite "a son of man"'. Secondly, Aramaic generalisations do not have to be true of all people; indeed they are not necessarily true.[248] Burkett, however, does not discuss Aramaic sentences.

Such criticisms are inappropriate in method. It is *part* of my proposed hypothesis that all Son of man statements in English, all Menschensohn statements in German and at least the majority of ὁ υἱὸς τοῦ ἀνθρώπου statements in Greek are true of Jesus alone. This explains why this hypothesis is uncongenial to scholars who have a strong sense of logic, a good knowledge of Christian tradition and little or no knowledge of Aramaic. It is central to the proposed hypothesis that Aramaic usage was *different* from that of other languages, especially in that (א)שׁ(א) בר cannot lose a general or generic level of meaning. It follows that this hypothesis cannot be understood, let alone assessed, by means of Son of man statements in any language other than Aramaic.

When we look back over the scholarship of the last fifty years, we see a massive explosion of knowledge in subjects which form the background to the reconstruction of Jesus' sayings in their original language. The Dead Sea scrolls have provided a decisive increase in our knowledge of Aramaic and other languages used in Israel towards the end of the Second Temple period. The discovery and editing of many other texts has massively increased our knowledge of the Aramaic language. Major tools of study have made our task more possible. Scholars in the fields of Bilingualism and Trans-lation Studies have greatly increased our understanding of how bilinguals and translators function. Work on the LXX, the Targums and the Peshitta has increased our understanding of the large group of translators whose work most closely approximates

---

[247] Casey, 'Jackals', 8–9, 20–1.
[248] See pp. 111–18 below.

that of translators who worked to produce information about Jesus in Greek.

The same does not apply to the actual reconstruction of sayings of Jesus. The best book on the subject is still Black, *Aramaic Approach*, the first edition of which was published in 1946. Much recent work has taken scholarship backwards instead of forwards. The time is therefore ripe for a new attack on these problems. We must begin by elaborating a new methodology.

2

METHOD

The purpose of this chapter is to propose a methodology for reconstructing Aramaic sources which lie behind the synoptic Gospels. We must begin by surveying the languages which were in general use in Israel during Jesus' lifetime: Latin, Greek, Hebrew and Aramaic.

Latin was the language of the Roman imperial power. It is consequently found in inscriptions. One of the most famous was set up by Pontius Pilatus, Praefectus Iudaeae during at least the latter part of Jesus' ministry. It comes from a building in Caesarea, the Roman capital of Judaea and the normal residence of the Praefectus Iudaeae:[1]

]S TIBERIEUM
PON]TIUS PILATUS
PRAEF]ECTUS IUDA[EA]E

This is the language of power, and we may not infer from it any widespread use of Latin.

Other people in Israel who will have known some Latin include Herod Antipas, the tetrarch of Galilee during Jesus' ministry. He was educated in Rome for several years (see Jos. *AJ* XVII.20),[2] and he maintained Herod the Great's description of his supporters as Herodiani.[3] How much he used this language, however, we do not know.

It follows that Jesus is not likely to have had the opportunity to have learnt Latin, and that it would have been of little use to him if he had.

Greek was much more widely used, throughout Israel. It had

---

[1] For photograph and fresh discussion, see G. Labbé, 'Ponce Pilate et la munificence de Tibère', *Revue des Etudes Anciennes* 93, 1991, 277–97.

[2] H. W. Hoehner, *Herod Antipas* (MSSNTS 17. Cambridge, 1972), pp. 12ff.

[3] See pp. 186–9 below.

begun to spread through Israel after the conquests of Alexander the Great. A number of Greek cities were founded, and some older cities were hellenised. For example, Josephus describes Gaza, Gadara and Hippos, at the end of the first century BCE, as Ἑλλη-νίδες . . . πόλεις (*AJ* XVII.320). In the third century, direct evidence of hellenisation is provided by the Zenon papyri. Here we find Tobiah, an aristocratic Jew, conducting business affairs in Greek. By the time of the Maccabees, many Jews had hellenised, a process which included the building of a gymnasium and under-going aspects of Greek education (1 Macc. 1.11–15; 2 Macc. 4.7–17). We must infer that assimilating Jews in Jerusalem learnt Greek. At the same time, the book of Daniel was written in Aramaic and Hebrew, and used Greek only for the Greek musical instruments favoured by Antiochus Epiphanes: קיתרוס = κίθαρις, פסנתרין = ψαλτήριον and סומפניה = συμφωνία (Dan. 3.5, cf. 3.7, 10, 15). None of these words has a proper Aramaic ending. This shows an attitude of extreme hostility to Greek on the part of faithful Jews.

The influence of Greek continued as time went on. At the time of Jesus, it will have been used by the Roman administration when-ever they did not use Latin. Greek was also used at the court of Herod Antipas. His cities Sepphoris and Tiberias were basically Greek cities. As in the Maccabean period, however, this establishes the use of Greek in Israel, but not the extent of its use among faithful Jews.

It is for this reason that five pieces of evidence may be thought to be of crucial significance. Firstly, there are Dead Sea scrolls in Greek. These include copies of the scriptures. This shows that there were Jews who wanted to know what the scriptures said, who could not understand them in Hebrew, and who needed them in Greek rather than in Aramaic. However, we do not know who these people were, or how numerous they were. Jews as assimilated as Herod Antipas will have wanted copies of Jewish sacred texts available, otherwise they could not have passed as proper Jews. They may well have wanted them in Greek, because that was the language of most of civilisation as they perceived it. Jews came to Jerusalem from the diaspora in the whole of the Roman empire, including Greece and hellenised places such as Alexandria. It is entirely likely that some synagogues were in consequence Greek-speaking. Whoever was responsible for the Dead Sea scrolls may have been providing translations of the scriptures quite deliberately for such people. This is strongly suggested by the late date of non-scriptural documents written in Greek. If Greek were widespread in Israel, and genuinely in use at Qumran, we would expect other Greek documents to be found. This does happen after 70 CE, but that was a major crisis which may well have resulted in more widespread use of Greek among Jews.

This is the importance of our second piece of evidence, the Greek material from Masada.[4] This includes jar inscriptions, some and probably all of which labelled produce for Herod the Great: this shows Greek as a language of international trade in the Roman empire, and understood by some people in Israel. There are a small number of papyri, one perhaps from 25–35 CE, others possibly later and one indicating a delivery of produce to a man called Judah. There are also some twenty ostraka from the ancient period, far fewer than in Aramaic and Hebrew. At least some of the ostraka are Jewish, and date from the period of the revolt against Rome. This provides some evidence of the use of Greek by Jews outside Jerusalem. The extent of this usage is, however, limited.

Equally important are the tomb inscriptions in Greek. There are many of these, notably from Jerusalem. Here too, however, we must be careful. The majority of Greek tomb inscriptions from Israel date from long after 70 CE, so they do not provide evidence of the situation at the time of Jesus. Those from Jerusalem before its fall do indeed indicate that some people spoke Greek, but they do not tell us how many or who these people were. They may have immigrated from the diaspora, or they may be hellenised Jews from among the richer aristocracy, they may be from Greek-speaking synagogues and these may not have been all that common. We should not draw dramatic conclusions from counting the proportion of those which survive in Greek, because we may be counting those rich enough to be buried in more durable materials, and it may have been precisely these who were more hellenised than the population as a whole.

Our fourth piece of evidence is traditions about normative or orthodox Jews from our period. Unfortunately, however, most of these are late and unreliable. For example, we are told that Gamaliel had 500 students of Greek. But this tradition is late (b. Sot 49b, cf. t. Sot 15.8), and unconfirmed by early sources. We

---

[4] H. M. Cotton and J. Geiger (eds.), *Masada II: The Yigael Yadin Excavations 1963–1965. Final Reports. The Latin and Greek Documents* (Jerusalem, 1989).

do know that Gamaliel I's students included St Paul (Acts 22.3).
Paul was fluent in Greek, but he also spoke Aramaic and read
Hebrew, and while he was studying under Gamaliel he was an
orthodox Jew. It may be that the late traditions are not altogether
accurate presentations of earlier situations like this, made in the
light of later experience when more Jews did speak Greek.

Our fifth piece of evidence is that of individuals outside the
Gospels. Our best-known Jerusalem Jew is Josephus. Josephus was
a well-educated aristocratic Jew from a priestly family. As such, he
did learn Greek, but it was his second language, and he needed
stylistic help when writing it (*C. Ap.* I.50, cf. *AJ* I.7; XX.263–5).
This means that he was aware of suffering interference from his
native Aramaic.

Taking all this evidence together, we must infer that in certain
circumstances a first-century Jew would have learnt Greek as part
of his education in Israel, and could have taught in Greek. This
would have happened if he had been born to assimilating aristocratic Jews in a major hellenised city, and had gone on to discourse
at the court of Herod Antipas. It is likely to have happened also
over a somewhat more orthodox spectrum than that. We do not,
however, have evidence to persuade us that Greek was in use
among normal Jews in Jewish places such as Nazareth and Capernaum.

This takes us to the lingua franca of Judaism in Israel, which was
Aramaic. Aramaic was a relatively old language, generally classified
as emerging from the general Semitic background in the ninth or
eighth century BCE. It was the administrative language of the
Persian empire, and consequently Jewish documents are extant in
Aramaic from the fifth century BCE onwards. This is the reason
why Aramaic was used for Ezra's instructions and some other parts
of the book of Ezra. When Ezra read the Torah after his return, he
needed Levites to explain what it meant. They are first mentioned,
after the men and women of the congregation, as כל מבין (Neh.
8.2), literally 'everyone who caused to understand', then likewise
המבינים (8.3). More explicitly, when Ezra read the Law, מבינים
את־העם לתורה (8.7) and most fully מפרש ושׂום שׂכל ויבינו
במקרא, literally 'translating and giving understanding, and they
caused to understand during the reading' (8.8).[5] We must infer that

---

[5] I have interpreted the Hiphil of בין consistently in these references. This gives us
three sensible groups, men, women, and those who helped them understand, a third

Ezra's audience did not understand the Hebrew text, and that the Levites explained it to them in Aramaic. It follows that by this time Aramaic was the normal language among Jews. It remained in widespread use in the diaspora in the East, outside the Roman empire.

We have more Aramaic documents extant from Israel, at intervals from the third century BCE until the time of Jesus. They include the Dead Sea scrolls, fragmentary remains of a large quantity of documents.[6] Among these are Daniel 2–7, stories deliberately written in defence of Judaism when it was being attacked by hellenisers, and other popular Jewish literature such as the Genesis Apocryphon. While some of the Aramaic material comes from a sub-group centred on Enoch, it is not otherwise sectarian. Apart from calendrical information which everyone needed, it is not especially learned either. It follows that Aramaic was a language spoken by ordinary Jews in Israel. The dates of the copies of some of these documents run through into the first century CE, that is, into and past the lifetime of Jesus.

Of particular importance are the Targums from the Dead Sea. The extensive remains of the Targum to Job are sufficient to show that a complete Targum was made. It is quite a literal translation. It follows that there were Jews who wanted to know what the book of Job said, but who could not understand it in Hebrew. Their native tongue must have been Aramaic. Equally important is 4Q156, containing what survives of an Aramaic translation of Lev. 16.12–21, part of the instructions for observing Yom Kippur. The people who needed this text must have been faithful Jews: again, Aramaic must have been their native tongue. Similar remarks would apply to the Aramaic fragments of Tobit, if these were a translation from an original Hebrew, but it may be that the Hebrew fragments have been translated from an Aramaic original.[7] There are also a few non-literary works. These include ostraka from Jesus' lifetime, recording details of the delivery of items such as cakes of dried figs.[8] This shows Aramaic in very mundane everyday use.

---

essential group. We should not follow commentators who take the first examples of בין differently, thereby producing a very odd group with the men and the women.

[6] See pp. 33–7 above.

[7] Cf. Fitzmyer, 'Aramaic and Hebrew Fragments of Tobit'.

[8] A. Yardeni, 'New Jewish Aramaic Ostraca', *IEJ* 40, 1990, 130–52; K. Beyer, *Die aramäischen Texte vom Toten Meer: Ergänzungsband* (Göttingen, 1994), pp. 197–9.

The Aramaic of documents written before 70 CE shows significant interference from Hebrew, a natural result of centuries of diglossia among learned Jews. There is, however, no significant interference from Greek, as there was to be later. We must infer that, at the time of Jesus, Aramaic was not generally spoken by people who were bilingual with Greek.

The inscriptions in the Temple are another significant piece of evidence. A warning to Gentiles survives in Greek. Mishnah reports several other inscriptions, giving them mostly in Hebrew, the language in which Mishnah is written. However, the inscriptions on the shekel trumpets are among those which it reports in Aramaic, תקלין עתיקין and תקלין חדתין (m. Sheq 6.5). This can only be explained if Aramaic was the lingua franca of Israel. We also have transmitted to us three letters dictated by Gamaliel (t. San 2.6//y. San I.2.18d.12–19//b. San 11b). One is about the intercalation of a month, because the lambs were too young and the birds so small. This was therefore probably before the fall of Jerusalem, so Gamaliel is probably Gamaliel I, the elder contemporary of Jesus. One letter is written to Jews in upper and lower Galilee. That this is the language in which a prominent rabbi wrote to the Jewish communities in these areas shows that Aramaic was the lingua franca of Israel. Some inscriptions also survive in Aramaic. They include those in the tomb of Caiaphas.[9] This shows Aramaic as the natural language used in the tomb of a family of which more than one member served as high priest.

Josephus, who was brought up as a member of a distinguished priestly family in Jerusalem, wrote the first draft of his *Jewish War* in Aramaic. He needed Greek-speaking assistants to help with the style of his work, even when he wrote years later in Rome (*C. Ap.* I.50, cf. *AJ* I.7; XX.263–5). This is normal for someone whose first language was Aramaic, and who learnt Greek as part of his education. At the siege of Jerusalem, Titus, who was fluent in Greek (Suet. *Div. Tit.* 3; cf. Jos. *Vit.* 359), told Josephus to negotiate with the Jews τῇ πατρίῳ γλώσσῃ (*BJ* V.360–1), so their only common language was Aramaic (cf. VI.96; 327; *C. Ap.* I.49). This is supported by Luke's report that the people of Jerusalem called a place τῇ ἰδίᾳ διαλέκτῳ αὐτῶν Ἀκελδαμάχ, τοῦτ᾽ ἔστιν,

---

[9] Z. Greenhut, 'The "Caiaphas" Tomb in North Talpiyot, Jerusalem', *'Atiqot*, 21, 1992, 63–71. For a more sceptical view of the identity of the tomb, see W. Horbury, 'The "Caiaphas" Ossuaries and Joseph Caiaphas', *PEQ* 126, 1994, 32–48, with bibliography.

Χωρίον Αἵματος (Acts 1.19). This is a reasonable presentation of the Aramaic חקל דמא. Late sources have a few reports of early rabbis using Aramaic. For example, m. Ed 8.4 (//b. AZ 37a) records some judgements of Jose ben Joezer of Zereda in the second century BCE:

על אייל קמייצא דכי ועל משקי בית מטבחיא דאינון
דכיין ודי יקרב במיתא מסתאב

> Concerning the ayil-locust that it is clean, and concerning the flows in the slaughter-house that they are clean, and that he who touches a corpse becomes unclean.

It is probable that such traditions were always handed down in Aramaic because that is how they were originally delivered.

Aramaic continued to be used in Israel after the fall of Jerusalem. The Greek of the Babata archives and the Hebrew of the letters of Simeon son of Kosiba both contain enough Aramaisms to show that Aramaic was the first language of some Jews whose second language was Greek or Hebrew. The Palestinian Talmud contains many sayings in Aramaic attributed to rabbis long before it was written down. The Christian Palestinian Syriac lectionary shows Christians in this area continuing to use Aramaic too. The Targums show that there continued to be many Jews who wanted to understand the scriptures, and whose native tongue was Aramaic.

These points form a massive argument of cumulative weight. Jesus will have been brought up with Aramaic as his native tongue, and he will have had to use Aramaic to teach normal Jews in Galilee and in Judaea.

Finally, we must consider the position of Hebrew. Hebrew was the lingua franca of Israel in the pre-exilic period. Consequently, the scriptures were written in Hebrew. We have seen that it was replaced by Aramaic as the lingua franca of Israel, and that parts of the books of Ezra and Daniel were consequently written in Aramaic. Hebrew none the less continued in use as a living literary language. Joshua son of Sirach wrote the book which we call Ecclesiasticus c. 200 BCE. Parts of Daniel are written in Hebrew: the concentric structure of chapters 2–7 makes it probable that these Aramaic chapters existed first,[10] and that the remaining

---

[10] A. Lenglet, 'La Structure littéraire de Daniel 2–7', *Bib* 53, 1972, 169–90; P. M. Casey, *Son of Man: The Interpretation and Influence of Daniel 7* (London, 1980), pp. 7–9.

chapters were written by people deliberately returning to Hebrew when the hellenising crisis involved the persecution of Jews who were faithful to the Torah.

Most of the Dead Sea scrolls are written in Hebrew. They include 4QMMT, a learned and detailed halakhic letter directed to the priests who were running the Temple in Jerusalem.[11] This means that Hebrew was considered suitable by some learned and faithful Jews as a vehicle for communicating with other learned and faithful Jews. Other works include learned commentaries on scripture, and non-canonical psalms. These Hebrew texts are not marked by significant interference from Greek, and the degree of interference from Aramaic is sufficiently accounted for by a long period of diglossia. These documents therefore constitute decisive proof that some learned Jews wrote sound Hebrew as a living literary language. They also make it probable that some Jews spoke Hebrew. It may even have been some people's first language. In view of all this, we must infer that Hebrew was used by scribes in the Temple too. It is thus entirely possible that some people such as Pharisees and Temple scribes could not only read the scriptures in Hebrew, but conduct learned debates in Hebrew too. Some Hebrew documents from the Dead Sea were not written by particularly learned people. These, however, contain more Aramaisms, an indication that Aramaic was almost certainly the first language of the authors. This shows that some people used Hebrew, but not that it was the first language of anyone other than scribal families.

Hebrew continued in use, and may have increased in use by the time of Mishnah, which is written entirely in Hebrew. It consists almost entirely of learned material. This is not the case with the Talmuds, both of which are written partly in Aramaic and partly in Hebrew. Sayings in Hebrew are attributed to early rabbis. For example, m. Av 1.12 attributes the following saying to Hillel:

היו מתלמידיו של אהרן אוהב שלום ורודף שלום אוהב
את הבריות ומקרבן לתורה.

> Be of the disciples of Aaron, loving peace and pursuing peace, and loving people and bringing them near to the Torah.

---

[11] A. Qimron and J. Strugnell, with Y. Sussmann and A. Yardeni, *Qumran Cave 4. V. Miqṣat Maʻaśe Ha-Torah* (DJD X. Oxford, 1994).

It is possible that sayings like this were always transmitted in Hebrew because they were originally spoken in Hebrew.

It follows that Hebrew was in use at the time of Jesus. It was probably a spoken language among learned Jews, and the scriptures were certainly read in the original Hebrew by some people. It is not probable that Jesus would have been brought up to speak it in Nazareth, but it is probable that anyone absorbed in the Jewish faith in Israel would have learnt to read the scriptures in Hebrew, and might have learnt to speak it if he intended to become involved in debate with learned scribes. It would not be useful for teaching the crowds.

General evidence therefore dictates that Jesus was brought up to speak Aramaic, and makes us take seriously the possibility that he also knew Greek and/or Hebrew. We must turn next to the evidence of the Gospels.

The synoptic Gospels are written in Greek, and never mention interpreters. Some have inferred that Jesus taught in Greek.[12] There are three reasons why we must not do so. Firstly, we have seen that Greek was used in certain specialised circumstances, and was not a suitable language for teaching the crowds. The Gospels, however, have the teaching of the crowds as a central facet of Jesus' ministry. Moreover, they give us no clear indication that any of the central group of disciples had a Greek education. We must therefore infer that when Jesus taught in Aramaic, the Gospel writers do not tell us so.

Secondly, the Gospels were written to communicate the Gospel to Christian churches, in a form which lies inside the broad range of the Greco-Roman βίος.[13] We know from Acts and the Epistles that Greek was the language of many churches throughout the Roman empire. We must infer that our Gospels were written for Greek-speaking churches. This is why they are written in Greek. Thirdly, we shall discuss in detail features of the synoptic Gospels, including transliterated Aramaic words, which can only be explained if Jesus taught in Aramaic. It follows from these three points that the mere fact that Jesus' words in the Gospels are almost entirely in Greek does not mean that he spoke them in Greek.

Did Jesus speak Greek at all? This is more difficult to determine.

[12] See pp. 9–11, 63–8 above.
[13] R. A. Burridge, *What are the Gospels? A Comparison with Graeco-Roman Biography* (MSSNTS 70. Cambridge, 1992).

Mark has him be a τέκτων (Mark 6.3), usually translated 'carpenter', but it has a somewhat broader range of meaning, like the Aramaic נגר which underlies it. He was a craftsman, and may have worked in stone as well as in wood. He may not have been able to stay in business by working in Nazareth for Nazarenes alone. He may therefore have worked in Sepphoris, a large city rebuilt by Herod Antipas during Jesus' lifetime, and just four miles over the hill from Nazareth. Joseph may have known some Greek for this kind of purpose, and Jesus may have been brought up with the Greek necessary for conducting business negotiations. In the absence of direct information, we cannot be sure about this.

There are two other occasions when Jesus may be thought to have communicated in Greek. He has a conversation with a woman described as Ἑλληνίς, Συροφοινίκισσα τῷ γένει (Mark 7.26). If she was Syrophoenician by race, and came from near Tyre (Mark 7.24), Aramaic may have been her second language, or she may have been brought up bilingual before marrying into a Greek social group. Alternatively, since the Gospels never mention interpreters, they may have simply assumed that they were present when needed. The other occasion is Jesus' trial before Pilate. Here we may be quite certain that the proceedings were not conducted in Aramaic. It does not help that our accounts of them are unreliable.[14] If, however, Pilate really communicated with Jesus and expected him to reply, he will have used an interpreter.

Two of the inner circle of twelve have Greek names, Andrew and Philip, and these are extant in an early list in which only Simon's nickname Peter is given only in Greek translation (Mark 3.16–19). Unlike Cephas/Peter, Andrew and Philip did not play a significant role in Greek-speaking churches, so they are not likely to have become known by Greek names and to have had Aramaic names too. We should probably infer two bilingual members of the twelve. A strong case can also be made for Jesus' use of a single Greek word, ὑποκριτής. When sayings of Jesus were first translated into Greek, this meant 'actor' rather than 'hypocrite'. This makes excellent sense in passages such as Matt. 6.2, 5, where its use with reference to overtly observant Jews would have formed extremely sharp polemic, for the theatre symbolises especially well the Hellenism against which they sought to protect Jewish observances.

---

[14] This opinion cannot be justified here. For discussion, with bibliography, see R. E. Brown, *The Death of the Messiah* (2 vols., ABRL. London/New York, 1994), vol. I, pp. 665–87.

The Aramaic חנף does not occur in Aramaic texts until later. It does not mean 'actor', and the Hebrew חנף is properly rendered with ἀσεβής in the LXX (Job 8.13; 15.34; 20.5; 27.8; Prov. 11.9; Isa. 33.14), rather than with ὑποκριτής (Job 34.30; 36.13, neither really original to the LXX, but from Theodotion), because of the much bigger overlap in semantic area. The sharper force of ὑποκριτής also fits the dramatic imagery of Matt. 6.2, 5, which clearly refers to the sort of behaviour found in cities. We should therefore conclude that Jesus used this Greek word polemically. Like the Greek words in Daniel, however, this shows rejection of Greek, rather than acceptance, normal use or extensive knowledge of it.[15]

We must conclude that Jesus probably knew more than one word of Greek. He did not, however, generally teach in Greek, so to understand his words we shall need to reconstruct them in their original Aramaic.

The Gospels confirm our expectation that Jesus did not know any Latin. They give no serious signs that he knew or used it. The trial before Pilate is not an exception, if it was conducted in Latin, for the same reason already given for not using it as evidence that Jesus spoke Greek: Pilate may have employed interpreters. There are one or two Latin loanwords. These include δηνάριον (Mark 12.15//Matt. 22.19//Luke 20.24; Matt. 18.28; 20.2, 9–13; Luke 7.41; 10.35). This is simply the ubiquitous denarius, so called because that was its name, and actually used as a Roman symbol in the debate of Mark 12.13–17//Matt. 22.15–22//Luke 20.20–6. Jesus will have used the occasional Latin loanword, like everyone else at the time.

By contrast, the evidence that Jesus taught in Aramaic is abundant. Some of his words are recorded in Aramaic. For example, Mark 14.36 records his prayer in the Garden of Gethsemane. The first word is ἀββα, the Aramaic אבא, 'Father'. The fatherhood of God was an important aspect of Jesus' teaching, and the early church would not have invented a prayer that he might not die, when his atoning death was central to them. We must infer

---

[15] It is remarkable that such a solution to the obvious linguistic difficulties of ὑποκριτής is not even entertained by most of the secondary literature, notably not by J. Barr, 'The Hebrew/Aramaic Background of "Hypocrisy" in the Gospels', in P. R. Davies and R. T. White (eds.), *A Tribute to Geza Vermes: Essays on Jewish and Christian Literature and History* (JSOT. SS 100. Sheffield, 1990), pp. 307–26, esp. 324, n. 3.

that Jesus prayed in Aramaic, and the prayer has been translated, like everything else, because the Gospel was written for Greek-speaking Christians. Similarly, Mark 15.34 records his cry of Ps. 22.1 from the cross. The last word is σαβαχθανι, which is neither Greek nor a quotation of the Hebrew עזבתני. It is the distinctively Aramaic שבקתני, used later in the Peshitta and the Targum of this verse. It follows that Jesus not merely spoke Aramaic: he spoke to God in Aramaic even when he was speaking to God alone, even when so doing by means of the Hebrew scriptures. It follows that Aramaic was his first language.

Jesus also gave Aramaic epithets to the inner circle of three disciples, Peter, Jacob and John. Mark put 'Peter' in Greek, noting that his original name was Σίμων (Mark 3.16). He calls him Peter thereafter (except for 'Simon' in a word of Jesus at 14.37). Paul, however, has Κηφᾶς in Epistles written in Greek (1 Cor. 1.12; Gal. 1.18 etc.). Κηφᾶς is not Greek, but the Aramaic כפא, 'rock' (1 En. 89.32; 11QtgJob XXXII.1; XXXIII.9). We must infer that Jesus called Simon כיפא, and that people continued to use this name after Jesus' death. Mark has translated it into Greek, for it is one of the rare puns that works in both Aramaic and Greek, so he was known as 'Peter' in some churches (cf. John 1.42). Jacob and John were called בני רעם, 'sons of thunder'.[16]

Jesus' disciples are occasionally recorded as using an Aramaic word too. For example, Judah of Kerioth identified Jesus when he betrayed him with the address Ῥαββι (Mark 14.45). This is not Greek, and will reflect the Aramaic (or Hebrew in this case) רבי. At Mark 14.12, 14, both Jesus and two of his disciples are recorded using the word πάσχα, Passover. This is the distinctively Aramaic form פסחא.

As well as Aramaic words, Jesus' teaching shows features which can only be explained if he spoke Aramaic. The outstanding one is the idiomatic use of the term 'son of man'. The Greek ὁ υἱὸς τοῦ ἀνθρώπου is not known in texts previously written by monoglot Greeks. It can only be understood as a translation of the Aramaic בר (א)נש(א).[17] Some sayings, when reconstructed completely, also turn out to be examples of a particular Aramaic idiom, according to which a speaker could use a general statement with בר (א)נש(א) with particular reference to himself, or himself and a group of other

---

[16] See pp. 197–8 below.
[17] See pp. 118–21, 130–2 below.

people. We shall see this in detailed discussions of Mark 2.28; 9.12; 10.45; 14.21. These sayings must therefore have originated in Aramaic.

Other signs of interference include the use of certain words. For example, in the Lord's prayer we are to ask God to forgive τὰ ὀφειλήματα ἡμῶν (Matt. 6.12), literally our 'debts', but a metaphor for our 'sins', so a literal translation of the Aramaic חובינא. We must say that we have already forgiven τοῖς ὀφειλέταις ἡμῶν, literally 'our debtors', and a metaphor for 'those who have sinned against us', and so a literal translation of חייבינא.[18] Some of Jesus' parables, in which debt functions as a metaphor for sin, show him making extensive use of this same metaphor in story mode (cf. Matt. 18.23–35; Luke 7.36–50; 16.1–9). It follows that the Matthean version of the Lord's prayer properly reflects Jesus' usage. Interference is also found in the structure of sentences. For examples, passages such as Mark 1.39–43 and 11.15–17 show a large amount of parataxis, and verbs placed near the beginnings of sentences. While both these phenomena occur in crude and/or Semitising Greek, in true stories about events in Aramaic-speaking communities they are more likely to be due to the translation of Aramaic sources.[19]

Some features of Mark's Greek are characteristic of the work of bilinguals. For example, at Mark 9.43, 45, 47 we read καλόν where a monoglot Greek-speaker would use a comparative. Aramaic has no comparative, so the use of καλόν is due to interference in someone who was used to saying טב. Again, at Mark 14.72 we read ἐπιβαλών at a point where no monoglot Greek-speaker would want to say 'throwing'. In Syriac, however, שׁדא is used of 'throwing' threats and curses, much as in English we may 'hurl' abuse. In the absence of an appropriate word just at this point, we must infer that Mark had a written source which read ושׁרא בכא: 'And he began to weep.' He misread this as ושׁדא בכא: 'And throwing [sc.

---

[18] For an Aramaic reconstruction of Matt. 6.12–13a//Luke 11.4, see p. 60 above.

[19] The investigation of M. Reiser, *Syntax und Stil des Markusevangeliums* (WUNT II, 11. Tübingen, 1984), is too limited to demonstrate otherwise. Reiser acknowledges other evidence of Semitic influence in Mark (*Syntax und Stil*, pp. 11, 164). His selection of authors for comparison includes later works, including Christian works whose authors had the Greek Bible in the background. His statistical comparisons often cover the whole of Mark, and therefore are not valid against a theory that only parts of it are translation material. For reconstruction and interpretation of the Aramaic source of Mark 11.15–18a, see P. M. Casey, 'Culture and Historicity: The Cleansing of the Temple', *CBQ*, 59, 1997, 306–32.

more abuse], he wept'. This made sense to him because the idiomatic use of שׁדא was already present in Aramaic, and he translated with ἐπιβαλών because he was suffering from the double level of interference inevitable in translators. While שׁדא could be misheard as well as misread, and שׁדא could interfere with ἐπιβαλών in a bilingual's head as well as in a written text, this degree of interference is more probable in a translator than in someone writing freely.

This Gospel contains a few phenomena so marked that they must be regarded as mistakes. ἐπιβαλών is perhaps best so classified. The expression ὁδὸν ποιεῖν (Mark 2.23) is another one. It ought to mean that the disciples were building a path rather than going along one. The Aramaic עבר, however, means to 'go along', and is easily misread as עבד, which may generally be translated with ποιεῖν because of the massive overlap in semantic area between these two words. This also entails that Mark was using a written Aramaic source.[20]

In considering evidence of Aramaic sources, we must remember the evidence of the Dead Sea scrolls that Hebrew had penetrated into Aramaic more than we had previously realised because of a lengthy period of diglossia. We must therefore accept that what we had previously thought of as Hebraisms may be evidence of written sources in Aramaic. The outstanding example is Mark 14.25 Θ οὐ μὴ προσθῶμεν πιεῖν, supported by D 565 a d f arm οὐ (μὴ) προσθῶ π(ι)εῖν. We must infer a source לא נוסף למשתה. The construction is in a sense a Hebraism, for it is common in Hebrew, but יסף is an old Aramaic word, and this construction is used already at 4Q198 (Tobit 14.2), cf. 11QtgJob XXV.8, so its presence in an Aramaic source should not be regarded as problematical. The reading οὐ μὴ προσθῶμεν πιεῖν is also an extreme example of interference in an author who uses πάλιν twenty-eight times in such a short document. We should again infer the double level of interference characteristic of translators of texts.

It follows from this array of evidence that Jesus spoke Aramaic, that he taught in Aramaic, that accounts of his life and teaching were transmitted in Aramaic, and that Mark's Gospel contains some literal translation of Aramaic source material.

The evidence of Jesus' use of Hebrew is more difficult to evaluate. The most general features of his ministry suggest that he was

---

[20] See p. 140 below.

steeped in the scriptures. He drew on the wellsprings of the prophetic tradition. However, John the Baptist had been the only major prophet for centuries, so Jesus must have been familiar with the works of the prophets themselves. The two major abstract concepts in his teaching, the kingship and fatherhood of God, are both biblical. On the other hand, these things might be learnt orally in an observant home, helped by listening orally to the exposition of the scriptures at Jewish meetings every sabbath and on other occasions. The decisive argument is his detailed reliance on scripture to establish major points, especially significant matters of halakhah.

For example, when challenged by Pharisees because his disciples were plucking grain on the sabbath, Jesus cited in their defence the example of David in 1 Samuel and the purpose of the sabbath at the creation (Mark 2.23–8).[21] He had an unusual exegesis of the end of Malachi 3, according to which the prophecy of Elijah coming again before the end had been fulfilled in John the Baptist. His exposition of this (Mark 9.11–13) can only be understood in the light of his understanding of other passages, including Isaiah 40 and Job 14.[22] His unusual and possibly unique prohibition of divorce was justified by his appeal to texts from the creation narrative of Genesis (Mark 10.2–9, citing Gen. 1.27; 2.24). His control of the halakhah in the court of the Gentiles was a prophetic act, made possible by his charismatic preaching on biblical texts which included Isaiah 56 and Jeremiah 7.[23] He employed vigorous exegesis of the revelatory text of Exod. 3.6 as if it were a decisive argument which established his belief in the resurrection of the dead (Mark 12.26–7). He relied upon the scriptures, including Psalm 41 and the Hallel psalms, for predictions of his betrayal, death and resurrection.[24]

All this bears witness to his detailed knowledge of the scriptures, his complete trust in the truth of the scriptures, and his absolute confidence in his own innovative exegesis. He must therefore have known the text. We can imagine all this in a language other than the original Hebrew. Had he taught in Alexandria, for example, we can imagine such confidence in the LXX. In first-century Israel, however, only the original Hebrew text (with Aramaic in Ezra and

[21] See pp. 151–7 below.
[22] See ch. 3 below.
[23] Casey, 'Cleansing of the Temple'.
[24] See pp. 231–3, 247 below.

Daniel) was sufficiently canonical for him to have relied on it like this. For him to have used Aramaic versions like this, we should have to suppose that there were virtually canonical Targums for the whole of the Hebrew Bible. It is clear from the evidence of the preservation of texts that this was not the case. We must therefore infer that Jesus knew the scriptures in the original Hebrew.

We should not hold Mark 15.34 against this. As we have seen, this shows him quoting Ps. 22.1 in Aramaic rather than Hebrew at a moment of extreme stress. We must infer that Aramaic was his first language, but not that it was the language in which he *read* the scriptures. In all the incidents noted above, he will have *expounded* the scriptures in Aramaic. That he should *repeat* a scripture in Aramaic is therefore entirely natural. We must infer that he read the scriptures in Hebrew, and expounded them in Aramaic. Luke 4.16–20 may be thought to support this. Here Jesus goes to a Jewish meeting on the sabbath, is handed a scroll of Isaiah and reads from it, a process dependent on his being able to read Isaiah in Hebrew. An unsupported Lukan narrative is, however, rather limited support.

If Jesus read the scriptures in Hebrew, could he then speak Hebrew? This does not necessarily follow, and is very difficult to determine. Judging by the accounts of the ministry, we have little reason to suppose that he would have much occasion to speak Hebrew. There are two small indications of his use of Hebrew, both deriving from responses to opponents who very probably did. One is the accusation by 'scribes who came down from Jerusalem' that he cast out demons by בעל זבול (Mark 3.22). These people are likely to have been able to speak Hebrew, and זבול is extant in Hebrew, but not in Aramaic sources. Jesus will have used the same expression at Matt. 12.27//Luke 11.19. The other such occasion is at Matt. 11.19//Luke 7.34, which includes a quotation from his opponents. In the Greek text, Jesus says that he comes ἐσθίων καὶ πίνων, and his opponents accuse him of being ἄνθρωπος φάγος καὶ οἰνοπότης. In Aramaic, it is impossible to find two seriously different expressions for these two things, but this is essential for the passage to make sense. When I reconstructed it, therefore, I used the Hebrew of Deut. 21.20 as part of the accusation, which I reconstructed thus:[25]

הא אנש זלל וסבא, חבר למכסין ולחטין.

[25] Casey, 'General, Generic and Indefinite', 39–40.

This shows Jesus able to repeat an accusation based in the Hebrew scriptures, as we should expect from someone who read the scriptures in Hebrew.

On the other hand, Jesus did not use Hebrew in his debate with Pharisees at Mark 2.23–8. This follows from the use of the Son of man saying at 2.28, which makes sense as an example of the idiomatic use of (א)בר (א)נש found in Aramaic, but not in Hebrew. For the same reason, he cannot have spoken in Hebrew when responding at Mark 3.28, cf. Matt. 12.32//Luke 12.10, to the scribal accusation that he cast out demons by בעל זבול.

If Jesus had little occasion to speak Hebrew, there are just these two small indications of his using it in the synoptic tradition, and two indications that he did not use it when he might have done; we should infer that he did not generally speak Hebrew. While we must keep our eyes open for the occasional use of Hebrew by scribal opponents and in appropriate responses by him, we must reconstruct his sayings in Aramaic, not in Hebrew. As we have seen further indications that Aramaic was in general use and that there are signs of its use in narrative sections of Mark too, we must use Aramaic for reconstructing such parts of the narrative as seem to go back to Aramaic sources.

Our next problem is the kind of Aramaic we should use. We must suppose that Jesus spoke Galilean Aramaic. Virtually no Galilean Aramaic of the right period survives, however. Later sources are centuries later, and much of what goes under the heading of Galilean Aramaic does not really come from Galilee.[26] Moreover, there is no guarantee that Mark's Aramaic sources were actually transmitted in Galilean Aramaic, rather than by one or more disciples who spoke Judaean Aramaic.

This problem is insuperable in theory, but fortunately it is no longer of great importance in practice. This is largely due to the discovery of the Dead Sea scrolls, which provide us with a large slice of Aramaic vocabulary, and standard syntax, from shortly before the time of Jesus. These words and constructions are virtually all found in other dialects too. It follows that they were known in the time of Jesus, and that they are likely to have been known in Galilee. Most of the Dead Sea scrolls have now been published, together with convenient glossaries.[27] It is therefore

---

[26] See pp. 35–6, 39 above.
[27] Beyer, *Die aramäischen Texte*; Fitzmyer and Harrington, *Manual of Palestinian Aramaic Texts*; Beyer, *Ergänzungsband*.

quite easy to check whether most words occur in the Aramaic of our period (though the reading of rare words must be checked with photographs). If we do this, we succeed in the massively difficult task of viewing the sources in their original language, a major step towards seeing them in their original culture.

It matters little that Jesus probably pronounced some of his gutturals in a different way from the way we shall write them. Matthew clearly thought that something about Peter's speech gave him away in the high priest's courtyard (Matt. 26.73), and Matthew was in a good position to work this out. The difference must surely have been his pronunciation. A late source has a son of Galilee ask for an אמר:

> אמרו לה, גלילאה שוטה, חמר למירכב או חמר למישתי
> עמר למילבש או אימר לאיתכסאה?

> They said to him, 'Stupid Galilean, an "ass" to ride or "wine" to drink, "wool" to wear or a "lamb" to kill?'
> (b. Erub 53b)

This story makes sense only if later people from outside Galilee felt that Galileans badly confused sounds including א, ח, and ע. This would be recognisable at any time. If it were already the case in the first century, however, it would make no difference to the meaning of Jesus' sentences, as we can reconstruct them from Gospel sayings. It would make no difference to narrative whatever. Equally, there are likely to have been a few differences in words. For example, scholars trying to reconstruct Jesus' sayings in 'Galilean' Aramaic have used חמא where I shall use חזא. However, most examples of חמא are much later than the time of Jesus in date, and it is very doubtful whether most of them are genuinely Galilean. This is why I shall use חזא, which is extant in the Dead Sea scrolls, and earlier and biblical Aramaic, as well as Samaritan Aramaic, and has not died out in Christian Palestinian Aramaic and other dialects. What is equally important, however, is that the semantic area of both words is almost identical, approximately equivalent to the English word 'see'. It would therefore make no serious difference if we were to use a word from the wrong dialect.

This situation must be contrasted with two others. We have seen abundantly that, from an historical perspective, using the wrong language is disastrous. This is most obvious with בר (א)נש(א). The semantic area of this expression is unchanged in any serious sense from Sefire III.16 through 1QapGen XXI.13 to later Jewish Aramaic and Syriac, and it is an expression extant in Galilean Aramaic, however that is defined. Where a change of dialect does not affect the meaning, the change of language to ὁ υἱὸς τοῦ ἀνθρώπου was serious, and efforts to understand it as if it were English or German have been disastrous.[28] Equally, using any dialect without any controls is disastrous. We cannot possibly suppose that the verb אתברנש was available for Jesus to use – it is a specifically Syriac development, brought about by the need to discuss his incarnation in theological terms. Moreover, we have seen that scholars who play tricks with words can play them more abundantly if they avail themselves of the Aramaic of all periods. We therefore must not do this.

It follows that the Dead Sea scrolls are our major resource. They are from the right language, the right culture, and very near to the right date. Moreover, there are now sufficient of them extant and published to supply a high proportion of the vocabulary and syntax of the Aramaic sources of the synoptic Gospels. However, they do not supply everything. What do we do when the necessary vocabulary is missing? At this point, we must use material from other dialects with caution. We may consider first Aramaic words extant from earlier documents. These were certainly in existence before the time of Jesus, and the Aramaic language was spread in a relatively stereotyped and official form, because it was the official language of the Persian empire. The probability of words extant in old sources still being extant is therefore high. Moreover, we know that Akkadian words were sometimes taken over into Aramaic, but unmentioned until late sources.[29] This happens most with unfamiliar words such as šib-bur-ra-tú, later Aramaic and Syriac שברא, 'rue'. It none the less reinforces the main point, that the rate of change was slow, so that old sources are a reasonable resource for us.

We may turn next to the Palestinian Talmud. This is the right language and culture, only somewhat later in date. It contains many words which are also extant in the Dead Sea scrolls and earlier sources, and many sayings which are attributed to rabbis long before the final date of its composition. For example, many basic words such as אמר, ברך and גבר are found abundantly in

---

[28] See pp. 69–71 above.
[29] In general, see S. A. Kaufman, *The Akkadian Influences on Aramaic* (Assyriological Studies, 19. Chicago, 1974).

both. Sayings attributed to early rabbis include this one, attributed to R. Simeon son of Yohai at y. Sheb 9.1/12.38d:

צילר מבלעדי שמיא לא יבדא. כל שכן בר נשא.

> A bird is not destroyed without heaven – how much more a/the son of man!

We cannot be confident that R. Simeon said exactly this in 148 CE, and it does not mean that we can predate without further ado the expression מבלעדי, or take כל שכן to be normal Aramaic rather than Hebrew. None the less, most words in this saying are a normal part of earlier Aramaic, and it ends with the idiomatic use of בר נשא in a general statement which has particular reference to the speaker. We should not refuse to regard this as relevant to Gospel sayings merely because of its somewhat later date, when its Sitz im Leben, a man with good reason to fear death, is so close to sayings in other Aramaic dialects and in the teaching of Jesus.

We may also turn to the Palestinian Syriac lectionaries. The major one, that of the Gospels, gives us a translation of many passages into Aramaic, a dialect in the right place, of a slightly different culture, and somewhat later date. We must be careful, therefore. Obviously, an expression such as ברה דגברא (for example Matt. 9.6; Luke 9.58; John 6.53) is entirely secondary to the process of translating the Greek Gospels *into* Aramaic, and we must always watch for this effect. At the same time, these sources use many words which we know from the Aramaic of the right period. For example, ברנש is used of people other than Jesus, such as Levi in the narrative of Matt. 9.9, and the centurion referring to himself at Luke 7.8. The plural בנינשא is also restored, referring to people in general (for example Matt. 9.8; Luke 18.27). The term γέγραπται is rendered with כתיב (for example Matt. 2.5; Luke 19.46), which is the right word exactly. It is therefore always worth looking in this source when we cannot find a word we need in the Aramaic of the right period.

Finally, we should consult Aramaic of any period and dialect when we are stuck for rare words – 'dill', 'moneychangers' and the like. Such words may not change over a very long period of time, and it makes very little difference if we make the wrong choice of a single word of no particular theological significance. We must at such a point bear in mind the purpose of this enterprise. We need reconstructions so that we can see our sources, and particularly the teaching of Jesus, in its original cultural setting. If we get the wrong word for ὁ υἱὸς τοῦ ἀνθρώπου, we are in serious trouble. If we get the wrong word for 'dill', no serious harm is done. We are equally well advised to use late sources when the evidence of the Gospels is strong enough. We have noted the expression ἀπὸ μιᾶς at Luke 14.18. This can only be explained if the idiomatic Syriac expression מן חדא, which means 'all at once', was in use in the Aramaic of our period, its lack of attestation in early sources being due to the small quantity of extant material.[30] It is at this stage of the enterprise that we should not refrain from careful use of any of the Syriac versions either.

Work done in three other fields of study is also important for a proper understanding of the changes which have taken place between the original telling of the words and deeds of Jesus in Aramaic and their present formulation in Greek: Bilingualism, Translation Studies, and work of a similar kind done on biblical versions.

Bilingualism, or even multilingualism, is an inevitable result of living where more than one language is spoken. Consequently, people may be functionally bilingual without having full command of both languages. They may learn both together as they grow up, or acquire a second language for a particular purpose when grown up. They may move into a monoglot environment, and over a period of years they may forget aspects of their first language, especially items of vocabulary which are not often used. In a summary account soundly based on the massive number of recent studies of people who use more than one language, Hoffmann describes fifteen different kinds of people, including schoolchildren from Italian immigrant families living in the United States who use English both at home and outside but whose older relatives always address them in Italian; Turkish immigrant workers in Germany who speak Turkish at home and with friends and work colleagues, but who communicate in German with superiors and authorities; and the Danish immigrant in New Zealand who has had no contact with Danish for the last forty years.[31] These kinds of people are typical of many, and they have in common that they do not need the whole of both languages. Consequently, the majority of

---

[30] See pp. 42–3, 53–4 above.
[31] C. Hoffmann, *An Introduction to Bilingualism* (London/New York, 1991), pp. 16–17.

bilinguals are not fully competent in the whole of both their languages.

This is one reason why bilinguals are not necessarily good translators, even if they are proficient in the use of two or more languages in the circumstances in which they normally use them. We must bear in mind that Gospel translators may have had similar experiences to those described above, because they are so basic to the lives of people who live in multilingual environments. When therefore we find that the translator responsible for Mark 3.17 had forgotten the Aramaic word for 'thunder', we find something perfectly normal in a bilingual. He may have spoken Greek at home, or spoken only Greek for the previous ten years, so he had called thunder βροντή always or for years, and had forgotten רעם, if he ever knew it.[32]

All bilinguals suffer from interference. The most obvious form of this is the least relevant to us – phonological interference, what most people call a foreign accent. We have no idea whether Mark or his translator spoke Greek with an Aramaic accent, so we cannot make use of this. The most important forms of interference for us are those which are visible, sufficiently different from the speech and writing of monoglot users of the language for us to be able to see them. One of the least obvious forms of interference is accordingly relevant whenever it can be measured – the use of a linguistic item more commonly than monoglot speakers. For example, Danish students are reported using the English definite article more often than monoglot speakers of English. This reflects 'the fact that Danish and English seem to have slightly different conceptions of what constitutes generic as opposed to specific reference'.[33] Bilinguals often use a linguistic item more frequently because it has a close parallel in their other language. For example, there is a tendency for English loanwords among some speakers of Australian German to be feminine – die Road, die Yard etc. – and this is probably due to the similarity in sound between the German *die* and the accented form of English 'the', whereas the German masculine *der* and neuter *das* sound different.[34] While we cannot

[32] See pp. 197–8 below.

[33] S. Larsen, 'Testing the Test: A Preliminary Investigation of Translation as a Test of Writing Skills', in S. Larsen (ed.), *Translation: A Means to an End* (The Dolphin 18. Aarhus, 1990), pp. 95–108, at 102.

[34] M. Clyne, *Perspectives on Language Contact, Based on a Study of German in Australia* (Melbourne, 1972), pp. 11, 15.

conduct the kind of statistical analysis of usage possible in the treatment of recorded conversations in the modern world, we all know that increased frequency of καί is to be expected in people who are accustomed to saying ו. We now have a larger pattern into which to fit many phenomena of this kind, not only those known to the older secondary literature. This is also the correct pattern for Aejmelaeus' demonstration that ὅτι is used incorrectly and too often in the LXX as a rendering of כי precisely because it is so often used correctly.[35]

This observation accords with another major result of the modern discipline of Translation Studies. Whereas bilinguals suffer from interference anyway, translators suffer from it much more strongly, because the text which they are translating always reinforces the interference. Švejcer summarises the basic points:

> As a bilingual, the translator is exposed to far greater interference (other conditions being equal) than one who, in using heterolinguistic systems, produces his utterances on the basis of his own programme rather than a source-language text . . . in translating it is a translation variant that is subject to choice . . . The factors which determine the choice are also different: in translation the choice is 'programmed' by the content of the original, whereas in the verbal activity of a bilingual it is determined by the external conditions of the communicative event.[36]

This may result in overliteral translation. For example, the LXX translator of Gen. 6.14 put νοσσιάς for קנים because it is usually the Greek equivalent for this Hebrew word. He probably did not imagine a pair of lions living in a bird's nest at the top of Noah's ark, but if he did, he put νοσσιάς all the same because literal translation was his preferred solution to that kind of difficulty. Neubert summarises our knowledge of modern translators in a similar situation, noting that translators may read their translations with the original texts still in the back of their minds. Consequently, translations, through interference, qualify as second-rate target texts: they read differently from original texts.[37] At Gen. 6.14, the translator's use of νοσσιάς will have been controlled by קנים in a

[35] Aejmelaeus, 'OTI *causale*'; see p. 56 above.
[36] Švejcer, 'Literal Translation', p. 39.
[37] A. Neubert, 'Interference between Languages and between Texts', in Schmidt, *Interferenz*, pp. 56–64, at 56–7.

way that the use of νοσσιάς in a monoglot Greek speaker could not be. The use of ὁ υἱὸς τοῦ ἀνθρώπου as a translation of בר (א)נש(א) may fruitfully be viewed as a more extensive example of the same phenomenon: when a bilingual translator read his version of sayings such as Mark 2.28 and 14.21, he could see the original idiom which he had translated in a way that was not possible for a monoglot speaker of Greek.

As well as translating very literally from the source into the target language, translators sometimes retain one or more words from the source text in their translation, transliterating them if the source and target languages have different alphabets. In this way, translators have produced a massive variety of phenomena. For example, part of Curtius' German translation of *The Waste Land* reads as follows:

> Hier, sagte sie,
> Ist Ihre Karte, der ertrunkene phönizische Seemann.
> ('These are pearls that were his eyes!' Sehen Sie!)[38]

Here the translator has added quotation marks and left a quotation from *The Tempest* in the original English. He also added a footnote explaining that this is a quotation from Shakespeare, *Der Sturm*, thus translating the title where he had not translated the quotation. He evidently felt that the quotation needed to be appreciated in its original language, despite the original English being printed on the facing page.

The translation of an English essay by G. Ash, on the Czech situation in 1989, posed a problem which could be perceived similarly or differently.[39] One sentence has people with 'red, white and blue badges saying "Havel for president"'. The French translator translated this: 'des badges aux couleurs bleu–rouge–blanc sur lesquels on peut lire "Havel président"'. This translates everything, and is not entirely literal, so as to be clearer and to be more idiomatically French than a word-for-word translation would be

---

[38] T. S. Eliot, *Das wüste Land. Englisch und deutsch*, tr. R. Curtius (Wiesbaden, 1957). Curtius does not number the lines, which are 46–48 in T. S. Eliot, *The Complete Poems and Plays* (London, 1969), p. 62.

[39] C. Schäffner and B. Herting, ' "The Revolution of the Magic Lantern": A Cross-cultural Comparison of Translation Strategies', in M. Snell-Hornby, F. Pöchhacker and K. Kaindl (eds.), *Translation Studies: An Interdiscipline. Selected papers from the Translation Studies Congress, Vienna, 9–12 Sept. 1992* (Amsterdam/ Philadelphia, 1994), pp. 27–36, at 33–4.

(albeit with the English loanword 'badges'). In particular, it translates the inscription on the badge. The German translator, however, thought that the inscription on the badge ought not to be translated, to the point where she originally misinterpreted her source on the assumption that it had not translated it either: 'rot–weiß–blaue Buttons mit der englischen Aufschrift *Havel for President'*. When her translation was republished, she discovered her mistake, and made a second attempt: 'rot–weiß–blaue Buttons mit der Aufschrift "*Havel na Hrad*" (Havel auf die Burg)'. Here she has endeavoured to find the original Czech inscription, and has seen fit to give it in Czech, and to follow it with a literal German translation, which presupposes that the original English translation was rather free. The behaviour of these translators is a perfect example of the rather arbitrary nature of the decision whether to retain the original language, and whether to translate it as well if it is retained. We are on the same level as the decision of an author as to what to write – we may find major reasons for a decision, or we may find that the translator's decision is dependent on their idiolect or even their whim.

Another example of different decisions being taken arises from the francophone African novel *Xala*.[40] A description of a man and his wife includes the following: 'D'où son titre d'"El Hadji" au masculin et pour sa femme d'"Adja"'. This was translated into German as follows: 'Daher sein Titel El Hadji, der Pilger, und für seine Frau "Adja", die Pilgerin'. Here the author of the novel expected his French-speaking readers to recognise the transliterated Arabic terms, and did not translate them. The German translator did not expect his readers to recognise Arabic terms, and responded by keeping the terms, transliterated from Arabic as in the French original of the novel, and translating them into German. He could have decided simply to translate them. The many exotic names in *Asterix the Gaul* have given rise to different decisions by translators into several different languages.[41] For example, *Abraracourcix* was retained in Italian and Dutch, but became *Majestix* in German, Swedish, Danish and Norwegian, and *Vitalstatistix* in English. No

---

[40] C. Schmitt, 'Translation als interkulturelle Kommunikation: Zum Problem der Übersetzung frankoafrikanischer Literatur ins Deutsche', in J. Albrecht et al. (eds.), *Translation und interkulturelle Kommunikation* (FAS A, 8. Frankfurt-on-Main, 1987), pp. 89–118, at 99–103.

[41] S. Embleton, 'Names and their Substitutes: Onomastic Observations on *Astérix* and its Translations', *Target* 3, 1991, 175–206, at 181–2.

one would argue from the culture-specific quality of 'vital statistics' that *Vitalstatistix* was the original name of an English-speaking character: we must be careful not to make similar mistakes when characters in Greek Gospels have Greek names.

All these examples underline the literary nature of the translation process, and the personal quality of the decision whether to retain an original word and whether to translate it as well.

It is not surprising that LXX translators occasionally resorted to transliteration.[42] For example, at Genesis 22.13 LXX we read ἐν φυτῷ σαβεκ for בסבך, both a translation and a transliteration of סבך. At Judg. 5.16, both texts have Ρουβην for ראובן, an example of the common habit of transliterating names. The A text also has τῶν μοσφαθαιμ for המשפתים, whereas the B text translates τῆς διγομίας. This again illustrates the extent to which the decision whether to transliterate has an element of arbitrary judgement. In this case the decision of the A translator was probably due to his not knowing a rare word, but not to guess at something that would make sense in fluent Greek for the target audience is still an actual decision. We may contrast the translation of the rare word נשף at Isa. 21.4. Despite τὸ ὀψέ (Isa. 5.11) and ἐν μεσονυκτίῳ (59.10), the translator of Isa. 21.4 reckoned that it should have been נפש, and he made a perfectly good Greek sentence by rendering it ἡ ψυχή μου. This is a deliberate attempt to ensure that the text makes sense to the target audience. One of the most extraordinary examples of transliteration is Theodotion's response to the Aramaic עיר. This is a word for a kind of heavenly being, often rendered into English as 'Watcher'. For עיר וקדיש (Dan. 4.10, 20) the LXX used ἄγγελος, but Theodotion revised this to ιρ καὶ ἅγιος. Here the LXX translator went for an interpretative translation which made perfect sense for the target audience. The revisers have preferred to represent the text more exactly, transliterating the rare עיר, though without anything for ע, and translating the straightforward קדיש with ἅγιος, as near to a precise translation as one can get. We cannot tell whether they did not know the meaning of עיר, or regarded it as an Aramaic technical term for a particular sort of angel, to be communicated verbatim and mysterioso.

We now have a complete frame of reference within which to see

[42] Cf E. Tov, 'Transliteration of Hebrew Words in the Greek Versions of the Old Testament', *Textus* 8, 1973, 78–92.

Mark's transliterations. At 14.36, ἀββα ὁ πατήρ, he has transliter-ated and added a translation, expecting that everyone would be aware of this because ἀββα was used in this way in Greek-speaking churches (Rom. 8.15; Gal. 4.6). At Mark 15.34, he has put ὅ ἐστιν μεθερμηνευόμενον between the unfamiliar Aramaic words and his translation, so that everyone would know what the unfamiliar words meant. He has assumed that everyone would know that Aramaic was the language from which they were transliterated. At Mark 5.41 he has used the same words between the transliterated ταλιθα κουμι and an explicitative translation, with the added words σοὶ λέγω. When we have surveyed the habits of translators in general we can see that this does not entail any expectation that he would transliterate more words of Jesus when they were par-ticularly solemn, or particularly anything else.

These two major sets of phenomena, interference in bilinguals and the increase in interference prevalent among translators, make it quite clear that the form of a language spoken by bilinguals and produced by translators is not the same as the form of that same language spoken by monolinguals. Moreover, the form of a second or further language produced by bilinguals and translators changes as they become more competent and experienced. Consequently, scholars who work in these fields have begun to use the term 'interlanguage', which can be fruitful for us. Appel and Muysken, tracing the term back as far as 1972, though widespread use of it is more recent, describe it and comment as follows: 'the version or the variety of the target language which is part of the implicit linguistic knowledge or competence of the second-language learner. He or she proceeds through a series of interlanguages on the way to complete mastery of the target language. Of course, most second-language learners never reach this stage.' Interference is one of the major features which they select for discussion.[43] What this clarifies is that we cannot expect Gospel writers to have produced normal koine Greek if they were bilingual, and doubly so if they were translating.

Another major result is that translators generally have to deal with two cultures, not just two languages. They may then write for the target culture, and make changes accordingly. Neubert

[43] P. Appel and P. Muysken, *Language Contact and Bilingualism* (London, 1987), p. 83, tracing the term 'interlanguage' back to L. Selinker, 'Interlanguage', *International Review of Applied Linguistics* 10, 1972, 209–31. It was already introduced by L. Selinker, 'Language Transfer', *General Linguistics* 9, 1969, 67–92, at 71.

describes the difference like this: 'In plain words, *translation recasts the original for different people*, after an unavoidable *time lag* and, as a rule, at a *different place*. It is displaced communication.'[44] This is obviously true of the synoptic Gospels. They were written for Christians rather than Jews. A lengthy time lag is obvious for Luke. A few years had already gone by before Mark was written, a few more before Matthew was composed. The Gospels were not written in Jerusalem, let alone Capernaum, but somewhere in the diaspora. Some of the translating was done before the composition of the Gospels themselves, but this is still displaced communication for the benefit of the target audience.

Such changes are sufficiently widespread to have given rise to the *skopos* theory of translation, for which the changes for the target culture form the main point.[45] For example, Séguinot studied the translation of ten articles in *Le Monde* for *The Guardian Weekly* in 1981, looking for changes which 'clearly arose from a change in the communicative situation'.[46] She reckoned 175 discrepancies between the source and target versions of the texts, and classified these as increased readability/explicitness (50 per cent), adaptation to target audience (21 per cent), reductions in emotive and figurative language (21 per cent), increased objectivity (4 per cent), and reductions in journalistic style (4 per cent). Here the needs of the target culture have evidently been of prime importance. The same applies to translators of our period. For example, at Num. 24.17, the LXX has ἄνθρωπος for שֵׁבֶט, and *Tg. Onqelos* has מְשִׁיחָא. Both these renderings are deliberately interpretative. The LXX makes clear that Israel will be led to victory by a man. *Tg. Onqelos*, written later when Messianic expectations had crystallised round the figure of a future Davidic king, identifies the victor as the Messiah.

Some kind of change is inevitable when the source text is particularly culture-specific. This is well illustrated by two German translations of the following passage from *Alice in Wonderland*:

---

[44] A. Neubert, *Text and Translation* (Übersetzungswissenschaftliche Beiträge 8. Leipzig, 1985), p. 8.

[45] See especially K. Reiß and H.-J. Vermeer, *Grundlegung einer allgemeinen Translationstheorie* (Linguistische Arbeiten 147. Tübingen, 1984).

[46] T. C. Séguinot, 'The Editing Function of Translation', *Bulletin of the Canadian Association of Applied Linguistics* 4, 1982, 151–61, as reported by Neubert, *Text and Translation*, pp. 72–3, and A. Neubert and G. M. Shreve, *Translation as Text* (Translation Studies 1. Kent, Ohio, 1992), pp. 87–8.

'Perhaps it doesn't understand English', thought Alice; 'I dare say it's a French mouse, come over with William the Conqueror.'

Remané translated this as follows:

'Sie versteht mich nicht', sagte sich Alice. 'Vielleicht ist es eine französische Maus, die mit Wilhelm dem Eroberer zu uns nach England gekommen ist.'

The first problem is 'English', when the text is being translated into German: Remané has put 'mich' instead. She has translated 'William the Conqueror' literally, and kept the reference in its original cultural context by adding 'zu uns nach England'. Different decisions were taken by Enzensberger, in a translation published the same year:

'Vielleicht versteht sie kein Deutsch', dachte Alice; 'ich könnte nur denken, sie ist eine französische Maus und mit Napoleon herübergekommen.'

This translator has opted for a much larger cultural shift. He has replaced 'English' with 'Deutsch', which makes excellent sense in a German text. The cultural shift is completed by replacing 'William the Conqueror' with 'Napoleon', so that German readers can imagine the uncomprehending mouse coming to Germany instead of England.[47]

Some of these examples are partly explicitative translations, translations which try to clarify the meaning of the text. Blum-Kulka noted a trend among bilingual graduate research assistants working on the Harvard Literary Skills project for the Target Language texts to be longer than the Source Language texts. Her examples include this:

SL: The teacher began, 'g', 'l', 'o', 'n'.

TL: La maîtresse dit, 'Ecrivez "g", "l", "o", "n".'[48]

---

[47] L. Carroll, *Alice in Wonderland and Through the Looking Glass* (New York, 1946), p. 18; *Alice im Wunderland*, tr. L. Remané (Munich, 1973), p. 38; *Alice im Wunderland*, tr. C. Enzensberger (Frankfurt-on-Main, 1973), p. 25; as reported by C. Nord, 'Scopos, Loyalty, and Translational Conventions', *Target* 3, 1991, 91–109, at 101–2.

[48] S. Blum-Kulka, 'Shifts of Cohesion and Coherence in Translation', in J. House and S. Blum-Kulka (eds.), *Interlingual and Intercultural Communication: Discourse and Cognition in Translation and Second Language Acquisition Studies* (Tübinger Beiträge zur Linguistik 272. Tübingen, 1986), pp. 17–35, at 20.

Here the replacement of 'began' with 'dit', and the addition of 'Ecrivez', should be ascribed to a perceived need to clarify the text by making the situation clear. This is the pattern into which we must fit Mark 5.41. Here a similar attempt has been made to clarify the translation of the Aramaic טליתא קום by means of the addition σοὶ λέγω.

Translators are faced with all these problems at the same time. Some, such as the translator of the Testament of Ephraem, are consistently free. In line 124, for example, he rendered ברנשא with ἄνδρα, and for כל ברנש at T. Ephraem 944 he put τῆς τοῦ θεοῦ ἐκκλησίας. The first example is free enough, and the second shows that there is no felt need to keep to the same rendering of a single expression. The second example is also highly interpretative, and vigorously directed at the target culture. An original text could not be reconstructed from either passage.

Other translators are consistently literalistic. Perhaps the best known in our field is Aquila. Others include the syrohexapla to the Old Testament and the Harklean version of the New. In the case of the syrohexapla, it is difficult to see how else the translators could have proceeded. If they did not seek to render overliterally to make clear to Syriac readers *exactly* what the Greek said, there was no point in their efforts, since more fluent translations would simply be more like other translations. The Harklean arose from similar determination. The Peshitta was the standard translation of the separate Gospels. Philoxenus of Mabbug, however, had already found it too free and arranged for a revision in the direction of the original Greek. Thomas of Harkel took this so far that the results are often literal to the point of not being correct Syriac. For example, at Mark 14.58, the Peshitta reasonably has לתלתא יומין for διὰ τριῶν ἡμερῶν. The Harklean revision is ביד תלתא יומא, which is not satisfactory Syriac. This kind of literalism is very helpful if one is trying to reconstruct an original text: it greatly increases the proportion of cases in which only one original text could possibly have given rise to such a translation.

Many translators vary in the extent of their literalism. The LXX is like this if treated as a single translation, which of course it is not. It is, however, a close parallel to the Gospels, in that the later translators knew at least some of the work of the earlier ones. Looking at the rendering of בן אדם in the LXX as a whole, we find that it generally went for υἱὸς ἀνθρώπου, but that there are two exceptions, Isa. 56.2, ἄνθρωπος, and Ps. 146.3, υἱοὺς ἀνθρώπων. Of these, Isa. 56.2 is just free enough to pass as normal monoglot Greek, and Ps. 146.3 is somewhat literalistic and interpretative at the same time. I have already noted the three different translations of נשׁף in LXX Isaiah alone.[49]

Another result of the variety of problems which face a normal translator is important for us: they may adopt strategies. To translate freely, or literally, can be adopted as a strategy. A strategy may be undertaken at a verbal level, as for example Aquila's decision to render the Hebrew את with the Greek σύν plus accusative, when את means that the next word will be the object of the previous verb. The only clear strategy in the synoptic Gospels concerns the translation of בר (א)נשׁ(א). We shall see that we must infer the following strategy: we use ὁ υἱὸς τοῦ ἀνθρώπου for בר (א)נשׁ(א) when it refers to Jesus, and not otherwise. The few exceptions (Mark 3.28; 9.12; Matt. 10.32–3) are responses to particular problems.[50] This is very important for understanding the whole of the synoptic tradition, for a translation strategy can only be employed when extensive portions of the literature in which it is found are in fact translated. This strategy alone enables us to infer substantial translated sources used by Matthew, Mark and Luke, whether by them personally or by their sources.

All these points must be borne in mind when we consider the nature of the traditions which confront us in the synoptic Gospels. We may find work on the LXX particularly helpful, though it must be used with caution. The LXX and parts of 1 Enoch are the nearest to the Gospels in date and in cultural change from a Semitic language to Greek-speaking people influenced by Hellenism. If the translators of Gospel sources had any training at all, a matter which may not be taken for granted, they will have been trained on the LXX. We know that they almost certainly consulted the LXX, from the evidence of the Gospels. For example, the quotation of Isa. 29.13 at Mark 7.6–7 follows the LXX. It is always possible that some such quotations are secondary, and produced by the Gospel writers. Overall, however, such is the use of the LXX in the Gospels that it is very difficult to suppose that the translators did not use it. They are therefore liable to have inherited its translation techniques.

At the same time, we may not use the LXX too literally. In the

[49] See p. 98 above.
[50] See pp. 111–21, 130–2 below.

first place, it is possible that our translators merely used it as their scriptures, without making any study of its translation techniques. Secondly, in any given instance they may have reacted against it, because monoglot speakers of Greek felt that it was not literary enough. For example, they might have taken pains to add more particularly Greek features, such as particles and genitive absolutes. Alternatively, they might have opted for one sort of translation over against another. For example, the Hebrew אם, which often overlaps in semantic area with the Greek εἰ and at the same time with the English 'if', is also used as a strong negative. Some LXX translators translated it in these cases with εἰ (for example Gen. 14.23; 2 Sam. 11.11; Ps. 94.11(MT 95.11)), a usage contrary to the normal speech patterns of monoglot Greeks and clearly due to the strong form of interference natural to translators. Equally, however, the translators of some books show a variety of negatives (for example μή Gen. 21.23; οὐκ 1 Sam. 24.22; οὐ μή Gen. 42.15; ἦ μὴν οὐκ Num. 14.23). If our translators knew the LXX thoroughly, they would have had a choice of known renderings. I shall suggest that the equivalent Aramaic אן lies behind μήτι at Mark 14.19.

It should be clear from this discussion that language is an integral part of culture. This is taken for granted in every other field of study known to me. For example, Lehiste summarises: 'Language is the chief carrier of nonmaterial culture. Thus, it may become the most obvious symbol of the group.'[51] At a more individual level, Banks heads an essay with this quotation: 'In the last analysis, any sociopsychological image of the self, in fact the very possibility of a self concept, is inextricably dependent on the linguistic practices used in everyday life to make sense of our own and others' actions.'[52]

This is why we have seen that translators make so many changes in their source texts when they render them into the target language. Even when words have approximately the same semantic areas in two different languages, we may find that it is simply customary to say something different. Kubczak instances the simple case of a German person getting on a bus and asking, 'Ist

---

[51] I. Lehiste, *Lectures on Language Contact* (Cambridge, Mass., 1988), p. 44.

[52] S. P. Banks, heading to 'Achieving "Unmarkedness" in Organizational Discourse: A Praxis Perspective on Ethnolinguistic Identity', in W. B. Gudykunst (ed.), *Language and Ethnic Identity* (Philadelphia, 1988), p. 15, quoting J. Potter and M. Wetherall, *Discourse and Social Psychology* (London, 1987), p. 95.

dieser Platz frei?', a perfectly normal German question.[53] It consists of four common words each of which has a straightforward English equivalent. It could therefore be literally translated into English, 'Is this place free?' The trouble with this is that an English person getting on a bus is not very likely to say this. We might accordingly translate, 'Is this seat taken?', which is normal English and closer to the original German than, say, 'Uuuhh, anyone sitting here?' Wierzbicka notes a number of cultural differences between Polish and English in the area of politeness phenomena.[54] She translates literally into English a polite request by a Polish host to a distinguished Australian guest, Mrs Vanessa Smith, asking her to take the seat of honour (using 'Mrs' for the Polish 'pani', which can be combined with first names):

> Mrs Vanessa! Please! Sit! Sit!

Here the short imperative 'Sit!' sounds to most of us like a command rather than a polite request – indeed a command directed at an unruly bitch rather than a distinguished person. This sort of difference always sets a translator a problem, and they respond with different degrees of literalness and of change. When we study the Gospels, we must be aware of the different options which were available to our translators, and we may not assume that they did what we think they should have done.

Consequently, there are many examples of translators making culturally orientated mistakes. Drescher has discussed translations of the works of Dickens into German.[55] In chapter 2 of *The Old Curiosity Shop*, Mr Swiveller declares that last week 'was a fine week for the ducks, and this week was fine for the dust'. A German translation published in 1965 has this: 'letzte Woche gutes Enten-jagdwetter gewesen sei, diese Woche aber sei es recht staubig'. The play on sound between 'ducks' and 'dust' was bound to be lost, just the kind of effect which is so often lost in translation. But what does it mean that it was a fine week for ducks? Most English people know that it had been pouring with rain. The German translator has clearly thought hard about what English people do so that we

---

[53] H. Kubczak, 'Ist aus systemlinguistischer Perspektive Übersetzung möglich?', in Albrecht et al, *Translation*, pp. 47–62, at p. 49.

[54] A. Wierzbicka, 'Different Cultures, Different Languages, Different Speech Acts: Polish vs. English', *Journal of Pragmatics* 9, 1985, 145–78.

[55] H. W. Drescher, 'Dickens's Reputation in Germany: Some Remarks on Early Translations of his Novels', in Albrecht et al., *Translation*, pp. 307–14.

can have a fine week for ducks, and has concluded that we love hunting them! Some of us do, but the result is a quite mistaken piece of explicitation.

Explicitation may run riot when there is no object or activity in the target culture corresponding to a word in the source text. Baker notes the difficulty of translating the English 'airing cupboard' into many languages whose speakers do not have such a thing. She also transmits this 'meaning' of the Brazilian word *arruação*: 'clearing the ground under coffee trees of rubbish and piling it in the middle of the row in order to aid the recovery of beans dropped during harvesting'.[56] While the context will always supply some of this, the translation of this word into English is inherently problematical. When problems occur on a large scale, translators may decide to replace something difficult with something familiar in the target culture. Baker discusses the translation of the opening of Hawking's *Brief History of Time*:[57] 'A well-known scientist (some say it was Bertrand Russell) once gave a public lecture on astronomy.' At the end, 'a little old lady at the back of the room' informed him that 'The world is really a flat plate supported on the back of a tortoise.' The Spanish translator felt that this was accessible enough to be translated literally. The Greek translator, however, did not feel that this would go down well with Greek readers, and substituted a piece of English culture which they would know well and which would still catch their attention at the beginning of the book. The well-known scientist becomes Alice in Wonderland, and the little old lady becomes the Queen, whose notion of the earth as a giant playing card is quite dotty in a way that fits her character. We can therefore see that from the point of view of translating the book as a whole this is a piece of cultural substitution which performs the same function as the original opening. At a literal level, however, it says something quite different from the source text.

When we have taken all this into account, we are in a position to understand the massive variety of phenomena which are found in the field of Translation Studies. When we return to the Gospels, we shall not approach them with narrow preconceptions based on our own experience or those of virtually monoglot professors who privilege New Testament Greek because it is the language of their

[56] M. Baker, *In Other Words: A Coursebook on Translation* (London, 1992), pp. 21–2.
[57] *Ibid.*, pp. 31–3, 261–3.

sacred text. We must be aware of both the slavish literalism that translators can resort to and the alterations which they may bring about in the interests of the target culture.

Now that we have seen what sources we must use, and which insights from other fields of study we must employ, we can lay down a standard procedure for reconstructing Aramaic sources from the witness of our Greek Gospels. It consists of seven stages.

1. We select for this purpose passages which show some signs of having been translated literally. The most extreme are mistakes, such as ἐπιβαλών at Mark 14.72. We have seen that ἐπιβαλών translates שׁדי, a misreading of שׁרי, the Aramaic for 'began'. I therefore reconstructed ושׁרי בכא, 'And he began to weep.'[58] This gives us standard behaviour by a bilingual translator suffering from interference. He translated שׁרי with ἐπιβαλών because of the large overlap in semantic area between these two words, which made him read Aramaic idiom into his Greek translation. We might therefore represent what he meant literally in English: 'And hurling [sc. threats and curses], he wept.' Monoglot Greek-speaking audiences would not understand this.

In such a case we have to anticipate several of the further stages of reconstruction in order to select the passages in the first place. This will always be so where there are mistakes in our Gospel text. The translators were, however, too good for us to rely heavily on this criterion. We must also take into account features such as parataxis and the early position of verbs in the sentence. Such linguistic features are found in ordinary Greek too, especially in the papyri. There are, though, many passages, such as Mark 11.15–18a, where we also have non-linguistic reasons for believing in the truth of the story, which is set in Israel, where Aramaic was the lingua franca.[59] In such a case, an Aramaic source is more likely to have caused such features. Whenever any linguistic feature is both a Semitism and a feature of everyday Greek, a translator has twice as many reasons as an author for using it, since the source text will cause him to select a feature of everyday Greek. We must therefore look for features which characterise Aramaic texts, and not discount them if they are also found in everyday Greek. It follows that we should also consider non-linguistic reasons for

---

58 See pp. 85–6 above.
59 Casey, 'Cleansing of the Temple'.

believing in the accuracy of Gospel reports, since these indicate that
our reports come from the original cultural environment.

2. We then begin the detailed work of making up a possible
Aramaic substratum. For this purpose, we must use in the first
instance the Aramaic of the Dea Sea scrolls. We have seen that it is
close to the right date and cultural environment, which is of central
importance. It is the wrong dialect for Jesus' speech, but this is
much less important than has generally been thought. To do this,
we must carry the Aramaic of the Dead Sea scrolls in the back of
our heads. While there are useful glossaries,[60] they cannot substitute for our memories, because we can look up in them only words
which we have already thought of. *In extremis*, we can read the
whole of the glossaries, but it is inefficient to do this too often.

Where words are not found in the scrolls, we must use other
Aramaic with care. There is, for example, no word which could
have given rise to κολλυβιστῶν (Mark 11.15), and since the scrolls
contain no discussions of changing money or the like, this is
obviously due to a gap in our source material, not to the late date
of the Syriac מערפנא or the Babylonian Aramaic פתורא. It is at
this stage that we may consult the Syriac versions of the Gospels,
including the Palestinian Syriac lectionary. When we do so, we
must be particularly careful to bear in mind that these versions are
translations *into* Syriac, not reconstructions. We may not imagine
that Jesus *must* have said מערפנא because we find it at Matt. 21.12
pesh hark, Mark 11.15 sin pesh hark, John 2.15 pesh hark. These
translations into the wrong dialect give us a possibility which we
cannot confirm. We must also check whether any word in these
versions occurs in earlier Aramaic, or in Akkadian, to see whether
we can infer its existence in the right period. For example, there is
no equivalent for the description of Jesus as τέκτων at Mark 6.3 in
the Dead Sea scrolls, because they do not have any discussions of
carpenters and/or stonemasons. Both pesh and hark have נגרא, as
do cur pesh hark with reference to Joseph at Matt. 13.55. נגר is also
well attested in later Jewish Aramaic. When we discover that it is
also attested in earlier Aramaic and in Akkadian, we need look no
further: it was certainly the word used of Jesus. We should not,
however, predate the metaphorical use of it with reference to a
scholar found in later Jewish sources. This would not make good

[60] Beyer, *Die aramäischen Texte*; Fitzmyer and Harrington, *Manual of Palestinian
Aramaic Texts*; Beyer, *Ergänzungsband*.

sense of the passage, it would not explain the translation τέκτων, and the sources are too late.

3. Our third task is to check that the draft reconstruction is sufficiently idiomatic. Some specifically Aramaic locutions are bound to have been removed during the process of translation into Greek. For example, the rarity of a resumptive pronoun such as αὐτοῦ picking up οὗ at Mark 1.7 shows that most examples have been eliminated, presumably thereby producing a slightly shorter text, whereas translations generally tend to increase in length. Similarly, confronted with the quite Greek οὐκ ἔχει ποῦ at Matt. 8.20//Lk 9.58, I suggested בה . . . ד אן לה איתי לא.[61] We cannot normally infer that such suggestions are accurate verbatim. What we should claim is that Jesus must have spoken, and our sources must have written, idiomatic Aramaic. If, therefore, this is what we reconstruct, we shall obtain an accurate impression of the source even where details are uncertain. Our fifth procedure will be a particularly important check and balance against too much creativity on our part.

4. We must interpret the resulting reconstruction from a first-century Jewish perspective. We must pay particular attention to any respect in which it differs from the Greek translation. This is most striking with בר (א)נש(א), a normal term for 'man' with a general level of meaning, quite different from ὁ υἱὸς τοῦ ἀνθρώπου, a Christological title of Jesus alone. Sometimes it is later Christian tradition which has to be removed. At Mark 2.10, I reconstructed שבק from Mark's ἀφιέναι.[62] This must be interpreted from the semantic area of the Aramaic שבק, not the English 'forgive' or the German *vergeben*, but this should already have been clear from the perfectly sound Greek translation ἀφιέναι. The mere fact of an Aramaic source takes us one stage back in the tradition, but not necessarily back to Jesus himself. We must then use all the necessary criteria to determine whether Jesus said and did what our sources attributed to him. The Aramaic sentences will be found especially helpful in reconstructing the cultural context of Jesus' ministry. They cannot, however, function properly without a full cultural context.

5. We must go through the passage again from the perspective of an ancient translator. If he was faced with the proposed

[61] Casey, 'Jackals', 7.
[62] Casey, *Son of Man*, pp. 160–1.

reconstruction, might he reasonably have put what we have got? We must pay careful attention both to the overall sweep of the translation and to all the small details. In doing this, we must make use both of research into the known habits of ancient translators and of modern insights into the nature of the translation process itself. We shall feel happiest when our translator could *only* have done what we posit, but we must not impose this as a general standard of judgement, because there are many situations in which translators have a genuine choice. We must be on the look-out both for consistent habits and for strategies, but we must be careful not to invent either of them.

6. We must see whether we can infer any deliberate editing by the Gospel writers themselves. This is especially important with Q passages, where we have to determine whether we are dealing with one translation or two. It is also important with Mark, though often more difficult to determine. We can safely infer it for the central group of passion predictions (Mark 8.31; 9.31; 10.33–4). It has often been noted that these predictions as a whole show editing to conform them to the passion story, and an Aramaic reconstruction is a more general statement than the present predictions.[63]

7. Having completed a whole hypothesis, with a reconstruction interpreted in the light of Jesus' Jewish culture and a translation plotted out in accordance with the needs of a translator who belonged to the target culture, we must make an overall assessment of the probability of what we have suggested. I shall suggest that in the case of the passages studied in chs 3–6 of this book, the probability that we have abbreviated but accurate accounts written by Jews from Israel who were present at the time is quite unassailable. Accordingly, I propose that the methods expounded here are an essential element in any reasonable attempt to recover the Jesus of history.

---

[63] Casey, 'General, Generic and Indefinite', 43–9.

3

JESUS' SCRIPTURAL UNDERSTANDING OF JOHN THE BAPTIST'S DEATH: MARK 9.11–13

The interpretation of Mark 9.11–13 has flummoxed everyone. In verse 12, we are told that Elijah restores all things, and in verse 13 that he has come, but neither John the Baptist nor anyone else came and restored all things. The second half of verse 12 refers to the suffering and rejection of the Son of man. Mark seems to hop from Elijah to Jesus and back to Elijah again, and searching the scriptures for the suffering and rejection of the Son of man has only led scholars to regurgitate pious Christian tradition. In verse 13, we are told not only that Elijah has come, but apparently that they did to him what they wanted, as it is written of him. If finding the suffering of the Son of man in scripture is difficult, the fate of Elijah boggles the exegetical mind.

The purpose of this chapter is to solve this set of problems by reconstructing Mark's Aramaic source, and tracking out the decisions made by a translator in difficulties. We must begin with the use of the term (א)שׁנ(א) בר. The main point is that (א)שׁנ(א) בר is a normal term for 'man'. There are thousands of examples of this, and all the uses which have caused trouble for New Testament scholars stem from it. When we have reviewed the range of usage of (א)שׁנ(א) בר in natural Aramaic, we can proceed to the reconstruction of Jesus' Son of man sayings. If such reconstructions fit properly into the known use of (א)שׁנ(א) בר, we must infer that (א)שׁנ(א) בר was used like this earlier than the examples in extant texts. That it was used more broadly than in extant early texts follows from the date of the earliest example (Sefire III.16) several centuries before the time of Jesus, and from the general nature of its use in the few examples from our period (1QapGen XXI.13; 11QtgJob IX.9; XXVI.3; cf. Dan. 7.13; and in the plural Dan. 2.38; 5.21; 1 En. 7.3; 22.3; 77.3 [4Q Enastr[b] 23]; 1QapGen XIX.15; 4QGiants 426; 11QtgJob XXVIII.2). In this chapter, we shall see that it is only when Mark 9.12 is reconstructed in its original

Aramaic that we can recover what Jesus actually said and meant. In subsequent chapters, we shall study Mark 2.28; 10.45; 14.21. In these cases we shall see that the Greek translations make excellent sense for the target culture, but that some of the original Jewish assumptions of these sayings of Jesus have been lost in the translation process.

In the first place, then, בר (א)נש(א) is a normal term for 'man'. Examples of this include many general statements, such as passage 1.

1. 1QapGen. XXI.13: MT איש (Gen. 13.16):

> ואשׂגה זרעך כעפר ארעא די לא ישכח כול בר אנוש
> לממניה

> And I will multiply your seed like the dust of the earth which no son of man can count.

Here the fact that בר אנוש represents the Hebrew איש must mean that it was felt to be especially suitable for a general statement. This passage was written as near to the time of Jesus as we can get with Aramaic source material.

Since the term בר (א)נש(א) was a general term for 'man', it is used in tractates about humankind, and in the most general references to the composition of human beings and the variety of our life experiences. This is illustrated in passage 2.

2. Bardaisan, *The Book of the Laws of the Countries*, p. 559, lines 11–14:[1]

> כינה דברנשא הנו דנתילד ונתרבא ודנקום באקמא ודנולד
> ודנקש כד אכל וכד שתא וכד דמך וכד מתתעיר ודנמות.

> This is the nature of (the son of) man, that he should be born and grow up and reach his peak and reproduce and grow old, while eating and drinking and sleeping and waking, and that he should die.

Passage 2 is the oldest general discussion of humankind extant in Aramaic sources. This is the only reason why it is the earliest text in which בר (א)נש(א) has all the most basic human experiences.

Death is such a natural part of life that the death of the son of man is found in Jewish Aramaic sources as soon as they are

---

[1] For the text, see Bardesanes, *Liber Legum Regiorum*, cuius textum syriacum vocalium signis instruxit, latine vertit F. Nau, annotationibus locupletavit Th. Nöldeke, in F. Graffin (ed.), *Patrologia Syriaca* vol. 2 (Paris, 1907), pp. 490–657.

sufficiently extensive. Passage 3 is a general statement inserted into the story of how Ḥaninah ben Dosa was bitten by a snake when he was praying, with the result that the snake died. I quote MS Leiden Or. 4720: those texts which transmit בר נש in the indefinite state do not offer any difference in meaning.

3. y. Ber 5. 1/26 (9a)

כד הוות נכית לבר נשא אין בר נשא קדים למיא חברברא
מיית ואין חברברא קדים למיא בר נשא מיית.

> When it bites a/the (son of) man, if the (son of) man reaches (the) water first the snake dies, and if the snake reaches (the) water first, the (son of) man dies.

Since בר (א)נש(א) is a normal term for 'man', the minimal requirements for its use are that human beings are referred to, and that there is a general level of meaning. It is not, however, necessary for son of man statements to be literally true of all people. This is illustrated by passage 3, which is false and refers only to people who have been bitten by a snake. It is conspicuously not true of Ḥaninah ben Dosa, who survived through his prayerful relationship with God, not by making a rapid dash for the nearest pond. Passage 4 further illustrates the kind of limited references which are quite normal in the use of son of man statements:

4. John of Dalyatha, *Letters* 49. 13[2]

מן בתר הנא שוחלפא אתא בתרה שוחלפא אחרנא
דלבשא לה לברנשא נורא מן פסת רגלה ועמדא למוחה
דמא דחאר ברנשא הו בה לא חזא לפגרא מרכבא אן
להד נורא דלביש.

> After this transformation, there follows another transformation in which fire clothes the (son of) man from the soles of his feet up to his brain, so that when the (son of) man looks at himself he does not see his composite body, but only the fire with which he is clothed.

This is part of an account of an experience of ascetic visionaries, not part of the normal experience of everyone.

The particular nuance which is central for most of the son of

---

[2] For the text, see R. Beulay, *La Collection des lettres de Jean de Dalyatha: Edition critique du texte syriaque inédit, traduction française, introduction et notes*, PO 39 (Turnhout, 1978), pp. 254–538.

man statements correctly attributed to Jesus is that these general statements can be used because the speaker wants to make a point about himself, or himself and a group of other people. This is illustrated by passages 5–7.

5. Sefire III.14–17

והן יסק על לבבך ותשא על שפתיך להמתתי ויסק על
לבב בר ברך וישא על שפתוה להמתת בר ברי או הן יסק
על לבב עקרך וישא על שפתוה להמתת עקרי והן יסק
על [ל]בב מלכי ארפד בכל מה זי ימות בר אנש שקרתם
לכל אלהי עדיא זי בספרא זנה.

And if you think of killing me and you put forward such a plan, and if your son's son thinks of killing my son's son and puts forward such a plan, or if your descendants think of killing my descendants and put forward such a plan, and if the kings of Arpad think of it, in any case that a son of man dies, you have been false to all the gods of the treaty which is in this inscription.

This example was written centuries before the time of Jesus, in the name of the king of Ktk. It uses בר אנש in a general statement which refers to the king and his descendants. In view of the cultural context, it is most unlikely that it was intended to refer to the death of anyone other than people on the side of the king of Ktk, and it probably refers only to the king and his descendants. Precise description is not part of this idiom, the effectiveness of which depends on the plausibility of the general level of meaning. When this passage is taken together with many later passages, such as passages 2, 3, 6 and 7, it should be obvious that dying is a universal experience characteristic of בר (א)נש(א), and that this was already so long before the time of Jesus.

6. Testament of Ephraem, lines 121–4

מן דסאם לי בגו היכלא   לא נחזא היכל מלכותא
דלא מוטר שובחא סריקא   לברנשא מלא שוא לה

Whoever lays me in the church, may he not see the Church of the kingdom!
For empty praise is no use to a/the son of man who is not worthy of it.

Lines 121–2 belong to a whole section which uses the first person singular. It is consequently clear that the son of man statement in lines 123–4 also refers particularly to Ephraem, writing c. 370 CE and contemplating his forthcoming death. It remains a general statement.

7. GenR LXXIX.6

צִיפּוֹר מִבִּלְעֲדֵי שְׁמַיָּא לָא מִיתְצְדָא. חַד כְּמָן וּכְמָן נֶפֶשׁ
דְּבַר נָשׁ.

A bird is not caught without the will of heaven: how much less the soul of a son of man.

After saying this, R. Simeon emerged from his cave with his son. It follows that this is a general statement which applies particularly to the speaker and one other person.

It is clear from these examples that this idiom was in use for centuries before and after the time of Jesus. This is natural, because it consists of a simple application of general statements to fulfil a normal human need, that of speaking indirectly about oneself. If therefore sayings of Jesus emerge as examples of this idiom when straightforwardly reconstructed, we should accept them as examples of it.

It is equally important for understanding the Aramaic source of Mark 9.11–13 that these general statements may be used because of their particular application to someone else. I have noted elsewhere Targumic examples of general statements with בַּר (אֱ)נַשׁ(א) used with particular reference to Adam, the chief butler, Joseph, Moses, and Zerah and his army.[3] Passage 8 is one of these.

8. *Tg. Neofiti I* Gen. 40.23

שְׁבַק יוֹסֵף חִסְדָא דִלְעֵל וְחִסְדָא דִלְרַע . . . וְאַתְרְחִיץ בְּרַב
מְזוֹגְיָה בְּבְשַׂר עָבִיר . . . וְלָא אַדְכַּר כְּתָבָא דִכְתִיב בְּסֵפֶר
אוֹרָיְתָא דַיְיָ . . . לַיְיט יְהוֵי בַּר נָשָׁא דִּי תְרַחֵץ בְּבִשְׂרָא.

Joseph abandoned the grace which is from above and the grace which is from below . . . and he put his trust in the chief of the butlers, in flesh which passes away . . . and he did not remember the scripture which is written in the book of the Law of the Lord . . . 'Cursed be the son of man who puts his trust in flesh.'

Here *Tg. Neofiti I* uses בַּר נָשָׁא, apparently to render הַגֶּבֶר at Jer. 17.5, thus inserting a general statement which applies particularly

---

[3] Casey, 'Use of the Term בַּר (אֱ)נַשׁ(א) ', 88–9, 104.

to Joseph. Passage 9 also illustrates the fact that בר (א)נש(א) may
be used in a general statement which has especial reference to
someone other than the speaker or narrator.

9. y. Ber 8. 1/11 (12a)

> רבי אבהו כד הוה אזיל לדרומה הוה עבד כרבי חנינא
> וכד הוה נחית לטיבריא הוה עבד כרבי יוחנן דלא מפלג
> על בר נש באתריה.

When R. Abbahu went to the south, he did according to
R. Haninah, and when he went to Tiberias, he did
according to R. Johanan, so that he might not differ from
a (son of) man in his place.

Here בר נש refers especially to R. Haninah and R. Johanan. The
narrator makes a general statement which presupposes that one
should follow the halakhah of the local rabbi, which also conforms
one's behaviour to that of the local Jewish community. Thus the
general level of meaning is central in providing an explanation of
R. Abbahu's behaviour.

When sufficient Aramaic is extant, people particularly referred to
with the term בר (א)נש(א) include Elijah, John the Baptist and
Jesus. This is illustrated in passages 10–12.

10. Ps.-Ephraem, Homily on Elijah and the Widow of Sarepta,
p. 102, lines 129–30[4]

> חזא אלהא לברנשא דלא מרחם על בר זוגה
> ושדר מלאכא ודברה לנפשה דברה מארמלתא

129 God saw a/the son of man who did not have compassion on his fellow being,
130 and he sent an angel and took the soul of the widow's
son.

Elijah has performed a miracle to feed the widow and her son, but
he still has the heavens shut up so that there is no rain, a situation
which has caused the earth to object, addressing him as בר נשא
(line 73). In passage 10, the use of ברנשא retains a general level of
meaning – it is assumed that it is generally wicked for people not to
have compassion on other people. At the same time, the statement
is made for its particular application to Elijah, as is graphically
illustrated by the following line.

---

[4] Cited according to the editio princeps of S. P. Brock, 'A Syriac Verse Homily on
Elijah and the Widow of Sarepta', *Le Muséon* 102, 1989, 93–113.

11. Ephraem, *Commentary on the Diatessaron* XIII.10. 3–5[5]

לא הוא לם מן בר אנשא נסבנא סהדותא מטל דאית לי
סהדותא דרבא מן דיוחנן. ואן מן בר אנשא לא נסב יוחנן
מנא קדם אתא?

'Now I do not receive witness from a (/the son of) man
because I have a witness which is greater than that of
John.' And if he did not receive (witness) from a (/the son
of) man, why did John come first?

The quotation is a word of Jesus from the Diatessaron, which used
John 5.34, 36. At some stage, the anarthrous ἀνθρώπου was
rendered with the definite state בר אנשא, which is perfectly sound
because of the generic level of meaning of this term. Ephraem's
commentary retains בר אנשא to keep the general level of meaning,
but it has point only if it is a special reference to John the Baptist.

12. Narsai, *Homily on the Birth of Our Lord from the Holy
Virgin*, lines 474–6[6]

474 וחרר אנון בחד [ביד manuscripts] ברנשא בפגרא
ונפשא
475 בהדא תנוי שקל ברנשא מן ברת אנשא
476 וזינה ברוחא דנפרוק גנסא מן חסינא

474 And he [sc. God] set them [sc. sinful humanity] free in
body and soul by one [manuscripts: by the hand of a/the]
(son of) man.
475 With this intention he took a (/the son of) man from a/
the daughter of man/men
476 And supported him with the spirit so that he might
redeem his race from the strong one.

All the references to Jesus which I have seen in Aramaic come from
the Syriac-speaking church. The vast majority either make or
rather deliberately assume a point about his humanity, as does this
one.

All these examples form part of a coherent range of material.
בר (א)נש(א) can be used in general statements which refer especially

---

[5] I cite section, paragraph and line of paragraph from L. Leloir (ed.), *Saint
Ephrem. Commentaire de L'Evangile concordant: Texte syriaque (Ms Chester Beatty
709)* (CBM 8. Dublin, 1963).
[6] For the text, see F. G. McLeod (ed.), *Narsai's Metrical Homilies on the Nativity*,
PO 40 (Turnhout, 1979), pp. 36–69.

to the speaker, or the speaker and a group of other people, or another person, or to the human nature of a person, because it is a general term for 'man'. We must not imagine a series of restrictions which Aramaic speakers had to observe. On the contrary, this is a flexible term with a range of meaning, and that is why it can be used idiomatically to give plausibility to otherwise unusual or difficult comments, such as the rejection or death of a particular person.

In a recent article, Burkett has tried to show that this approach to the Son of man problem in the Gospels is wrong,[7] and related criticisms are found in other recent secondary literature. I have shown that his criticisms of my exegesis of other passages are inaccurate, because they are based on English translations, not on the Aramaic reconstructions which are central to my proposed hypothesis.[8] We must refute some of his other criticisms before we can proceed to the reconstruction of Mark 9.11–13.

Burkett classifies all non-titular usages of 'son of man' together. This can be fruitful, because all examples of the Hebrew בן אדם and the Aramaic בר (א)נש(א) are non-titular. Equally, however, it can be misleading because it can lead to assertions that recent theories are really the same as work published a century or more ago. We shall see that Burkett falls into this trap, particularly in alleging that my proposed solution involves a *mis*translation of בר (א)נש(א) to produce ὁ υἱὸς τοῦ ἀνθρώπου.

Burkett casts doubt on the widespread agreement that some form of בר (א)נש(א) underlies ὁ υἱὸς τοῦ ἀνθρώπου, referring to this as an 'assumption'.[9] It is not an assumption. It is a widespread agreement, based on facts which were considered obvious. Firstly, we have surveyed at length the abundant reasons for supposing that Jesus spoke Aramaic.[10] Secondly, the Greek expression ὁ υἱὸς τοῦ ἀνθρώπου is not normal monoglot Greek, and could be understood as a literal translation of a Semitic expression. Thirdly, the Greek υἱός overlaps greatly in semantic area with the Aramaic בר and the Hebrew בן. It is extensively used in the LXX to render בן, in both literal and figurative senses, including expressions which are not normal monoglot Greek, but literal translations (for example υἱός δυνάμεως for בן־חיל, 1 Sam. 14.52). Fourthly, the Aramaic

[7] Burkett, 'Nontitular Son of Man'.
[8] See pp. 69–71 above.
[9] Burkett, 'Nontitular Son of Man', 515.
[10] See pp. 76–8, 83–6 above.

(א)נש(א) overlaps extensively in semantic area with the Greek ἄνθρωπος. Fifthly, the Hebrew בן אדם, the equivalent of the Aramaic בר (א)נש(א), is normally rendered υἱὸς ἀνθρώπου in the LXX, by several different translators. Sixthly, the Gospel expression ὁ υἱὸς τοῦ ἀνθρώπου evidently did not cause difficulty in understanding at the time. It must therefore represent a normal Aramaic expression rather than an unusual one. This requirement is satisfied by בר (א)נש(א). Seventhly, some Gospel sayings (notably Mark 13.26; 14.62) make use of Dan. 7.13, where בר אנש is certainly the underlying Aramaic expression.[11]

Burkett then produces a set of objections which entail rejecting everything we know about the translation process. He first suggests a strong probability that all examples were of the definite state בר אנשא, on the simple ground that the Greek translator used two articles. Noting my previous objections to this view, he comments, 'But if the expression were the idiom that Casey claims, the translator would have known that it included Jesus in its reference and would have had no need to add articles.'[12] This comment presupposes an inaccurate model of translators. We have seen that bilingual people generally experience interference between the languages which they use, and that this is increased when they translate from one language into another, because the features of the source language are present before them to cause the interference. We have also noted that interference causes bilingual translators to use some linguistic features more frequently than monoglot speakers. The generic use of the Greek article is of this kind. It is genuine Greek, and therefore liable to be used in translating Aramaic nouns which are used generically. In ὁ υἱὸς τοῦ ἀνθρώπου, it is always correctly and conventionally used before ἀνθρώπου, only two words away from the first article. Consequently, with both articles, bilingual translators could perceive both levels of the Aramaic idiom. They could therefore feel satisfied that they had done as well as possible.

We have also seen how translators often write deliberately for their target culture. The Gospels were written for Christians, who

---

[11] Casey, *Son of Man*, ch. 8. Burkett suggests בר גברא, or the Hebrew בן הגבר, with certainty for the fourth Gospel and tentatively for the synoptics. This should not be accepted for many reasons, including that this unfamiliar expression does not cause discussion, the proposed dependence on Prov. 30.1–4 is not convincing, and the proposed translation with ὁ υἱὸς τοῦ ἀνθρώπου cannot be accounted for. More detailed discussion must be offered elsewhere.

[12] Burkett, 'Nontitular Son of Man', 516, n. 61.

happily received another Christological title. Mark already has ὁ
υἱὸς τοῦ ἀνθρώπου in clear references to the figure of Dan. 7.13
(Mark 13.26; 14.62, cf. 8.38). The translation and editing of the
central group of Son of man passion predictions (Mark 8.31–3;
9.30–2; 10.32–4; cf. 9.9) show particularly clear signs of explicitative translation and editing with the needs of the target culture
firmly in mind, to the point where literal reproduction of the source
text has been left far behind.[13] The translators and editors of other
Son of man sayings will have known that if monoglot Greek
speakers did not perceive Jesus' original Aramaic idiom, they
would still have perceived the most important level of meaning, the
references to himself. Their task was therefore different from that
of LXX translators of בן־אדם, and they did as well as possible for
their fellow Christians by making clear the specific reference to
Jesus, which was essential for them, rather than an Aramaic idiom,
which did not matter so much.

Burkett proceeds to divide בר (א)נש(א) into three 'meanings', all
of which he expresses in English.[14] The trouble with this is that no
Aramaic word really had separate 'meanings' which can be organised round English words. Some words are sufficiently analogous
for us to say, for example, that אמר means 'say', but we should
never imagine that this establishes a word-for-word equivalence.
What בר (א)נש(א) did have was a range of usage which is generally
consistent, and it is this which I have illustrated. Partly as a result
of his classification of 'meanings', Burkett attributes to me the view
that the Aramaic has been 'mistranslated', a view which I have
never expressed and do not hold. This also follows from insuffi-
ciently careful classification of my view together with others,
especially from the older scholarship, who did hold this view.[15] I
have always maintained, what Burkett offers in criticism, that 'the
translators knew their business and gave ὁ υἱὸς τοῦ ἀνθρώπου as
the best equivalent of the underlying Aramaic'. Unlike Burkett,
however, I have approached this from the meaning of Aramaic
sentences, not of English words. In the light of recent work on the
translation process, and standard scholarship on the LXX, I have
accordingly mapped out the changes which took place in the
translation of a specifically Aramaic idiom into Greek, instead of

[13] Casey, 'General, Generic and Indefinite', 40–9.
[14] Burkett, 'Nontitular Son of Man', 516.
[15] E.g. J. Wellhausen, *Skizzen und Vorarbeiten* VI (Berlin, 1899), p. 197.

imagining that competent translation could remove the differences between languages.

Burkett then states another unsatisfactory criterion. 'In order for the thesis of mistranslation to be plausible, these scholars must show that the Greek expression as it stands does not yield an adequate meaning.' This is wrong at two levels. In the first place, it would treat as literally accurate any successful interpretative translation. So, for example, at Num. 24.17, both LXX ἄνθρωπος and *Tg. Onqelos* מְשִׁיחָא 'yield an adequate meaning', but they actually translated שֵׁבֶט, not אנוש/אדם and המשיח respectively.[16] Such changes result from translators responding to the needs of the target culture, to which they generally belong: once again, Burkett has denied the nature of the translation process. Secondly, the notion 'yield an adequate meaning' is dependent on later Christian tradition for the meaning which ὁ υἱὸς τοῦ ἀνθρώπου has. At the time, it was not an expression used by monoglot Greeks, who would be more likely to ask what it meant than Burkett's formulation suggests.

Finally, Burkett declares that the most serious objection is exegetical. We have, however, seen that in presenting this objection, he does not discuss proposed Aramaic reconstructions at all, but English translations.[17] It follows that his objections have no validity. We may therefore proceed with בר (א)נש(א) as the Aramaic which gave rise to ὁ υἱὸς τοῦ ἀνθρώπου, and we shall understand בר (א)נש(א) in the light of the thousands of Aramaic examples from which we have drawn typical illustrations.

I now propose the following reconstruction of the Aramaic source of Mark 9.11–13:

11 ושאלין לה ואמרין, למה אומרין ספריא דאליה עיתד
למאתא לקדמין?
12 ואמר להון, אתה אליה לקדמין ומתיב כולא, והיכה
כתיב על בר אנש דיכאב שׂגיא ואתבסר.
13 ואמר אנה לכון דאף אליה אתה ועבדו לה דצבו כדי
כתיב עלוהי.

And (they were) asking him and saying, 'Why do (the) scribes say that Elijah is going to come first?' [12]And he said to them, 'Elijah comes first and turns back all, and how it is written of (a/the son of) man that he suffers much and is

---

[16] See further p. 100 above.
[17] See pp. 69–71 above.

rejected! [13]And I tell you that, moreover, Elijah has come, and they did in the case of him whom they desired according as it is written concerning him/it.'

For the first ὅτι, I have reconstructed למה, 'why?'. This produces a question by the disciples which makes excellent sense, and receives an intelligible answer. It also makes dubious Greek, in that ὅτι is used as a direct interrogative, whereas monoglot speakers of Greek used it only as an indirect interrogative.[18] This is a straightforward example of interference in a bilingual translator. He will have equated למה with ὅτι in his mind, and this extension of the usage of ὅτι will have been directly due to the influence of למה, and doubly likely to happen when he was translating. He seems to have used ὅτι as a direct interrogative elsewhere: cf. Mark 2.7, 16; 9.28.

In its Markan context, this question is asked by Peter, Jacob and John, but this setting appears secondary. The question must, however, have come from disciples who had heard the opinion of the scribes. Our understanding of this question has not been helped by the assumption of the Christian tradition that it must mean that Elijah would come before the Messiah. Recent work has shown that there was no such expectation specific to the Messiah,[19] but that should not be surprising since this term had not yet crystallised as a title.[20] There certainly was expectation that Elijah would come, and both known examples (Sir. 48.10; 4Q558) take up the text of Mal. 3.23–4, in which it is quite clear that Elijah will come before the day of the Lord. Jesus was well known for preaching the imminent coming of the kingdom of God (cf. Mark 9.1), and he was the central figure of the Jesus movement. We must infer that scribes hostile to the movement had resorted to the scriptures, and had argued that God could not be about to establish his kingdom, with Jesus as the central figure, because the scriptures said that Elijah would come first. Since all agreed that the scripture was true, and everyone was in the situation created by the Jesus movement,

---

[18] Black, *Aramaic Approach* ([3]1967), pp. 119–21.

[19] M. M. Faierstein, 'Why Do the Scribes Say that Elijah Must Come First?', *JBL* 100, 1981, 75–86; J. A. Fitzmyer, 'More About Elijah Coming First', *JBL* 104, 1985, 295–6, referring to D. C. Allison, 'Elijah Must Come First', *JBL* 103, 1984, 256–8.

[20] M. de Jonge, 'The Use of the Word "Anointed" in the Time of Jesus', *NT* 8, 1966, 132–48; M. de Jonge, 'The Earliest Christian Use of *Christos*: Some Suggestions', *NTS* 32, 1986, 321–43; Casey, *From Jewish Prophet to Gentile God: The Origins and Development of New Testament Christology* (The Edward Cadbury Lectures at the University of Birmingham, 1985–6. Cambridge/Louisville, 1991), pp. 41–4.

there was no need for our source to be more specific than the word לקדמין ('first'). In due course, the scribal view was maliciously attributed to Jesus by people who mocked him when he was being crucified (Mark 15.35–6).

The term δεῖ should not be regarded as a serious problem, though there is no Aramaic word with a corresponding semantic area. I have suggested that עתיד could give rise to it. The word עתיד means 'ready, prepared', and it is extant in Aramaic before the time of Jesus at Daniel 3.15, where Shadrach, Meshach and Abednego will be let off if they are 'ready', 'prepared' to worship Nebuchadnezzar's image (LXX and Theod. ἔχετε ἑτοίμως for איתיכון עתידין). In its take-up of Malachi, the Geniza text of Sir. 48.10 has נכון, the semantic area of which includes 'ready'. In later Aramaic, עתיד is used idiomatically to indicate the future, even the remote future. It was therefore very suitable to indicate the future event of Elijah's coming, and its use in the Peshitta of Sir. 48.10 illustrates what a suitable word it is to take up in Aramaic the prophecy of Mal. 3.23–4. This range of meaning made it difficult for the translator to proceed without making a conscious decision. He did well not to prefer ἕτοιμος. At least some of the scribes will not have believed that Elijah would come at any moment, for they were using the prediction of his coming as an objection to the eschatology of the Jesus movement. Moreover, in verse 12 Jesus agrees with the scriptural prediction, but he did not think that Elijah was ready to come either – he thought that he had come already. The translator has taken the same kind of option as the translator of Dan. 2.28–9 LXX and Theod., where δεῖ is part of an explicitative translation of an Aramaic imperfect. He has indicated the certainty of the scribes that the scriptural prediction will be fulfilled, and thereby correctly represented them.

The first part of Jesus' reply accepts that the prophecy in the book of Malachi is to be fulfilled. It has occasionally been treated as a question, and this view has recently been recreated by Marcus, with reference to a range of Jewish source material.[21] One of the problems inherent in treating the sentence as a question is that Jesus would challenge the truth of scripture only if he had a good reason to do so. Marcus seeks to solve this problem by assimilating

---

[21] E.g. Wellhausen, *Evangelium Marci*, pp. 75–6; J. Marcus, 'Mark 9, 11–13: "As it Has Been Written"', *ZNW* 80, 1989, 42–63; J. Marcus, *The Way of the Lord: Christological Exegesis of the Old Testament in the Gospel of Mark* (Edinburgh, 1993), pp. 94–110.

this passage to some passages of Mekhilta and other Jewish sources which resolve supposed contradictions between different scriptural passages. Marcus translates Mark 9.12a: 'He said to them, "Is it true that, when he comes before the Messiah, Elijah will restore all things?"'[22] This is inaccurate, both in its introduction of the Messiah and in its insertion of the questioning phrase, 'Is it true that'. This phrase is a reasonable translation of וכי in some passages of Mekhilta which reconcile apparent contradictions between passages of scripture, and the crucial point is that it has no equivalent in the Markan text. One of the passages used by Marcus is Mekhilta Pisḥa III.1.1ff:

דברו אל כל עדת ישאל וגו' רבי ישמעאל אומר וכי
שניהם היו מדברים והלא כבר נאמר ואתה דבר אל בני
ישראל וגו ומה ת"ל דברו אלא כיון שהיה משה מדבר היה
אהרן מרכין אזנו לשמוע באימה ומעלה עליו הכתיב
כאילו שמוע מפי הקידש.

'Speak (pl) to the whole congregation of Israel etc' (Exod. 12.3). R. Ishmael says: Is it true that (וכי) both of them spoke? And is it not already (הלא כבר) written, 'And you (sg), speak (sg) to the children of Israel etc' (Exod. 31.13)? And what does scripture mean (ומה ת"ל) 'Speak (pl)' (Exod. 12.3)? But (אלא) as soon as Moses spoke, Aaron inclined his ear to listen with awe, and the scripture reckons it to him as if he heard it from the mouth of the Holy One.

The only one of the formal indicators in this passage to be found in the text of Mark is אלא, and this is not enough. While the precise nature and presence of them does vary somewhat, the absence of any equivalent to וכי is especially damaging and points up the inaccurate nature of Marcus's English translation, which inserts what is conspicuously not there. Mark does not even have μή or any other indication that the sentence is a question. This is the second problem inherent in any interpretation of the sentence as a question. Nothing at all is not a good way of indicating a challenge to the most obvious meaning of a scriptural passage, in a sentence so easily interpreted as expressing agreement with it.

Jesus' comment naturally uses the Aphel of תוב to recall the Hiphil of שוב. There is no direct Aramaic equivalent of the Waw

[22] Marcus, 'Mark 9, 11–13', 47; *Way of the Lord*, p. 99.

Consecutive plus perfect וֹהשׁיב: I have suggested the timeless narrative participle מתיב, for which a translator might naturally put a Greek present. The Aramaic מתיב כולא cannot, however, be accurately and completely translated, for any translation into Greek or English loses the cultural resonances present in Jesus' deliberate reference to the text of Mal. 3.23–4, probably to Sir. 48.10, and certainly to the tradition which Sir. 48.10 represents. To see what Jesus meant, we must go back to the scriptural text(s) which he interpreted. The Aramaic מתיב picks up הֹשׁיב from Mal. 3.24, and to understand it we must look at the whole clause:

והשׁיב לב אבות על בנים ולב בנים על אבותם.

And he will turn back the heart of the fathers to the children and the heart of the children to the fathers.

To this we must add Sir. 48.10. The original text of this has not survived. The major witnesses are as follows:

1. Late Hebrew text from the Cairo Geniza:

הכתוב נכון לעת להשבית אף לפני . . .
להשׁיב לב אבות על בנים ולהכין שׁ . . . . . . ל.

2. LXX:

ὁ καταγραφεὶς ἐν ἐλεγμοῖς[23] εἰς καιροὺς κοπάσαι ὀργὴν πρὸ θυμοῦ, ἐπιστρέψαι καρδίαν πατρὸς πρὸς υἱὸν καὶ καταστῆσαι φυλὰς Ιακωβ.

3. Peshitta:

והו עיתד דנאתא קדם דנאתא יומה דמריא למהפכו בניא
על אבהיא ולמסברו לשבטי יעקוב.

While doubts about details inevitably remain, it is clear from the combined evidence of these witnesses that the hope of Malachi was repeated, and interpreted with something about preparing/restoring the tribes of Israel/Jacob.

We can now see what Jesus really believed: he believed that these prophecies were fulfilled in the successful popular ministry of John the Baptist. He used מתיב because Mal. 3.24 used הֹשׁיב, and he used כולא as a summary of both texts and/or of the tradition which Sir. 48.10 represents. This was perfectly comprehensible to

---

[23] There are numerous variants here, so that the reading is doubtful, but discussing it would not help at this point.

Aramaic-speaking Jews who knew their scriptures. They would not take כולא as literally as commentators have taken πάντα. People who believed that Daniel's 'third kingdom' ruled כל־ארעא (Dan. 2.39) did not suppose that the Persians ruled Greece and Rome, and when Lamech wanted to know כולא (1QapGen II.5), he was not asking for the whole of human wisdom – he just wanted his wife Bitenosh to reassure him that he was the father of her son. Aramaic is only one of several languages in which words which are sometimes used comprehensively are also used in a more restricted way – English examples include 'everyone',[24] and בר (א)נש(א) is another Aramaic example. Aramaic-speaking Jews would therefore have no difficulty in interpreting כולא of the comprehensively successful popular ministry of John the Baptist.

The translator rendered מתיב with ἀποκαθίστημι, for it was the obvious choice. It overlaps massively in semantic area with the Hebrew שׁוב and the Aramaic תוב, and generally renders שׁוב in the LXX. Suffering the double level of interference inevitable among translators, he could hardly have gone for anything else. It is possible that he wrote the form ἀποκαταστάν(ε)ι (*א D), but this detailed uncertainty does not undermine the validity of any of the main points. In any case, neither the translator nor Mark was copying LXX Mal. 3.23, since this has the form ἀποκαταστήσει. This form is read at Mark 9.12 by C Θ 565 579 pc, which is not strong enough attestation to be the original reading, and which is therefore evidence of later assimilation of our text to LXX Mal. 3.23.

So far, so good. Jesus interpreted John the Baptist's successful ministry as a fulfilment of prophecy of a successful return of Elijah. John the Baptist, however, had been arrested and executed by Herod Antipas, and the prophecies of Elijah said nothing about that. In one sense, Jesus was in the same boat as the NT scholar – he could not find prophecies of John the Baptist's rejection by the Jewish authorities, arrest and execution. As a first-century Jew devoted to the scriptures, however, he had a resource which NT scholars have been most reluctant to use – general statements in the same scriptures. Jesus' overriding need was to understand John the Baptist's rejection and execution within the framework of God's purposes. Mal. 3.1 was surely bound to lead him to Isa. 40.3, which he must then interpret of John the Baptist too. He must surely

---

[24] Casey, 'Jackals', 10–11.

continue, past the prophecy of John's successful ministry preparing the way of the Lord in the wilderness straight to a metaphorical presentation of the transitory nature of human life:

כול הבשׂר חציר וכול חסדיו כציץ השׂדה . . .

All flesh (is) grass and all their acts of kindness like the flower of the countryside.

Isa. 40.6–8 must then surely remind him of the classic presentation of the suffering of man in Job 14.

Job 14 has everything which an ancient exegete needed. It begins with a blunt general statement about man:

אדם ילוד אשה קצר ימים ושבע רגז.

Man who is born of woman is shortlived and full of turmoil.

The rabbinical Targum has בר נשׁ for אדם. This Targum is too late in date to have influenced Jesus, but the rendering is a common one because of a genuine overlap in semantic area,[25] and this is significant because it means that Jesus might have used בר (א)נשׁ(א) in a general statement based on this text, even without the further reasons which we shall find for him to have done so.

The next verse is equally important:

כציץ יצא וימל ויברח כצל ולא יעמוד.

Like a flower he comes out and withers, and he flees like a shadow and will not stay.

The word ציץ is the same as at Isa. 40.6, 7, 8, and the whole context is similar. This is the link which a faithful Jew, learned in the scriptures, could not fail to make. In the middle of the chapter, we read at some length of man's death, essential for understanding the death of John the Baptist. The last verse is also especially significant:

אך בשׂרו עליו יכאב ונפשׁו עליו תאבל.

Indeed his flesh suffers upon him, and his soul mourns over him.

Here the word בשׂר forms another verbal link with Isa. 40.6, and

---

[25] Casey, 'Use of the Term בר (א)נשׁ(א) ', 93–5.

כאב is the word which Jesus used for 'suffer'. The noun מכאב is now extant at 4QTLevi VIII.1; VIII.3, with . . . [מכאב] at VII.3, so there should be no doubt that כאב could be used in the Aramaic of our period, and meditation on this Hebrew scripture is precisely what would make Jesus choose it.

Malachi 3 would also send Jesus to Jer. 6.27ff. Mal. 3.2–3 says of the messenger, identified at 3.23 as Elijah:

> כי־הוא כאש מצרף וכברית מכבסים: וישב מצרף ומטהר
> כסף וטהר את־בני־לוי וזקק אתם כזהב וככסף והיו
> ליהוה מגישי מנחה בצדקה.

> For he is like a refiner's fire and like fullers' lye, and he will
> sit refining and purifying silver, and he will purify the sons
> of Levi and he will refine them like gold and like silver and
> they will bring an offering to the LORD in righteousness.

At Jer. 6.27–30 this process seems to have begun but not finished. The piece may be perceived as addressed to John the Baptist/Elijah, and it ends with the wicked still unremoved, and the word מאס is used, and could be interpreted either of the wicked or of the people:

> לשוא צרף צרוף ורעים לא נתקו: כסף נמאס קראו להם
> כי מאס יהוה בהם.

> Refining he refines in vain, and the wicked are not drawn
> off: they shall be called rejected silver, for the LORD has
> rejected them.

This leads into Jeremiah 7, of which Jesus made vigorous use when he cleansed the Temple (Mark 11.17).[26] It contains a conditional threat to the whole Jewish people, and to the Temple. Jer. 7.29 uses מאס again:

> כי מאס יהוה ויטש את־דור עברתו.

> For the LORD has rejected and abandoned the generation
> of his fury.

The rejection of the people in Jeremiah 6–7 is quite sufficient to justify the general statement בר (א)נש(א) . . . אתבסר, made as an interpretation of scripture. It was this rejection which required John the Baptist's death, and would require Jesus' death also, with whoever would die with him (cf. Mark 8.31; 10.38–9; 14.31).

---

[26] Casey, 'Cleansing of the Temple'.

I have suggested אתבסר as the word which Jesus used to pick up מאס, and which the translator rendered ἐξουδενηθῇ. It has the right semantic area. It occurs before the time of Jesus at 4Q542 I.6, and subsequently in several dialects, including Jewish Aramaic. I have left יכאב in the imperfect, as at Job 14.22.The tenses of these verbs used by Jesus, and by Mark's source, must, however, be regarded as quite uncertain. The translator used two aorist subjunctives to focus on the suffering and rejection of a/the Son of man as a single matter rather than a long process, and he might have done this whatever the tenses in his source.

We have now recovered some of Jesus' biblical exegesis. He interpreted Malachi 3 and Isaiah 40 of the successful ministry of John the Baptist; Isaiah 40 and Job 14 of the death of man; Job 14 of the suffering of man; and Jeremiah 6–7 of the rejection of the Jewish people. We now have a second reason why he should use the term (א)נש(א) בר in a general statement which had particular reference to John the Baptist/Elijah: his suffering and rejection are written in the scriptures in general statements, not in specific references. The idiomatic use of (א)נש(א) בר is the third reason. His Aramaic-speaking disciples would know as they listened that John the Baptist was being particularly referred to, because he was the main figure under discussion. At the same time, Jesus predicted his own death during the ministry.[27] Since the disciples' question reflects a scribal reaction to the position of Jesus at the centre of a popular and successful Jesus movement, we should infer that he had already done so, as in the Markan narrative. He will therefore have included himself in this general statement, and his disciples could hardly fail to realise this. If the Markan narrative is in the right order, this will have been especially obvious after Peter's objection (Mark 8.32–3). It would become even more so after the discussion of Jacob and John's request to sit on his right and left in his glory (Mark 10.35–45). This passage is permeated by the perception that some of the disciples would die with him, and Jacob and John's immediate acceptance of their fate (Mark 10.39) shows that they had learnt much from something, surely including Jesus' rebuke of Peter and the present incident.

Jesus saw his own fate in the scriptures in the same kind of way, in passages such as Psalms 41; 118.22–3 referring to him

---

[27] Casey, 'General, Generic and Indefinite', 40–9; see pp. 202–3, 205–6, 211–18, 229–32, 239–42 below.

individually (Mark 12.10–11; 14.18, 20) and in general statements such as Ps. 116.15 (cf. Mark 14.21).[28] Verbal links with the passages which we have just discussed include מאס again at Ps. 118.22, מות at Job 14.10, 14 and Ps. 41.6; 116.3, 15; 118.17–18, and קום at Job 14.12 and Ps. 41.9, 11. We must surely add Ps. 116.15 to the general statements which helped Jesus to understand the death of John the Baptist. Other passages are also possible (cf., for example, Isa. 53; Psalms 39, 69), but they all have disadvantages and cannot be verified. The links between these ones are so secure and their interpretation so clearly in accordance with ancient exegetical method that we may be confident of his interpretation of them. Finally, this cannot be a question which mysteriously receives no answer: it makes sense only as an abbreviated statement of what Jesus said in answer to an entirely reasonable question from some of his disciples.

Why, then, does Mark 9.12 not actually mention death? Because John the Baptist's death was not the main problem. All people die, and if John the Baptist's successful ministry had prepared the way for Jesus and John had died a natural death when his ministry had been complete, his death could have been seen unproblematically at Isa. 40.6; Ps 116.15; Job 14.10, 14 and elsewhere. The problem was the rejection of John by many of Israel's leaders, and his suffering at their hands. That is why כאב and בסר were used to reflect scriptural texts in the source of Mark 9.12. John the Baptist's death was accordingly different from the death of Jesus, mentioned literally by him at Mark 8.31; 9.31; 10.34, 45, and metaphorically at Mark 10.38–9; 12.7–8; 14.8, 21, 24; Luke 13.32–3. Jesus' death was seen by him as an important event which would enable God to redeem Israel. Positive assessment of his death was always necessary to the early church, doubly so when Gentiles entered the churches without becoming Jews, and this explains both the preservation of his predictions and the extension and editing of one of them through the centre of Mark's Gospel. The source of Mark 9.12 was primarily about the fate of John the Baptist and only secondarily about that of Jesus, and John's death had no such function.

What Jesus meant is now clear. It faced the translator with a very difficult problem. He had evidently decided, probably in discussion with others, to use ὁ υἱὸς τοῦ ἀνθρώπου as a translation of בר (א)נש(א) when it referred to Jesus, and not otherwise. The positive

[28] Pp. 229–33 below.

half of this decision is fully in accordance with the known habits of translators, then and now.[29] It gives straightforward evidence of literal translation. Neither ὁ υἱὸς τοῦ ἀνθρώπου nor the anarthrous υἱὸς ἀνθρώπου is found in natural Greek. Its component elements, however, are close equivalents to the component elements of בר (א)נשׁ(א). There is massive overlap between the semantic areas of the Aramaic בר and the Greek υἱὸς, and likewise between the semantic areas of the Aramaic (א)נשׁ(א) and the Greek ἄνθρωπος. Moreover, the Hebrew בן אדם, clearly the equivalent of the Aramaic (א)נשׁ(א) בר, is normally rendered υἱὸς ἀνθρώπου in the LXX, by several different translators. In examples of the idiom exemplified in passages 5–7, the Greek articles are also appropriate, because the Greek article is both generic and particular. The first article is accordingly as near as possible to the Aramaic idiom, in which a general statement is used with particular reference to an individual, and the second article, always τοῦ, is simply generic.[30]

Moreover, the behaviour of Gospel translators is significantly paralleled by some LXX translators. Tov notes that 'υἱός follows בן, even in such combinations as 1 Sam 26:16 בני מות, "those who deserve to die", literally: "sons of death" – υἱοὶ θανατώσεως.'[31] The plural οἱ υἱοι τῶν ἀνθρώπων represents the anarthrous בני אדם more often than not (for example Pss. 11.4; 12.2, 9). Here both articles are generic. The less literalistic ἄνθρωποι was available, but rarely used (Isa. 52.14; Prov. 15.11). The LXX was the Bible of the Christian churches. Both in keeping the term υἱός, and in using the articles the Gospel translators of בר (א)נשׁ(א) followed a path known to the target culture from their sacred text.

The negative half of the translator's strategy follows from the absence of the term from most of the synoptic Gospels. On general grounds, if the tradition contained בר (א)נשׁ(א) as a reference to Jesus, it will have contained it when it was not a reference to him as well, and it will have had it in the plural too. In attempting to avoid confusion, other words have been used instead, surely including ἄνθρωπος both in the singular and the plural. The translator had

---

[29] Cf. P. M. Casey, 'Idiom and Translation: Some Aspects of the Son of Man Problem', *NTS* 41, 1995, 164–82.

[30] For more detailed discussion of the articles, including responses to other criticisms, see Casey, *Son of Man*, pp. 230–1; 'Jackals', 14–15; 'General, Generic and Indefinite', 31–4; 'Method in our Madness, and Madness in their Methods: Some Approaches to the Son of Man Problem in Recent Scholarship', *JSNT* 42, 1991, 17–43, at 40–1.

[31] Tov, 'Septuagint', p. 180.

got stuck once before, and came up with Mark 3.28. Here he was faced with (א)שׁנ(א) בר in a general statement which had particular reference to Jesus,[32] but he did not like the sense, for he thought that speaking against Jesus was unforgivable. He therefore compromised, and put the plural, τοῖς υἱοῖς τῶν ἀνθρώπων. This is both literal and explicitative. The plural ensures that there is no especial reference to Jesus, and this is reinforced by the sense of the verse as a whole. The translator and all Christians believed that the Holy Spirit was active in Jesus' ministry, so the verse conveys the sense that speaking against Jesus' ministry, as 'scribes who came down from Jerusalem' (Mark 3.22) had done, was unforgivable. Thus the sense of Jesus' words is accurately conveyed, and only the original idiom has been lost.

At Mark 9.12, the translator's source faced him with an even more difficult problem. It cannot be translated in such a way as to leave monoglot Greek-speaking Christians with the impression that it is a general statement with particular reference to Elijah/John the Baptist, and with reference to Jesus too. So the translator had to retain something, drop something, or write a lengthy explanation instead of a translation. He was not writing lengthy explanations on principle – he was translating his source. As a committed Christian, he believed that Jesus' death was more important than that of John the Baptist, so he decided that reference to it must be retained. He did this as he had previously decided to do, by translating (א)שׁנ(א) בר with ὁ υἱὸς τοῦ ἀνθρώπου. If the first article were taken as generic, as the second must be, bilinguals could see the original idiom. The translator had therefore done as well as possible. We may feel that his work illustrates a general observation made by modern students of translation: 'Strategies do not solve translation problems – they are merely plans that can be implemented in an attempt to solve problems.'[33] This further illustrates the normality of the processes by which Mark's text was produced.

The translator also had to be careful about אתה, which Jesus

---

[32] For a reconstruction, see Casey, 'General, Generic and Indefinite', 36–7; cf. B. Lindars, *Jesus Son of Man* (London, 1983), pp. 34–8, 178–81.

[33] H. G. Hönig, 'Holmes' "Mapping Theory" and the Landscape of Mental Translation Processes', in K. M. van Leuven-Zwart and T. Naaijkens (eds.), *Translation Studies: The State of the Art. Proceedings of the First James S. Holmes Symposium on Translation Studies* (Amsterdam, 1991), pp. 77–89, at p. 85, quoting D. C. Kiraly, 'Toward a Systematic Approach to Translation Skills Instruction', Ph. D. thesis, Urbana, Illinois (1990), 149.

pronounced as a participle but which could be read as a third-person singular perfect, as it must be in the following verse. That would be unfortunate, for at verse 12 Jesus is merely agreeing that the scriptural prophecy of the coming of Elijah receives its fulfilment. It is not until verse 13, when he has pointed out that there are other scriptures which tell of his suffering and rejection, that our source genuinely uses a past tense of the coming of Elijah. The translator has moved Elijah to the beginning of Jesus' speech, added an idiomatic Greek μέν to contrast with the following verse, rendered the participial אתה with the aorist participle ἐλθών, and used ἐλήλυθεν for the perfect אתה in the following verse. In these respects, the resultant rendering is clear. His rendering of על with ἐπί is overliteral, and is to be explained by the large semantic overlap between these two words, as well as by the care which he was taking. Finally, his rendering of היכה with πῶς is extremely straightforward. It will not have occurred to him that the result could be read as a question which receives no answer.

At 9.13, I propose that Mark's ὅσα ἤθελον is an explicitative translation of דצבו, which is also difficult to translate. It could mean 'what they wanted', and in choosing ὅσα the translator ensured that this is how monoglot Greeks would interpret his translation. I propose that Jesus in fact intended a reference to חפצים at Mal. 3,1. The Targum has צרן, pesh צבין. Like the rabbinical Targum to Job, these cannot have influenced Jesus, but they indicate that the overlap in semantic area between the Hebrew חפץ and the Aramaic צבא makes the Aramaic צבא the natural word for Jesus to have used in order to make reference to חפצים at Mal. 3.1. The writer of the Aramaic source will have thought that this was clear because he had Mal. 3 in his mind. Jesus' actual speech is as usual too short, so we should not trouble over the question whether the disciples could have picked up the reference. If they knew the scriptures well enough they could have done so, and Jesus will really have said something longer which is consequently likely to have been clearer.

With the reference to Mal. 3.1 established, we must be careful about the force of לה. In Aramaic, the particle ל is often used in a way that has no proper equivalent in English, and is only approximately equivalent to the so-called ethic dative in Greek, the nearest Greek equivalent and therefore naturally used in translation. All that ל does in Aramaic is to establish some kind of reference to the person concerned. That is all that our source intended here. We

must be equally careful about עלוהי. Though the suffix is techni-
cally masculine rather than feminine, there is no neuter in Aramaic,
so the suffix does not distinguish between men, objects and abstrac-
tions. It is accordingly vaguer than αὐτόν or 'him', and can refer to
the whole series of events, not simply to John the Baptist/Elijah.

We can now find the scriptures referred to in this verse – they are
the same as the ones in the previous verse. People delighted in John
the Baptist, who carried through the successful popular ministry
prophesied in Malachi 3, and referred to more briefly at Isa. 40.3
and Sir. 48.10. The generalised plural also refers to the other
scriptures discussed above. He suffered and died like all men in Job
14. Since the people were not sufficiently refined as in Jeremiah
6–7, they were rejected, and some of them shed the innocent blood
of John the Baptist. Any other scriptures that we are no longer able
to find will have been included here too.

The opening phrase of the translation is emphatic but unexcep-
tionable. If we are right to reconstruct the simple ו, ἀλλά is to be
associated with μέν as part of the translator's task in ensuring the
contrast between the two verses. This was all the more necessary in
the light of his decision to render בר (א)נש(א) with ὁ υἱὸς τοῦ
ἀνθρώπου. This now refers primarily to Jesus, and the translator
will have been aware that monoglot Greek-speaking Christians
would perceive no other reference. A strong contrast at the beginning of verse 13 was therefore essential to the translator, as it was
not to Mark's source. None the less, we cannot exclude the
possibility that Jesus said, and/or Mark's source wrote, להן or
אלא: this level of uncertainty is inevitable, and while it is often
unimportant, it should be explicitly recognised. καί is reasonable
for אף, as, for example, at LXX Lev. 26.16; Judg. 5.29; Isa. 43.7.
Any Greek-speaking person bilingual with Aramaic and/or Hebrew
was likely to use καί more often than monoglot speakers of Greek,
and it is evident from the text of Mark's Gospel that such people
were involved in its composition.

The perfect ἐλήλυθεν is at first sight surprising for the Semitic
perfect אתה – we might have expected ἦλθεν for a single past
event, just the change which Matthew made. We have seen that this
was caused by the double occurrence of אתה. The translator put
the perfect because he was being careful to distinguish between the
participle אתה and the perfect אתה. He thus used a completed past
tense for the coming of Elijah/John the Baptist, which was now
over but had continuing effects, and this was to be contrasted with

the scribes' view of the fulfilment of Malachi 3, necessary but still in the future. We have seen that μέν in verse 12 must result from the translator's care to ensure this distinction, and I have suggested that ἀλλά is a strong translation of וֹ for the same reason. For the perfect עבדו he put the more predictable aorist ἐποίησαν, which Matthew duly retained.

There is only one serious problem: ὅσα ἤθελον. Firstly, we must note that it is a perfectly possible interpretation of דצבו, so that this is the kind of shift in meaning always liable to happen in translation. Secondly, the translator was concerned to ensure that there was a reference to the death of John the Baptist in scripture, as his source told him. As a bilingual, he could see an idiomatic reference preserved as well as possible in verse 12, but he will have known that monoglot speakers of Greek would not see it unless they were told. This is one reason why he should interpret דצבו as ὅσα ἤθελον. The plural without a subject enabled him to interpret it of leading figures who rejected John (Matt. 21.32, cf. Mark 11.27–33), and of Herod Antipas and others who put him to death. He will also have remembered his use of θέλω in his dramatic and gossipy account of John's death (Mark 6.19, 22, 25, 26). Like so many translators, he simply did not see the problems which his translation would cause for other people much later. At the end of the verse, he had to choose αὐτόν or αὐτό to represent the suffix of עלוהי, and he preferred the masculine because of his primary need to ensure references to Elijah/John the Baptist, who would no longer be perceived by congregations who heard ὁ υἱὸς τοῦ ἀνθρώπου rather than בר (א)נש(א). He used the overliteral ἐπί for על, as he had done in the previous verse. Finally, we must infer that Mark's text was not revised after the translation was done. This should be treated as part of the evidence that his Gospel was never finished.

This verse, like the others, has an excellent Sitz im Leben in the teaching of Jesus, who was baptised by John the Baptist. It has no Sitz im Leben in the early church, for it is written in such a way that it could cause confusion between the roles of John and Jesus. It cannot possibly have originated in Greek, for any reading of the Greek text as if it were written of set purpose produces dreadful confusion, whereas the Aramaic source is quite lucid, and the behaviour of the translator comprehensible, indeed quite conventional. We must therefore conclude that Mark's Aramaic source gives us an accurate account of Jesus' teaching, even if it is an abbreviated account.

This gives us an additional argument for the priority of Mark. This passage was already a strong argument when Matthew and Mark were studied in Greek. The discussion of Davies and Allison justifies their summary: 'We find it well nigh impossible to fathom why anyone would revise Matthew's text to give us the perplexities of Mark. But that Matthew, faced with Mark's troublesome words, ironed out the difficulties and cleared everything up, is altogether natural.'[34] The above discussion is quite a different kind of argument for the same conclusions. If Mark's text is intelligible as a conventional translation of an Aramaic source which gave a lucid account of an original debate which has a proper Sitz im Leben in the ministry of Jesus but not in the early church, Mark cannot have been abbreviating Matthew. If the translation is none the less such that monoglot Greeks who were not involved in its production would want to revise it, it is entirely coherent that Matthew revised it and Luke left it out.

Finally, both the nature of the Aramaic source and the unrevised quality of the translation imply a much earlier date than is conventional for this Gospel. The source was a very abbreviated account which could only be written for someone who was supposed to know Jesus' unrecorded biblical exegesis: the translation has not been revised by someone writing for monoglot Greeks. This could only happen within a few years of the crucifixion, when most Christians were Jewish and authors could assume a considerable knowledge of the Jesus of history.

The following conclusions should therefore be drawn. The traditional problems involved in interpreting Mark 9.11–13 can be solved by reconstructing Mark's Aramaic source. In response to the disciples' question, Jesus accepted the opinion of the scribes that the scriptural prophecies of Elijah's coming would be fulfilled. Since he and they also had to understand John the Baptist's death, he added a general statement referring to other scriptures which he also saw fulfilled in him. These scriptures included Isaiah 40, Jeremiah 6–7 and Job 14. Jesus interpreted Elijah as John the Baptist, and, with another reference to the foundational scripture in Malachi 3, he asserted that these scriptures had been fulfilled.

The major source of exegetical trouble has been the treatment of this passage as if it were written by a monoglot Greek-speaking Christian. It was in fact written by a bilingual translator who

---

[34] Davies and Allison, *Matthew* vol. II, pp. 710–18: I quote from p. 710.

followed his strategy of rendering (א)שׁנ(א) בר with ὁ υἱὸς τοῦ ἀνθρώπου whenever it referred to Jesus. In this passage, the primary reference of (א)שׁנ(א) בר was originally to John the Baptist/Elijah, but additional reference to Jesus was also implied, and this was most important to the translator because of his commitment to Jesus, whose suffering and rejection were central events leading up to his atoning death. Other problems resulted from the translator's need to compensate for this understandable decision. Consequently, we can recover what Jesus meant, and the scriptural passages to which he referred, only if we reconstruct Mark's Aramaic source. When we have done so, we find a very brief account of evidently early date.

4

TWO SABBATH CONTROVERSIES: MARK 2.23–3.6

Mark 2.1–3.6 consists largely of conflict stories. It has often been suspected that they were collected together at a relatively late stage in their transmission. On the other hand, connections between them have been pointed out. Those between 2.23–8 and 3.1–6 are especially striking, because they are assumed rather than stated. Mark's account of both incidents also contains a number of features which indicate literal translation of an underlying Aramaic source. It is this source which we must seek to reconstruct.

23 והוה בשבתא עבר בזרעיא ותלמידוהי שריו למעבר אורח ולמקטף שובליא.

24 ופרושיא אומרין לה, הא, למא עבדין בשבתא מה די לא שליט.

25 ואמר להון, לא קריתון מה די עבד דויד כדי צרך לה וכפן הוא וחברוהי.

26 על לבית אלהא ביומי אביתר כהן רב ואכל לחמא די אנפיא די לא שליט למאכל להן לכהניא, ויהב אף לחברוהי.

27 ואמר להון, שבתא בדיל אנשא אתעבדת ולא אנשא בדיל שבתא.

28 שליט נא הוא בר נש אף בשבתא.

1 ואוסיף למעלל לכנישתא, והוא תמן אנש דיבישתא לה ידא.

2 ונטרין לה הן בשבתא יאסאנה, דיאכלון קרצוהי.

3 ואמר לאנשא דידא יבישתא לה, קום בגוא.

4 ואמר להון, השליט בשבתא למעבד מה טב או לאבאשה, נפש לאחיה או למקטלה. ושתקין אנין.

5 וחזא עליהון ברגז ועציב על קשיות לבביהון ואמר לאנשא, פשט ידא. ופשט ותוב לה ידא.

6 ונפקין פרושיא בה שעתא ויהבין עיצה עם הרודיאני עלוהי היך יהובדונה.

²³And he was, on the sabbath, going through the cornfields and his disciples began to go along a path and to pluck the ears of corn. ²⁴And Pharisees said to him, 'Hoy! Why are they doing, on the sabbath, something which is not permitted?' ²⁵And he said to them, 'Have you not read what David did, when he was hungry and in need, he and his associates? ²⁶He went into the house of God, in the days of Abiathar – a great/chief priest! – and ate the shewbread, which is not permitted except to priests, and gave also to his associates?' ²⁷And he said to them, 'The sabbath was made for man, and not man for the sabbath. ²⁸Surely, then, a man is master even of the sabbath.'

¹And he went again to the synagogue. And there was there a man who had a withered hand. ²And they were watching him, to see whether he would heal him on the sabbath, so that they might accuse him [literally eat his pieces]. ³And he said to the man whose hand was withered, 'Get up (and come) into the middle.' ⁴And he said to them, 'Is it permitted on the sabbath to do what is good, or to do evil, to save life/a person or to kill him?' And they were silent. ⁵And he looked over them with anger, and he was grieved at the hardness of their hearts, and he said to the man, 'Stretch out the hand.' And the hand stretched out and returned to him. ⁶And the Pharisees went out in that hour with the Herodiani and gave counsel against/concerning him how they might destroy him.

The first sentence goes straight to the point. בשבתא is the second word of Mark's source, to tell us with absolute clarity that these disputes are about what should and should not be done on the sabbath. Καὶ ἐγένετο is not attested in non-biblical Greek as an introduction to a past event, but it would come naturally to anyone familiar with the LXX, and from this perspective it forms a natural rendering of the opening ויהוה (cf. 1 En. 6.1). The rendering of the singular שבתא with the plural τοῖς σάββασιν had been normal for a long time. It arises from the fact that the ending of the Aramaic שבתא may be assimilated to a Greek neuter plural and this is especially well illustrated at LXX Exod. 16.29. Here the Hebrew singular השבת is rendered with the Aramaising plural τὰ σάββατα, and the purely grammatical nature of the plural is shown by the explicitative addition of the singular τὴν ἡμέραν ταύτην in apposition to τὰ σάββατα. It follows that, in passages like these, noone has misunderstood anything. Rather, the plural form τὰ σάββατα, used of a single sabbath, entered Jewish Greek because Aramaic was the lingua franca of Israel. So Josephus, who often uses τὸ σάββατον in the singular, also has κατὰ δὲ ἑβδόμην ἡμέραν, ἥτις σάββατα καλεῖται (*AJ* III.237; cf. I, 33; XII.4; XIII.12). Hence the use of τοῖς σάββασιν by Mark's translator for the singular שׁבתא, the ending of which would encourage him to use the plural rather than the singular through the normal process of interference.

Jesus and his disciples were perfectly entitled to be in the fields on the sabbath. The only sabbath limit likely to have been observed in Galilee at that time is the 2,000-cubit limit known directly from later rabbinical sources (cf. Acts 1.12).[1] This allowed people to go for a walk of any length, provided that they did not go more than 2,000 cubits (over half a mile) beyond the boundary of the town, village or whatever place they were in, and that is quite far enough for the disciples to have been 'going through the cornfields'. For example, b. Shab 127a has the story of Rabbi finding somewhere too small for his disciples, and consequently going into a field and clearing it of sheaves. The halakhic discussion concerns the legitimacy of clearing the sheaves: that he goes into the field is taken for granted.

Mark's Aramaic source proceeds to give the specific reason for the disciples' presence in the fields: 'And his disciples began to go along a path, and to pluck the ears of corn.' Mark's ὁδὸν ποιεῖν is notoriously unsatisfactory Greek, as is the subordination of τίλλοντες, since it tells us the main point of the dispute. The subordination of τίλλοντες to ὁδὸν ποιεῖν will have resulted from the Greek translation of an original parataxis: the crucial factor is then the misreading of עבר as עבד. Reading the text as למעבד, the translator rendered it literally with ποιεῖν. This kind of literal rendering is quite common both in general and among the translators of our languages and period: in a similar way, the LXX translator of Judg. 17.8 rendered לעשׂות דרכו as τοῦ ποιῆσαι ὁδὸν αὐτοῦ. The Aramaic source must therefore have read something very like that suggested above.

This reconstructed source describes the offence which the disciples were supposed to have committed with sufficient precision

---

[1] On the sabbath limit, see L. H. Schiffman, *The Halakhah at Qumran* (SJLA XVI. Leiden, 1975), pp. 90–8.

for us to see the original situation with clarity, provided that we ask the right question. What assumptions must the author have held that enabled him to think he had explained the situation when he said no more than this? The major point is then the system of Peah: our source thought he had told us that the disciples were going along a path in between the fields to pluck the grain which was left for the poor. He assumed that he had said enough because he wrote in a Jewish environment in which Peah was a conventional institution, part of the social security system of ancient Israel. In that environment, everyone knew that people went along a path plucking grain from other people's fields because they were poor and consequently hungry. Hunger had to be mentioned explicitly by Jesus, and by our source, at 2.25, to make sure that the David incident was a clear exemplum. The system of taking Peah was, however, so well known in Israel that the narrator, having declared that people 'began to go along a path and to pluck the ears of corn', assumed that he had made himself clear. Mark followed his source without deliberate alteration.

The basic regulations for Peah are biblical. 'When you reap the harvest of your land, you shall not complete the border (פאת) of your field, nor shall you gather the gleanings of your harvest. And you shall not glean your vineyard nor shall you gather the fallen grapes of your vineyard: you shall leave them for the poor and for the sojourner' (Lev. 19.9, cf. 23.23). The translation of פאת as 'border' rather than 'corner' is not obvious, and we do not have direct empirical data to tell us exactly how Peah was left at the time of Jesus. We know that the semantic area of the word covers 'border', 'edge', 'side', as well as 'corner'. The Peshitta evidently understood the custom as leaving the edges unharvested, since it renders פאת with ספרא, and Jewish influence was so pervasive in the environment where this translation was made that this evidence must reflect actual practice. This is indirectly supported by the LXX, whose free renderings θερισμόν (Lev. 19.9) and τὸ λοιπὸν τοῦ θερισμοῦ (Lev. 23.22) are natural in the absence of a genuinely suitable Greek word for the border of a field, whereas the interpretation of פאת as 'corner' should have led the translator to add to the thirty-two LXX occurrences of γωνία. Paths not only gave access to corn and a way through it: they also marked the boundaries between fields so that Peah had to be given for each field. M. Peah 2.1 lists a private road (דרך), a public road, a private footpath (שביל) and a public footpath in use both in summer and in the rainy season as among the features which cause a division with regard to Peah, and this is so obvious an interpretation that we may not dismiss it as a later development. Thus even later rabbinical discussion which maintains that Peah must be left בסוף שׂמה, even if it is left elsewhere too, would also result in a situation where people would normally and regularly go along a path in order to collect it (cf. m. Pea 1.2: t. Pea 1.6//Sifra Qed I. 10// y. Pea IV. 3.5//b. Shab 23a). We should deduce from this evidence one of the assumptions of our source. Since this part of the Mosaic Law allowed the poor to go along a path and to pluck the ears of corn, he assumed that we would know from this description that these disciples were poor and hungry. We can now see also why Jesus was not plucking the corn – he was not poor enough to do so.

One other biblical text must be taken into consideration, since it has been thought to give an alternative justification for the disciples' action: 'When you go into your neighbour's standing grain, you may pluck the ears with your hand, but you shall not put a sickle to your neighbour's standing grain' (Deut. 23.25). Unfortunately, this does not specify the circumstances in which you may go into your neighbour's standing grain. Later rabbis restricted this right to hired labourers, but it is improbable that this restriction was already in force at the time of Jesus.[2] Most commentators suggest that this custom was for the sustenance of travellers, but some have suggested that it was a universal right, and an ancient one. The latter view may not be founded on Deut. 23.26 interpreted in 'isolation'; the compiler might have written the opening of the verse with any of these customs in mind, for his purpose was to regulate a known custom, not to describe it, and he did not intend his words to be interpreted out of their social context without regard for his assumptions. Josephus probably applied the passage to the sustenance of travellers, but the customs referred to in his enthusiastic description (*AJ* IV. 231–40) are not wholly clear. If 4Q159 refers to Deut. 23.25–6, it established dire poverty as a qualification, but this interpretation is also uncertain.[3]

These uncertainties over details must not be allowed to upset the clarity with which we can see the main points. Jesus' point that David and his companions were 'hungry and in need' is a feasible

---

[2] Cf. B. Cohen, 'The Rabbinic Law Presupposed by Matthew xii. 1 and Luke vi. 1', *HThR* 23, 1930, 91–2.

[3] Cf. F. J. Weinert, '4Q 159: Legislation for an Essene Community Outside of Qumran?', *JSJ* 5, 1974, 179–207.

point to make if, and only if, his disciples were hungry and in need. The well-known and widespread custom of Peah explains why the author of our source thought his description of their action of going along a path plucking the grain would convey the information that they were hungry and in need. It would also imply that they were poor. It is not impossible that a different regulation allowing hungry people to eat from other people's crops was in mind, but this is less probable because the description of them as going along a path was less likely to be transmitted, and the taking of Peah provides a simple explanation of the fact that Jesus himself was not plucking the grain. In that case, since they are not said to be far from home, it is still most likely that the disciples were generally poor rather than temporarily in need. Further, it is precisely this regulation which would combine with the universal knowledge of the qualifications for taking Peah to make it unnecessary to mention that disciples taking Peah were poor, since the halakhah probably allowed them to go along a path plucking the grains of corn if they were only temporarily in need. As the sages said of a householder who took poor people's dues because he was in need when travelling, 'he was poor at the time' (m. Pea 5.4). The point in dispute was therefore the right of hungry people to pluck corn on the sabbath, and the mention of their going along a path made the situation clear for people familiar with the relevant customs. The situation of the disciples is moreover of direct relevance when we consider Jesus' defence of them. Whether they were permanently in dire poverty or not, the fact that they were hungry and in need explains why he unhesitatingly defended them with such vigour.

This verse also provides another new argument for the priority of Mark. As we have seen, the peculiarities which have struck scholars who have treated him as if he were a monoglot Greek-speaking Christian can be explained as the natural work of a translator of a written Aramaic source. It follows that Mark was not editing Matthew and/or Luke. Neither of them repeats ὁδὸν ποιεῖν, but that is natural because it is not correct monoglot Greek for the required sense. Both add that the disciples ate. They do not, however, mysteriously agree: they use different forms of ἐσθίω in different positions because they were vigorous independent editors who could both see that their target audiences needed to be told what the disciples plucked the grain for, whereas this was too obvious to the Jew who wrote Mark's Aramaic source for him to consider it worthy of mention. Luke, unlike Matthew, also added ψώχοντες ταῖς χερσίν, because he thought his target audience needed to be told how one can eat raw grain plucked in a field. From a Griesbachian perspective, Riley comments: 'To *make (their) way* is perhaps a Latinism, from *iter facere*, to journey, and a sign of secondary writing; in any case, the words coming after *going through the grainfields* are tautologous. This is quite in Mark's manner, but it results in the word *began* being attached to the wrong verb.'[4] Everything is wrong with this. The central point is that it merely *catalogues* what Mark would have to be thought to have done if the Griesbach hypothesis were right: it does not *explain* his behaviour at all. This is most obvious with Mark adding something tautologous, which he has to be thought of as doing often, while omitting most of Jesus' teaching as he found it in Matthew and Luke. To do so while attaching *began* to the wrong verb makes him not merely a fool, but a fool too inexplicable for us to believe in. In the real Mark's Aramaic source, שׁריו was correctly connected to למעבר, because the disciples had to go along a path to be able to take Peah. This was then literally translated, as we have seen. On Riley's model, however, Mark had no reason to introduce ὁδὸν ποιεῖν at all, and to interpolate an unnecessary Latinism when he hardly has any others makes him a quite peculiar bilingual. We must conclude that Riley's account of Mark is incredible. The proposed Aramaic source, however, makes excellent sense in its own right, and the behaviour of the translator is also wholly in accordance with the known behaviour of translators.

The objection, or rather the very presence, of the Pharisees is one of the reasons which many scholars have given for their refusal to believe in the accuracy of Mark's account. In an influential and much-repeated passage, Beare comments,

> That the setting is in any case artificial hardly needs to be argued, were it not that commentators still take it as a genuine fragment of reminiscence . . . how, then, does one explain the presence of the Pharisees? Are we to suppose that they kept company with the disciples on their sabbath afternoon strolls, as a regular practice; or that some of them just happened to be passing by the very fields in which the disciples were plucking the grain?[5]

[4] H. Riley, *The Making of Mark: An Exploration* (Macon, 1989), p. 29.
[5] F. W. Beare, 'The Sabbath was Made for Man', *JBL* 79, 1960, 130–6.

There are two perfectly sound reasons why the Pharisees might have been present. Firstly, orthodox Jews[6] who lived in Capernaum were liable to join the Pharisees, and any Pharisees who did live in Capernaum were perfectly entitled to go for a stroll on the sabbath, just like Jesus and his disciples. The point of the sabbath limit was to tell you how to avoid infringing the commandment to remain in your place (Exod. 16.29); within the sabbath limit the Pharisees could either stroll or walk for a set purpose, for the sabbath limit told them that they were not going on a journey. Nor is it too coincidental that they should meet Jesus' disciples doing something they disapproved of. They perceived themselves as guardians of the Law at a time when we can verify the increase in sabbath Law in which they themselves played a significant part, while Jesus took his prophetic message to the people of the land. That was sufficient to make conflict inevitable. We should not invent the notion of their keeping company with the disciples on sabbath strolls as a regular practice, because our primary source does not suggest this. The fields within the sabbath limit were a quite limited area, and it is not unlikely that such an incident would occur once. There is just the one report of a dispute of this kind in the Gospels: we should not refuse to believe it merely because of the general improbability of its being a weekly occurrence.

There is a second reason why the Pharisees may have been there: they were quite free to go and see whether Jesus was teaching in accordance with the Law. In Mark's narrative, he has already healed on the sabbath and eaten with tax-collectors and sinners. While we cannot confirm Mark's placing of all these events in their present sequence, both activities were such outstanding features of Jesus' ministry that it is entirely plausible that some Pharisees would have come and observed him. This is explicit in the following narrative, where they are said to be watching him in case he heals

---

[6] I use the term 'orthodox' in the sense defined in Casey, *From Jewish Prophet to Gentile God*, pp. 17–18. The centre of this definition is that these people not only observed the Law, but vigorously sought to apply it to the whole of life. This led them to discuss and codify additional enactments. It should be obvious that I have not suggested that they were normative, or that they always agreed with each other. Consequently, I have not been impressed by criticisms which presuppose this from a Christian perspective. My definition was drawn up for academic rather than confessional reasons, and should be judged by whether it is a fruitful analytical tool, not by whether it agrees with a Christian view of orthodoxy. A more detailed response to such criticisms must be given elsewhere.

on the sabbath again (Mark 3.2), and we shall see that these two narratives were originally connected.

The ground of the Pharisaic objection was that the disciples were plucking corn on the sabbath, and should not have been doing so because this was 'work'. The plucking of corn is the only action mentioned which could form the ground of an objection, and we shall see that the subsequent arguments are intelligible as a response to it. This is the reason why it is described so carefully in the opening verse. It is generally assumed that the Pharisaic opinion was already part of universal Jewish halakhah. For example, Banks describes the plucking as 'an act which unquestionably violated all current practice of the sabbath laws'.[7] This is most improbable. Before the time of Jesus, Jub. 2.23, coming from the orthodox wing of Judaism, specifies twenty-two kinds of work prohibited on the sabbath. More than a century after the time of Jesus, m. Shab 7.2 specifies thirty-nine kinds of work prohibited on the sabbath. Despite the partly agricultural background of m. Shabbat, which explicitly prohibits sowing, ploughing, reaping (קוצר), binding sheaves, threshing, winnowing, choosing, grinding and sifting (7.2), 'plucking' is not mentioned. At y. Shab VII.2, תלש is prohibited in an opinion attributed to third-century rabbis, but, as in the anonymous parallel at t. Shab 9.17, this occurs in a list of the different terms used for reaping different items (grapes, olives, dates and figs), and it is by no means clear that the authors, tradents and compilers of the saying had in mind the plucking of ears of corn, rather than the uprooting of plants such as endives (תלש is used of picking endives at t. Shab 9.17). Moreover, תלש is omitted from the parallel list at b. Shab 73b. We must therefore infer that תלש was not in universally accepted regulations in Israel in the tannaitic period, and was consequently omitted from Mishnah and from the tannaitic list of b. Shab 73b: it was added by third-century rabbis as recorded in y. Shab VII.2, and consequently collected into t. Shab 9.17.

One passage of Philo does prohibit plucking, and is often cited at this point. Philo asserts that contemporary respect for, and observance of, the sabbath was widespread, and that it was extended to neighbours, slaves and even animals:

---

[7] R. Banks, *Jesus and the Law in the Synoptic Tradition* (MSSNTS 28. Cambridge, 1975), p. 114, n. 2.

For the rest extends also to every herd and to whatever was made for the service of man, like slaves serving him who is by nature their master. It extends also to every kind of tree and plant, for it does not allow us to cut a shoot, a branch or even a leaf, or to pluck any fruit whatever (καρπὸν ὁντινοῦν δρέψασθαι). They are all released and as it were have freedom on that day, under the general proclamation that no one shall touch (κοινῷ κηρύγματι μηδενὸς ἐπιψαύοντος). (*Life of Moses* II. 22)

We must accept that this passage prohibits plucking on the sabbath. We must, however, be careful before we apply it to Israel, and even more careful before we generalise too much concerning the groups of Jews who would follow this halakhah. We have seen evidence from Israel which strongly suggests that the prohibition of plucking did not enter generally accepted halakhah until it was promulgated by rabbis in the third century CE. A second reason supports this. Philo derives the prohibition of plucking from a more general principle, μηδενὸς ἐπιψαύοντος. This principle is not known from elsewhere either. If the halakhic judgement, and the principle on which it is based, are both unknown from Israel in this period, Philo is not sufficient evidence that they were known outside Alexandria.

What Philo does illustrate is the orthodox tendency found in various quarters in the development of the halakhah at this time. Jubilees, CD, the Pharisees, the compilers of Mishnah, Tosephta and the Talmuds, and the hellenised Philo, all had in common a very profound and unshakeable commitment to observing the immutable divine Law that Jews do not work on the sabbath. This central commitment was very similar to the central commitment of orthodox Jews in the modern world, and one of its manifestations is the expansion of detailed regulations governing sabbath observance. Accordingly, the Pharisees' attitude to the disciples' action does not require us to suppose that even they already had a detailed regulation prohibiting the plucking of corn on the sabbath, though they may have had. It more certainly presupposes that their central commitment to the sabbath rest was so profound and of such a kind that they were shocked to see Jews plucking corn because this violates the sabbath. This commitment was later to express itself in the orthodox prohibitions of various kinds of plucking on the sabbath, just as it expressed itself in contemporary Alexandria in

Philo's principle that no one should touch, and the prohibition of taking anything from plants which is derived from it.

If the disciples were poor people in need, and therefore hungry, the Pharisees might have been expected to have made allowances for them. We should infer that, as so often with Jesus' opponents, they were stricter than that. Some orthodox Jews had long ago written down their non-biblical halakhah: 'A man shall eat on the sabbath day only what has been prepared, and from what is decaying in the fields' (CD X.22–3). This restricts people to prepared food and fruit which must have fallen off the day before,[8] and so the opposite of what needs to be plucked. We should infer that the Pharisees took a similar view. They were themselves accustomed to fasting, so they would not have been impressed by the mere fact that poor people were hungry. They would rather have taken the view that they should eat only food which they should have prepared the previous day.

To understand the action of Jesus' disciples, and his defence of them, we must consider their central commitments. Since the disciples were poor and did take Peah on the sabbath, they must have been normal Jews, the sort of people whom the rabbis would later call עם הארץ. These people were as far removed from Philo as from the Pharisees. They may have taken it for granted that you could pluck to eat, and they may not have imagined that this was work. If the Pharisees did not normally live in the area, it is all the more likely that their opinions were not known, and if they did, the עם הארץ did not obey the Law in the Pharisaic manner even when they obeyed it as a whole. That is to say, they did not share the kind of commitment to the protection of Judaism which expresses itself in the orthodox expansion of regulations: they obeyed basic laws such as circumcision and not in general working on the sabbath, but they were always liable to do what stricter Jews thought they should not do.

Jesus' life-stance was significantly different again. He came from the prophetic wing of Judaism, and the centres of his life were God himself and love of one's neighbour. He did not share the concern of the Pharisees and others to defend Judaism by means of the expansion of regulations. Thus he observed the sabbath, but he vigorously defended his right to heal on that day, and he was not shocked that people who were hungry and in need should pluck

---

[8] Schiffman, *Halakhah*, pp. 98–101.

corn in order to have enough to eat on that day: rather, with prophetic authority he defended their right to satisfy their most basic needs on the day which God had created for them to rest on and to enjoy.

Furthermore, differences of opinion on minor matters of hala-khah were widespread among observant Jews, even when they shared a more orthodox life-stance. For example, m. Sheb 10.7//m. Ukz 3.10 shows the question whether one might take honey from a beehive on the sabbath still undecided (cf. b. Sheb 66a, 80b), while the schools of Hillel and Shammai disagreed whether you could put out nets on Friday which would catch animals on the sabbath (m. Shab 1.6). The men of Jericho ignored the view of the Sages that, on the sabbath, they should not eat fruit which lay fallen under a tree (m. Pes 4.8), and they did this specifically for the benefit of the poor (t. Pes 2.21, b. Pes 56a). At one level, the question at issue in Mark 2.23–8 is that kind of detail. This makes it all the more inappropriate to deduce universal halakhah from our meagre observant sources, since even evidence that some observant first-century Galilean Jews prohibited the plucking of corn on the sabbath would not show that others did not disagree with them. Yet further, the question at issue may be perceived as whether a prohibition of plucking corn is to be overridden by human hunger. Our source does not express it in these terms, because neither Jesus nor Mark's Aramaic source viewed the world from a rabbinical perspective, but the perspective is fruitful for us because it under-lines the fact that none of our early sources deals with this matter: even Philo, who clearly prohibits plucking of all kinds, does not give a decision about the fate of poor and hungry people taking Peah.

Finally, the evidence of our primary source should be treated as decisive. When Jesus might be thought to be challenging Penta-teuchal Law, Mark records him faithfully, with the reasons for the apparent challenge and his justification from the creation narrative of Genesis (Mark 10.2ff.). On occasions when he launched slashing attacks on the known oral Law of the Pharisees, our primary sources represent him as doing just that (for example Mark 7.8ff.). In defending the disciples at Mark 2.23–8, however, he does neither of these things: rather he produces two coherent arguments to demonstrate that hungry people should not be prevented from plucking corn on the sabbath. Thus, all our evidence is consistent. There was no generally accepted regulation prohibiting the plucking of corn on the sabbath. The Pharisaic life-stance was, however, such that they felt that the sabbath rest was being violated when they saw the poor plucking ears of corn. They complained to Jesus, who sought to establish that it was in fact in accordance with God's will that hungry people got something to eat on the sabbath.

What is the Sitz im Leben of such a dispute? Already we have enough to place it in the life of the historical Jesus, for this is exactly the kind of halakhic dispute that the Pharisees would land on a Jewish teacher; indeed it is the sort of dispute that they conducted among themselves. Equally, it is not a matter of such interest to the early church that they would produce it. Acts, the Epistles and Revelation all show that the fundamental issues were whether Gentiles had to become Jews in order to become Christians, and how Gentile Christians and Jewish Christians could relate to each other. Consequently, the major flashpoints were circumcision, a decisive step often perceived to be that of a Gentile becoming a Jew, and eating, which might involve eating alien food and other unwelcome customs. When the sabbath does feature in these disputes (Col. 2.16), it is something which has passed away in Christ, a quite different type of dispute from one over detailed halakhah. In these circumstances, a story about Jesus' disciples plucking grain on the sabbath is not relevant enough to have been produced.

Beare argues that

> the saying [sc. 2.27] originated not with Jesus, but with the apostolic church of Palestine, in controversy with the Pharisees, who took exception to the failure of Christian Jews to keep the sabbath. The Christian reply to the accusation . . . has then come to be regarded as a saying of Jesus himself, and the little story of the disciples in the grainfields has been created as a frame for the saying.[9]

We shall see that Beare's argument begins from misinterpretation of 2.27. The supposed dispute, in which Pharisees took exception to the failure of Christian Jews to keep the sabbath, is a conjecture based on this passage, and thus a classic example of the form-critical circle. It is a ludicrous conjecture, because all Christian Jews known to us from the early church in Israel kept the Law, as Jesus did, and only after prolonged controversy did most of them agree

---

[9] Beare, 'Sabbath', 135.

that Gentile Christians need not do the same. The selection of plucking grain, rather than an obvious and universally accepted form of working on the sabbath, such as carrying burdens or going on a journey, is in these circumstances inexplicable. Then the Pharisees object only to the minor offence, and do not in fact bring the general accusation of not keeping the sabbath, as they surely would have done in the fictional setting proposed by Beare. We may contrast John 5.9–18; 9.16. Here, where history has been rewritten, clear breaches of the sabbath are indicated and Jesus is said to have abrogated it, just what is necessary to meet the situation invented by Beare. We must conclude that Beare has written fiction rather than history.

The Pharisees' question is immediately followed by Jesus' first argument in defence of his poor disciples. 'Have you never read what David did . . .?' οὐδέποτε has no very literal equivalent in Aramaic (or in Hebrew, with the result that the LXX has only two examples with a known Semitic underlay). It is therefore to be regarded as a strong translation of the simple negative לֹא, as at Exod. 10.6 LXX. We should omit πῶς from Mark with B D 2427 r¹ t. Most manuscripts assimilate to Matthew, and Luke (ὡς) also felt the need to add something, whereas the Aramaic source is better without anything, and was literally translated. 'He went into the house of God ἐπὶ Ἀβιαθὰρ ἀρχιερέως.' This is one of the great mistakes of the Markan narrative, one of the bits that gave both Matthew and Luke such a fit that they left it out altogether. The origin of the mistake may be discovered by reconstructing Mark's Aramaic source: ביומי אביתר כהן רב. Abiathar was much more important than Ahimelech, and his presence may reasonably be deduced from the narrative in 1 Samuel. כהן רב is an accurate description of what Abiathar was famous as, and does not necessarily carry the implication, clear in Mark's Greek, that he was רב כהן at the time of the incident. Furthermore, כהן רב may have meant only that he was one of the most important priestly authorities, the ἀρχιερεῖς of the later Markan narrative. Abiathar was in either case outstanding, and correct observance of the Law in his days could safely be assumed. This was significant because he was conspicuously not Zadok, the founding father of the Sadducees, and the Pharisees were bound to accept Jesus' description of him. The translator's rendering with ἐπί plus genitive is sound, and paralleled by the rendering of מימין with ἐπὶ τοῦ at Job 38.12 LXX. He failed to notice that the rendering ἀρχιερέως without an article produces an expression which may naturally be read as a mistake. This is a normal mistake in a bilingual.

According to Jesus, David gave the bread to his companions. The MT helped most rabbis and some exegetes to believe otherwise, but it is intelligible only as a somewhat corrupt and truncated text, which may be translated: 'I have no ordinary bread to hand – there is only holy bread. If the young men have kept themselves from women' (1 Sam. 21.5). The missing words are found in 4Q52, which reads מאשה ואכלתם ממנו (fragments 3 and 4, line 3): 'from women, you (pl.) may eat of it'. This is partly supported by the LXX, which seems to have originally read καὶ φάγεται, a literal translation of ואכל, the first four letters of ואכלתם in 4Q52.[10] Following 4Q52, we may therefore read the second part of Ahimelech's reply אם נשמרו הנערים אך מאשה ואכלתם ממנו: 'If the young men have kept themselves from women, you (pl.) may eat of it.' It follows from this that the young men were to eat of it: Jesus will have known a text of Samuel similar to that preserved in 4Q52.

The major difficulty in verses 25–6 has been the logic of the argument. In the original narrative, Ahimelech hesitated over whether to allow David and his companions to eat the bread, and allowed them to do so on being assured that they had not been made unclean by sexual intercourse during the previous days. Jesus, however, says quite bluntly that only the priests are allowed to eat the shewbread. The only possible sources for this restriction are Jesus' perception of the current halakhah in the Temple at Jerusalem, and its scriptural basis. The halakhah dealing with the shewbread had a firm and ancient basis in scripture, and it is natural that the very same passage prescribes the changing of the shewbread on the sabbath and restricts its eating to the priests: 'Every sabbath day he shall arrange it before the LORD continually on behalf of the children of Israel as an eternal covenant. And it shall be for Aaron and for his sons and they shall eat it in a holy place' (Lev. 24.8–9). Both points are found together in Josephus' very clear account of the halakhah in the Temple at Jerusalem:

---

[10] It is difficult to evaluate the evidential status of the reading καὶ φάγονται, and of the more accurate καὶ φάγετε (Eus. ad Ps. 33, syro-Hexapla apud Barhebraeus ad loc.), perhaps a correction to the LXX on the basis of a correct reading in a Hebrew text. For the text of 4Q52, and discussion, see F. M. Cross, 'The Oldest Manuscripts from Qumran', *JBL* 74, 1955, 147–72, esp. 167–8. On the textual tradition of 4Q52, see E. C. Ulrich, *The Qumran Text of Samuel and Josephus* (HSM 192. Missoula, 1978).

They are baked two by two separately on the sabbath eve. Early on the sabbath morning (τῷ δὲ σαββάτῳ πρωΐ), they are brought in and placed on the holy table, facing each other, in two rows of six each. Two golden bowls full of incense are placed over them, and they remain there until the following sabbath. Then others are brought in in place of them, while the original ones are given to the priests as food (οἱ δὲ τοῖς ἱερεῦσι πρὸς τροφὴν δίδονται). (*AJ* III.255–6)

The changing of the shewbread on the sabbath is also indicated at 1 Chr. 9.32, and it is confirmed by later evidence (cf., for example, m. Suk 5.7–8; m. Men 11.7; b. Pes 47a). We may not suppose that Jesus knew only part of the scripturally based halakhah concerning the shewbread: if he knew that only the priests ate it, he knew also that it was changed on the sabbath. Furthermore, one of the general facts we know about Jesus and the Pharisees is that they shared a profound knowledge of the Torah. Consequently, Jesus not only knew the Temple halakhah based on Leviticus 24, but he could assume that the Pharisees knew it too. When this knowledge is applied to the story in 1 Samuel 21, it follows that the story must be dated on the sabbath, because this is the day on which Ahimelech would have had only the shewbread available for feeding David and his companions. Thus the dating of the incident to which Jesus refers on the sabbath was a cultural assumption which he could take for granted as known to the Pharisees.

Why, then, does our source not mention the sabbath at this point? The explanation of this is partly literary and partly cultural. From the literary point of view, the sabbath is already mentioned five times in six verses, and the nature of the dispute as a sabbath dispute has been carefully delineated by the description of the disciples' action as taking place בשבתא, the second word of our source, and by the Pharisees' question, 'Why are they doing on the sabbath something which is not allowed?' Thus, from the literary point of view, Jesus and the Pharisees will have assumed, for the reasons already given, that the incident took place on the sabbath, and these two reasons reinforce each other. A few passages of rabbinical literature make similar use of incidents from the lives of the patriarchs. 'Let our masters teach us. Shall a man who is being pursued by Gentiles and robbers profane (יחלל) the sabbath? Our masters taught that a man who is being pursued by Gentiles or robbers profanes the sabbath and saves his life. And thus we find concerning David: whcn Saul sought to kill him, he fled from him and escaped' (Tan. Mas. 1//NumR XXIII.1). This passage clearly sets up a problem of sabbath observance, as Mark's source does for anyone who shares its cultural assumptions. This is solved by reference to the example of David, as in the first of Jesus' arguments at Mark 2.25–6. There is, however, no precise reference to the biblical narrative because it is assumed that everyone knew the story and knew that part of David's flight took place on the sabbath (cf. 1 Sam. 21.11): furthermore, from a literary point of view, the nature of the point at issue has been stated with such clarity that there is no need to mention the sabbath a third time with reference to David's flight. It does not matter that this narrative was written down much later than the time of Mark's Aramaic source, because in all significant respects it comes from the same cultural context.

More explicit rabbinical discussions of this incident are also illuminating, because they clarify Jesus' reasons for choosing it as the basis of one of his arguments against the Pharisees. He chose it because it shows that David did not abide by Pharisaic Law, and scripture does not criticise him for this: rabbinical exegesis shows a variety of ways of avoiding this unwanted conclusion. We may begin with Yalqut Shim'oni II.130.

> 'I have no ordinary bread here. There is only the sacred bread. If the young men have kept themselves from women' (1 Sam. 21.5). He said to him, 'Do you not know that a man who touches a woman is not allowed to eat holy things?' David said to him, 'For three days we have had nothing to do with women', as it is written, 'We have been restrained from women for the last three days and the things of the young men are holy' (1 Sam. 21.6). Now it was the sabbath, and David saw that they were baking the Bread of the Presence on the sabbath, as Doeg had taught them. He said to them, 'What are you doing? Baking it does not override (דוחה) the sabbath, but only arranging it, as it is written "on the sabbath day he shall arrange it" (Lev. 24.8).' Since he found there only the Bread of the Presence, David said to him, 'Give it to me so that we may not die of hunger, for danger to life overrides the sabbath' (ספק נפשות דוחה שבת, m. Yom 8.6). How much did

David eat on that occasion? R. Huna said, 'David ate nearly seven Seahs, because he had bulimia (בולמוס).'

Firstly, the incident of 1 Sam. 21.2f. is explicitly placed on the sabbath. This sets up the following halakhic decisions, beginning with the decision, here attributed to David, that the baking of the bread does not override the sabbath. We have already seen from Josephus that the bread was in fact baked on Friday, and the halakhic point is debated at some length at b. Men 95b. Secondly, the possibility that David broke the Law is circumvented by supposing that his life was in danger from hunger. This is not suggested by the biblical story, but it can easily be read into it from the perspective of a rabbinical life-stance. Thirdly, the halakhic decision that the bread may be eaten, another decision here attributed to David himself, explicitly takes the form of justifying David's action on the sabbath: 'Give it to me so that we may not die of hunger, for danger to life overrides the sabbath.' This is especially important in understanding Mark's narrative, because it is often alleged that the law breached by David in eating the Bread of the Presence was not a sabbath law, and this has been treated as an incoherence in the Markan narrative.[11] The Yalqut does not function in accordance with that kind of analysis: the point is to find a general principle to justify David's action, and since the narrative is placed on the sabbath, sabbath Law is perfectly satisfactory. Just as Jesus was able to create a difficulty for the Pharisaic position by arguing that David had (on the sabbath) breached what was not obviously a sabbath law, so the Yalqut was able to justify his action (in breaching what was not obviously a sabbath law) by means of an overtly sabbath regulation. We must deduce from Mark's narrative that Jesus' argument belongs to the same cultural environment as the Yalqut, a cultural environment which in significant respects remained unchanged for more than a millennium. In that environment, a strict classification of laws into sabbath and non-sabbath laws was not followed in interpreting David's action, for such a division of application would be contrary

---

[11] Cf, e.g., Beare, 'Sabbath', 133–4; J. D. G. Dunn, 'Mark 2.1–3.6: A Bridge between Jesus and Paul on the Question of the Law', *NTS* 30, 1984, 395–415, at 407; rev. edn *Jesus, Paul and the Law* (London, 1990), pp. 10–36, at pp. 22–3; and as an incoherence in Jesus' argument, D. Daube, *The New Testament and Rabbinic Judaism* (London, 1956), pp. 67–71; D. M. Cohn-Sherbok, 'An Analysis of Jesus' Arguments Concerning the Plucking of Grain on the Sabbath', *JSNT* 2, 1979, 31–41, at 36.

to the nature of Jewish halakhah. We should not find Jesus' argument incoherent, and the Markan narrative a mosaic of separate pieces, on the ground that the argument does not follow an analytical mode foreign to the environment in which the argument was produced.

Fourthly, R. Huna's opinion was clearly understood by the compiler of the Yalqut to explain why David ate the shewbread on the sabbath, not merely the fact that he ate it. The saying is a revised version of the one attributed to R. Huna at y. Yom VIII.5, and the placing of the incident on the sabbath was probably the original interpretation and that of the compiler of y. Yom VIII.5. The festival context of m. Yom 8.5 does not appear to be relevant, so the collection of the saying at this point will be due rather to the mishnaic opinion that anyone suffering from bulimia is to be fed on the sabbath even with unclean things until his eyes brighten (m. Yom 8.6). It is, moreover, this conventional sabbath halakhah which is most likely to have given rise to the saying. Once David's action is seen to be caused by desperate hunger, there is no need to move the incident from the sabbath, where, as we have seen, the assumptions of rabbinical culture would naturally place it. It is thus probable that David's action was explained away by his desperate hunger on the sabbath already in the third or fourth century.

The other major rabbinical discussion of this incident is at b. Men 95b. The discussion largely concerns the question whether the shewbread should be baked on the sabbath or on a weekday, and much of it is carried through in terms of detailed exegesis of the late and corrupt MT of 1 Sam. 21.6–7. R. Simeon's opinion that David found the priests baking the shewbread on the sabbath implies that he arrived on the sabbath. The Gemara then justifies his eating the shewbread with an ingenious argument from the law of sacrilege. R. Judah's opinion, apparently presupposing that David arrived on Friday afternoon, gives a different reason why he should not have eaten the (freshly baked) shewbread, namely that it was sanctified in the oven, and this difficulty is then resolved by supposing that he was critically ill, for saving life overrides most laws. This solution is similar to that of the Yalqut, where the same basic principle overrode both this law and the sabbath Law. Two other late Jewish opinions should be noted. R. David Kimchi, commenting on 1 Sam. 21.7, records the opinion of his father that the loaves eaten by David were not the bread of the Presence but the loaves of Thanksgiving: Ps.-Jerome records a Jewish opinion that David did not in fact eat the bread.[12] From an exegetical point of view, both these opinions are extraordinarily farfetched, and their significance is that they show how far rabbinical exegetes could go to avoid infringing their central commitment to the Law. It is presumably for the same reason that Josephus omitted to mention the shewbread, saying only that David obtained provisions for his journey (*AJ* VI.243–4).

Thus all the later Jewish material illustrates Jesus' wisdom in selecting this incident for this argument. It creates severe difficulties for the Pharisaic view of the Law. We should infer that this was its function. The Pharisees came from the orthodox wing of Judaism, and the difficulties caused by strict and expanding halakhah for accepting the patriarchal narratives are evident long before the time of Jesus. Jubilees is reduced to repetitive raving by the fact that Reuben was not burnt alive for having sexual intercourse with Bilhah (Jub. 33.2–20), and its author was clearly very concerned that people might deduce (and perhaps had deduced) that it was sufficient to repent and be forgiven without the penalty written in the Law being exacted (Jub. 33.15). Similar trouble was caused by Judah's sexual intercourse with Tamar (Jub. 41.8–28) and the number of David's wives (CD V.3ff.). The excuses given for the patriarchs' behaviour, or for the fact that they were not punished in accordance with the letter of current Law, serve only to illustrate the hermeneutical problem caused by the application of strict halakhah to biblical narratives, and by the assumption that the behaviour of biblical heroes may be imitated. This problem for the Pharisaic life-stance is so organic to it that Jesus was bound to perceive it, and he aimed his first argument straight at it: the argument will have required an answer. We may not predate the rabbinical answers. If the Pharisees had been arguing for years that David's life was in danger from ravenous hunger, Jesus' argument would have been pointless. In fact, b. Men 95b is our earliest rabbinical discussion, and we must deduce from this combination of facts that the orthodox life-stance had not yet produced a well-known answer to the problem which Jesus raised for it. Whether the Pharisees produced any answer we are not told, for the very different reason that it was not in accordance with the interests of our primary sources to record what the Pharisees may have said.

---

[12] For Ps.-Jerome, see A. Saltman, *Pseudo-Jerome, Quaestiones on the Book of Samuel* (SPB XXVI. Leiden, 1979), p. 96.

Jesus' second argument was designed to play a more positive role:

שבתא בדיל אנשא אתעבדת ולא אנשא בדיל שבתא .
שליט נא הוא בר נש אף בשבתא.[28]

The general background is that of conventional Jewish thought about the creation, especially the normal view that man was intended to dominate the created world. The classic texts are Gen. 1.26, 28 and Ps. 8.6–9, and two pseudepigraphical expressions of this belief are especially relevant. The orthodox author of 4 Ezra concludes his rather lengthy account of creation, 'And over these [sc. created beings] Adam, whom you appointed as ruler (ducem, מדברנא) over all the works which you had created' (2 Esd. 6.54). The author of the related 2 Baruch similarly looked back from the shattered present to the divine intention at creation: 'And you said that you would make for your world (a/the son of) man (ברנשא) as the manager (מפרנסנא) of your works, to make it clear that he was not made for the world, but the world was made for him' (2 Baruch 14.18). The late date of these passages is of no concern because they express a genuinely biblical theology of creation. In this way, observant Jews could declare man's lordship over creation, and since they believed that this was wholly consistent with the election of Israel and the importance of doing the Law, they could also say, even in the same documents, that the world was created for the righteous or for Israel (cf. 2 Esd. 6.55, 59; 7.11; 2 Baruch 15.7; 21.24; Ass. Mos. 1.12).

The second factor in normal Jewish thought is the idea of the sabbath as a great gift of God. This is biblical, 'for YHWH has given you the sabbath' (Exod. 16.29), and of the massive later evidence it is sufficient to quote Jubilees: 'And he gave us a great sign, the sabbath day, that we should work six days, but keep sabbath on the seventh day from all work' (Jub. 2.17). This is the sense in which the sabbath was made for man. That it was given at the time of the creation is not only straightforward OT belief, but continued to be felt so strongly that the rabbis could call the weekly sabbath 'the sabbath of creation' to distinguish it from the sabbath year (for example MekhY Kaspa III; Exod. 23.12). As in the case of creation as a whole, the sabbath could be said to be for Israel rather than for mankind, the more so as it was usually viewed as a distinctively Jewish institution. This should not, however, be over-interpreted, as it was in a classic and influential manner by T. W.

Manson, who surveyed some of the more ethnically orientated expressions of Jewish celebration of the gift of the sabbath to Israel and, by way of arguing that Son of man must have been a title in the original version of Mark 2.27, roundly declared: 'As a matter of historical fact the Sabbath was not made for man in general. At the time when the saying was uttered the sabbath was a distinctive peculiarity of the Jews: and our evidence goes to show that they regarded it as such and resented any non-Jewish observance of it.'[13]

This comment manifests a false and apparently widespread assumption about the nature of the relationship between language and culture. From the fact that the sabbath was an identity factor of Judaism, being treated as such by both Jews and Gentiles, it does not follow that words such as 'man' cannot be used in otherwise conventional Jewish statements about it. There are two kinds of sentence in our primary sources which demonstrate this particular case empirically. The first is well illustrated by Philo, *Dec.* 99. Here Philo declares that God once for all made a final use of six days for the completion of the world and had no further need of periods of time. Contrast ἀνθρώπων δ᾽ἕκαστος: 'each man, since he shares in mortal nature and needs masses of things for the necessities of life, must not slacken in providing for his needs to the end of his life, but should rest on the sacred seventh days'. Here the use of 'each man' with reference to the specifically Jewish sabbath arises naturally from the context of the creation of man. This is the truly biblical thought of Gen. 1.26, 28; Ps. 8.6–9, and the wholly Semitic pseudepigrapha 2 Esd. 6.54; 2 Baruch 14.18. The second kind of sentence is found in a large number of legal judgements in orthodox Jewish sources. 'Clothes vendors who go out on the sabbath with cloaks folded (and) lying on their shoulders are liable to a sin-offering. And they [sc. the sages] said this not of clothes vendors alone but of every man (כל אדם), but that it is in the nature of merchants to go out like that' (b. Shab 147a). The sages were not dealing with the behaviour of Gentiles! Rather, the cultural context of Talmudic Law makes it so obvious that observant Jews are referred to that the description can safely be used of them without confusion. A more extreme example is provided by m. Shab 6.6: 'Arabian women go out veiled and Median women with cloaks looped up over their shoulders. And so everyone (כל אדם), but the

---

[13] T. W. Manson, 'Mark II. 27f', *CNT* 11, 1947, 138–46, at 145, followed by Beare, 'Sabbath', 132.

sages spoke about normal customs.' Here the cultural assumptions of the document are so strong that observant Jewish women in Arabia and Media can be referred to as Arabian women and Median women, and observant Jewish women as a whole as כל אדם.

Neither the date nor the language of these examples is important, because in all significant respects they belong to the same cultural context as Jesus of Nazareth. Mark 2.27–8 makes perfect sense against the background of a standard Jewish theology of creation, and the use of words for 'man' is all the more natural in the context of a dispute which hinges partly on the importance of bodily needs which are common to all people. An additional reason for Jesus to use these words is that it enabled him to utilise the Aramaic idiom of Mark 2.28 and thus declare his authority to ward off unwanted sabbath halakhah only by associating himself with the mastery of man in the created world in general. At this point it is therefore significant that reference to the superiority of man over beast forms the basis of some of the arguments which Jesus used elsewhere to justify his interpretation of sabbath halakhah (Matt. 12.11–12// Luke 14.5; Luke 13.15–16).

The genuine statement of Mark 2.27–8 should not, however, be overinterpreted, and to see it in its cultural context we must consider one further aspect of Jewish culture. In setting forth halakhic decisions, other Jewish teachers sometimes expressed themselves in dramatic statements which can be misinterpreted in the same Gentile way as Mark 2.27, if they are removed from their original context. I have found three examples concerned with sabbath halakhah: two of them occur at Mekhilta Shabbat I, Exod. 31.12–17.

> Whence do we know that saving life overrides (ידחה) the sabbath? R. Aqiba says, If capital punishment overrides (דוחה) the Temple service which overrides the sabbath, how much more saving life overrides the sabbath. R. Jose the Galilean says: When it says, 'Only my sabbaths you shall keep' (Exod. 31.13), 'only' makes a distinction. There are sabbaths on which you rest, and there are sabbaths on which you do not rest (יש שבתות שאתה שובה וייש שתבות שאין שובה). R. Simeon ben Menasya says: Look! It says, 'And you shall keep the sabbath, for it is holy to you' (Exod. 31.14). The sabbath is delivered

to you and you are not delivered to the sabbath (לכם
שבת מסורה ואין אתם מסורין לשבת).

The first relevant saying in this passage is the one attributed to Yose
the Galilean. Removed from its context of Jewish Law, this might
be interpreted in a straightforward literal way to mean that sabbath
observance is optional: one should observe some sabbaths, but
there is no need to observe every sabbath. In favour of interpreting
it 'in isolation', we may point out that it has a different author from
the saying before it (R. Aqiba) and the saying after it (R. Simeon
ben Menasya). This would, however, be quite wrong. The saying
must be interpreted in its cultural context, and the correct cultural
context is provided by its present literary setting. The only sabbaths
on which you do not rest are those on which you save life. The
security of this assumption is fundamental to the production of this
saying, for if the matter were in doubt, so dramatic an expression of
the certainty that life may be saved on the sabbath would not be
safe. The alternative version of the saying attributed to R. Yose in a
different literary context at t. Shab 15.16 further clarifies the fact
that correct interpretation of these apparently dramatic statements
entails careful attention to their literary context, because this may
supply the correct cultural context even when it is secondary.

The saying of R. Simeon son of Menasya is justly famous for its
similarity to Mark 2.27. The difference between 'you' and 'man' is
not as fundamental as the basically similar declaration that the
sabbath was for people. In each case, the exact wording is partly
controlled by the detailed context: R. Simeon's saying uses the
second person plural because this is used in Exod. 31.13–14,
whereas Jesus used 'man' because the dispute was about a human
need, the argument was derived from God's action in creating man
as well as the sabbath, and it enabled him to use a particular
idiomatic way of justifying his right to interpret the basic command
not to work on the sabbath. There is a basic similarity of function
too: in both cases the more lenient of two possible halakhic
decisions is being given. Jesus was declaring that his hungry
disciples could pluck grain on the sabbath, against the Pharisaic
view that they could not, a dynamically similar situation to
R. Simeon's declaration that saving life overrides the sabbath,
against a possible view that it did not (cf. 1 Macc. 2.31–8; Jub.
50.12). R. Simeon's saying must be interpreted strictly in its cultural
context. It is from, and only from, its cultural and literary context

that we know that general undermining of sabbath halakhah may not be derived from it. It is collected a second time in Mekhilta Shabbat I, Exod. 31.12–17. At b. Yoma 85b, another version of it is attributed to R. Jonathan son of Joseph (R. Simeon son of Menasya then has the following saying). This tells us little beyond the fallibility of rabbinical attribution and the independent collection of generally homogeneous material. It does not enable us to deduce that the saying was a proverb, still less that it was as old as the time of Jesus. It does, however, show that the saying was sufficiently functional in the context of Jewish halakhah to be included in more than one collection of sabbath sayings.

The third sabbath saying of this kind is the most stunning of all:

עשׂה שׁבתך חול ולא תצרך לבריות

Make your sabbath profane, and do not depend on people.

Is this not a radical prophet, authoritatively declaring freedom from sabbath casuistry in favour of respect for other people? In fact it is R. Aqiba, and at b. Shab 118a, the source which has the longest literary context for the saying, he is laying down the halakhic decision, in his own name, that a man who is already dependent on a gift from the community's charitable resources should not ask for more than his basic standard requirements, i.e. probably not more than fourteen meals a week, including two rather than three on the sabbath.

The precise force of the saying is difficult to recover because it is somewhat 'isolated' even in this context. It has all the appearance of being added to the existing discussion by the compiler, or perhaps by an earlier rabbi. Its transmission as an isolated saying is made quite obvious by b. Pes 112a, where it is collected no fewer than three times. The first occurrence is placed in a generally similar context, in that it deals with a person who is so poor that he has to be given the four cups of wine for celebrating Passover (m. Pes 10.1). At its third occurrence, it is one of a collection of otherwise 'isolated' sayings of R. Aqiba, and both the first two occurrences virtually treat it as an isolated saying. Even so, the isolation of this saying from its cultural context would be ruinous, and the longest literary context, secondary though it be, none the less provides the correct cultural context. In that context, the only sense in which the sabbath is to be profane is that you are not to eat more than two meals on it, and the only sense in which you are not to depend on people is that you are to depend on them for two rather than three meals on the sabbath, and, if the whole literary context is the correct cultural context, for fourteen meals a week rather than for more than that. If the saying is removed from this kind of context, and basic principles are then drawn from over-literal interpretation of it, the results are simply remote from the culture under study.

With all aspects of the cultural background in mind, we may proceed to the technical problems involved in reconstructing the Aramaic source behind Mark 2.27–8. The first saying is not very difficult. The only serious point to make is that אישָׁא must be the word behind ἄνθρωπος in 2.27. This straightforward reconstruction makes perfect sense of the original source and of the translator. Some scholars[14] have suggested בר (א)נשׁ(א) in 2.27, but this makes the behaviour of the translator difficult to understand.

At 2.28, the term ὁ υἱὸς τοῦ ἀνθρώπου does dictate בר (א)נשׁ(א), used idiomatically in a general statement which refers particularly to the speaker and a larger group of people. It does not, however, tell us whether (א)נשׁ(א) was in the absolute or emphatic state, for two reasons. Firstly, examples of the idiom in Aramaic texts show no difference in meaning according to the use of the absolute or emphatic state. Secondly, the behaviour of the translator continues to follow the strategy uncovered in the previous chapter, of using ὁ υἱὸς τοῦ ἀνθρώπου whenever he thought that examples of this idiom referred to Jesus.

The next problem is κύριος. An obvious possibility is מרא, which was naturally used by the Syriac versions to translate κύριος, and by Meyer in his attempt at a reconstruction.[15] Wellhausen's שליט is, however, greatly to be preferred,[16] because it fits so well both with the general level of meaning and with the earlier part of the dispute. It is the same word as in the Pharisees' question, and it had already been used in Jesus' first argument. It is likely that it had already been used on an earlier occasion, where the words attributed to Jesus (Mark 2.10) may reasonably be reconstructed as follows:[17]

ותנדעּן די שליט בר אנשא למשבק חטאין על ארעא

[14] E.g. Meyer, *Muttersprache*, p. 93; p. 12 above; Manson, 'Mark 2.27ff'.
[15] Meyer, *Jesus Muttersprache*, p. 93; p. 12 above.
[16] Wellhausen, *Skizzen und Vorarbeiten* VI, p. 203.
[17] Casey, *Jesus Son of Man*, pp. 159–61; Lindars, *Son of Man*, pp. 44–7, 176–8.

Colpe argues against שׁליט behind Mark 2.28 on the ground that it is mostly absolute, and usually goes with ב. These arguments should not be accepted. Some examples are not absolute, the number of examples is too small for these proportions to be relevant, and we should put ב after it (Wellhausen put ד). Colpe prefers מר, רב or a derivative of בעל, but this leads him to so lofty a meaning that he attributes the saying to the community.[18] This highlights the methodological importance of arguing for שׁליט on the ground that it fits better with the general level of meaning implied by the use of בר (א)נשׁ(א) . Given the use of שׁליט earlier in the argument, it is natural that Jesus should have used it to ram home his final point. שׁליט takes ב to give the sense of 'mastery over', so we can write בשׁבתא for τοῦ σαββάτου. Jesus' last word is then exactly the same as the other central term in the Pharisees' question, and it is this which is highlighted at the beginning of our source's introduction to the narrative. אף is straightforward for καί. It does indeed follow from verse 27, which stated the purpose of the creation of the sabbath as for man's benefit, that man is master on the sabbath, as well as in respect of the shewbread and the forgiveness of sins, and therefore entitled to eat of the fruits of God's creation. בשׁבתא means 'on the sabbath' as well as 'over the sabbath', so that the sentence declares the authority of man, from which the authority of Jesus and the defence of the disciples are derived, in an indirect way. For ἐστίν we may reasonably write הוא, bearing in mind that its semantic area normally and conventionally includes a copulative usage approximately equivalent to the Greek εἰμί.

The connecting ὥστε has caused great problems to interpreters, for ὥστε plus indicative does not have a natural Semitic equivalent, and consequently we find no more than three examples in the LXX. At Esther 7.8, it is an extraordinary elliptical rendering of הגם: 2 Kgs. 21.12 and Job 21.27 are more relevant, because in both cases the translators have rendered freely in accordance with the sense (one might say they were rendering אשׁר and הן respectively). We must deduce that our translator has done the same. Man's mastery declared in 2.28 is in a profound but not remote theological sense dependent on the will of God shown in creation and declared at 2.27, so the translation with ὥστε plus indicative correctly gives the sense. It follows that we do not really know what the underlying

[18] C. Colpe, 'ὁ υἱὸς τοῦ ἀνθρώπου', *TWNT* VIII (1969), p. 455.

Aramaic word was, even though we can reconstruct the sense. In the suggested reconstruction of Mark's source, I have put גֹא, though I cannot assume more than 51 per cent probability for my best guess. Another possibility is ארו: we might expect the translator to render it with ἰδού, but the very fact that he has produced ὥστε plus indicative shows he has rendered freely, and we have seen that Job 21.27 would give us a good parallel. Again, the simple ו is possible, and כלקבל דנה would be another sound suggestion. It follows that we may not rely on some of the details of the proposed reconstruction to expound the precise force of Jesus' statement.

We can now consider finally the nature of the idiom in the Aramaic sentence underlying Mark 2.28. This sentence runs smoothly as an example of an idiom whereby a speaker used a general statement to refer to himself, or himself and a group of associates. Moreover, in this instance the general level of meaning follows necessarily from the general statement of 2.27. Consequently, these two verses form an excellent example of the absolute chaos that would be involved in any attempt to use בר (א)נש(א) as a title while it was still a normal term for 'man'. Jesus thus claimed for himself only what is at least potentially the case for other people too, a significant point because it makes any claim of authority on his part an indirect claim which lays stress on the authority given by God to men rather than on his own person. The reference to the speaker, however, combined with the vigour of his comments, means that at the same time Jesus took responsibility for his disciples' actions, as the Pharisees assumed that he would by directing the question to him in the first place. At this level, his final sentence says that he, as a (son of) man, is master on/over the sabbath. The ambiguity of ב in בשבתא further ensures the indirectness of the expression, but there is no doubt about its thrust. Jesus claims the authority to ward off the Pharisaic criticism and allow his poor and hungry disciples to pluck grain on the sabbath. After he has created a major problem for the Pharisaic view at 2.25–6, the ground which he gives for this authority is the theological statement of 2.27, in accordance with which any man who is obedient to God has the mastery over the sabbath which God made for him at the creation. If שליט is right, the mode of expression also throws the criticism of the Pharisees back in their faces: if perchance Jesus really said מרא, the overall thrust of his argument is not seriously different. The general nature of the statement also implies that Jesus' disciples in some sense have mastery on/over the sabbath, and the sense in which this is true may be deduced from the context. Firstly, in a theological sense, they have the mastery given to them by God at creation because they are obedient to their heavenly Father. We may assume the disciples' devotion to Jesus' teaching and consequently to the Fatherhood and kingship of God, and thus the assumption running throughout Jesus' teaching that this is more important before God than obedience to Pharisaic halakhah, which is here warded off. Secondly, in a practical sense, they are entitled to feed themselves on the sabbath, taking advantage of the provisions deliberately laid down by God for the poor and hungry in the Law of Moses.

We must, however, be careful not to exaggerate, either by legitimating later Christology from Jesus' genuinely authoritative behaviour or by confusing his opponents with the whole of Judaism. Jesus came from the prophetic wing of Judaism, which did no more than the עם הארץ to exalt the sabbath above human needs. The son of man statement is not a weakening of 2.27 because this does not declare freedom over against sabbath Law, much less against the Law in general. On the contrary, man's mastery over the sabbath presupposes his total obedience to the will of God revealed in the Law of Moses. The view that 2.27 is more radical than this results from removing it from its context and interpreting it against a background of Gentile Christianity, which does not obey the Law and which needs a higher Christology than that of Jesus or the apostles to enable it to hold together. Like the rabbinical decisions attributed to Jose the Galilean, Aqiba and Simeon ben Menasya, Mark 2.27–8 must be seen in its cultural context, and this is provided by the reconstruction of its literary context in the original language. This enables us to see that Jesus was concerned not with his authority or with attacking Jewish Law, but with the defence of his poor and hungry disciples.

We have seen that this whole narrative has an excellent Sitz im Leben in the life of Jesus. The early church cannot have created it. The sabbath was not a major flashpoint in early church disputes, and when it was controversial, the controversy was over whether it should be observed at all, together with the other identity factors of Judaism (cf. Gal. 4.10; John 5.9ff., 9–10). Such controversies resulted from the admission of Gentiles to the churches: they did not occur between Christian Jews and Pharisees in Israel because the earliest church in Israel observed the Law. Once we have interpreted Mark 2.27 correctly as part of a dispute about whether you should pluck grain on the sabbath (not about the abrogation of the sabbath), we can see that it cannot have originated to deal with early church controversies. Our sources do not confirm any dispute between the earliest Christian Jews and other Jews over details of the Law. An actual controversy between them over plucking grain on the sabbath would have missed every significant point, not least because Christian Jews and non-Christian Jews alike varied in the extent to which they kept the details of the Law. If Mark 2.27 alone were authentic, a controversy about plucking grain would not have been created to illustrate it because in this context too it would have missed the point. The complete form-critical circle, in accordance with which the passage itself is treated as evidence for an implausible early church dispute which it is thus held to have been created for, has never been accompanied by an adequate account of the supposed creative process. These considerations are wholly in harmony with the other points made in this chapter. An incident which makes proper sense only when the narrative is reconstructed in Aramaic and interpreted against the background of Jewish culture is also incomprehensible as the product of the early church. The narrative is abbreviated, but on all these grounds we should conclude that it is authentic.

Finally, Mark's source must have been written by a Jew from Israel. It is intelligible only if we make assumptions which would have been normal in his environment. The first is that if people are described as going along a path through the fields and plucking grain, they were poor people taking Peah, who were necessarily hungry and in need. The second assumption is the scripturally based Temple halakhah which made it obvious that 1 Sam. 21.2–7 related an incident which took place on the sabbath. The third assumption is that when the sabbath is mentioned five times in six verses, it does not have to be mentioned again at verses 25–6, given the assumption that the David incident took place on the sabbath. The fourth assumption is that there is a sense in which man is master of the sabbath, provided that he is obedient to God. The fifth assumption is the acceptance of Jewish Law as the divine revelation to Israel. This is the environment within which the dramatic statement of 2.27 could be made without any thought of its being misunderstood as a weakening of sabbath Law, let alone the Law in general. The reconstruction of the Aramaic source is essential to the understanding of 2.28, which does not contain a

Christological title, and does not openly declare the status of Jesus. It does, however, assume his authority to defend his disciples by means of his interpretation of the Law, an authority derived from the theological position of man as beneficiary of the sabbath (2.27), and shared with the disciples who were by the same token allowed to pluck the grain. A further assumption is that the permission to do this was also part of divine Law.

If, and only if, this complex of assumptions be made, the argument of the whole passage becomes intelligible. The Pharisees were shocked at the disciples' behaviour and questioned it. Jesus' first recorded argument was sufficient to create a major difficulty for their view, since it showed the patriarch David violating their legal restrictions by eating the shewbread on the sabbath, and the scriptural account clearly assumes that he was right to do so. Jesus' second argument then wards off the Pharisaic criticism with a basic declaration of the purpose of the sabbath. The only feasible Sitz im Leben for this dispute is in the life of Jesus, a situation in which the issue whether poor and hungry disciples might pluck corn on the sabbath could be perceived as sufficiently important to cause a memorable dispute. The only perceptible influences of the early church are those of abbreviation and translation, and these are not serious enough to prevent us from recovering the original situation and two of Jesus' arguments, provided that we attack the problem in the right way. To do this, we have to reconstruct the whole pericope in its original language, and reconstruct the cultural assumptions made by Jesus, the disciples, the Pharisees, and the tradents and compiler of this passage.

This passage has been held by many scholars to be a serious obstacle to the standard view that Mark was the first Gospel to be written, and that it was subsequently edited independently by both Matthew and Luke. These scholars have been impressed by the supposedly large number of minor agreements between Matthew and Luke against Mark.[19] I propose to re-examine most of them, in the light of my reconstruction of Mark's Aramaic source. Both Matthew and Luke were vigorous editors. Where the text of Mark shows features of translation from Aramaic and of Jewish assump-

---

[19] E.g. E. P. Sanders, 'Priorités et dépendances dans la tradition synoptique', *RSR* 60, 1972, 519–40, at 530–5; H. Aichinger, 'Quellenkritische Untersuchung der Perikope vom Ährenraufen am Sabbat Mk 2, 23–28 par', in A. Fuchs (ed.), *Jesus in der Verkündigung der Kirche* (SNTU 1. Linz, 1976), pp. 110–53; M. D. Goulder, *Luke: A New Paradigm* (2 vols., JSNT. SS 20. Sheffield, 1989), vol. 1, pp. 336–9.

tions which were no longer clear, and where it simply appears different to monoglot Greeks from its original appearance to a bilingual translator, Matthew and Luke alter, omit and explain. Both were committed Christians, who wrote decent Greek. Consequently, they agreed in their alterations to some passages more often than would be predicted on the basis of pure chance. This is such a passage because it was difficult to translate from Aramaic-speaking Judaism into Greek-speaking Christianity, and the translator's efforts to do so left an unusual number of items which monoglot Greek-speaking Christians would want to alter. It is accordingly of equal importance that they both made a number of alterations which are unique to each of them.

In editing Mark 2.23, Matthew and Luke both omit ὁδὸν ποιεῖν. We have seen that, from a monoglot perspective, this is incorrect Greek. Matthew and Luke must therefore do something. Does this phrase give the ground of the supposed offence? No, this was that the disciples were plucking, so the phrase is not central. Why is it there? It is a literal translation of למעבד אורח, a slight misreading of למעבר אורח. In Mark's source, this gave the important information that the disciples were taking Peah, so it was originally central. Its significance has been lost, not only in the literal translation, but in the cultural shift from Judaism in Israel to Christianity elsewhere. For both Matthew and Luke, the disciples are justified by the mighty figure of Jesus. Both of them express this by making Jesus personally Lord over the sabbath. From his more Jewish perspective, Matthew has a new halakhic argument from the Temple service, and a new application of Hos. 6.6 (Matt. 12.5–6). Neither Matthew nor Luke, therefore, requires a revised version of ὁδὸν ποιεῖν. Its content is irrelevant to their needs, and abbreviating Mark's account as both of them do as they go along, both have omitted it. It follows that, so far from being an argument against the priority of Mark, this common omission can only be fully understood on the basis of the priority of Mark and the cultural resonances of his Aramaic source.

Matthew and Luke both say that the disciples ate the grains of corn. We have seen that they use different parts of the verb (Matthew ἐσθίειν, Luke ἤσθιον) in a different position, so this is not very strong evidence of a common source. It is also part of the same cultural shift as the omission of ὁδὸν ποιεῖν. With universal knowledge of the customs involved in taking Peah no longer available to their audiences, both Matthew and Luke are in danger of relating the disciples doing something incomprehensible. Worse, their audicnccs might imagine that the disciples were plucking corn to carry it home and make bread, and might find it obvious that they were working on the sabbath. This is why both Matthew and Luke have explained that they ate the corn there and then, and Luke has felt it necessary to explain how they could. This is not an agreement due to a common source or the knowledge of one by the other. It is one common element in independent editing necessitated by the cultural shift from Judaism in Israel to Christianity elsewhere.

In editing Mark 2.24, Matthew and Luke both alter ἔλεγον to εἶπαν. Which tense to use is a matter of style. When we view Matthew and Luke's Gospels as a whole, we find that they use the imperfect of λέγω in these circumstances much less than Mark does. Accordingly, they often alter Mark's imperfects to aorists. For example, they agree to alter ἔλεγεν to εἶπεν at Mark 3.23// Matt. 12.25//Luke 11.17, whereas at Mark 3.22, Matthew alters ἔλεγον to εἶπον (Matt. 12.22) and Luke to εἶπαν (Luke 11.15). These kinds of agreement are due to the simplicity of an alteration to a stylistic feature which Matthew and Luke are known to share abundantly. Sometimes, they make different alterations. For example, at Mark 4.2 Luke again has εἶπεν for Mark's ἔλεγεν (Luke 8.4), whereas Matthew has put an aorist ἐλάλησεν in place of Mark's imperfect ἐδίδασκεν, and has replaced the imperfect ἔλεγεν with the participle λέγων. Even the decision to replace the imperfect is a strong tendency, not an inflexible rule. For example, at Mark 2.16, Matthew retains Mark's ἔλεγον (Matt. 9.11), whereas Luke has a main verb ἐγόγγυζον rather than Mark's participle ἰδόντες, and in place of ἔλεγον he has the participle λέγοντες (Luke 5.30). At Mark 4.30, on the other hand, Luke retains Mark's ἔλεγεν while Matthew adds the introduction Ἄλλην παραβολὴν παρέθηκεν αὐτοῖς, and for Mark's ἔλεγεν he has the participle λέγων. In these circumstances, the common alteration of ἔλεγον to εἶπαν may not be regarded as evidence of a common source, or of knowledge of Matthew by Luke. It is rather evidence of two vigorous editors who share some stylistic features, and who consequently make the same alteration to a given word some of the time.

The same applies even more strongly to the common alteration of λέγει to εἶπεν at Mark 2.25//Matt. 12.3//Luke 6.3. Mark's use of the historic present is by normal standards excessive, and the majority of his examples are provided by λέγει and λέγουσι. It is natural that Matthew and Luke often alter these present tenses to aorists. Sometimes they do so independently. For example, at Mark 1.38 Luke replaces Mark's λέγει with εἶπεν (Luke 4.43), while Matthew omits the narrative. At Mark 8.17, on the other hand, Matthew replaces Mark's λέγει with εἶπεν (Matt. 16.8), while Luke omits this whole section of Mark. Since Matthew and Luke make this same alteration often, they sometimes do so at the same point. This is evidence of deliberate editorial alteration, not of a common source.

There is a negative agreement in the same verse: Matthew and Luke both drop Mark's χρείαν ἔσχεν καὶ. Matthew also drops αὐτός, while Luke alters ὅτε to ὁπότε. The longer expression has some point in the original source, where צרך לה means that David needed something, and כפן הוא וחברוהי explains why. Readers of Mark, however, have often considered his expression redundant, and we should infer that Matthew and Luke did so. They both chose the precise ἐπείνασεν αὐτὸς καὶ οἱ μετ᾽ αὐτοῦ because this makes it quite clear that David's men ate the bread because they were hungry, and this provides a reasonable analogy to the behaviour of Jesus' disciples.

In editing Mark 2.26, both Matthew and Luke omit ἐπὶ Ἀβιαθὰρ ἀρχιερέως. We have seen what the problem is. The literal translation of Mark's Aramaic source results in a false impression, that Abiathar was actually high priest at the time of the incident, which he was not. Matthew and Luke were therefore bound to make some kind of alteration. Taking their Gospels as a whole, they tend to shorten Markan material because they have much else to say. In this case, the text does not tell us why Abiathar should be mentioned. Correcting the date to the time of Ahimelech would accordingly be meaningless. Once again, Matthew and Luke agree because they are vigorous editors, not because they have a common source. This time, the transition out of Jesus' original culture and the translation process have combined to make a mistake and produce a meaningless expression which they both dropped.

There are two more small agreements in the same verse. Where Mark has τοῖς σὺν αὐτῷ, both Matthew and Luke have τοῖς μετ᾽ αὐτοῦ. This is due to the influence of the previous verse, where Matthew and Luke both followed Mark in writing οἱ μετ᾽ αὐτοῦ. This increase in consistency is always liable to appeal to editors who are revising their sources stylistically, and bears witness to these evangelists' knowledge of the previous verse, not to a separate source. Matthew and Luke also add some form of μόνος, but it should be noted that they do not have it in quite the same position, nor is it in the same case, for Matthew, unlike Luke, altered the construction of this part of the verse without changing its meaning. A large amount of evidence of this kind would be impressive, but that two vigorous editors should coincide in the addition of an unnecessary word is not enough to show that they are not independent.

A negative agreement is the omission of Mark 2.27. Matthew left out the whole verse, and Luke retained only the introductory καὶ ἔλεγεν αὐτοῖς. A related agreement is the common omission of Mark's ὥστε at the beginning of Mark 2.28. These agreements are due to a combination of two factors: a change in meaning of the passage because of its translation from Aramaic into Greek, and a change of culture from Judaism to Christianity. The original source was a general statement from which the general level of meaning in the בר (א)נש(א) statement underlying verse 28 could be seen to follow. This general level of meaning was not, however, available to monoglot Greeks who read the existing text of Mark, in which ὁ υἱὸς τοῦ ἀνθρώπου is a Christological title. Moreover, the Christology of Matthew and Luke is higher than that of Mark, and both wrote in the light of a successful Gentile mission. They therefore took Mark 2.28 to mean that Jesus himself was Lord over the sabbath, and consequently it was his authority which enabled him to lay down the halakhah over against the Pharisees. Seen in this light, Mark 2.28 does not follow from 2.27. This explains the common decision of Matthew and Luke to drop both 2.27 and the conjunction ὥστε, for in their view these were both wrong.

Both Matthew and Luke also drop καί and alter the order of words to put ὁ υἱὸς τοῦ ἀνθρώπου in the dominant position at the end. The dropping of καί is a natural decision by independent editors because it has no proper reference. The reason for this is necessarily conjectural, but I have suggested with reasonable probability that Mark's source had שׁליט both here and at Mark 2.10. The original force of אף was accordingly to make reference back to an incident where Jesus had already declared that בר (א)נש(א) was שׁליט to release/undo/forgive a person's sins when he released his limbs for normal use. At Mark 2.28, he declared that בר (א)נש(א) was שׁליט in respect of the sabbath too. The loss of this reference makes Mark's καί unnecessary. Together with the removal of 2.27

and the higher Christology which Matthew and Luke both assume, the placing of ὁ υἱὸς τοῦ ἀνθρώπου at the end of the sentence further emphasises Jesus' authority.

We are now in a position to reassess the minor agreements between Matthew and Luke in this passage. They are caused by a combination of two related factors, translation from Aramaic into Greek and cultural shift from Judaism to Christianity. Vigorous editing by Matthew and Luke has been caused by the presence of linguistic features unsuitable for monoglot Greeks, and by the position of Matthew and Luke in early Christianity. The resulting passages have been edited to be suitable for monoglot Greek Christians. Accordingly, the minor agreements are not an argument against the priority of Mark. On the contrary, the reconstruction of Mark's Aramaic source is an essential task which alone enables us to give a full explanation of them.

The second dispute is set in the synagogue – presumably, therefore, later the same morning. As faithful Jews, Jesus and the Pharisees would go to synagogue on the sabbath, and if they were in a small place like Capernaum, the Pharisees should not have had too much difficulty in ensuring that they were at the same meeting. While verse 2 has no subject mentioned, the combination of 2.24 with 3.6 means that we must infer the Pharisees as the subject of verse 2, since they, rather than people in general, would be seeking to accuse them. If 3.1–6 were transmitted separately, this would not be satisfactory: we must infer that our source transmitted the two narratives together.

For συναγωγήν, I have reconstructed כנישתא. There is no doubt that this is the right word for 'synagogue' in later Jewish Aramaic, in which it also means 'gathering', 'assembly'. The root כנש is extant long before the time of Jesus, as well as in Daniel (3.3, 27) and the Dead Sea scrolls (for example 1QapGen XII.16). The form כנשת, meaning 'assembly', is found in 4QGiants (8.18; 9.5). There is therefore no serious doubt about the word used by Mark's source, and we may be quite certain that Jesus went to a Jewish assembly on the sabbath. We should probably imagine the scene in a distinctive building used for Jewish meetings of all kinds, though it is difficult to confirm this beyond all doubt (cf. Mark 1.21–9; Luke 7.5).

Why were the Pharisees looking for a second violation of the sabbath? Our source is comprehensible only if we make an assumption characteristic of later Jewish source material – a person cannot be prosecuted for one sabbath violation, but must be warned, and can only be prosecuted if they do it again (m. San 7.8; y. San VII.25c, 51–5). This is only sensible. The Jewish community can flourish if people are encouraged to observe the Torah, sabbath included. The biblical penalty for breaking the sabbath is, officially, death (Exod. 31.14; 35.2). If this were normally carried out without warning, it would wreck the Jewish community as disastrously as a major persecution. Hence we do not know of a single case from the whole of our period. Warning people, however, is a mode of encouraging observance. This is what the Pharisees will have thought they had done – they will have believed that their warning should stop Jesus from healing on the sabbath, and they took counsel to destroy him because they saw him as a disruptive influence, a man who broke the sabbath and claimed the authority of God in so doing, a claim which some people would accept when they saw him heal successfully. Our source could take all this for granted only if it transmitted 3.1–6 straight after another account when accusation was made of sabbath violation. We have a second reason for believing that these two narratives were transmitted together.

On what basis did the Pharisees consider that healing on the sabbath was violating it? It is not against the written Law. We have, however, seen that taking Peah was not against the written Law either, and that these Pharisees belonged to the orthodox wing of Judaism. They were expanding the written Law as they applied it to the whole of life, and just as they were shocked at the disciples plucking grain on the sabbath, so they were shocked that Jesus should heal on the sabbath. Later sources show concern that things which are connected with healing should not be done on the sabbath (m. Shab 14.3f.), with the major exception that saving life overrules the sabbath. We shall see that Jesus used this exception as the basis for his major halakhic argument in favour of healing on the sabbath. We have noted also that orthodox Jews during our period produced a number of halakhic judgements which are stricter that those which prevailed among the rabbis, including the prohibition of sex on the sabbath (Jub. 50.8). This is the Sitz im Leben for the Pharisaic judgement that healing is prohibited on the sabbath.

Major problems have been caused by methodologically unsound ways of trying to work out what the Law *really* was, instead of trying to reconstruct the different perspectives of Jesus and his Pharisaic opponents. For example, Dunn suggests that 'Jesus responds to the test case of performing an unnecessary healing in breach of the Sabbath.'[20] The text does not, however, suggest that Jesus considered the healing either unnecessary or in breach of the sabbath. On the contrary, he did it because he considered it essential to establish openly that healing was right on the sabbath, a position which he defended with vigorous halakhic argument, a central type of activity for a Jewish meeting on the sabbath. In the same way, but with the opposite result, Sanders notes that Jesus heals simply with a word of command, and comments, 'Talking is not regarded as work in any Jewish tradition, and so no work was performed.' He thus manages to infer that 'The story itself reveals no actual conflict over the sabbath.'[21] This is clean contrary to our text, which consists of a conflict story.

This dispute has no Sitz im Leben in the early church, which was concerned that Gentile Christians should not have to observe the sabbath, but was not concerned about this kind of detail. This is another powerful argument for the authenticity of the incident.

What was wrong with the man? Mark says ἐξηραμμένην ἔχων τὴν χεῖρα. This must represent something very like יבישתא לה ידא. It is possible that the narrator used צוי rather than יבישתא, but unfortunately neither word is a great deal of help to us. Something was wrong with the man's hand or arm – ידא, like χείρ, extends further than the English 'hand'. It was in some sense 'dried up', 'withered'. When Jesus carried out the healing, he told the man פשט ידא, which is a straightforward underlay for Mark's ἔκτεινὸν τὴν χεῖρα (3.5). We must infer that the man had not been using his hand/arm properly, and had not been stretching it out. One significant change emerges when we reconstruct Mark's account of what the man did when he was healed. We generally interpret ἀπεκατεστάθη as meaning 'was restored', which tells us that the man was healed, but nothing about how. In the LXX, however, ἀποκαθίστημι generally represents the Hebrew שׁוּב, which is natural because of the large overlap in the semantic area of the two words. It is difficult to see what it could represent here, other than the equivalent Aramaic תוב. Hence I have reconstructed: ופשט ותוב לה ידא. This, however, means something slightly different: 'And the hand/arm stretched out and returned to him.' This gives us a graphic picture of the man using his arm

---

[20] Dunn, 'Mark 2.1–3.6', 408 = *Jesus, Paul and the Law*, p. 23.
[21] E. P. Sanders, *Jewish Law from Jesus to the Mishnah* (London, 1990), pp. 21–2.

again, stretching it out and bringing it back to himself, and so using the muscles of his wrist and/or elbow as one should be able to. This effect can surely not be accidental: this adds to an argument of cumulative weight for the transmission of the story in an Aramaic version which has been literally translated.

As we try to find out what was wrong with the man, we must not impose upon our narrative the perspective of western biomedicine, what we in our society go to doctors and hospitals for. One thing we know with certainty is that Western biomedicine had not yet been invented. Therefore we must not translate the end of Mark 3.1 'who had a paralysed arm', and imagine him suffering from normally incurable paralysis. Whatever our narrator meant, it was not this. On the contrary, it was something that a traditional healer could heal. This is also shown by the attitude of Jesus' opponents. In the first place, they were watching to see whether he would heal *on the sabbath*, to accuse him of breaking the sabbath – they had no doubt that he could carry out the healing. Secondly, when the healing was performed, they did not have second thoughts, as faithful Jews would have when presented with a mighty act of God. They took counsel to destroy him, because from their perspective he had violated the sabbath by doing work on it, not by doing the impossible on it. This is reinforced by the fact that the narrator does not report any kind of amazement from the onlookers, though the healing was done in the full sight of everyone at a public meeting. We must infer that this is not a miracle story.

If we have a healing story which is not a miracle, we have two resources to help us work out what was the matter with the man – cross-cultural work on healers, and similar descriptions of illness in the same culture. In general, cross-cultural work on healers shows a massive variety of phenomena.[22] Many cultures have people to

---

[22] There is a very large bibliography, much of it written by specimens rather than analysts. I have found the following especially helpful or interesting: J. D. Frank and J. B. Frank, *Persuasion and Healing: A Comparative Study of Psychotherapy* (Oxford, 1961. Baltimore, [3]1991); E. M. Pattison, N. A. Lapins and H. A. Doerr, 'Faith Healing: A Study of Personality and Function', *Journal of Nervous and Mental Disease* 157, 1973, 397–409; D. Landy, *Culture, Disease and Healing* (New York, 1977); A. Kleinman, *Patients and Healers in the Context of Culture* (Berkeley/ Los Angeles/London, 1980); M. J. Christie and P. G. Mellett, *Foundations of Psychosomatics* (Chichester, 1981); L. Eisenberg and A. Kleinman (eds.), *The Relevance of Social Science for Medicine* (Dordrecht, 1981); A. J. Marsella and G. M. White (eds.), *Cultural Concepts of Mental Health and Therapy* (Dordrecht, 1982); D. C. Glik, 'Psychosocial Wellness among Spiritual Healing Participants', *Social Science and Medicine* 22, 1986, 579–86; M. Stacey, *The Sociology of Health and*

whom sick people go when they are ill, and who perform, or instruct them or their relatives to perform, a massive variety of rituals, including prayers and the taking of a massive variety of potions. The intellectual structures surrounding these events are also very varied, and include the placation or intervention of a wide variety of deities and spirits. The perception that someone is ill may depend on the person themselves, and/or on the social group to which they belong. The perception that they are better always includes a difference in the classification of the person, and may or may not include a change in symptoms.

From this perspective, there is no doubt that Jesus should be put in the general category of being a healer, even though an equivalent noun is not actually used of him in the Gospels.[23] There are many healing narratives in the Gospels, various people bring the sick to him to be healed, and when John the Baptist asked whether he was the person whose coming he had prophesied, Jesus cited his healing ministry as a major factor (Matt. 11.4–5//Luke 7.22). His position as a traditional healer is especially well shown in a visit to Nazareth, where he could do very little healing because of his traditional role as a craftsman (Mark 6.1–6). Exorcisms are especially prominent in the bottom layer of the tradition.[24] Jesus

---

Healing (London, 1988); Y. Bilu, 'Rabbi Yaacov Wuzana: A Jewish Healer in the Atlas Mountains', in M.-J. D. Good, B. J. Good and M. J. Fischer (eds.), *Emotion, Illness and Healing in Middle Eastern Societies* (*Culture, Medicine and Psychiatry* 12, 1, 1988), 113–35; C. Bass (ed.), *Somatization: Physical Symptoms and Psychological Illness* (London, 1990); I. E. Wickramasekera, 'Somatization: Concepts, Data, and Predictions from the High Risk Model of Threat Perception', *Journal of Nervous and Mental Disease* 183, 1995, 15–23; L. K. Hsu and M. F. Folstein, 'Somatoform Disorders in Caucasian and Chinese Americans', *Journal of Nervous and Mental Disease* 185, 1997, 382–7. Cf. S. L. Davies, *Jesus the Healer: Possession, Trance and the Origins of Christianity* (London, 1995), with bibliography; E. van Eck and A. G. van Aarde, 'Sickness and Healing in Mark: A Social Scientific Interpretation', *Neotestamentica* 27, 1993, 27–54.

[23] Cf. R. and M. Hengel, 'Die Heilungen Jesu und medizinisches Denken', in P. Christian and D. Rössler (eds.), *Medicus Viator: Fragen und Gedanken am Wege Richard Siebecks. Eine Festgabe . . . zum 75. Geburtstag* (Tübingen/Stuttgart, 1959), rep. in E. Suhl (ed.), *Der Wunderbegriff im NT* (WdE CCXCV. Darmstadt, 1980), 338–73; J. Wilkinson, *Health and Healing: Studies in NT Principles and Practice* (Edinburgh, 1980); and for background, L. P. Hogan, *Healing in the Second Tempel Period* (NTOA 21. Göttingen/Freibourg, Switzerland, 1992).

[24] H. C. Kee, 'The Terminology of Mark's Exorcism Stories', *NTS* 14, 1967–8, 232–46; P. W. Hollenbach, 'Jesus, Demoniacs, and Public Authorities: A Socio-Historical Study', *JAAR* 49, 1981, 567–88; B. D. Chilton, 'Exorcism and History: Mark 1:21–28', in D. Wenham and C. Blomberg (eds.), *Gospel Perspectives VI* (Sheffield, 1986), pp. 253–71; G. Twelftree, *Jesus the Exorcist* (WUNT 2, 54. Tübingen, 1993).

was so good at them that he sent out his disciples to do them (for example Mark 3.15; 6.7), other people did them in his name (Mark 9.38, cf. Acts 19.13–17), and scribes who came down from Jerusalem accused him of doing them with the help of Beelzeboul, a dispute which was so important that it appears in both Mark and Q (Mark 3.22–30; Matt. 12.24–32; Luke 11.15–22). Exorcism permits an exceptionally sharp characterisation of the role of a traditional healer. It presupposes that a person has been possessed by a demon. This is a particularly clear example of a sick person being labelled with a role. This role may be caused by their behaviour, their behaviour may be cited as evidence of it, and they may behave in ways which indicate that they have labelled themselves as possessed (for example Mark 5.9–12). The demon is then cast out in a ceremony. As a result of a successful exorcism, the person must be reclassified as a former demoniac from whom a demon has been cast out, and to some extent, depending on what they have been doing, they must alter their behaviour. For this purpose, they must be reintegrated into the social group. Hence instructions may be given to return home (for example Mark 5.19); a mother may be reassured that her daughter is no longer possessed (for example Mark 7.29); and we have a parabolic warning of what happens if the person is not then cared for in the community (Matt. 12.43–5// Luke 11.24–6).

Jesus' healings generally fall within the parameters of what is perceived to be possible by traditional healers who operate within communities of people who accept their powers. He does not heal broken limbs, prevent illness or grant immortality. He enables people who have been classified as ill to return to normal life.

The healing of Mark 3.1–6 is not an exorcism, but it has two features in common with some of them. Firstly, it is achieved by a word of command (cf., for example Mark 1.25; 9.25). Secondly, no one has any doubts that the healing can be done. Jesus calls the man out where everyone can see him, and has an halakhic argument with the Pharisees, who seek to punish him for violating their sabbath halakhah. Since the man co-operated with his healing, he must also have co-operated with or initiated the classification of him as ill. We must infer that he refused, or felt unable, to use his hand/arm.

The nearest parallel to the description of the same symptoms in ancient Judaism is the story of Jeroboam in 1 Kgs 13. When he ordered a prophet to be seized, ותיבש ידו אשר שלח עליו ולא יכל להשיבה אליו (1 Kgs 13.4): LXX καὶ ἰδοὺ ἐξηράνθη ἡ χεὶρ αὐτοῦ, ἣν ἐξέτεινεν ἐπ' αὐτόν, καὶ οὐκ ἠδυνήθη ἐπιστρέψαι αὐτὴν πρὸς ἑαυτόν: Tg ויבישת ויבשת אידה: pesh ידיה דאושיט עלוהי ולא יכיל לאתבותה ליה דאושת עלוהי ולא אשכח דנהפכיה לותה. Here the trouble is caused by direct divine intervention, and Jeroboam's hand was stuck out in the position in which he had used it to order the prophet to be seized. When he asked the man to pray for his cure, he asked for the specific effect ותשב ידי אלי (1 Kings 13.6): LXX ἐπιστρεψάτω ἡ χείρ μου πρός με: Tg ותתוב ידי לי. When Jeroboam is cured, ותשב יד־המלך אליו (1 Kgs 13.6): LXX καὶ ἐπέστρεψεν τὴν χεῖρα τοῦ βασιλέως πρὸς αὐτόν: Tg ותבת ידא דמלכא ליה. The description of what happened to Jeroboam's hand/arm has two striking things in common with the man of Mark 3.1–6. The term יבש is used of what was wrong with it, and when it was all right, he could send/stretch it out and bring it back again. It is possible that the author of our source had the Jeroboam incident deliberately in mind, but we cannot verify this. The comparison is striking because of lack of other parallels, but that may mean only that people did not write down, keep and transmit to us accounts of similar incidents. In either case, the Jeroboam story shows that our story is at home in Jewish culture. A man who could not stretch out his arm was a possible phenomenon, and a prophet who had access to God could restore him to normality.

From a cross-cultural perspective, the nearest parallel to these incidents is found in hysterical paralysis in late nineteenth- and early twentieth-century Europe. Hysteria was a fashionable illness at the time, so it was a natural choice for people who needed to be patients but who had nothing else wrong with them. Equally, hypnotism was a culturally acceptable form of manipulating people. Consequently, we have a number of accounts of hysterical paralysis,[25] some cases of which were curable under hypnosis. The culturally determined nature of these cases is especially well illustrated by those who could move their limbs under hypnosis, but could no more do so afterwards than they had done before. It is understandable that some earlier scholars sought to understand this case in that light,[26] but we should not impose so precise an understanding from another culture onto that of Jesus. All these cases

[25] See A. R. G. Owen, *Hysteria, Hypnosis and Healing: The Work of J.-M. Charcot* (London, 1971), esp. pp. 68, 124ff.
[26] See H. van der Loos, *The Miracles of Jesus* (NT. S VIIII. Leiden, 1965), pp. 439–40.

belong to the much larger phenomenon of somatised illness behaviour. Kleinman comments on his extensive field work in
Taiwan:

> Somatized illness behaviour is an important adaptive
> mechanism . . . It also seems for many to be personally
> adaptive as well . . . for some patients the illness behaviour
> is quite clearly maladaptive . . . Certain culture-bound
> disorders seem to be constructed in the same way: they
> represent loculated somatic delusions involving culturally
> specific Explanatory Models that shape a universal disease
> into a culturally specific illness.[27]

We must infer that Jesus was dealing with a case of somatised
illness behaviour. The man could not stretch out his arm because
this was an accepted mode of being ill in his culture. His hand/arm
is described as יבישתא because this was an acceptable description
of an illness in that culture. From a western biomedical perspective,
it is not an unreasonable description of a limb with atrophied
muscles, but this perspective was not available at the time. This is
why it is so important that everyone believed that Jesus could
perform the cure, and the narrator does not say that anyone was
surprised when he did so. It follows that the man was curable by a
traditional healer, and that we should not push the narrative into
the category of miracle story.

Jesus' first order to the man was קום בגוא. This was essential, not
just to perform the cure, but to have the halakhic argument with
the Pharisees. It has been translated literally to give the very
elliptical Greek expression, ἔγειρε εἰς τὸ μεσον. When Luke
rewrote this pericope, he consequently altered this to ἔγειρε καὶ
στῆθι εἰς τὸ μεσον, and Codex Bezae in Mark went for ἔγειρε καὶ
στήθει ἐν μέσῳ (similarly c e sa), while other variants show similar
awareness of a problem: Matthew, rewriting more completely,
dropped the whole expression. Reiser has sought to defend the
normality of Mark's Greek at the hand of a small number of
examples of ellipsis in Greek authors, almost all of which use
ἀνίστημι, which has a significantly different semantic area.[28] For
example, he notes Thucydides I.87.2, ἀναστήτω ἐς ἐκεῖνο τὸ
χωρίον. The problem with this is that ἀνίστημι had been in use for

---

[27] Kleinman, *Patients and Healers*, pp. 158, 163.
[28] Reiser, *Syntax und Stil*, p. 17.

centuries for people getting up in assemblies, whether to speak, to go out, or whatever. At this very dramatic moment, Sthenelaidas the ephor, having declared the Spartan shouts for and against war to be indecisive, sought to encourage people to vote openly for war by telling them ἀναστήτω, as one had often done, ἐς ἐκεῖνο τὸ χωρίον, on which Thucydides comments, δείξας τι χωρίον αὐτοῖς, and then for his opponents, the equally dramatic ἐς τὰ ἐπὶ θάτερα. This does not normalise Mark's use of ἐγείρω, as Luke bears witness.

Reiser's argument is thus unsound of method. No feature of a language is natural to monoglot speakers of it because ransacking the whole of it leads to a handful of examples which are not quite the same. Reasons for considering a whole piece to be a translation cannot be overthrown by showing that some of it is normal Greek: almost all translators try to translate into a normal version of the target language (Aquila and his ilk are notorious partly through being an exception to this general rule). The important fact which should replace Reiser's argument is that ellipsis in Greek will have combined with interference from the text encountered by the translator to make him untroubled when he wrote ἔγειρε εἰς τὸ μέσον.

Jesus' next question has some minor technical details which have been difficult to settle. I have followed one significant reading of Codex Bezae, which has τί ἀγαθὸν ποιῆσαι (with the support of b e), and I have taken this to be a literal translation of מה טב למעבד, 'to do what is good'. This is sound Aramaic. It is a general statement, and a reference to a particular good thing, the healing which Jesus was about to perform. It was translated literally, with the verb moved to its usual Greek position at the end of the phrase. Unfortunately, however, the resulting Greek could be taken to mean 'to do something/anything good'. This led Luke to write ἀγαθοποιῆσαι instead, and most manuscripts of Mark followed him (with ℵ W dropping the τί instead and W also replacing κακοποιῆσαι with οὐ, while E f¹ 700 moved the τί and the corrector of E omitted it). Once again, the reconstruction of the original Aramaic provides a good explanation of the variants. A good explanation of the reading of Bezae can hardly be obtained in any other way. We must also read ἐν before τοῖς σάββασιν, with Codex Bezae and several other manuscripts. The equivalent ב is essential in Aramaic, whereas ἐν is unnecessary in Greek, and its appearance in some manuscripts is difficult to explain except as the work of a translator. Thus we have additional arguments which require us to believe in Aramaic source material, and in the priority of Mark.

The centre of Jesus' argument is the expression נפש לאחיה, to save a life/person. Later rabbis wrote down the principle that saving life overrides the sabbath. For example, at m. Yoma 8.6, we read: ספק נפשות דוחה שבת. Jesus' argument makes sense only if we suppose that this principle was already accepted by the Pharisees. We know that the problem had occurred in a serious form almost two centuries earlier. During the Maccabean period, some orthodox Jews died rather than defend themselves on the sabbath (1 Macc. 2.29–38). This interprets the basic injunction not to work on the sabbath to include a ban on fighting even in self-defence, as in the written Law of Jub. 50.12. Mattathias and his followers then agreed that they would fight on the sabbath, to prevent the destruction of the Jewish community. This must have been the older halakhah, for the orthodox view would have caused equal havoc earlier if it had been held. It follows that Mattathias and his followers took a decision in accordance with normal and traditional Jewish custom. It was remembered as a decision. From the combination of these texts of different date, we must infer that Pharisees at the time of Jesus could be relied on to believe that saving life overrides the sabbath.

That the halakhic judgement was in this form is further shown by the sharp contrast with למקטלה. The penalty for sabbath-breaking was officially death, and we have already seen reason to believe that the Pharisees will have warned Jesus about this, and that our text could take this for granted. The combination of this fact with the normal ruling that saving *life* overrides the sabbath explains this sharp contrast. We might suppose, and these Pharisees surely will have supposed, that Jesus was not saving the man's life, and that therefore his action was not covered by the halakhic agreement that saving life overrides the sabbath. To understand Jesus' point of view, we must examine his argument in justification of another sabbath healing, that of a sick woman who was also unable to make proper use of her limbs (Luke 13.10–17). While parts of the narrative show signs of secondary editing, the crucial argument of Luke 13.16 can be reconstructed in its original Aramaic form, and its Sitz im Leben is surely where it is put, not in the early church.

דא בת אברהם, דאסרה סטנא הא שנין עשרה ותמניה, לא
יאי דאשתריתי מן אסורא דנא ביומא דשבתא.

This daughter of Abraham, whom Satan bound, look!, for
eighteen years, (is/was) it not fitting that she should be
released from this bond on the day of the sabbath?

Here we are in the area of overlap between demon possession and
what we would regard as other forms of illness. Jesus clearly took
the view that this woman could not use her limbs properly because
she had been bound by Satan. It is this view which explains the
strength of his commitment to healing on the sabbath, his description of it as נפש לאחיה and his opposition between this and
למקטלה. He believed that he was saving people from the devil.
Hence we might translate נפש לאחיה as 'save a person', and add
that it was more important to save people from the bond of Satan
than to keep them physically alive. What Jesus has done in his
halakhic argument with the Pharisees is to expand the meaning of
נפש לאחיה, which they agreed could be done on the sabbath, from
stopping someone from dying to saving a person from Satan. He
has done this in a proposition containing words with which the
Pharisees were bound to agree.

We can now return to the sharpness of למקטלה. We have seen
that the Pharisees must have warned Jesus about breaking the
sabbath, and that the official penalty for sabbath-breaking was
death. We shall shortly see them take counsel with the Herodians to
bring this about. This is what Jesus is contrasting with his own
action – he is saving a person, whereas they are bringing about
death. Not only therefore is he innocent – they are guilty, and
guilty of breaking the Law just when they think they are observing
it. It is this which explains the lead-in to this argument:

השליט בשבתא למעבד מה טב או לאבאשה

Jesus considered that he was doing good by saving the man from
the bond of Satan. He did not regard this as work, in the sense of
violating the commandment not to work on the sabbath. We might
have thought that לאבאשה was not in question, but it is more than
a simple contrast with doing good. The Pharisees' warning is in
question here again. They have every intention of doing evil on the
sabbath, and do so at the end of the passage when they take
counsel with the Herodians.

We now have a complete explanation of Jesus' halakhic argument. It presupposes the decision that saving life overrides the
sabbath. It extends this to saving a person on the sabbath by

healing thcm. It refers to this as doing good as part of a sharp contrast with the behaviour of the Pharisees, who are doing evil by plotting to bring about Jesus' death. We are then told that they were silent. We need this information partly because the arguments of Jesus' opponents are so rarely given to us, and we might imagine that here too they are simply omitted. The silence of the Pharisees is important because it further testifies to their determination to take action against Jesus. They could have had a halakhic argument with him. They preferred to be silent because, as we learnt in verse 2, they were waiting to accuse him. This is further evidence that the unmentioned subject of verse 2 is the Pharisees, not people in general. We then find Jesus angry that the Pharisees would not let him be the vehicle of divine action on the sabbath, and the narrator describes this as their hardness of heart. We should accept this as a correct insight into the views of the incident taken by the main participants. Jesus' annoyance finds vent elsewhere in severe criticism of his opponents, and it is clear that their opposition to him was very determined.

The healing incident follows. The man has already chosen to be on the side of Jesus rather than the Pharisees by obeying his order to come out into the middle. The whole incident requires co-operation between the man and Jesus, and this is presupposed already at verse 2. Jesus must have had the ability to perceive when people were able to come out of illness situations and be restored to normal life. His ability as an exorcist indicates that he was good at causing them to do so, not merely at perceiving when they would. He now issues the word of command, פשט ידא. The man was able to obey this command by stretching his arm out. His arm did not then become like that of Jeroboam, stuck out in that position, but also returned to him. The man has accepted that he is cured, and has made use of the muscles in his hand/arm. From an immediate perspective, therefore, he was cured. Jesus has now performed a healing on the sabbath, and action against him by the Pharisees follows in the next verse. As so often, however, there is no follow-up to the healing itself. Accordingly, we do not know how permanent the effect was.

The importance of this is especially well indicated at two levels. We have noted the Q parable, which shows knowledge that demoniacs might suffer serious relapse if not properly cared for after they had been through an exorcism (Matt. 12.43–5//Luke 11.24–6). In a classic investigation, Pattison and his associates asked a group of Americans who had been through a healing ceremony whether they were taking medicines. It was found that some of them did indeed take medicines for their remaining symptoms, even though they believed themselves to have been healed.[29] This underlines the nature of healing ceremonies. They are ceremonies, in which sick people are cared for, and following which they may declare themselves healed, regardless of whether there is any change in their symptomatology. When the ceremony is successful, the person is reclassified as no longer ill. The effects of this are, however, not necessarily permanent. This further illuminates the main point of this event, as a sabbath event. The main point is not whether the man was permanently healed, for this is not mentioned, and there is no question of a miracle. The main point is that the event took place on the sabbath, and was the occasion of a serious dispute between Jesus and Pharisaic opponents, who knew that he could perform healing ceremonies and believed that he should not do so on the sabbath.

The serious nature of this dispute is presented in the final verse. It has caused scholars many problems. We may begin with the language. The Greek word συμβούλιον means a council, not counsel, which may, however, be συμβουλία. I suggest that these two words have been confused by a bilingual translator who was faced with עיצה, which means both. Accordingly, Mark's Aramaic source really meant that the Pharisees 'gave counsel concerning/ against him'. This follows on very nicely from the narrative. We have seen that the Pharisees were hoping to accuse him if he carried out the healing. We now find them doing so. The confusion between συμβούλιον and συμβουλία is as straightforward an example of interference as one could ask for. The Aramaic על has a wide range of meaning: the translator's choice of κατά rather than περί is only sensible, in view of the context as a whole.

There are some problems with the attestation of עיצא, which does not occur in the Aramaic of the right period. The root first occurs in Aramaic in the form ליתעץ, 'will not take counsel', in a text from Deir Alla, long before the time of Jesus. Both עצה and the verb יעץ are common in the Hebrew Bible. The related forms יעט (Dan. 6.8; 11QtgJob V.8) and עטה (Dan. 2.14; 11QtgJob VII, 4) do occur in Aramaic in the two centuries before the time of Jesus. In the LXX, βουλή usually represents עצה and βουλεύομαι

---

[29] Pattison et al., 'Faith Healing'.

יעץ; συμβουλία is used to translate עצה (2 Sam. 1.12; 2 Chr. 25.16; Prov. 12.15), and σύμβουλος is used several times for יעץ. The rendering of עיצא with συμβουλία would accordingly have been impeccable. In later Aramaic, there is no doubt that עצא means 'council' as well as 'counsel' (for example *Tg. Neof.* Num. 26.9, representing the Hebrew עדה). I suggest that this is sufficient to make the use of συμβούλιον in place of συμβουλία comprehensible as the mistake of a bilingual translator.

For εὐθύς, I have suggested בה שעתא.[30] Mark has εὐθύς some forty-one times, which is excessive by the standards of normal monoglot Greek, and difficult to explain. The expression is well attested in the Aramaic of our period (for example Dan. 3.6, 15), and difficult to translate – efforts such as αὐτῇ τῇ ὥρᾳ (Dan. 3.6, 15 Theod.) and ἐν αὐτῇ τῇ ὥρᾳ (Luke 13.31) are explicable as normal examples of interference, but will not have satisfied everyone, because they are not normal monoglot Greek. If our translator used εὐθύς for some expression such as מיד or מחדא at Mark 1.10, and was faced with בה שעתא at 1.12, he may have felt *very* inspired at going for εὐθύς again, and thereafter. It is regrettable that we have no certain means of confirming the accuracy of this plausible story.

The next problem is Ἡρῳδιανῶν. This word does not occur elsewhere, except at Mark 12.13//Matt. 22.16. In form it is a Latinism, on the analogy of Caesariani, Tiberiani and later Christiani. The Herodiani were followers of Herod, the same people referred to by Josephus as τοὺς τὰ Ἡρῴδου φρονοῦντας (*AJ* XIV.450//*B.J.* I.326), and τῶν Ἡρωδείων (*B.J.* I.319). The Herod in question was by this time Herod Antipas, who was in charge of Galilee at the time. The word will not have changed since the days of his father, Herod the Great. The word 'Herodiani' does not otherwise occur because of the small quantity of our sources, and because in the two cited passages Josephus preferred more Greek expressions. The word Ἡρωδείων is in particular the direct equivalent of the Latin Herodiani. We should infer that it was used in the Aramaic source as well, hence הרודיאני, because this explains the behaviour of the translator. It was used by the source because this was what they were actually called, and there was not a straightforward Aramaic alternative.

Latinisms are not known in the Aramaic sources of our period

---

[30] Cf. Black, *Aramaic Approach* ([3]1967), pp. 108–12, esp. p. 109, n. 3.

because these contain very few discussions of Roman institutions and people. They are frequent in later Aramaic sources, which have many more such discussions. There are other purely lexical items in Mark's Greek (for example κοδράντης for quadrans, Mark 12.42, also Matt. 5.26). We should infer that loanwords for Roman things were commoner than we can see from contemporary extant Aramaic sources alone. Herod the Great and Herod Antipas both had strong Roman connections. Herod the Great's buildings with Greco-Roman names included the fortress of Antonia, after Antonius, and the city of Caesarea; the rebuilt Samaria was renamed as Sebaste, after the Greek form of Augustus. He also named two fortresses Herodium, after himself. This is just the sort of person who would produce Herodiani on the analogy of Caesariani.

Herod sent his son Antipas to be educated in Rome for several of his teenage years (see Jos. *A.J.* XVII.20).[31] When Herod Archelaus died, Antipas took over the dynastic name of Herod, and used it on coins and inscriptions. His Greek cities with Roman names included Tiberias, his new capital, after the emperor Tiberius, and Livias, later Julias, after the emperor's wife. This is just the sort of person to maintain the description of his supporters as Herodiani. This is precisely the situation required for speakers of Aramaic to refer to הרודיאני, whether they approved of them or held them in the same contempt as the musical instruments of Antiochus Epiphanes.

Many scholars have refused to believe that the Pharisees co-operated with the Herodians, on the ground that these two groups were not natural allies. This has sometimes been given as one reason for regarding the verse as redactional. In particular, it has been suggested that it originated a few years later, when Pharisees were on much better terms with Herod Agrippa II.[32] It is true that these groups were not natural allies, but our primary source material enables us to explain this unusual alliance. Herod was the secular authority in the area, and he had recently had another major prophet, John the Baptist, put to death (Mark 6.17–29; Jos. *A.J.* XVIII.116–19). This is the reason for Pharisees to contact the Herodians at that time, and to co-operate with them.

A further consideration is that putting Jesus to death for sabbath-breaking would be problematical. The enforcement of this

---

[31] Hoehner, *Herod Antipas*, pp. 12ff.
[32] E.g., B. W. Bacon, 'Pharisees and Herodians in Mark', *JBL* 39, 1920, 102–12.

penalty cannot have been a normal event. While the author(s) of
Jubilees were clearly very concerned to keep the death penalty, we
know of no instances from our period, and its replacement by seven
years' confinement at CD XII.3–6 is likely to be the institutionali-
sation of the known fact that it was not literally carried out.
Moreover, the view that Jesus had broken the sabbath twice
depends on taking a Pharisaic view of the halakhah. As we have
seen, neither taking Peah nor healing people on the sabbath was
against the written Torah, and Jesus behaved like a faithful Jew in
defending his disciples on the one occasion and performing a
healing on the other. It follows that the Pharisees would experience
grave difficulties in getting a conviction in a court. If, however, they
could persuade the secular authorities that Jesus was a menace, and
if in so doing they could present themselves as the guardians of the
Law who were responsible for interpreting it, then they might
persuade Herod Antipas to set up a court which they could control,
or to deal with him as he had with John the Baptist.

We should accordingly see the aftermath of this event at Luke
13.31–3. Luke had an Aramaic source for this ancient tradition,
and it may be reconstructed as follows:

31 ובה שעתה אזלין פרושין אמרין לה, פוק והלך מכא,
כי צבא הירוד למקטלך.
32 ואמר להון, הלכו אמרו לתעלא דנה, הא, מפק שידין
אנה ומשלם אסותא יומא דן ויום אחרן ובתליתיא שלם
אנה.
33 ברם עתיד אנה מהלך יומא דן ויום בתר יום, כי לא
יאי לנביה דיאבד ברא מן ירושלם.

[31]And in that hour Pharisees went and said to him, 'Get
out and go away from here, because Herod wants to kill
you.' [32]And he said to them, 'Go tell that jackal, Look! I
am casting out demons and performing healings to-day
and tomorrow, and on the third day I am perfected. But I
am going to proceed to-day and day after day, for it would
not be fitting for a prophet to perish outside Jerusalem.'

Here we see the strains and stresses of the temporary alliance
between Pharisees and Herodians. If Herod thought that John the
Baptist was a threat to the Herodian state (Jos. *A.J.*
XVIII.116–19), he was likely to take the same view of Jesus. The
alliance between Pharisees and Herodians, however, has not only

supplied him with a reason for killing Jesus, but also alienated some of the Pharisees. As such, Pharisees were merely orthodox Jews. If some felt so strongly that taking Peah and healing on the sabbath were, or should be, against the Law and that this should be enforced with the death penalty, others are likely to have felt that their view of how the Law should be observed should not be imposed on everyone, especially not on a prophetic teacher who brought so many Jews back to basic observances. They therefore came and warned Jesus. At the same time, they did not blame their fellow Pharisees, who did not have enough power to destroy Jesus unless they co-operated with the secular authorities. They blamed Herod, who had already killed John the Baptist and who would be responsible directly for measures against Jesus, if these were taken in Galilee.

Jesus' response comes from the same Sitz im Leben as the incident of Mark 3.1–6. He refers directly to his ministry of exorcism and healing, and to his forthcoming death. He was not polite about Herod – the jackal was a noisy, unclean nuisance of an animal, a predator which hunted in packs. This is very sharp polemic, and hence it is this which Jesus will have meant, and this is how he will have been understood. The word תעלא also includes foxes, commonly thought of in the Greek world as cunning, which was not an outstanding quality of Herod, so foxes will not have come to people's minds when they heard Jesus speak. They will have thought of noisy, unclean jackals hunting and killing.[33] The references to Jesus' death are indirect, like all those before the final sequence of events. The first prophecy uses שלם, to 'be perfected', a possible metaphor for death, and shown to be so here by the context. The second one uses a more straightforward word, יאבד, the same word as used by the narrator of Mark 3.6. In this saying, however, Jesus does not speak directly of himself, but uses a general statement about prophets. The stories about the deaths of prophets in Jerusalem were so extensive by this time as to make this a perfectly plausible general statement. Jesus used it to say that he would not be caught by Herod – he would die his divinely ordained death in Jerusalem, a process which in due course he helped bring about by cleansing the Temple.

We can now return to Mark 3.1–6. The plot between Pharisees and Herodians was to have Jesus put to death. This is the only

---

[33] Cf. Casey, 'Jackals', 8, with 20, n. 19.

occurrence of ὅπως in Mark. I have suggested that הֵיך gave rise to it. These two words overlap in semantic area and in function, and this is just what a translator would need to make him use a standard word which was not common in his idiolect.

Faced with the straightforward evidence of our primary sources, some scholars continue to find the whole story incredible. For example, Sanders surveys sabbath observance in general during our period, with some other aspects of the Law, and concludes that 'there is no indication that the Pharisees tried to impose their own rules on others', and 'no reason to think that the Pharisees sought the death penalty for minor transgressions of the sabbath'. This is one major reason why he follows the common view that Mark 3.6 is editorial, and concludes that 'any possible transgression on the part of Jesus or his followers was minor and would have been seen as such by even the strictest groups'. Sanders is followed by Meier, who puts their main conclusion bluntly: 'Thus, it is incredible that Pharisees or anyone else would seek to put Jesus to death for the event described in Mark 3:1–6.'[34]

There are five things wrong with this. The first is the underlying assumption that the relationship between Jesus and his opponents somehow *must* be the same as that between other Jews who differed over the interpretation of non-biblical expansions of the Law. Sanders never grounds this assumption in anything. Secondly, this assumption is clean contrary to our primary sources, which show vigorous conflict between Jesus and his opponents over a range of issues, including imaginative polemic. Thirdly, Sanders' argument does not take account of the cultural implications of this incident. If the Pharisees did not do something, they might find people following Jesus' interpretation of the Law instead of their own. Healing on the sabbath was not a minor matter because it lent itself so easily to the interpretation that God was demonstrating that Jesus was right and the Pharisees wrong, an interpretation which would undermine their authority altogether. Fourthly, after Jesus' death, conflicts between Jesus' followers and other Jews gradually became so serious that Christianity split from Judaism: this is coherent with the evidence of our primary sources that there was serious conflict during the ministry, whereas Sanders' assumption makes the whole situation more difficult to understand. Fifthly, we

---

[34] Sanders, *Jewish Law*, pp. 6–23; J. P. Meier, *A Marginal Jew: Rethinking the Historical Jesus* (ABRL. New York, 1991–4), vol. II, pp. 681–4.

should therefore consider exceptional circumstances in which there was serious conflict among Jews over the observance of the Law, instead of trying to understand the conflict between Jesus and his opponents on the basis of average circumstances in which there was no such trouble.

For example, when Hyrcanus fell out with the Pharisees, he abrogated their additional regulations and punished people who observed them (Jos. *A.J.* XIII.295–7). When Alexandra formed an alliance with the Pharisees, she ordered the people to obey them, and restored the regulations abolished by Hyrcanus (*A.J.* XIII.408). This is evidently a case of the Pharisees imposing their extra-biblical laws on other Jews. When Herod the Great set up a large golden eagle over the great gate of the Temple, it was chopped down by some young men at the instigation of two learned rabbis. They thought that the eagle was set up contrary to the Law, as Josephus did, but Herod accused them of robbing the Temple contrary to the Law. He had the two rabbis and the main culprits burnt alive, executed their associates and replaced the high priest (*B.J.* I.648–55; *A.J.* XVII.149–64). Here some Jews imposed their view of a detail of the Law by force, and the Jewish king killed them brutally on the ground that they had broken the Law.

We must therefore reject the objections of Sanders and Meier, and follow our primary source. As we have seen, this is eminently comprehensible, provided that we apply to Mark's Aramaic source the assumptions natural to Jesus' Jewish environment.

The following conclusions may therefore be drawn. Mark 2.23–3.6 is a literal translation of an Aramaic source. It has just enough mistakes for us to be sure that it was written, not transmitted orally by a bilingual. It also has evidence of the strategical decision to translate (א)שׁנ(א) בר with ὁ υἱὸς τοῦ ἀνθρώπου when it refers to Jesus, a decision which could only be made in the presence of extensive written sources. These points also form a new and decisive argument for the priority of Mark. To make sense of this source, we have to apply Jewish assumptions. When this is done, it gives us a coherent account of two disputes between Jesus and his Pharisaic opponents. These disputes concerned how the sabbath should be observed. They took place closely together, probably on the same day. Jesus' Pharisaic opponents were orthodox Jews, who believed in expanding the commandments to apply them to the whole of everyday life. Hence they believed that taking Peah and healing people violated the general commandment not to work on the sabbath. Jesus came in from the prophetic tradition. His commitment to God and people expressed itself in defending poor and hungry disciples who took Peah on the sabbath, and in healing people whom he believed that he thereby delivered from Satan in accordance with the will of God. He did not consider either of these things to be work.

The Sitz im Leben of these disputes is in the life of Jesus. Jesus lived in first-century Judaism, where the question of how to observe the Law was a permanent focus of Jewish life. It was a time when orthodox Jews were especially strict and powerful. These disputes have no Sitz im Leben in the early church, which was concerned about whether Christians, especially Gentile Christians, should observe the Law at all. These detailed disputes do not speak to that major issue. Moreover, the source makes numerous Jewish assumptions which could only be taken for granted if it was written in the expectation of being understood only by Jews. Mark's Aramaic source must therefore have been written in Israel at a very early date.

The outcome of these disputes was very serious. The Pharisees were so opposed to Jesus that they took counsel with the Herodians to destroy him. This was part of the reason for Herod's opposition to him. Other evidence shows Jesus avoiding the consequences of this opposition in Galilee, and expecting to die in Jerusalem. While some Pharisees were sufficiently concerned to warn him, such violent opposition was dangerous. We shall see that it was part of the cultural background to the final events. First, however, we must discuss a passage in which Jesus looked forward to his death.

5

THE QUESTION OF JACOB AND JOHN: MARK 10.35–45

Mark 10.35–45 is a remarkable passage. Here two of the twelve ask to sit on Jesus' right and left in his glory. Jesus declines their request, in terms which assume that he will in due course sit in glory, with someone on his right and someone on his left. He first asks them whether they will share his suffering, and subsequently gives teaching on service. This presupposes that his atoning death may be shared by others.

Scholars have found this passage so difficult that only the most conservative regard it as a unity. The point of the following Aramaic reconstruction is therefore in the first place to restore the passage as a unified whole. We shall also be able to recover most of the original interpretation, which differs significantly from that of most scholarship.

35 וקרבין לה יעקב ויוחנן בני זבדיה ואמרין לה, רבי,
צבינא דמה די נשאל מנך תעבדנה לן.
36 ואמר להון, מה צביתון לי דאעבדנה לכון.
37 ואמרו לה, הב לנא דניתב חד מן ימינך וחד מן שמאלך
בהדרך.
38 ואמר להון, לא ידעתון מא דשאלתון. התיכלון למשתה
כסא דאנה שתה, או לאתטבלה טבילא דאנה מתטבל?
39 אמרו לה, ניכול. ואמר להון, כסא דאנא שתה תשתון,
וטבילה דאנה מתטבל תתטבלון,
40 להן למיתב מן ימיני או מן שמאלא לא לי למיהב להן
להון דאתתקן להון.
41 ושמעו עשרה ושריו לאתזעפא על יעקב ועל יוחנן.
42 וקרא להון ישוע ואמר להון, ידעתון דסברין לממלך
על עממיא שלטין בהון ורברבניהון גברין עליהון.
43 לא כיני ביניכון, אלא מן דצבא למהוה רב ביניכון
להוה טליכון,
44 ומן דצבא למהוה ראש ביניכון, הוא להוא עבד לכלכון.

45 ואף בר אנשא לא אתא להשתמשא אלא לשמשה
ולמנתן נפשה פורקן חלף שגיאין.

[35]And Jacob and John, sons of Zebedee, approached him and said to him, 'Rabbi, we want you to do for us what we ask of you.' [36]And he said to them, 'What do you want me to do for you?' [37]And they said to him, 'Let us sit one on your right and one on your left in your glory.' [38]And he said to them, 'You do not understand what you have asked. Can you drink the cup which I will drink, or be immersed with the immersion with which I am immersed?' [39]They said to him, 'We can.' And he said to them, 'You will drink the cup which I drink, and be immersed with the immersion with which I am immersed, [40]but to sit on my right or my left is not mine to give, except to those for whom it has been prepared.'

[41]And the ten heard and began to be annoyed with Jacob and John. [42]And Jesus called them and said to them, 'You know that those who think to rule over the nations have power over them, and their great ones lord it over them. [43]Not so among you, but he who wishes to be great among you, he shall be your servant, [44]and he who wishes to be chief among you, he shall be a slave to you all.[45] What is more, a/the son of man does not come to be served but to serve, and to give his life/soul/self as a ransom for many.'

We do not have much information about the twelve, especially when we consider that what we do have implies their fundamental importance.[1] It is a reasonable inference that what is missing was not of positive interest to the early church, or rather perhaps to Gentile churches. Mark tells us that Jesus appointed twelve to be with him, and so that he might send them out to preach and to have power to cast out demons (Mark 3.14–15). This corresponds to the two central points of his ministry. Jesus' preaching and teaching ministry was directed at the whole of Israel, so it is logical that he should send his closest followers out to carry on that ministry. That there should be twelve of them corresponds symbolically to the twelve tribes of Israel. Exorcism and healing were central to his ministry, and of all kinds of healing, exorcism most

---

[1] For what we do know, see R. P. Meye, *Jesus and the Twelve: Discipleship and Revelation in Mark's Gospel* (Grand Rapids, 1968); W. Horbury, 'The Twelve and the Phylarchs', *NTS* 32, 1986, 503–27.

obviously is a healing ceremony carried out to enable people classified as socially unacceptable to return to the community.[2]

The account of the twelve during the ministry bears out this summary. They turn up with him at various points, including his final Passover (Mark 14.17, 20). They are sent out, which might have made them apostles, שליחין being the direct and natural equivalent for ἀπόστολοι. However, it was surely not the term normally used, since it is rare in the earliest sources (Mark 6.30 only; not in Q), it is conspicuously added by Matthew and Luke (Matt. 10.2; Luke 6.13, cf. 11.49; 17.5; 22.14; 24.10), and it has an obvious Sitz im Leben in the early church. We must infer that the inner group were known as the twelve, the term used by Mark when they are sent out (Mark 6.7) and in an old tradition about the resurrection, when they were surely eleven (1 Cor. 15.5). They were eleven because one of the twelve had betrayed him, a desperately memorable fact which the early church cannot have invented. The Markan account of their sending out mentions unclean spirits, or demons, twice (6.7, 13), and adds the preaching of repentance and healing the sick by anointing with oil (6.12–13). Thus the earliest source material is entirely coherent, and has an excellent Sitz im Leben in first-century Judaism, but not in the early church, for whom the twelve were not of continuing importance. The authenticity of this material should therefore be accepted.

It is quite alarming that some scholars think otherwise. I propose to discuss three major arguments. Firstly, there are variations in the names in the lists of the twelve as we find them at Mark 3.16–19// Matt. 10.2–4//Luke 6.14–16 and Acts 1.13.[3] This is a correct observation from which radical conclusions should not be drawn. In the best-attested texts of these sources, there is only one difference of personnel: both Luke's lists have Judas (son) of Jacob, whereas Matthew and Mark have Thaddaeus. Since neither figure is otherwise known, this is not due to a need to insert either of them secondarily. Luke clearly had a different piece of information from Mark and Matthew, and this may well be because he alone was interested in the composition of the twelve when Matthias was chosen to replace Judah of Kerioth. In this case both sources may be right: it is inherent in having twelve representatives of the twelve

---

[2] See pp. 176–80 above.
[3] P. Vielhauer, 'Gottesreich und Menschensohn in der Verkündigung Jesu', in W. Schneemelcher (ed.), *Festschrift für Gunter Dehn* (Neukirchen, 1957), pp. 51–79, at p. 62.

tribes that renegade or dead members must be replaced. If Thaddaeus left the movement and Jesus replaced him with Judah son of Jacob, we might well not have the story transmitted to us. Alternatively, the main point may be simply that most of the twelve are unknown from the period of the early church. This is also sufficient to cause someone to transmit a list of names with a mistake in it. Other variants in the names are very poorly attested. They therefore bear witness to continuing small changes due to defective memory and unfortunate creativity. They do nothing to alter the fact that the early church had no reason to create either the twelve or most of these names, because neither the twelve nor the names had a significant role in the early church.

Secondly, only one Q saying implies the number twelve (Matt. 19.28//Luke 22.30).[4] Radical conclusions do not, however, flow naturally from this extraordinary fact. We shall see that this particular saying does not have an adequate Sitz im Leben in the early church. We are therefore driven to conjecture. It is surely more probable that what Jesus said about and to a perfectly Jewish group, most of whom are otherwise unknown inter alia because they played no significant role in the early church, was not known to, or not suitable for, the early church.

Some arguments are derived from the structure of the material about the twelve in the Gospels. Wellhausen pointed out that the Markan account of the return of the twelve (Mark 6.30ff.) seems artificially constructed.[5] It is, however, well known that this Gospel as a whole has a structure some of which is secondary, and it has been reasonably conjectured that this is because Mark had no outline of the ministry. This does not reflect against the historicity of the pieces of material used by Mark. The return of the mission is an especially good example of this. It has the one example of ἀπόστολοι in Mark, a number which is not consistent with deriving it from Markan concern for apostleship. It occurs just at a moment when the twelve will have been properly called שליחין, because they had been sent out on the mission. The inconsequential information in 6.31 is not likely to be due to the interests of the early church either (though it could possibly be a reality effect).

We must conclude that radical attempts to remove the twelve from the historical record should not be accepted. The arguments

4 *Ibid.*, p. 62.
5 Wellhausen, *Evangelium Marci*, pp. 50–1; *Einleitung*, p. 140; followed, e.g., by Vielhauer, 'Gottesreich', p. 62.

used have been uniformly destructive, and have never coped with the Sitz im Leben of the twelve in Jesus' ministry to Israel, or with their lack of any Sitz im Leben in the early church.

Further information may be gleaned from the Q saying, Matt. 19.28//Luke 22.30. We have lost some of the opening part of it. Matthew has the Son of man sitting on the throne of his glory, surely a redactional presentation of the last times, so he did not like the way this was put in his source (cf. Matt. 16.28; 25.31). Luke has equally redactional references to 'my Father' and 'my kingdom'. We must infer that we have lost something eschatological which was too specifically Jewish for either Matthew or Luke. The Lukan version does also contain the words ἔσθητε καὶ πίνητε ἐπὶ τῆς τραπέζης μου. Luke had little reason to edit this in. If Jesus really said something longer on these lines, Matthew and Luke would both have reason to replace it with what we now read. It would also make an excellent occasion for the twelve to sit on twelve seats, and for all of them to drink new wine. What we have got is thus quite extraordinary: the twelve will judge Israel. Not Abel, not Abraham, not Moses, but the twelve. Abraham, Isaac, Jacob and much of the diaspora would be there, reclining as at feasts (Matt. 8.11–12//Luke 13.28–9), but not judging Israel. This puts Jacob and John's request at Mark 10.37 in its proper perspective. They merely ask for seats of honour when every man of the twelve, not God himself or the patriarchs, will judge the twelve tribes of Israel. As always in his teaching, the position of Jesus himself is implied rather than stated. It is evidently central, as Jacob and John understood, when they referred to his glory.

Jacob and John, sons of Zebedee, are singled out in the call of the first disciples. They are called straight after Peter, and his brother Andrew, at Mark 1.19–20, and these are the only four mentioned as called at this stage. After Jesus' first recorded exorcism in a synagogue, they went home with him to the house of Simon and Andrew (Mark 1.29). In Mark's list of the twelve, they are also mentioned next after Peter (Mark 3.16–17). In the Garden of Gethsemane, Jesus took Jacob and John on one side with Peter to watch and pray with him (Mark 14.32ff.). We must infer that they were central members of the twelve, which explains their request.

Jesus called Simon Cephas 'the Rock'.[6] He also gave Jacob and

---

[6] See p. 84 above.

John a special name, but this has proved difficult to understand.[7] Mark has Βοανηργές, ὅ ἐστιν υἱοὶ βροντῆς (Mark 3.17). βοανη is evidently an attempt to transliterate the Aramaic בני, 'sons of'. The transliteration of the shewa was necessarily problematical. Either α or ο was possible, but both together are ludicrous.[8] It follows that we have before us the work of one of the many bilingual people who are not good at transliteration. We should therefore not proceed by making up an Aramaic word for 'thunder' by transliterating Βοανηργές back *into* supposed Aramaic.[9] We must rather proceed from the known Aramaic word for 'thunder', רעם. This is extant as a verb at 4Q318, and at 11QtgJob XXXIV.5, where it represents the Hebrew רעם. This is just the sort of word that a bilingual might not know, or forget. If Greek was his first language, and he currently spoke it in Rome or somewhere, he might have heard thunder always called βροντή, or always for the previous fifteen years. He will therefore have had to ask the vowels, and how to transliterate ע. It would be reasonable to be told something about a short noise, γ and ε. He gave up on the first shewa, and put γ followed by ε. He then misread the final ם as ס. The orthography of the Dead Sea scrolls makes this a perfectly intelligible misreading.

The sons of thunder continued to be central after Jesus' death. Jacob was so important that he was martyred by Herod Agrippa I (Acts 12.1–2). John continued with Jacob the brother of Jesus and Peter as the central members of the Jerusalem church, known as the 'pillars' even to Paul (Gal. 2.9). In due course, therefore, Jacob and John, together with Peter, provided the central continuity between the Jesus movement and the early church. This testifies to the vigorous leaders who made the request of Mark 10.37. They may well have felt that their only serious rival for the position was Peter.

The opening of the narrative has two points of detail worth pausing over. For διδάσκαλε, I have suggested רבי. We must infer

---

[7] See D. R. G. Beattie, 'Boanerges: A Semiticist's Solution', *IBS* 5, 1983, 11–13.

[8] H. P. Rüger, 'Die lexikalischen Aramaismen im Markusevangelium', in H. Cancik (ed.), *Markus-Philologie: Historische, literargeschichtliche und stilistische Untersuchungen zum zweiten Evangelium* (WUNT 33. Tübingen, 1984), pp. 73–84, at 76–7, compares Μοασάδα at Strabo 16.2.44, but this only shows that Strabo could not transliterate very well either.

[9] Rüger, 'Die lexicalischen Aramaismen', p. 77, proposes to believe in an Aramaic rᵉgaš on the basis of *Tg. 1 Ks.* 18.41; *Tg. Isa.* 17.12f., in neither of which it means 'thunder', and undated and uncited sources from an unmentioned Arabic dictionary. We should not proceed like this.

from other passages that רבי was already a natural address for a teacher, and that the disciples so addressed Jesus (cf. Mark 9.5; 10.51; 11.21; 14.45). It is difficult to see what other Aramaic word could have been used. Secondly, the Aramaic מה has a semantic area including 'what' as well as 'whatever'. The translator had to make a choice, and he thought Jacob and John were so far gone that he opted for ὅ ἐάν plus subjunctive. If we wish to understand them, we should be more sympathetic. About to make a request which they must have known might be refused, they introduced it with a rigmarole, which is in effect a statement that they are going to ask Jesus to do something for them. Jesus then replied in the most straightforward way possible, by asking what it was that they wanted him to do for them. The brothers' request has a very straightforward piece of evidence of Semitic interference – the second εἷς. This is not natural Greek, but εἷς generally corresponds so closely to the Aramaic and Hebrew חד that it is a natural translation by a bilingual. Hence it is found also in the LXX (for example Exod. 17.12).[10]

It is intelligible that Matthew gave the request to their mother, removed the wording of the request altogether, re-edited the unsatisfactory wording of Jesus' question too, interpreted δόξῃ with βασιλείᾳ and left οἴδατε (Matt. 20.22) in the plural because the two brothers cannot be replaced by their mother throughout the following verses. The opposite alterations, which Mark would have had to make if he had been using Matthew, are not intelligible at all. Such details should be at the heart of the argument for Markan priority. The invention of their request in Greek (Mark 10.35 θέλομεν . . . ἡμῖν) is especially improbable, whereas its origin as a literal translation of normal idiomatic Aramaic is perfectly reasonable.

Given their position among the twelve, Jacob and John must surely have sat on his right and left from time to time. It may have been their usual place when Peter was absent. Their request makes sense only if taken literally. If heaven, or the kingdom, were a purely spiritual realm without place, space or time, being on Jesus' right and left would make no sense as a memorable request. It would help if we knew exactly what was meant by 'in your glory'. I have suggested בהדרך, which is something that people, kings and

---

[10] E. C. Maloney, *Semitic Interference in Markan Syntax* (SBLDS 51. Chico, 1981), pp. 156–9.

God can have, but it is not specific enough to help us. Matthew glossed Mark's phrase ἐν τῇ βασιλείᾳ σου, which is entirely reasonable. At his final Passover with his disciples, Jesus expected the kingdom to come soon, and to drink new wine in it (Mark 14.25). That would be a very suitable occasion for Jacob and John to be on his right and left. I have noted the implications of Matt. 19.28//Luke 22.30, which gives the twelve the role of judging the twelve tribes of Israel, and thereby implies a very glorious position for Jesus. We must also recall that, when Jesus predicted his death, he did so with a general statement and predicted the resurrection of himself and of others too (cf. Mark 8.31; 9.31; 10.33–4).[11] We must conclude that Jesus' 'glory' refers to his supreme position in the kingdom of God, after the resurrection, when the twelve would judge the twelve tribes of Israel.

We can also gain some insight from Luke 12.8–9//Matt. 10.32–3, cf. Mark 8.38//Luke 9.26. We can reconstruct the original sayings as follows:[12]

כל די יודי בי קדם אנשא בר אנש יודי בה קדם מלאכיא
די אלהא, וכל די יחפר בי קדם אנשא בר אנשא יחפר בה
קדם מלאכיא די אלהא.

> Everyone who acknowledges me before (a) man/men, a/the son of man will acknowledge him before the angels of God, and everyone who denies me before (a) man/men, a/ the son of man will deny him before the angels of God.

These sayings have two settings, the ministry of Jesus on earth, and the final judgement. People's attitude to Jesus on earth now will determine their fate in the final judgement, which is again indicative of the centrality of Jesus' position in the Jesus movement, and of its supreme importance. The final judgement is portrayed in a traditional way, with the heavenly court consisting of angels surrounding God (cf., for example, Dan. 7.9–14). It is supposed that there will be witnesses in the heavenly court, just as there are in an earthly one. Jesus refers to himself with the idiomatic use of בר (א)נש(א), which has two levels of meaning. At one level, this supposes that many people will acknowledge or deny the person on trial, depending on their attitude to Jesus during the period of the ministry. We have seen that to function in this idiom, the general

[11] Casey, 'General, Generic and Indefinite', 40–9.
[12] Casey, *Son of Man*, pp. 161–4, 193–4, 230–2.

level of meaning does not have to be true of everyone, and this is so here. The witnesses are everyone who matters, which in effect means the restored Israel. At the same time, there is a primary reference to Jesus himself. He will play a decisive role as witness at the final judgement. This would be the same general situation as when the twelve would sit on twelve thrones judging the twelve tribes of Israel.

This gives us a somewhat better idea of what Jacob and John meant when they referred to Jesus' glory (הדרך). They had in mind the events of the last times. They would sit at table with Jesus and the rest of the twelve, when they had risen from the dead. Jesus would be the decisive witness before the heavenly court in the judgement of people who had been faced with his decisive and divisive earthly ministry, and the twelve would sit on twelve thrones judging the twelve tribes of Israel. This is the cultural context for their request to sit on Jesus' right and left, and in that cultural context it is a much more intelligible and indeed reasonable request than commentators have generally allowed.

Jesus' reply is something of a rebuke, but not as severe a rebuke as commentators like to think. He began, לא ידעתון מא דשאלתון: 'You do not understand what you have asked.' This is not a declaration of their absolute incompetence, but an introduction to an exposition of what their request would involve, as we must infer from their response to his question in verse 39. Gundry argues that their question 'underscores their ignorance of his approaching passion', and Lane that 'they have understood his intention very superficially'.[13] There is no justification for these comments. On the contrary, their answer to Jesus' question shows that they understood his intentions perfectly well. Gundry cites Peter's protest after an earlier prediction (Mark 8.31–3) in favour of his view, but the main point is that Jacob and John's reaction is *different* from that of Peter, and this will be partly because Mark is correct in placing it later. It is very unfortunate that the help we might have got from having his next comment in Aramaic is not available to us, because we do not know what words he used where Mark uses βάπτισμα and βαπτίζομαι. We can, however, make a reasonable start with the 'cup', which has clear cultural resonances, not seriously different in Aramaic and in Greek.

---

[13] R. H. Gundry, *Mark: A Commentary on his Apology for the Cross* (Grand Rapids, 1993), p. 576: W. L. Lane, *The Gospel of Mark* (London, 1974), p. 378.

Jesus used this metaphor again, when he prayed to God his Father to take away 'this cup', evidently meaning his forthcoming suffering and death (Mark 14.36). We can be doubly sure that this is in mind at Mark 10.38–9, because it is taken up more explicitly at Mark 10.45, where a/the son of man is to give his life as a ransom for many. There is enough Jewish material to explain Jesus' use of this metaphor. In a massive expansion at Deut. 32.1, *Tg. Neofiti* has Moses say of בני נש, 'sons of men', 'people', דמייתין וטעמין כסא דמותה, 'who die and taste the cup of death'.[14] Similar expressions are found at *Tg. Neof.* Gen. 40.23, in other Targumic traditions to both passages, and at T. Abr. xvi. These texts are too late in date to have influenced Jesus, but they come from the same culture and should therefore be allowed as a proper illustration of the metaphor which he used. In the Hebrew Bible, the cup may refer to the wrath of the Lord: especially striking is Isa. 51.17, 22, where this cup is drunk by Jerusalem. This is the cup which was to be drunk by Jesus, and which Jacob and John declared their willingness to share.

There is similar material about the Maccabean martyrs, who were perceived to be in a similar position to Jesus. They died a death which they did not deserve, for they were righteously keeping covenant faith with God, but they took upon themselves the wrath of God and thereby enabled him to deliver Israel. The basis of this material is already present in the contemporary work, the book of Daniel. Their deaths are predicted at Dan. 11.35:

$$\text{ומן המשכילים יכשלו לצרוף בהם ולברר וללבן עד־עת}$$
$$\text{קץ כי־עוד למועד}$$

This text evidently supposes that their deaths will have a beneficial effect. Their reward is at Dan. 12.2–3, where they will be among those who rise from the dead and shine like the stars of heaven. To put it differently, they will be in glory. This position is further elaborated in subsequent literature.[15] For example, in 2 Maccabees we find the martyrs bearing the wrath of God. This is a different metaphor from our passage, but the same basic notion as that of Jesus, Jacob and John drinking the cup. The metaphor of the cup is used with reference to his forthcoming martyrdom by Isaiah at Mart. Isa. 5.14. Here Isaiah sends the other prophets

---

[14] R. le Déaut, 'Goûter le calice de la mort', *Bib* 43, 1962, 82–6.
[15] See pp. 213–16 below.

away, saying 'God has mingled the cup for me only.' Though this document is extant only in late texts, it is very probable that it is an independent Jewish use of the metaphor of the cup from approximately the time of Jesus.

We must therefore reach a definite conclusion about Jesus' question to Jacob and John, and their affirmative response. Being close to him in glory entailed giving their lives with him, taking on themselves the wrath of God so that God would be enabled to establish his kingdom.

It is in this light that we must make a much more conjectural attempt to understand the metaphor of baptism. The secondary literature is aware of טבל and טבילה, but these are really Hebrew words, and they occur in Aramaic only in later Jewish Aramaic, which resulted from continued diglossia among the learned. The translator of Luke 12.50, presumably independent of Mark's translator, also used βάπτισμα and βαπτισθῆναι, but this does not tell us what made him do so. It is worth while resorting to Targums to find a word, and I set out the evidence of this case partly as an exercise in method. If we look up טבל, we find that most examples are rendered with the Aramaic טבל, but this still does not make it the right word. It is a Hebrew word, which does not occur in the Aramaic of our period: it may therefore be found in Targums because of interference among the bilinguals who produced them. Moreover, our passage requires a very vigorous metaphor that can apply to death, whereas most biblical occurrences of טבל are of a minor act of dipping, such as a priest dipping his finger in blood. It is still worth cataloguing the other Aramaic words used to render טבל:

טמש *Ps.-J.* Exod. 12.22; Lev. 4.6, 17; 14.6, 16, 51; Num. 19.18; *Tg.* Ruth 2.14; *Pesh.* 1 Sam. 14.27; *Tg.* Job 9.31.
סחא *Neof.* Deut. 33.24; *Pesh.* 2 Kgs 5.14.
פלפל *Pesh.* Gen. 37.31.
צבע *Neof.* Gen. 37.31; *Neof.*, *Pesh.* Exod. 12.22; *Neof.*, *Frg. Tg.*, *Pesh.* Lev. 4.6; *Neof.*, *Pesh.* Lev. 4.17; 9.9; 14.6, 16, 51; Num. 19.18; *Pesh.* Deut. 33.24; Josh. 3.15; Ruth 2.14; 2 Kings 8.15; Job 9.31.
רבא *Onq.* Deut. 33.24.

It is also worth considering texts where any Greek translator used βαπτίζομαι. This gives us a wider range of meaning, with more overwhelming by floods and less minor dipping:

MT בעת Isa. 21.4: *Tg.* מחד, *Pesh.* זוע.

MT טבע: טבע טבע *Pesh.* Jer. 38.22; *Pesh.*, *Tg.* Ps. 9.16; 69.3; שׁקע *Tg.* Jer. 38.22.

MT שׁטף Lev. 6.21: *Onq.*, *Neof.*, *Sam.*, *Ps.-J.* שׁטף: *Pesh.* שׁוג.

We may not choose one of these words by counting the number of occurrences. Each occurrence might be due to a genuine overlap in semantic area, so we must consider each one on its merits. In practice, however, single occurrences are often due to special circumstances specific to one passage, and the following may be eliminated without much ado: שׁוג, רבא, פלפל, טבע, זוע, אחד and שׁקע.

This leaves us with four serious candidates, צבע, סחא, טמשׁ and שׁטף, all of which occur in both Jewish Aramaic and in Syriac. טמשׁ looks promising. It has the right semantic area – Jastrow describes it as the Aramaic equivalent of טבל. However, it is absent from Old Aramaic, Middle Aramaic, the Palestinian Talmud and Christian Palestinian Syriac, so it is not probable that it was the word used by Jesus. סחא does not occur in Old or Middle Aramaic. In Jewish Aramaic it means 'wash, bathe'; in Syriac, its semantic area includes both bathing and baptism. It must therefore be regarded as a serious possibility. צבע is extant from before the time of Jesus, meaning 'dip', hence 'dye', also 'get wet', in which sense it is used of Nebuchadnezzar being wet by the dew of heaven (Dan. 4.12, 20, 22, 30; 5.21). It continued in use in Jewish Aramaic and in Syriac. It is used for βαπτίζομαι in this passage by the Palestinian Syriac lectionary, which has מצבועיתא for βάπτισμα: both words are used elsewhere in Palestinian Syriac. These may be the words which Jesus used. שׁטף has the right semantic area. In Jewish Aramaic, it means 'wash', and in some late poetry it is used euphemistically for 'die'. It is not, however, extant in early sources. The real possibilities are therefore טבל, טמשׁ, סחא, צבע and שׁטף. The strongest candidates are perhaps טבל and צבע, but the major effect of this discussion is to underline the scanty nature of our evidence. In the above reconstruction I have opted for טבל and טבילא. We have extant the noun as well as the verb, and both are within a conservative estimate of the probable cultural resonances of Jesus' expression.

There is only a low degree of probability that this is right. The purpose of putting these words in is to complete the reconstruction of the passage as a whole, and thereby facilitate the process of seeing the whole passage in its original cultural context. This is a case where finding the Aramaic word is of no assistance to our exegesis, because there is too little Aramaic extant for us to find the word at all. It is fortunate that this does not happen often, and that it usually happens with unimportant words: otherwise the whole enterprise of doing Aramaic reconstructions would be pointless.

This leaves us with the following conclusions. Jesus referred to the suffering and death of himself, Jacob and John with two metaphors. The first reference began approximately התיכלון למשתא כסא דאנה שתה. This reconstruction has helped us to locate the cultural resonances of Jesus' metaphor. Jesus also used a second metaphor, which amplified the reference to his death and made the Greek translator feel that βαπτίζομαι and βάπτισμα were suitable renderings in Greek. We cannot be sure which words Jesus used, or the translator read. We therefore have to be content with the above description of the cultural resonances of Jesus' predictions, and cannot use an Aramaic original to draw them out further.

This brings us to the brief recorded reply of Jacob and John: ניכול. This has two remarkable features. Firstly, Jacob and John must have understood what they were asking for a great deal better than commentators have allowed. They must have understood the metaphorical references to Jesus' death. It follows that Mark is right to place this incident after some of the passion predictions. They also show no surprise at Jesus' question. They must therefore have understood that to sit on Jesus' right and left in his glory would entail suffering and death for them in the present life. That two of the inner circle understood this ought not to be a surprise. That it is a surprise stems partly from overliteral interpretation of Jesus' initial comment, Οὐκ οἴδατε τί αἰτεῖσθε. We should also remember that some Galileans were famous for their readiness to die, in circumstances which they saw as service to God (Jos. *AJ* XVIII.23–4, cf. XVIII.4–10; XX.102; *BJ* II.433ff.).

The second remarkable point is the simplicity of their affirmative answer. This is in striking contrast to Peter earlier in the story. When Jesus first predicted his suffering and death, Peter tried to rebuke him, and earned a stinging rebuke himself instead. We read this in Mark 8.31–3 because it was memorable, and it will have been very memorable to the inner circle of the disciples at the time. We must infer that Jacob and John had taken this to heart. This is how they had come to accept that Jesus must suffer and die. They will also have taken to heart teaching such as that in Mark 8.34–5, even if it was literally delivered on other occasions. We shall see that, at his final Passover, all the considerable number of disciples present had taken this on board. Led by Peter, they affirmed that they would die with him (Mark 14.29–31).

Jesus then affirms that Jacob and John will indeed share his fate. His affirmation of this is as straightforward as possible, and very inconvenient for Christians who wish to believe their tradition of the uniqueness of his atoning death. For example, Lane declares that his suffering and death 'belong to the unique messianic mission of the Son of Man'.[16] This contradicts the text, in which Jesus bluntly declares 'you will drink the cup which I drink': and it presupposes the understanding of 'Son of Man' as a Christological title clean contrary to the use of (א)שׁנ(א) בר in the language which Jesus spoke.

It has often been suggested that Jesus' prediction was a vaticinium ex eventu.[17] This extraordinary view should not be accepted. There is no early evidence that John son of Zebedee was martyred. By the time that later evidence was produced, the tradition that he lived to a ripe old age in Ephesus had been established for centuries. The tradition is secondary, but it was widespread by the end of the second century and became universal in the third.[18] This tradition would surely not have been produced if John had really been martyred in accordance with a scriptural prophecy attributed to Jesus. Accordingly, the very late evidence, mostly ambiguous or barely coherent, should not be interpreted to mean that he was martyred. In any case, stray pieces of evidence of very late date are always more likely to be mistakes than semi-miraculous preservation of authentic tradition. Secondly, if the early church or Mark were responsible for this pseudo-prophecy, they would surely have said something closer to their needs. By the time of Paul, baptism was into Christ's death (Romans 6) because his death was *different* from everyone else's, and martyrdom did not convey the same kind of function. The church also shows no interest in such matters as sitting on Christ's right and left.

The Aramaic reconstruction of verse 40 permits a simple solution to the mundane problems posed by Mark's Greek. להן may reasonably be reconstructed behind ἀλλά, because there is a large overlap

---

[16] Lane, *Mark*, p. 379.
[17] See, e.g., A. Loisy, *Les Evangiles Synoptiques* (Ceffonds, 1907), vol. II, pp. 237–8; Bultmann, *Geschichte*, p. 23.
[18] Casey, *Is John's Gospel True?*, pp. 154–70.

in semantic area, which explains the rendering, and it makes excellent sense. It means 'except' as well as 'but'. Once we realise this, the end of the sentence is normal, not drastically abrupt as Mark's Greek is. We have a straightforward Aramaic sentence in which Jesus says that he can only give the places on his right and left to those for whom this has been prepared. The passive אתתקן refers indirectly to the activity of God, who will decide who sits on Jesus' right and left. This provides another argument for Markan priority. Mark's Greek is easy to explain as a literal translation of his Aramaic source: that it arose from omitting τοῦτο and ὑπὸ τοῦ πατρός μου from Matthew is not credible.

Mark's Greek word for 'left' is εὐωνύμων (as at 15.27), whereas in verse 37 he has ἀριστερῶν (here only). Gnilka interprets this as evidence of a change of narrator.[19] We should not follow this, because translators do use two different words to translate a single one in the same passages, if they have both words in their idiolect. A precise parallel is found at 2 Chr. 4.6–8. The MT has מִשְׂמֹאול three times. The LXX translator put ἐξ ἀριστερῶν at 4.6, 7, and ἐξ εὐωνύμων at 4.8.

Jesus evidently did not know the identity of the people who would be on his right and his left, so we can only conjecture. Adam, Abraham, Moses and Peter should be among those who come to our minds. Moreover, Jacob and John have not been excluded. Our unresolvable conjectures have one useful function: they should remind us of how important this future occasion would be.

It is conventional to divide the passage into two between verses 40 and 41. One argument is the Markan nature of the supposed connecting links. For example, Best comments, 'Verses 41, 42a are in large part, if not entirely, Markan: ἄρχεσθαι is employed as an auxiliary and we have a participial form of προσκαλεῖσθαι with a verb of saying.' A second major argument derives from the partial parallel at Luke 22.24–27. Best comments, 'Verses 42b–45a are found in another form in Lk. 22.24–7 showing that they possessed independent existence at some period in their transmission.'[20] The omission of part or all of Mark 10.45 follows. Wellhausen already claimed that it was out of its context in Mark. He roundly declared that the change from service to redemption was a μετάβασις εἰς

[19] J. Gnilka, *Das Evangelium nach Markus* (2 vols., EKK II/1–2. Solathum/ Düsseldorf/Neukirchen, [4]1994), p. 99.
[20] E. Best, *Following Jesus: Discipleship in the Gospel of Mark* (JSNT. SS 4. Sheffield, 1981), p. 123, with some technical bibliography.

ἀλλὸ γένος, to be understood in the context of the Last Supper. Loisy suggested that Mark borrowed the theory of redemption, alien to the thought of Jesus, from Paul.[21]

These suggestions have often been repeated, but none of them should be regarded as convincing. In the first place, ἤρξαντο does little more than introduce ἀγανακτεῖν. We have seen that this is characteristic of the Aramaic שׁרי, and I have noted an example in Mark's Aramaic source at Mark 2.23.[22] Best never explains *why* auxiliary ἄρχομαι is a feature of Mark's Greek. This is surely because he took it from Aramaic tradition, and it is because it is much commoner in Aramaic than in Greek that Matthew and Luke reduced the number of examples so drastically (of Mark's twenty-six examples of ἄρχομαι plus infinitive, Matthew keeps six and Luke two: altogether, Matthew has about eleven, and Luke about twenty-five). The verb προσκαλοῦμαι is absolutely normal Greek, and if Mark or his translator did not use participial forms before verbs of saying, he would have more καίς than ever. If Mark was his own translator, his Greek will obviously have had the same features when he was translating as when he was editing, except that the process of translation will have increased the amount of interference. It follows that Best's reasons do not demonstrate that verses 41–42a are editorial.

Secondly, the partial parallel to this passage at Luke 22.24–7 does not show that part of our passage existed independently at any stage. It presupposes two features of Mark 10.35–45, which it does not mention because the Lukan setting is clear enough for them to be taken for granted. Unlike the Markan account of the Last Supper, that of Luke is addressed to the twelve alone. Hence Luke 22.24–7 must be addressed to them, but there is no mention of Jacob, John or the twelve. Further, Mark 10.45 is a decisive reason for associating Jesus' teaching with his death, but it is omitted by Luke, whose account of the dispute between the disciples is not properly motivated from beginning to end, not least because he omits the whole incident arising from Jacob and John's question. The Lukan version has also been straightened out in Greek: οἱ δοκοῦντες ἄρχειν has been replaced with the more straightforward βασιλεῖς, and Luke uses the specifically Greek εὐεργέται. The specifically Lukan introduction begins with one of

---

[21] Wellhausen, *Evangelium Marci*, p. 91; Taylor, *Mark*, ad loc.
[22] See pp. 29, 85, 183 above.

his favourite expressions, ἐγένετο δε. The Lukan version contains no other significant Semitisms, unless we follow the western text at Luke 22.27, with Black's suggestion that ηὐξήθητε represents רביתון, which resulted from a misreading or misunderstanding of רבעתון.[23] The western text is difficult, and it is not probable that its longer parts should be sorted out with this combination of creativity and puns. This is more probably a scribal actualisation of the text with reference to the disciples: 'in my service, you grew like one who serves', thereby following his example of service. We should therefore conclude that there are no clear Semitisms in the Lukan account. We thus have an argument of cumulative weight against the independence and authenticity of the Lukan version, even before we have considered the details of Mark's Aramaic source.

Thirdly, Mark 10.45 is perfectly placed where it is, and by no means specifically Pauline. Service and martyrdom are intertwined throughout the passage. This is because of the way it begins, with a request for superiority and Jesus' view that a leading role in the Jesus movement should involve martyrdom. It is entirely logical that this should lead him to give both further teaching on service and a final declaration that a whole group of people should be prepared to devote their lives to others to the point of death. Moreover, we shall see that when reconstructed in Aramaic, Mark 10.45 has a general level of meaning which monoglot Greek-speakers would not notice unless they were told. This links up directly with Jesus' response to Jacob and John, and thereby binds the passage together in a way that is not obvious in Greek. This is an especially powerful argument for the original unity of the whole passage. It also makes Pauline derivation especially unlikely. Moreover, it is notorious that Paul never uses ὁ υἱὸς τοῦ ἀνθρώπου, and he never uses λύτρον either.

We can now turn to the details of the second half of this passage. When Jesus has finished his short speech, we are told that the other ten of the twelve were annoyed with Jacob and John. The situation gives enough grounds for their annoyance, and it is perhaps more probable that it was Peter's primacy which was felt to have been challenged, rather than democratic assumptions which are more at home in our culture than in theirs. A similar problem is indicated at Mark 9.33–5. There is a problem with the actual word. I have

---

[23] Black, *Aramaic Approach* ([3]1967), pp. 228–9.

suggested לאתזעפא for Mark's ἀγανακτεῖν, because the Aramaic word זעף has the right semantic area (it is consequently used here by the Christian Palestinian Syriac lectionary). It does not occur in Aramaic before or in the Dead Sea scrolls. In the absence of a better word, however, it is best to regard this as coincidental, in view of the still small quantity of early evidence extant.

Jesus then called the twelve to him, which is natural because a potential quarrel needed defusing with further teaching imposed by the leader himself. Jesus began by defining bossy behaviour as alien, indeed as un-Jewish. In Mark's Greek, δοκοῦντες has caused problems, for its semantic area includes 'seem', and some commentators consider this usage ironical.[24] I have suggested that it renders סבר. The Aramaic סבר is used of the intentions of people who proceed to carry their intentions out (cf. Dan. 7.25, and as a loanword in Hebrew, Esther 9.1). It has a genuine overlap with the semantic field of δοκέω in the area approximated by the English 'think (to)', 'intend', so it is a perfectly feasible rendering. As so often, our problems with Mark's text come from treating it as if it were written by a monoglot Greek Christian. There are also technical problems with the words for dominant behaviour. I have suggested מלך under ἄρχειν, as probably at 1 En. 9.7. Here, as there, the translator may have felt that the conventional βασιλεύειν was too precise. For κατεξουσιάζουσιν, I have suggested גברין. This verb is used in an appropriate sense in later Aramaic and Syriac, and it is extant already at Sefire IIB.19, as at 1QapGen XX.18 and 4Q541 (cf. 4Q242.II.1). It will, however, be clear that the degree of certainty in these suggestions is quite low, and it may be that we have to do with less literal translation than usual, perhaps including more than one attempt at some form of שׁלט. These problems are not, however, of the kind that should be used to cast doubt on the existence of the Aramaic source. Furthermore, Jesus' rejection of foreign behaviour is so clear that we should not try to derive his teaching from scattered philosophical comments on the Hellenistic rulers whose behaviour is criticised.[25]

Jesus follows with one of those statements of fact which is also an order, which is linguistically easier when one does not have to use a verb: לא כיני ביניכון. Here I have used the Talmudic כיני, which would encourage the translator to put ἐστίν. It is, however,

---

[24] E.g. V. Taylor, *The Gospel According to St. Mark* (London, 1952), p. 443.

[25] As does D. Seeley, 'Rulership and Service in Mark 10:41–45', *NT* 35, 1993, 234–51.

possible that it was not already in use, since it is not found in earlier source material. It follows that Mark's source may have read כן, and that the translation may be explicitative. This leads in to the first main point, which defines service rather than lordship as characteristic of leadership in the Jesus community. This is a reasonable response both to Jacob and John, and to Peter and the others who found their request annoying. It leads straight into the son of man saying, which ties the whole passage together. As we have seen, the expression בר (א)נש(א) itself cannot lose its general level of meaning,[26] and we must uncover the general level of meaning to see not just what Jesus meant, but also any underlying assumptions that are not explicitly stated. It follows that אתא does not refer to the incarnation alone, but to the purpose of the lives of people in general. The next part of the saying is linked directly to the teaching which Jesus has just given. He asserts again that the purpose of life is service rather than lordship. This is not an empirical statement, but a declaration of God's purpose which the disciples are thereby ordered to carry out.

This service is then more precisely defined. This is the function of the simple ו, which may introduce a more precise version of what has been said, rather than a new point. The expression ולמנתן נפשו does not necessarily refer to death, but may include devoting one's life. We are, as it were, half-way to the final point, for פורקן חלף שגיאין must include such a reference. This is a statement of the function of martyrdom. There should be little doubt that פורקן was the original Aramaic underlying λύτρον. The verb פרק is extant at 11QtgJob XXVII.9, where it renders לחץ, apparently meaning 'set free, rescue, deliver'. It should be restored at 11QtgJob XXIII.6, which has פר[ן: this renders פדה (LXX σῶσον) of God's re-deeming/rescuing a man's soul from the Pit. At Dan. 4.24, it is used of Nebuchadnezzar doing something to his sins by righteousness: LXX and Theodotion both translate it as λύτρωσαι (Dan. 4.27), so an interpretation close to 'redeem' and analogous to λύτρον at Mark 10.45 was established long before the time of Jesus. פרק also occurs in Nabataean Aramaic at pap 5/6ḤevA nab I.10 in the first century CE, and later in both Jewish Aramaic and in Syriac. For example, it is used in a piece of Aramaic embedded in the Hebrew text of m. Ket 4.9, of a husband redeeming his wife from captivity. The noun פרקן occurs at Meg. Ta'an. 12, used of deliverance from

---

[26] See pp. 11–21 above.

the Gentiles, and later in Jewish Aramaic and in Syriac. For example, at Aphrahat, Dem. VI.14 (p. 292 line 24)[27] it renders ἀπολυτρώσεως (Eph. 4.30), meaning 'redemption'. We should infer that פּוּרְקָן was already in existence for Jesus to use, in an appropriate sense. The overlap in semantic area is so obvious that it is used to translate λύτρον by pal syr lec, sin, pesh, hark.

There has been a long tradition of associating this text with Isaiah 53, and interpreting λύτρον in the light of אָשָׁם at Isa. 53.10. Even without the above Aramaic available, Barrett and Hooker were able to show that this is not accurate.[28] Whereas λύτρον refers to the redemption of a person or thing, an אָשָׁם was offered when wrong had been done to someone else and restitution was to be made, the אָשָׁם being a guilt-offering by means of expiation. In the LXX, λυτρόω usually renders גאל or פדה, whereas at Isa. 53.10 אָשָׁם is rendered with ἁμαρτίας (Tg חובין, pesh חטהא). The Hebrew אָשָׁם is *never* rendered with λύτρον or any cognate word in the LXX, and none of the Hebrew words translated with λύτρον elsewhere in the Hebrew Bible is used in Isaiah 53. If Jesus had used אָשָׁם, a normal translator familiar with the LXX would almost certainly have used πλημμέλεια. We must not attribute to Jesus any word which involves going contrary to the evidence of our text, the semantic area of words and the known behaviour of translators. There is no mention of sins in Mark 10.35–45 because the death of Jesus, with or without Jacob, John and others, would enable God to redeem Israel; it was not to atone for the sins of individuals as in later Christian tradition. Neither נפשה nor שׁגיאין is sufficient to establish a reference to Isaiah 53, because both are too common. It remains possible that Jesus was informed by Isaiah 53, among many other texts, as he meditated on his death. This text cannot, however, have been especially prominent, because there is insufficient evidence of its use in the bottom layer of the tradition.

The use of Isaiah 53 in modern scholarship is a classic case of the hermeneutical circle, which is put with great clarity by France: 'To the Christian church the relevance of the Servant of Yahweh to the mission of Jesus has always been obvious; why should it be less

---

[27] Ed. I. Parisot, in R. Graffin (ed.), *Patrologia Syriaca*, vol. I.
[28] C. K. Barrett, 'The Background of Mark 10.45', in A. J. B. Higgins (ed.), *New Testament Essays: Studies in Memory of T. W. Manson* (Manchester, 1959), pp. 1–18; M. D. Hooker, *Jesus and the Servant* (London, 1959); C. K. Barrett, 'Mark 10.45: A Ransom for Many', *New Testament Essays* (London, 1972), pp. 20–6.

obvious to him?'[29] Because Jesus was not a Christian but a Jew, and consequently more influenced by first century Judaism than by later Christianity. Of course, he was also a vigorous and original biblical exegete, and if there were sufficient evidence that he used Isaiah 53, we would accept it. But the evidence seems sufficient to France because he is absorbed within the traditions of later Christianity. Consequently, he cannot deal with this saying in Aramaic, and must therefore miss the general level of meaning of the son of man saying and imagine the Hebrew אשם in the mouth of Jesus when neither כפר nor פורקן is sufficient to recall it.

Grimm and Hampel have suggested the use of Isa. 43.3f.; Ps. 49.8.[30] Here the linguistic overlap is stronger, but the difference in context and content is so great that direct dependence should not be accepted. That God should do something dire to Gentile nations is not properly connected with the self-sacrifice of Jesus and his disciples. For example, Isa. 43.4b reads:

ואתן אדם תחתיך ולאמים תחת נפשך

This has purely verbal equivalents of למנתן, בר אנשא, חלף and נפשה in the reconstruction proposed above, and at first sight this looks like a lot, and therefore a strong argument for literary dependence. What God is going to do in this passage, however, is to damage Gentiles in order to save Israel. This is so different from the whole idea of God delivering Israel because of the deaths of some Jews that, on further analysis, the connections must be attributed to the common element of the salvation of Israel, not to literary dependence.

The correct cultural background for understanding the atoning death of Jesus and of anyone else who might have died with him must surely be existing thought about the atoning deaths of people.[31] This underlines the unity of the passage, for the connection between the question of Jacob and John and the son of man

[29] R. T. France, *Jesus and the Old Testament* (London, 1971), p. 113.

[30] W. Grimm, *Die Verkündigung Jesus und Deuterojesaja* (Frankfurt-on-Main, [2]1981), pp. 238–55; V. Hampel, *Menschensohn und historischer Jesus: Ein Rätselwort als Schlüssel zum messianischen Selbstverständnis Jesu* (Neukirchener-Vluyn, 1990), pp. 326–34.

[31] Barrett, 'Background'; Hooker, *Servant*; J. Downing, 'Jesus and Martyrdom', *JThS* NS 14, 1963, 279–93; Barrett, 'Mark 10.45'; M. De Jonge, 'Jesus' Death for Others and the Death of the Maccabean Martyrs', in T. Baarda et al. (eds.), *Text and Testimony: Essays on New Testament and Apocryphal Literature in Honour of A. F. J. Klijn* (Kampen, 1988), pp. 142–51.

saying is the general level of meaning in the son of man saying. The main group of people concerned are the Maccabean martyrs. When faithful Jews were put to death during the Maccabean period, other faithful Jews needed to understand their deaths within the context of the purposes of God. We can see this being done already in the book of Daniel. In Daniel 7, the last chapter of the original Aramaic group of stories and visions, this goes only so far as reassurance that God will bring triumph after persecution. The same applies to the first two Hebrew visions, in chapters 8 and 9. Towards the end of the massive vision which concludes the book, however, two additional developments are found. The first (Dan. 11.35) refers again to these martyrs:

ומן המשכילים יכשלו לצרוף בהם ולברר וללבן עד־עת
קץ כי־עוד למועד

This text evidently supposes that the deaths of the righteous will have a beneficial effect. Exactly how this works could not be spelt out in detail, because this is the first positive evaluation of their deaths from a perspective which sees them within the purposes of God. The second development is their reward at Dan. 12.2–3, where they will surely be among those who rise from the dead and shine like the stars of heaven. This is close to the position which Jesus will occupy, 'in your glory', as the sons of Zebedee put it, with someone on his right and left, whether two of the twelve or not. Both these main points, the positive evaluation of the death of martyrs and their reward through resurrection, are thus established within Semitic-speaking Judaism more than a century before the time of Jesus.

This is elaborated in subsequent literature. There is some further material in 1 Maccabees, which was originally written in Hebrew in the second century BCE. In his farewell speech, Mattathias urges his sons δότε τὰς ψυχὰς ὑμῶν ὑπὲρ διαθήκης πατέρων ἡμῶν (1 Macc. 2.50). After recalling the exploits of traditional Jewish heroes, he again urges them ἀνδρίζεσθε καὶ ἰσχύσατε ἐν τῷ νόμῳ, ὅτι ἐν αὐτῷ δοξασθήσεσθε (1 Macc. 2.64). While this is not the same as the Markan passage, it does have in common with it the central notions of giving one's life for the will of God, and being glorified as a result. Of Eleazar, who died voluntarily so that he could kill an enemy elephant, the author comments, καὶ ἔδωκεν ἑαυτὸν τοῦ σῶσαι τὸν λαὸν αὐτοῦ (1 Macc. 6.44). This has the notion of self-sacrifice for the sake of Israel, and ἑαυτὸν will surely go back to נפשׁ.

The second book of Maccabees is equally early in date, and consists to a considerable degree of an epitome of the work of Jason of Cyrene. It is sometimes dismissed from consideration as background to the thought of Jesus and other Aramaic-speaking Jews, on the ground that it is hellenised, but we should not permit this. It was written, long before the time of Jesus, on behalf of the Jews of Jerusalem and Judaea who were faithful to the Law. It recommends the Jews of Egypt to keep the feast of Hanukkah, a new feast modelled on Tabernacles to commemorate the deliverance of Israel by the Maccabees, with the renewal of the observance of the Law including the cult in the Temple. It therefore does not matter if some of its thoughts about the atoning value of the deaths of the Maccabean martyrs have been partly influenced by Greek thoughts about noble deaths. It was part of observant Judaism in Jerusalem long before the time of Jesus. Its comments on the value of the deaths of Jewish heroes surely cannot have failed to penetrate Aramaic-speaking Judaism by the first century CE. If therefore this seems to be the background to some teaching attributed to Jesus, we should not regard it as inauthentic merely because we could classify it as hellenised. Rather, we should see this as the kind of hellenism that could penetrate into observant Judaism, not as anything to do with assimilation or as something that could only be said in Greek.

The accounts of martyrdoms in 2 Mac. 6–7 contain several references to resurrection. So for example, the fourth brother when at the point of death declares it right τὰς ὑπὸ τοῦ θεοῦ προσδοκᾶν ἐλπίδας πάλιν ἀναστήσεσθαι ὑπ' αὐτοῦ (7.14): Antiochus, however, will have no resurrection to life. The last brother prays that in him and his brothers the wrath of God, justly brought upon the whole nation, may cease: ἐγὼ δέ, καθάπερ οἱ ἀδελφοί, καὶ σῶμα καὶ ψυχὴν προδίδωμι περὶ τῶν πατρίων νόμων ἐπικαλ-ούμενος τὸν θεὸν ἵλεως ταχὺ τῷ ἔθνει γενέσθαι καὶ σὲ μετὰ ἐτασμῶν καὶ μαστίγων ἐξομολογήσασθαι διότι μόνος αὐτὸς θεός ἐστιν, ἐν ἐμοὶ δὲ καὶ τοῖς ἀδελφοῖς μου στῆσαι τὴν τοῦ παντοκρά-τορος ὀργὴν τὴν ἐπὶ τὸ σύμπαν ἡμῶν γένος δικαίως ἐπηγμένην (7.37–8). This also has the expression ψυχὴν προδίδωμι, used of what the martyr does. Following a similar prayer, we find Judas and his army successful, because the wrath of God had turned to mercy. The prayer is said to have included a plea to God τῶν καταβοώντων πρὸς αὐτὸν αἱμάτων εἰσακοῦσαι (8.3). Here therefore we find the martyrs bearing the wrath of God. Thus 2

Maccabees provides several close parallels to the position of Jesus, Jacob and John.

The fourth book of Maccabees is later in date and more hellenised, but it still comes from faithful Jews in the tradition of these earlier works, so it should be allowed to provide dynamic parallels to the situation of Jesus and those who might have died with him. Two passages are especially remarkable. At 6.28–9, one of the martyrs prays to God to be merciful to the whole people, and says, καθάρσιον αὐτῶν ποίησον τὸ ἐμὸν αἷμα καὶ ἀντίψυχον αὐτῶν λαβὲ τὴν ἐμὴν ψυχήν (6.29). At 17.20–2, the author even more clearly attributes the deliverance of Israel to the sacrificial death of the martyrs. He describes them as ὥσπερ ἀντίψυχον γεγονότας τῆς τοῦ ἔθνους ἁμαρτίας, and writes of τοῦ ἱλαστηρίου τοῦ θανάτου αὐτῶν. This type of development was surely just as likely to take place in Aramaic-speaking Judaism, given the view of these martyrs which we have already noted from earlier sources.

Finally, we should note that there is one document, the Community Rule from Qumran, in which people make atonement by living their lives in accordance with God's will. For example, at 1QS VIII.10 it is said of the inner group of the elect:

והיו לרצון לכפר בעד הארץ.

This is not the same as our passage, but it is a proper dynamic parallel which further illustrates that the unique teaching of Jesus arose naturally from its environment in first-century Judaism.

What about the reference of שׂגיאין? This must be deliberately generalised. If Jesus had wanted to say ישׂראל, he could have said it; and if he had wanted to declare that their deaths would atone for the sins of the world, he could readily have said כל עממיא or כל or בני אנשא or the like. To interpret שׂגיאין, we must therefore attend to the parameters of the ministry as a whole. His death would atone for Israel. Scribes and Pharisees who had counted themselves out of, rather than last into, the kingdom of heaven were out, and remarkable Gentiles who would worship subordinately in the cleansed court of the Gentiles were in. Basically, however, the covenant was between God and Israel, and that is the context in which Jesus himself saw his atoning death. We shall find further evidence of this in the account of his final Passover.

We can now see how effectively Mark 10.45 draws the whole passage together. It follows directly on from the immediately preceding teaching on service, for it carries the service required of leaders of the Jesus movement firstly to the devotion of the whole of their lives and then at once to the very point of death. This links up with Jesus' debate with Jacob and John. The general level of meaning of the term (א)בר(א)נש further reinforces Jesus' assertion that they will share his fate, and it is clear that death is included. The general level of meaning is also sufficiently loose to include the other members of the twelve. At the same time, it idiomatically refers primarily to the speaker, whose leadership in the whole incident was decisive. This general level of meaning not only is unavoidable in Aramaic, but is available only in Aramaic. We see once again that the slicing of Gospel passages into fragments depends partly on reading them in the wrong language. The cultural resonances of several points are lost when the passage is treated as the work of monoglot speakers of Greek. Another such resonance is the reward of service presupposed by Mark 10.45. It takes for granted that Jesus will be in glory, and the twelve knew when they heard him give this teaching that they would rise from the dead and be with him in glory, whether or not they already expected to judge the twelve tribes of Israel.

Finally, we must consider the work of the translator of this last verse. He had a familiar problem, the impossible translation of בר (א)נש(א). He followed his customary strategy. He knew that it referred to Jesus, so he used ὁ υἱὸς τοῦ ἀνθρώπου. The reference to Jacob and John, and less directly to the others, would be lost on uninstructed monoglot Greeks, but that could not be helped. The translator could not have done better with an impossible problem. But what about אתא? It can be read as a perfect, or as a participle with present force, and either could be used in a general statement. What should he do? He carried on with the reference to Jesus, whose death was a past event, and rendered the possible perfect with an aorist, as translators from Aramaic into Greek must be in the habit of doing. His behaviour was entirely reasonable. It is unfortunate that New Testament scholars read this translation as if it were the creation of a monoglot speaker of Greek. This ensures a meaning referring to Jesus alone in accordance with later Christian tradition, but the resonances with Jesus' own Jewish traditions and the connection with the rest of the passage have been lost.

Once again, the original source has made Jewish assumptions. Its Sitz im Leben is in the ministry of Jesus, not in the early church. Its author must be a Jew from Israel who had a genuine interest in what happened. There is nothing to tell us whether he was one of the twelve or not, though one of them must have been the ultimate source. To write an abbreviated but accurate and unvarnished account of this incident implies an early date. It is difficult to screw anything more precise out of this passage, but it would be consistent with the other passages studied if we concluded that it was probably written within ten years of the event, at most.

We have reunified this passage, and read Mark's source against the cultural background of Jesus and the twelve. It tells a completely true story of a debate between Jesus and his disciples. This debate began when Jacob and John asked to be seated at his right and left when he was in his glory. Jesus responded by saying that they would share his death. He continued with teaching on service and position in the Jesus community. Contrasting the behaviour of Gentile rulers, he gave them orders that any of them who wanted to be great among them should in fact be sure that they served the community. He concluded by drawing the whole debate together. For this purpose, he used a general statement with the idiomatic use of (א)נש(א) בר which enabled him to make particular reference to himself and the twelve as well, naturally including Jacob and John. This declares that the purpose of life is service to others, and that this must be carried up to the point of death. This presupposed that death would be followed by resurrection, when the twelve would share his glory. For further information about his view of his death and theirs, and its connection with the coming of the kingdom, we must turn to his final Passover with his disciples.

6

JESUS' FINAL PASSOVER WITH HIS DISCIPLES: MARK 14.12–26

The Last Supper has been a significant focus of interest for scholars and lay people alike. Both have usually considered it to be the occasion of the institution of the Lord's Supper, or Eucharist. The oldest narrative source of the Last Supper is agreed to be the Gospel of Mark. Jeremias argued that the Semitisms in this narrative indicate its age and authenticity. Pesch carried this argument further, distinguishing carefully between Paul's *Kultätiologie*, his 'cult aetiology', and the *berichtende Erzählung* of Mark, his 'narrative report'.[1] Pesch also brought forward further arguments for supposing that Mark's narrative had a Semitic original. The purpose of this chapter is to reconstruct and interpret Mark's Aramaic source.

12 וביום חד לפטיריא, כדי פסחא דבחין, אומרין לה
תלמידוהי, לאן צבא אנת דנאזל ונתקן לך דתאכל פסחא.
13 ושלח תרין מן תלמידוהי ואמר להון, הכו לקריתא
ויפגע בכון אנש והוא קולה דמיא שקל. אזלו אחרו,
14 ולאן יעלל, אמרו לבעל ביתא דאמר רבונא, אן בית
אבתותי אן פסחא אכל עם תלמידי?
15 והוא יהחזא לכון עלית רב, משתוא עתיד. ותמן אתקנו
לנא.
16 ונפקו תלמידוהי ואתו לקריתא ואשכחו להון כדי אמר
להון. ותקנו פסחא.
17 ורמש הוא, ואתא עם תרי עשרתא.
18 ורבעין אנון ואכלין ואמר ישוע, אמן אמר אנה להון
דחד מנכון ימסרני, הוא דאכל עמי.
19 שריו לאתעצבה ולמאמר לה חד חד, אן אנה.
20 ואמר להון, חד מן תרי עשרתא, הוא דצבע עמי בחדא

[1] Jeremias, *Eucharistic Words*; R. Pesch, *Das Abendmahl und Jesu Todesverständnis* (QD 80. Freiburg/Basle/Vienna, 1978).

מזרקה.
21 אזל בר נש ככתיב עלוהי, ואוי לאנשא הוא דבר נש
מתמסר בידה. טב לה אן לא יליד גברא הוא.
22 ואכלין אנון ונסב לחם וברך וקצא ויהב להון ואמר,
נסבו, דנה הוא גשמי.
23 ונסב כס וברך ויהב להון ואשתיו בה כלהון.
24 ואמר להון, דמי דנה, דקימא הוא, מתאשד על שגיאין.
25 אמן אמר אנה לכון דלא נוסף למשתא מפרי גפנא עד
יומא הוא דבה אשתינה והוא חדת במלכותה די אלהא.
26 והללו ונפקו לטור זיתיא.

[12]And on the first day of unleavened bread, [literally And on day one for unleavened breads] when they were sacrificing the Passover (victim), his disciples said to him, 'Where do you want us to go to, and prepare for you that you may eat the Passover?' [13]And he sent two of his disciples and said to them, 'Go to the city and a man will meet you, and he (will be) carrying a pitcher of water. Go after him, [14]and where he enters, say to the owner of the house, "The rabbi says, 'Where (is) the house of my-spending-the-night, where I will eat the Passover with my disciples?'" [15]And he will show you a large upper room, set out ready. And there prepare for us.' [16]And his disciples went forth and came to the city. And they found according as he said to them. And they prepared the Passover. [17]And it was evening, and he came with the twelve. [18]And they (were) reclining and eating and Jesus said, 'Amen I say to you, that one of you will hand me over, he who "eats" with "me".' [19]They began to be sad and to say to him one by one, 'Certainly not I!' [20]And he said to them, 'One of the twelve, he who dips with me into a dish. [21]A/The (son of) man goes as it is written concerning him, and woe to that man by whose hand a/the (son of) man is betrayed/handed over. (It would be) good for him if that man had not been born.' [22]And they (were) eating and he took bread, and said a blessing, and broke (the bread) and gave (it) to them and said, 'Take! This it/is my body.' [23]And he took a cup and said a blessing and gave (it) to them, and all of them drank in it. [24]And he said to them, 'This (is/was) my blood, it (is) of the covenant, shed for many. [25]Amen I say to you that we will not drink again from the fruit of the vine until that

day on which I drink it and it (will be) new in the kingdom
of God.' [26]And they sang the Hallel, and went out to the
Mount of Olives.

Verse 12 begins with a description of the date on the first day of
unleavened bread, when they were sacrificing the Passover. The
word πάσχα is distinctively Aramaic, part of the evidence that the
background to the oldest Gospel narratives is Aramaic rather than
Hebrew. The date is problematical. The Passover victims were
officially slaughtered on the afternoon of Thursday, 14th Nisan.
The first day of the feast of Unleavened Bread did not, however,
begin officially until dark, the Thursday evening which marked the
beginning of 15th Nisan, when the Passover was eaten (for example
Lev. 23.6; Jos. *AJ* III.249–50). Moreover, Mark seems to have got
it right only a few verses earlier. Mark 14.1 gives a date two days
before Passover and Unleavened Bread, which starts them both at
the same time. We should probably infer that Mark was not writing
freely in both verses. Several scholars, including Jeremias, have
gone further, and argued that at 14.12 Mark misread a written
Aramaic source. Jeremias has קמי before דפטיריא. He argues that
קמי meant 'before', and was wrongly taken to mean 'first', so that
Mark's source meant 'on the day before Unleavened Bread'.[2] The
expression קמי ד is, however, Talmudic in date. It is possible that
קדמי, which is extant from our period (for example Dan. 7.4),
could be used in the same two ways, but this is impossible to prove
on account of lack of evidence. Moreover, at *AJ* II.317, Josephus
has the feast of Unleavened Bread last for eight days rather than
seven, presumably including 14th Nisan, when observant Jews
removed leavened bread from the house. At m. Pes 1.4, R. Meir
and R. Judah debate how long you may *eat* leavened bread, both of
them assuming that you must burn any which is left at the
beginning of the sixth hour, which is earlier than the official time
for the sacrifice of the Passover victims. Hence at *BJ* V.99, Josephus
has the day of unleavened bread come round (ἐνστάσης) on 14th
Xanthicus. It is more probable, therefore, that our source, and
Mark, deliberately referred to 14th Nisan as the first day for
Unleavened Bread. Alternatively, both Mark and Josephus may
have been influenced by the notion that the day begins at midnight
or in the morning, which makes possible the perception that the

---

[2] *Ibid.*, p. 18.

feast of Unleavened Bread really begins on 14th Xanthicus. It follows that we cannot be certain of the exact words of our source. I have used a quite different expression from that of Jeremias, to make again some points of method. Firstly, we cannot be content with Talmudic Aramaic, which is too late in date. Secondly, existing scholarship is far too interested in producing puns and misunderstandings in texts which make good sense. Thirdly, when we reconstruct Aramaic sources, it appears at once that in a number of cases, there is uncertainty as to the exact word used. This puts in perspective attempts to use precise observations on Greek words to recover the original meaning of Jesus or of the earliest narrators: we should be much more careful to consider what we are doing. Finally, the 'original' meaning imagined by Jeremias is rather contorted. It might well be taken to mean 13th Nisan, which would mean that they sacrificed their lamb or goat on what was regarded as the wrong day, as we shall see many people did. That would be very unfortunate, to the point that Jeremias' view should be rejected.

In spite of these problems, there should be no doubt about what our source meant, or about its general accuracy. It began with a general description of the approximate time when the leavened bread was removed, and followed it up with a precise description of the time and place 'when they were sacrificing the Passover'. I do mean place as well as time. The phrase כדי פסחא דבחין conveys a massive amount of information, provided we notice that our source takes for granted basic facts about Jewish culture. Jesus and his disciples were in the inner court of the Temple. As leader of the group, Jesus slit the throat of a one-year-old lamb or goat, referred to as פסחא/πάσχα, and let its blood drain into a gold or silver bowl held by a priest (cf. m. Pes 5.5–10). The priest passed the bowl back to a priest who was beside the altar, where he dashed the blood against the base of the altar, further soaking the bottom of his once white robes. The air stank of blood and of burning fat, somewhat covered by incense. The Levites, and perhaps many other people, sang the Hallel psalms, to the accompaniment of trumpets and other musical instruments. This did not sound like Handel's *Messiah*. To our ears, it would be a strange, loud and raucous noise. The animal was flayed, and the next major step was obvious: it had to be taken to the place where it was to be eaten, and there it had to be roasted and so on. Jesus' disciples had to ask where this was, because they did not know. Mark has already told us the

reason for this – chief priests and scribes were seeking to kill him
(Mark 11.18; 12.12; 14.1–2, 10–11), a fact that would be obvious to
a man who had cleansed the Temple and taken part in the
subsequent arguments with them (Mark 11.15–17, 27–33;
12.1–11), especially as he had more theological reasons for expecting to die.[3]

New Testament scholars have not generally been sympathetic to
this cultural context. For example, Taylor, with no thought for the
Aramaic background he has just discussed, announces that the
imperfect ἔθυον 'denotes repeated action': on that basis, he translates 'when it was customary to sacrifice the Passover lamb'.[4] This
arbitrary use of Greek grammar to remove the action from its
known setting should not be accepted. First-century Jews, who
included all the earliest Christians from whom alone any authentic
traditions about these events could originate, knew what the main
public ceremony of this major pilgrim feast was: the sacrifice of
lambs and goats. This was indeed a repeated action: it was done
several thousand times every year; but this is no reason for
imagining Jesus and his disciples anywhere other than where the
originators of the tradition knew they were, in the Temple. We
must translate, 'when they were sacrificing the Passover'. Once we
anchor the story in its right place on earth, and continue with the
assumptions natural to first-century Jews giving us the information
which we find in Mark, a dramatic but entirely earthborne narrative
follows. The necessary question about where to go is naturally
asked by תלמידוהי, which does not imply all or most of the
disciples taking the initiative in any serious sense, as Mark's Greek
has sometimes been taken to mean.[5] In their question, I have
followed Bezae's reading σοι, with western support, and reconstructed the idiomatic Aramaic לך. Greek copyists evidently felt it
to be redundant.

The observant Jew who wrote this source was also reassuring
himself and everyone else that Jesus sacrificed the victim on the
biblically appointed day. This could by no means be taken for
granted. The crucial piece of evidence comes from the opening of
the Mishnaic tractate *Zevahim*. We must begin with m. Zev 1.4:

הפסח ששחטו בשחרית בארבעה עשר שלא לשמו, רבי

---

[3] Pp. 199–205, 211–15 above.
[4] Taylor, *Mark*, p. 537.
[5] See, e.g., Gundry, *Mark*, p. 821.

יהושע מכשיר כאילו נשחט בשלשה עשר. בן בתירה
פוסל, כאילו נשחט בין הערבים.

The Passover (victim) which they slaughter in the morning
on the fourteenth (of Nisan) which (is) not (sacrificed)
under its (proper) name, R. Joshua declares it valid as if it
were slaughtered on the thirteenth. Ben Bathyra declares it
invalid as if it were slaughtered 'between the evenings'
(Exod. 12.6).

The problem posed is that of the validity of a Passover victim
slaughtered during the morning of the correct day, 14th Nisan,
rather than at the official time during the afternoon, the current
interpretation of the biblically appointed time 'between the evenings' (Exod. 12.6). The victim has been sacrificed under a different
heading, and we must infer that this is *because* it was being
sacrificed at a time contrary to the biblical regulations. Ben Bathyra's judgement is what we might expect, and it is simply laid
down, without attribution, at m. Pes 5.3. Just as if one were to
slaughter it at the right time but not under its own name, which no
one in their right mind would do, so if it is slaughtered at another
time not under its own name it is not valid either. R. Joshua's
judgement is accordingly quite amazing, and so is his analogy with
victims slaughtered on the previous day. His judgement takes it for
granted that Passover victims slaughtered on the thirteenth were
valid. What is the Sitz im Leben of this judgement? It cannot be
after 70 CE, because after the destruction of the Temple it would be
better to imagine everything done in accordance with the biblical
regulations. The assumption makes excellent sense at the end of the
Second Temple period, when there were so many pilgrims in
Jerusalem that the victims could not possibly all have been sacrificed on the afternoon of 14th Nisan. It follows that everyone knew
that many victims were sacrificed on 13th Nisan, and that this was
accepted practice. R. Joshua's judgement likewise only makes sense
if many victims were actually sacrificed on the morning of 14th
Nisan. This fits in with the attributions: both may be identified as
rabbis who lived in Jerusalem before the fall. Joshua ben Hananiah
was a relatively liberal rabbi, who became important at Jabneh
after the fall. He will have been originally responsible for the
transmission of his judgement.

We are now in a position to interpret the very opening of the
Mishnaic tractate *Zevaḥim*.

כל הזבחים שנזבחו שלא לשמן כשרים אלא שלא עלו
לבעלים משום חובה, חוץ מן הפסח ומן החטאת. הפסח
בזמנו והחטאת בכל זמן.

All the sacrifices which they sacrifice which are not under
their (proper) name are valid (but they do not free their
owners from their obligation), except for the Passover
[victim] and the Sin-offering. The Passover (victim) in its
time, and the Sin-offering at any time.

The opening principle provides the explanation of how the priests
and scribes decided that Passover victims slaughtered under
another heading are valid: there was a general principle to that
effect. The second is quite clear – Sin-offerings are valid *only* if they
are labelled Sin-offerings when they are brought for sacrifice. But
why is the Passover invalid if sacrificed under another heading,
only 'in its time'? Surely no one would be so foolish as to try to
offer their Passover offering during the feast of Tabernacles? No
indeed, the point must surely be to accept that Passover victims are
valid if slaughtered under another name on 13th Nisan and the
morning of 14th Nisan.

It might be objected that sacrificing the Passover under another
heading would make it valid, but in accordance with the principle
stated it would not free the owner from his obligation, so he would
have to offer another victim, which would make the earlier sacrifice
pointless. This objection should not be sustained. It is not made in
any source I have seen, and what is crucial is that it would not
explain the exceptional place of Passover victims in the opening
statement, or the point of R. Joshua's judgement at 1.4. It may
have been the opinion of stricter rabbis, but we should infer that it
was not the practice of numerous Jews, who did not follow the
conventional practice of slaughtering their lamb or goat on the
afternoon of 14th Nisan either. Quite what they thought of the
biblical regulations we do not know. They may have been less than
fully observant, but with R. Joshua behind them and an opposing
rabbinical opinion recorded they are more likely to have had a
different exegesis of בין הערבים (Exod. 12.6). The dual/plural
could readily have been interpreted of 13th and 14th Nisan. They
would then have sacrificed their victims under a different heading
simply to get round priests whose exegesis they may have regarded
as inaccurate and very inconvenient.

We can now see why our source had to begin וביום חד לפטיריא.

It meant Nisan 14. It assumed that we know that this was the first day on which unleavened bread was eaten, and that if it drew our attention to this, we would assume that Jesus sacrificed the Passover in accordance with the biblical regulations as generally understood, in the afternoon.

Verses 13–15 give us Jesus' instructions to two unnamed disciples, transmitted to us because they are quite unexpected, and explain how Jesus succeeded in celebrating his final Passover with his disciples, despite the ultimately successful plot against his life. He sent two of his disciples, enough to carry the animal comfortably. The Aramaic מן is reflected in the ἐκ of Codex Bezae, with Latin support, removed from other manuscripts because it is not necessary in Greek. This is straightforward evidence of the originality of at least some of Bezae's Semitisms, and a reminder that we probably owe to rule-orientated Alexandrian scribes the loss of some evidence of Semitisms in the original text of the Gospels. The disciples are called תלמידוהי because they were two of his disciples, not two of the twelve. The difference between the term 'disciples' (Mark 14.12, 13, 14, 16) and 'the twelve' (verses 17, 20, also verse 10) has been used to slice this passage into different pieces, which ruins our appreciation of the cultural assumptions made by Mark's source. For example, Knox used such evidence to delineate a 'Twelve-source' and a separate 'Disciples' source': for Nineham, this terminology 'at least suggests that this section [sc. verses 12–16] is a late-comer to its present context'. So strong is the Christian tradition that only Jesus and the twelve were involved that Anderson comments on verse 17, 'The statement that **he came with the** *twelve* takes no account of the sending ahead of the two disciples in verse 13', and Gnilka concludes that verse 17 does not belong to old tradition.[6]

None of this should be regarded as convincing. Throughout this narrative, Mark says the twelve when he means the twelve, and the disciples when he refers to a wider group. It was very important that Judah of Kerioth was one of the twelve (Mark 14.10); that all the twelve came with Jesus to the Last Supper (14.17); and that Jesus foretold his betrayal by one of the twelve (14.20). There was, however, no need for the twelve to roast the goat, or lamb, so

---

[6] W. L. Knox, *The Sources of the Synoptic Gospels. I. St Mark* (Cambridge, 1953), chs. 2, 14; D. E. Nineham, *Saint Mark* (Harmondsworth, 1963), p. 376; Anderson, *Mark*, p. 310; Gnilka, *Markus*, vol. II, p. 235.

disciples who did not belong to the twelve asked for detailed instructions at the appropriate moment, and carried them out (14.12, 13, 16). As we shall see, the exclusion of women and other faithful disciples would have been so remarkable as to be worthy of mention: the two were to ask for a room for Jesus to eat 'with my disciples' (14.14) because more than the twelve were there.

There is a problem with the directions, which I have not been able to resolve. Given that they were in the Temple in Jerusalem, הכו לקריתא may have told the disciples exactly where to go, but I have not been able to confirm this. The man will have been recognisable because water-pots were normally carried by women, an assumption which our author took for granted. We shall see that cultural assumptions of this kind are essential for understanding this source. The man will have been looking out for them, and the nature of these arrangements surely implies that they were a mode of escaping detection. Again, the use of רבונא, rather than any clear identification of Jesus, must surely have been to ensure that, having got away safely from the Temple in the massive crowd, the two disciples could not be secretly followed, and the final Passover interrupted by their arrest. It also functions as a safety device, if by some mischance there should be another man waiting, carrying a water-pot.

The word κατάλυμα is a problem, but it should be considered a minor one. Its eight LXX occurrences with clear underlays represent six or seven different Hebrew words, and there is no obvious equivalent in the Aramaic of our period or earlier. I have therefore selected a later Aramaic expression, one of which a literal translation would not be sensible, so κατάλυμα would be a good solution to the problem posed by בית אבתותי. The degree of certainty is, however, negligible. Fortunately, this makes no serious difference.

There is one more precious piece of information to be gleaned from verse 15. Why a *large* upper room? Not for thirteen men to stretch their legs, not with Jerusalem bursting at the seams. The large upper room makes good sense only if there were to be many people there. This is confirmed at verse 17, where Jesus comes with the twelve, making fifteen people actually mentioned by our source. There is further confirmation at verse 20, where the definition of the traitor as one of the twelve is not very sensible if only the twelve were there. We must infer the presence of a sizeable group of disciples. Women are not mentioned because the presence of women at Passover is too obvious to be worthy of mention. Jesus was not likely to have excluded some of his most faithful followers from his final Passover, and had he really determined to celebrate his final Passover with only the twelve, he would have had a remarkable reason, and our source would surely have remarked upon his remarkable behaviour. It follows that we do not know how big the company was. If we imagine thirty, we have a margin of error, but if we follow the conventional thirteen, we are simply wrong. It is probable enough, but less certain, that there were children there too. In that case, one of them will have asked for, and received, an explanation of the feast (cf. Exod. 12.26; m. Pes 10.4).

Verse 16 records the success of the arrangements, ending with the preparation of the Passover. We are not told unwanted detail, and we should not infer, for example, that the disciples did not speak to the man and followed without his knowing.[7] Our source makes only the main point, that, despite the extremely difficult circumstances noted earlier in Mark's narrative, Jesus and his disciples took part in the public celebration of Passover, and ensured by stratagem that they could eat the meal itself before his arrest. The word אחספ/πάσχα again refers to the lamb or goat, which has now been mentioned four times.

After this very clear statement that, following the slaughter of the Passover victim, two disciples went and prepared it, neither our source nor Mark himself had any reason to repeat, between verses 17 and 25, that this is a Passover meal. The notion that these verses formed a separate source is based on no firm evidence, but on an abstracted notion that Gospel narratives were handed down in small pieces. This is a most unsatisfactory frame of reference, into which differences between verses 12–16 and 17–25 have been fitted as if *any* difference in successive episodes proved a different source, and could not rather be due to conveying significant information. This applies particularly to the important information that Jesus came with the twelve, when it was evening. He came to eat at that time because it was a Passover meal, and this had to be eaten after dark. The twelve are mentioned here because it was important that they were all present, a reasonable perception when one of this inner group was about to betray him, and all the other eleven ran away when he was arrested.

Our source passes to the meal itself. 'And they (were) reclining

---

[7] T. A. Mohr, *Markus- und Johannespassion* (AThANT 70. Zurich, 1982), p. 150.

and eating' tells us that the Passover meal had begun. Jeremias noted that reclining was a significant feature of Passover meals, and scholars who have disputed the relevance of this, by pointing out that people reclined on some other occasions, have missed the point.[8] Several features of this narrative provide an argument of cumulative weight for its being a Passover meal, the decisive point being the clear designation of this meal as a Passover meal in the account of the preparation for it. It is methodologically unsound to take small points like reclining one at a time, argue that there are circumstances where each separately might take place, declare verses 12–16 are really from somewhere else, and find ourselves left without the Passover meal so carefully prepared for in the beginning of this passage.

The next important event is the shocking fact of the forthcoming betrayal of Jesus to the authorities who were so obviously out to get him. The first form of the prediction has חד מנכון, an appropriate form for the first announcement. For παραδώσει, I have continued to use סמר,[9] despite the lack of attestation in the Aramaic of the right period. It is abundantly attested in later Jewish Aramaic with the right semantic area, and it was felt so appropriate in Christian Palestinian Aramaic that the Palestinian Syriac Lectionary uses it at points including the passages parallel to this, Matt. 26.21, 24; Luke 22.21–2. It is also found in Samaritan Aramaic and in Syriac. It is therefore very probable that its lack of attestation earlier is due to our still rather meagre Aramaic sources, which do not discuss the betrayal of anyone.

Mark's definition of the traitor as ὁ ἐσθίων μετ' ἐμοῦ looks odd at first sight, but we should follow those commentators who see the key to this expression in Ps. 41.10. I have suggested an underlying הוא דאכל עמי, which has the same effect of singling out one person, yet by means of an activity which all those present were doing. The particular person referred to, however, is the person of the psalm, 'the man of my peace, in whom I trusted, who eats my bread, he has made great his heel against me'. That is a reasonable description of one of the twelve betraying Jesus: the reference to bread has been altered, because the unleavened bread had not yet

---

[8] E.g. G. Ogg, 'The Chronology of the Last Supper', in D. E. Nineham et al., *Historicity and Chronology in the New Testament* (London, 1965), pp. 75–96, at p. 85.

[9] So, for example, Lindars, *Jesus Son of Man*, pp. 68–9; Casey, 'General, Generic and Indefinite', 40–2; Hampel, *Menschensohn*, pp. 288–300.

been started. We shall see this matter taken up again at verse 20. The betrayal of Jesus by Judah of Kerioth could be seen at Ps. 41 verse 7: 'And if he comes to see me, his heart speaks falsehood, he gathers wickedness, he goes outside, he speaks of it.' This gets Judah to the chief priests and scribes, who may be seen at verse 8: 'All those who hate me whisper together against me, they devise evil against me.' Their intention is given in verse 9, together with their denial of Jesus' resurrection, a denial equally comprehensible in Sadducees who did not believe in the resurrection and in scribes and Pharisees who thought that he was too wicked to go to heaven: 'A thing of Belial will constrain him, and when he lies down, he will not rise again.' Then Judah of Kerioth, as we have seen, at verse 10, 'Yes, the man of my peace, in whom I trusted, who eats my bread, has made great his heel against me.' There follows a plea for resurrection in verse 11, 'And you, LORD, be gracious and raise me up.'

All this is surely too simple, and too extensive, to be unintentional. We must infer that everyone knew psalm 41, and that the betrayal of Jesus was written in scripture. No one suggested that they could prevent him from being betrayed. Simon the Rock had remonstrated with him once, and earned a very severe rebuke. Subsequently, Jacob and John had accepted promptly the notion that they would die with him (Mark 10.39). We will notice also that the plea for resurrection, unlike the original form of his predictions, is a plea for him alone to be raised. Like them, it uses the verb קום, and is consequently quite opaque as to the mode of raising. The verse is also quite opaque as to time. This is one of the scriptures which the disciples could hardly avoid returning to after the crucifixion, when they came to believe that God had indeed raised him up, according to the scriptures. It was not, however, picked up by Matthew. Without the reference, the description is not sensible, since several people were eating with him. Matthew therefore removed this phrase and inserted Matt. 26.25, which identifies Judas himself as the traitor. That Mark himself should remove Matt. 26.25, and add in Greek ὁ ἐσθίων μετ' ἐμοῦ, is not credible. We have another small argument in favour of Markan priority.

Despite all this, a group of normal human beings began to be sad, and to say one at a time, אן אנה, 'Certainly not me!' There is no very literal equivalent of Mark's μήτι. I have suggested the equally idiomatic אן, of which there is no literal and accurate translation. Some translators of the equivalent Hebrew אם preferred εἰ (for example LXX Ps. 94.11, for the Hebrew אם at MT Ps. 95.11, and so at Heb. 3.11), which is overliteral to the point of being unsatisfactory Greek. Some translators did, however, produce various negatives (for example μή Gen. 21.23; ἤ, after preceding μή, Num. 11.12; οὐκ 1 Sam. 24.22; ἤ μὴν οὐκ Num. 14.23; οὐ μή Gen. 42.15), and this is where Mark's translator belongs. The Greek μήτι has a range of meaning which includes a fairly strong denial. Mark's translator therefore did as well as possible, and we should accept the more vigorous form of denial into the historical record. It is not probable that μήτι would be used by a monoglot Greek-speaker writing freely, because he would be more likely to ensure an unambiguously stronger form of denial. μήτι is not sufficiently like אן or any other Aramaic term to be a result of interference in a bilingual writing freely. The use of μήτι therefore adds cumulative weight to the argument that the Markan account is translated from a written Aramaic source. The unsatisfactory Greek εἷς κατὰ εἷς must therefore be understood likewise as a translation of חד חד. This kind of interference, always possible in the normal speech of a bilingual, is doubly likely in translation, because the translator always has the text in the host language in front of him to increase the interference.

We should take שְׁרִיו, 'They began', literally. As *disciples* began to affirm that they would not betray him, Jesus narrowed down the group from whom the traitor came to the inner circle of twelve. This makes no sense if only the twelve were present. With a bigger group, thirty, or more, possibly fewer, it makes excellent sense, defining the scriptural prediction, making the betrayal the more shocking, yet also reassuring faithful disciples that their affirmations were accepted. I have again followed Bezae, this time with the support of the majority of manuscripts, in reading ἐκ, which is unnecessary in Greek, but a possible and perfectly natural translation of מן. The rest of the definition is more difficult. I suggest that it was intended to take the reference to Ps. 41.10 further. Mark has ὁ ἐμβαπτόμενος μετ'ἐμοῦ εἰς τὸ ἕν τρύβλιον. We should read ἕν with B C* Θ 565, because τὸ ἕν is a translation of חדא. Mark's source, בחדא מזרקה, means simply 'into a dish'. This is another piece of evidence that Mark had an Aramaic source. The article ὁ is the problem, for, like ὁ ἐσθίων in verse 18, ὁ ἐμβαπτόμενος appears grammatically to pick out a single person, whereas the content of the phrase refers to an activity which several people were doing. I have suggested that we reconstruct Mark's source in the same way, to give a second reference to Ps. 41.10. We have seen that the first reference, at Mark 14.18, had to omit the bread. This second reference reminds everyone of it, everyone, that is, to whom the daily life of first-century Judaism was real daily life. At hundreds of normal meals, all the twelve had dipped bread with Jesus into a dish. On Passover night alone, they dipped into the dish without bread. This reference singles out the traitor as a man dipping into a dish with Jesus, thereby reminding the whole company how often he had dipped bread with Jesus, and locating him as 'the man of my peace . . . who eats my bread' (Ps. 41.10).

A full discussion of Judah's motivation cannot be undertaken here, but some brief comments must be made for the sake of clarity. The crucial event was the Cleansing of the Temple.[10] It was an ambiguous event in the sense that it could be seen as disrupting the arrangements for the collection of the Temple tax, and for the sale of sacrificial birds at a major pilgrim feast. It caused the chief priests and scribes to take the final action against Jesus. We should infer that it was the last straw for Judah as well. The chief priests could not arrest Jesus in public because that would cause a riot, but they were so opposed to his action that they wanted to arrest him secretly. How to do this was a grave problem which Judah solved for them by offering to betray him at a convenient opportunity (Mark 14.10–11). This opportunity arose when Jesus remained in the Garden of Gethsemane to fulfil his Passover obligation to remain in greater Jerusalem for the night. Thus the Markan narrative is consistent and coherent, and we should take it to be based on authentic tradition. It is difficult to see how Judah could have kept his hostility to Jesus' action altogether secret. We should infer that Jesus knew perfectly well that Judah would betray him, and made it known that he would be in the Garden of Gethsemane.

Once again, Matthew's editing of Mark is intelligible. He has removed the Semitism εἷς κατὰ εἷς, added the address κύριε, omitted Εἷς τῶν δώδεκα because he imagined that only the twelve were there (Matt. 26.20), added τὴν χεῖρα so that we can imagine only Judas and Jesus dipping into a dish together, and removed ἕν. That Mark should have edited Matthew to produce what we have got is a quite unreasonable supposition. In particular, the Semit-isms εἷς κατὰ εἷς and τὸ ἕν are not likely to be produced by anyone editing Matthew's perfectly sound Greek text, whereas they are

---

[10] Casey, 'Cleansing of the Temple'.

natural in a bilingual in the act of translating an Aramaic source. This further enhances the obvious arguments for the priority of Mark.

The reference to scripture is carried further at verse 21. Here the Aramaic (א)נֹשׁ(א) בר cannot lose its level of generality, though this is not the main point of the saying. Jesus can have been in no doubt that he was going to suffer a humiliating death, but this was to have a fundamental redemptive function. He therefore had good reason to state the prediction of his death in scripture, and the doom awaiting the traitor, by means of a general statement. At the same time, no one will have been left in doubt that Jesus' own death was primarily referred to. Psalm 41 is one scripture clearly in mind. Others must surely have included the second group of Hallel psalms. These include the clear general statement of Ps. 116.15, 'Glorious in the eyes of the Lord is the death of his pious ones.' Surely none of them could sing that verse without thinking of the importance of Jesus' death. They could also include themselves, in so far as they had formed, or were forming, their intention to die with him. Creative exegesis was quite normal for observant Jews, and could lead to more precise references. Part of the final Hallel psalm, Ps. 118.14–17, could easily be read like this: 'The LORD is my strength and song, and he is for me, for Jesus . . . The right hand of the LORD raises up . . . I shall not die because I shall live.' The doom pronounced on the traitor was also made by means of general statements. The first is at one level a condemnation of traitors, and hence universally acceptable. This made it feasible for Jesus to proceed with the condemnation of the traitor. This is in accordance with scriptural passages such as Ps. 40.15–16; 41.11; 118.7f. The word καλόν is a literal translation of the Aramaic טב, but it cannot function as actual evidence of an Aramaic source. Aramaic does not have a comparative, but καλόν need not be interpreted as one.[11] Further evidence genuinely is provided by the reference of ὑπάγει, which is not a normal Greek word for dying, whereas the Aramaic אזל is used with this reference. The context requires this reference to be included here.

Gundry objects to this interpretation of ὑπάγει on two grounds: the infrequency of its reference to death and the fact that אזל is not so rendered by the LXX.[12] Both objections should be regarded as

---

[11] Maloney, *Semitic Interference*, pp. 192–6.
[12] Gundry, *Mark*, p. 838: I assume that אצל is a misprint for אזל.

methodologically unsound. אזל is an extremely common word, abundantly attested in Aramaic texts written before the time of Jesus, including the Dead Sea scrolls. It is therefore quite wrong to make the validity of its use with reference to death dependent on a high proportion of its occurrences having that reference: the question at issue should rather be whether the proposed reference is securely attested, and that is not in doubt. Perhaps the most famous example is a saying of Rabbi at y. Kil 9, 4/4, 32b//y. Ket 12, 3, 35a//GenR 100, 2:

לא כמא דבר אינש אזל הוא אתי.

It is not as a son of man goes that he (will) come (again).

In this passage, the reference of אזל to death is unambiguous. There are plenty of examples of this in Jewish Aramaic and in Syriac. We should not demand that this particular reference be found in examples from before the time of Jesus, because too little Aramaic is still extant for such a detailed demand to be reasonable. It is sufficient that the word is clearly attested in earlier sources, and that the euphemistic use of it with reference to death both is clear in later sources and emerges naturally when Mark 14.21 is reconstructed. This is more important than the possible example in the very fragmentary book of Giants (it should not be read at Tobit 3.15).[13]

The LXX evidence is suspicious enough for us to analyse the occurrences, seven in Aramaic and five in Hebrew. The translator of Ezra preferred πορεύομαι for literal going (4.23; 5.8, 15), as did the translator of 1 En. 29.1. This was a possible alternative, to the point that Luke 22.22 could be an alternative translation by someone who did not understand the scriptural reference. That one biblical and one other translator preferred πορεύομαι does not, however, mean that there is anything wrong with ὑπάγει, or consequently with the proposed reconstruction: it merely illustrates that words for 'going' and 'coming' in Aramaic and Greek have several overlaps in their semantic areas. The translators of Daniel omitted the idiomatic occurrence at Dan. 2.24, which has no

---

[13] See Giants 10.25 in Beyer, *Ergänzungsband*, p. 121. אזל is read at Tob. 3.15 by Beyer, *Ergänzungsband*, pp. 137, 305, but Fitzmyer correctly restores אבב]דו, which explains the Greek translation ἀπώλοντο: see J. A. Fitzmyer, 'A. Tobit', in M. Broshi et al., *Qumran Cave 4 XIV: Parabiblical Texts, Part 2* (DJD XIX. Oxford, 1995), pp. 13–15.

genuine Greek equivalent, and is otherwise rendered with ἔρχομαι (6.20 Theod.), ἀπέρχομαι (2.17 LXX, 6.19 Theod.), εἰσέρχομαι (2.17 Theod.), probably πορεύομαι but possibly ἵστημι (6.20 LXX) and ὑποστρέφω (6.19 LXX). There are two notable features in these renderings: the use of ἔρχομαι and its compounds, and the interpretative nature of some of the renderings. ἔρχομαι and its compounds are like πορεύομαι, in that there is a genuine overlap in semantic area with אזל. It is therefore entirely reasonable that Theodotion put ἀπῆλθεν and ἦλθεν in place of ὑπέστρεψεν and ἔστη (Dan. 6.19–20). None of these renderings would be satisfactory at Mark 14.21. ἔρχομαι is not suitable because its semantic area overlaps with 'come' as well as 'go', so it would be very confusing; ἀπέρχομαι could be taken literally, which would be equally disastrous; the other renderings are more obviously inappropriate.

The five Hebrew examples of אזל reduce on inspection to three, for Prov. 20.14 belongs to an omitted section, and κατεφρόνησας at Jer. 2.36 shows that the translator derived תזלי from זלל, not from אזל. Each of the other examples is a unique figurative rendering: 1 Sam. 9.7 ἐκλείπω (which renders forty-seven different words, including הלכה, כרת and תמם several times each); Deut. 32.36 παραλύω (which renders רפא three times, and several other words once each); Job 14.11 σπανίζω (which renders אפס once, and stands in place of חתם at Dan. 9.24 LXX). It is unreasonable to expect any of these renderings to be repeated by another translator. Taken with the freer renderings of the Aramaic אזל, however, they remind us that the translator of Mark's Aramaic source did have another option – he could have translated more freely. He might, for example, have used ἀποθνήσκω. We have, however, discovered that we do not have that sort of translator. The difficulty of rendering בר (א)נש(א) had led him to form a strategy, according to which he translated it with ὁ υἱὸς τοῦ ἀνθρώπου whenever it referred particularly to Jesus, as it obviously does here. It also led him to be especially careful, and therefore generally very literal, in his rendering of the rest of the sentences containing it. From this perspective, ὑπάγει is an excellent and straightforward rendering of אזל. It would also be preferred by any translator who was forming Markan usage, for Mark has ὑπάγω fifteen times altogether, and πορεύομαι only in the compound παραπορεύομαι some four times, always literally (cf. 2.23; 9.30; 11.20; 15.29). This is just the sort of person who would choose ὑπάγει rather than πορεύεται to translate אֹזֵל at Mark 14.21. He was quite different from Luke (ὑπάγω five; πορεύομαι about fifty).

Of the five Greek renderings of the Aramaic אֹזֵל, and three of the Hebrew, only one, πορεύομαι, used at Luke 22.22, is even possible, and it is not in any way better than ὑπάγει. This illustrates once again that LXX data must be carefully analysed, not blindly followed, when applied to the behaviour of the translators of Gospel sources. At first sight, the information that אֹזֵל is never rendered with ὑπάγω in the LXX looks like an important objection to the proposed meaning and translation process; on careful examination it turns out to be of no significance whatever.

Following Jesus' condemnation of the traitor, our source moves to some time during the meal. Having told us that it is a Passover meal, it did not see fit to give an account of the meal, but rather to pick out the points it found important in it. Hence the movement straight from the announcement of the betrayal to the interpretation of the unleavened bread, the next unusual event. This has caused dreadful trouble for scholars, so we must pause to consider the nature of our source. What is omitted is not just the lamb or goat, so explicitly prepared for in verses 12–16, or only the bitter herbs. After verse 16, there is no explicit mention of the Passover, and in the whole Markan narrative, there is not a single reference to the Exodus from Egypt. Many scholars have assumed that what is not mentioned explicitly by Mark did not happen, and was not mentioned by Jesus. So, for example, we may imagine that 'none of the accounts of the Last Supper states that it was in fact a passover meal'.[14] Indeed, Mark 14.17–25 'does not even expressly mention Jerusalem', and 'there is no mention of the *lamb* that figured very prominently in the Passover ritual'.[15] With Passover gone, Mark 14.22–25 'appears to be a liturgical account derived from an early Palestinian source': thus the Markan account reveals 'the singularly original manner in which Jesus conceived the nature of His redemptive death and related the Eucharist thereto'.[16] There is no mention of the Eucharist in Mark. None the less, 'The command "Do this in memory of me" seems intended to make explicit in Luke and Paul what was already doubtless regarded as self-evident in the tradition of Mark

---

[14] M. D. Hooker, *The Gospel According to St Mark* (London, 1991), p. 338.

[15] Anderson, *Mark*, pp. 308–9.

[16] Taylor, *Mark*, pp. 663, 543.

and Matthew.'[17] 'Probably the Evangelist himself . . . regarded the Lord's Supper as the replacement for the Passover ritual meal.'[18] These quotations illustrate the social function of Gentile Christian scholarship. Mark tells us that the Jesus of history celebrated his final Passover with his disciples: 'critical' scholarship has the Eucharist instituted by the Christ of faith. We have the hermeneutical circle again!

Such assumptions have made nonsense of the narrative, with careful and explicit preparation for eating the Passover followed by eating a meal which is not a Passover meal, but which none the less contains many features of Passover meals, from beginning after dark in verse 17 to staying in greater Jerusalem at verse 26. We must take the opposite view. This source was written by an Aramaic-speaking Jew from Israel, who was writing for people who shared *his* cultural assumptions. He thought he told us that this was a Passover meal in verses 12–16. He expected us to know what a Passover meal was like. Therefore he did *not* write an account of the meal. Rather, he narrated those aspects of the meal which enable us to understand how and why Jesus died. This is why the account of the meal contains the prediction of his betrayal, which shows that he knew he would die, and how he would be arrested; the references to scripture, which show that his death was in accordance with God's will, as he knew; the interpretation of unleavened bread and wine, which explain the redemptive function of his forthcoming death, and show his knowledge of this; the prediction of the coming of the kingdom, which shows he knew he would die very soon and gives more information about the effect of his redemptive death; and the movement to the Mount of Olives, ready for further predictions and the account of his arrest. Everything else that is mentioned makes sense against the background of the Passover meal, and is mentioned only for clarity.

We may therefore reconstruct the basic elements of the Passover meal as the proper background for the comments of our source. At some stage, there will have been the story of the deliverance of Israel from Egypt, possibly recited from Exodus 12. Symbolic interpretations of the main elements of the Passover meal will have been included. According to m. Pes 10.5, Gamaliel laid down that

---

[17] X. Léon-Dufour, *Sharing the Eucharistic Bread: The Witness of the New Testament* (1982. ET New York/Mahwah, N.J., 1987), p. 84.

[18] Anderson, *Mark*, p. 308.

to fulfil the Passover obligation, mention must be made of three things, the lamb or goat, the unleavened bread and the bitter herbs. This must surely be Gamaliel I, the contemporary of Jesus. It is not probable that he gave this judgement if customs were already uniform. The same decision is explicit in the habit attributed to their contemporary Hillel, of making a sandwich of the unleavened bread, lettuce and Passover offering (t. Pes 2.22; b. Pes 115a). This is not some strict Pharisaic halakhah. The victim itself and the unleavened bread were central features of this major pilgrim feast, and the bitter herbs are biblical: 'and they shall eat the flesh that night, roasted with fire; with unleavened bread and bitter herbs they shall eat it' (Exod. 12.8). We must infer that Jesus gave traditional interpretations of the lamb or goat, and of the bitter herbs, as part of his exposition of God's redemption of Israel from Egypt. Like Gamaliel, who will have been leading a Passover group elsewhere in Jerusalem, he will have said something to the effect that we eat bitter herbs because the Egyptians embittered the lives of our fathers in Egypt. Similarly, over the Passover offering, he will have said something to the effect that this is the Passover, for our Father in heaven passed over the houses of our fathers in Egypt. He may have quoted Exod. 12.27: 'It is the sacrifice of the Passover for the LORD, who passed over the houses of the children of Israel in Egypt, when he slew the Egyptians and spared our houses.' This hermeneutical framework was essential if he was to use the interpretation of bread and wine to predict and interpret his forthcoming death. On any hypothesis, Jesus was surrounded by Jewish disciples. They had come on pilgrimage to Jerusalem to celebrate this major feast, when all Israel looked back to their deliverance from Egypt, and some at least looked forward to their deliverance in the future. He was therefore bound to make reference back to their deliverance from Egypt by the mighty hand of God, on whom alone they could rely for their deliverance in the future. He was bound to do so; everyone always did so; that he did so was not remarkable. We have the sort of source which, for that reason, did not need to mention it when it could take it for granted while it made the main points relevant to understanding Jesus' death. This is presented in two new pieces of interpretation, both of which have caused problems.

The first is the interpretation of the unleavened bread. Verse 22 begins with the resumptive ואכלין אנון, 'And they were eating'. This takes us further on into the meal. I hope it is clear from my

Aramaic reconstruction that this is a natural way to write the narrative, not a 'seam' which justifies splitting the story into pieces which can then be interpreted without their original context. The reading εὐλόγησεν καί of Bezae, with very little support, is again a literal translation of the reconstructed text, and the majority εὐλογήσας should be regarded as a secondary 'improvement'. At a normal festival meal, the leader of the group had to bless the bread when people began to eat it. This is *not* that opening blessing. It is a special blessing of God immediately prior to the symbolic presentation of Jesus' redemptive death. We should infer that Jesus had already referred to the deliverance of Israel from Egypt, with appropriate interpretation of the lamb and bitter herbs. There has been a vigorous debate concerning whether the Aramaic behind Mark's σῶμα was בשׂר or גוּף. I have suggested גשׁם. There should be no doubt that it is a very suitable word. It means 'body', and at Dan. 3.27, 28 it is used of the bodies of Shadrach, Meshak and Abednego, whose bodies were not harmed by the attempt to martyr them in the burning fiery furnace. Both the LXX and Theodotion (3.94–5) translate with σῶμα, as at Dan. 7.11. At Dan. 4.30 and 5.21, the LXX paraphrases, and Theodotion uses σῶμα again. It follows that גשׁם was in use in the language in the right sense, and would give rise to Mark's σῶμα. The same cannot be said of בשׂר. Though it would make sense in the saying of Jesus, the conventional association between σάρξ and αἷμα would surely have ensured that בשׂר was rendered with σάρξ, as so often in the LXX. The use of σάρξ at John 6.51–6 is not relevant, because this has been creatively written to be as anti-Jewish as possible.[19] We cannot quite rule out גוּף, or indeed פגרא, for both occur earlier with reference to dead bodies, but neither occurs in quite the right sense until texts of later date. I conclude that Jesus almost certainly used גשׁם. The order of words must be less certain, but I have made a straightforward suggestion which accounts for the production of Mark's text, and something like it is so clear that we may proceed to interpret what Jesus meant.

In the Passover context, the identification of the unleavened bread as Jesus' body is necessarily symbolic. As other interpretations looked back to the redemption of Israel at the Exodus, so this one looks forward to Jesus' redemptive death. The instruction to take of the bread he had broken must indicate some kind of shared

[19] Casey, *Is John's Gospel True?*, pp. 41–51.

experience. This was always true of the unleavened bread, as well as the lamb or goat, and the bitter herbs. The whole feast of Passover was an experience of shared redemption in the past, at least sometimes accompanied by the shared experience of looking forward to redemption in the future. We may infer that the disciples would share in the benefits of Jesus' redemptive death. We have seen some evidence that they might have died with him (cf. Mark 10.39; 14.31).[20] A little more information will come in verse 24.

Verse 23 is less problematical in itself, though it has caused trouble to exegetes. Many scholars have posited a gap in the meal at this point, because they have supposed that the unleavened bread was interpreted as soon as it was served, they have followed m. Pes 10 in supposing that four cups of wine were served at Passover, and they have interpreted verse 25 very literally, so that Jesus would not have another sip of wine after he said these words, rather than another meal's worth after this meal. We have, however, seen that the unleavened bread was not interpreted until the meal was well under way. Mishnah was not written down until well over a century after the fall of Jerusalem, a period during which Jewish people altered Passover so as to celebrate it outside Jerusalem without the sacrifices in the Temple.[21] The four cups are likely to be later schematisation. A gap at this point is not indicated by our source, which did tell us when we moved further on into the meal at verse 22. I cannot see that Jesus had any reason to interpret separately the two elements which he interpreted symbolically of himself. We should infer that he took a cup more or less straight after the unleavened bread over which he had said a blessing. One fact which was significant to our source is that the disciples all drank from a common cup before the interpretation of the wine was given. This again indicates the same kind of shared experience of redemption that was normative at Passover.

I have reconstructed ברך behind both εὐλόγησεν in verse 22 and εὐχαριστήσας here. It is much the most suitable word to have been used by Mark's source and to have given rise to both translations. It follows that the translator first used the normal LXX translation, and then had a second go with a more Hellenistic word. We have already seen that it is normal for translators to use

---

[20] See pp. 201–6 above.
[21] B. M. Bokser, *The Origins of the Seder: The Passover Rite and Early Rabbinic Judaism* (Berkeley, 1984).

two different words for a single word in their source text, and that the translator of Mark 10.37–40 used both ἀριστερῶν and εὐωνύμων for שמאל.[22]

There followed an interpretation of the wine. This has also proved very difficult to reconstruct. The problem has been the expression τὸ αἷμά μου τῆς διαθήκης. Scholars have tried to reconstruct this as דמי דקימא or the like, which is unsatisfactory Aramaic, because a suffix cannot be attached to a noun in the construct state, nor can a noun with a suffix generally precede ד or די when this is the standard equivalent of the English word 'of'. This problem arises from a widespread error of method, that of translating Gospel sayings *into* Aramaic, whereas we should be reconstructing Aramaic sayings which would cause translators to produce the sentences which we find in the Gospels. I have therefore reconstructed דמי דנה, דקימא הוא. A translator must alter the order of these words to make reasonable Greek, and the Markan phrase is a sound and natural translation of this. It is not, however, perfect monoglot Greek, in which the noun αἷμα should not be followed by one dependent genitive and then another. This is more likely to be done by a translator than by a bilingual writing freely. It therefore adds cumulative weight to the argument for this passage being a translation of an Aramaic source.[23]

We can now proceed to interpret the whole saying. Jesus began with the symbolic identification of the wine with his blood. The symbolic context is too strong for the disciples to have felt seriously that they had drunk blood.[24] At the same time, this was a potential problem, sensibly reduced by giving the interpretation *after* they had all drunk from the common cup. This illustrates how literally we should take our source, and it is another small indication that its real Sitz im Leben is in the event at the time. The imagery is necessarily sacrificial, looking forward to the redemptive significance of Jesus' forthcoming death, just as they looked backwards to the redemption from Egypt. The second statement expands somewhat on the scope of Jesus' death: דקימא הוא, 'it is of the covenant'. This indicates that Jesus' death is important in the relationship between God and his people, Israel. When the people of Israel took upon themselves the observance of the Law, Moses

---

[22] See p. 207 above.
[23] For detailed discussion, see P. M. Casey, 'The Original Aramaic Form of Jesus' Interpretation of the Cup', *JThS* NS 41, 1990, 1–12.
[24] Cf. P. M. Casey, 'No Cannibals at Passover!', *Theology* 96, 1993, 199–205.

threw sacrificial blood over them and declared, 'Behold the blood of the covenant' (Exod. 24.8). The blood shed at circumcision could be called the blood of the covenant (for example t. Shab 15.9), and the blood of the Passover sacrifice had been fundamental in the deliverance of Israel from Egypt. A later source was able to draw on this same complex of tradition and declare in the name of the Lord, 'For the merit of the covenant blood of the circumcision and of the Passover blood, I have redeemed you out of Egypt, and for their merit will you be redeemed at the end of the fourth world empire' (Sayings of Rabbi Eliezer, ch. 29). Jesus' interpretation also looks back and forward. Jesus' death would be important in the relationship between God and Israel. This is pushed somewhat further with the rest of the sentence, מתאשד על שגיאין, 'shed for many'. There have been numerous attempts to extract precise meaning out of 'many'. For example, Gnilka describes 'Die Vielen' in German terms as 'ein Begriff', and slides through Qumran usage of רבים with reference to the community to declare that in view of the Servant Songs the term cannot be narrowed down ('eingeengt') to Israel. The description 'eingeengt' is quite prejudicial, and the use of Deutero-Isaiah to shift the meaning of 'die Vielen' is hardly *historical* research, but the detailed presentation of German Christian tradition.[25] This is another example of the hermeneutical circle. The word שגיאין must be interpreted with care, as at 10.45. It is not a direct reference to Gentiles, nor is it a deliberate restriction of the covenant to ethnically Jewish people. Basically, however, the covenant was between God and Israel, and that is the context in which Jesus himself saw his redemptive death.

There follows another saying which has proved very difficult to reconstruct. For לא נוסף למשתה, 'we shall not drink again', I have followed a text based on the most Semitic readings of D, Θ and a few other manuscripts, since I cannot otherwise understand their origin, whereas the majority readings are natural corrections to more normal Greek. The construction might be regarded as a Hebraism, for it is common in Hebrew, but יסף is an old Aramaic word, and this construction is used already at 4Q198 (Tobit 14.2); cf. 11QtgJob XXV.8, so its presence in an Aramaic source should not be regarded as problematical. The reading οὐ μὴ προσθῶμεν πιεῖν is also a severe example of interference in an author who uses πάλιν twenty-eight times in such a short document. We should

again infer the double level of interference characteristic of translators of texts. It makes no sense as an alteration to the text of
Matthew. Once again, we have an additional argument for the
priority of Mark. The word ἐκείνης, supposed here to be a
translation of הוא, is unnecessary in Greek. The words πίνω καινόν
have also caused trouble. After Dalman's comments, Black declared that this expression 'is impossible in Aramaic and can
scarcely have been original'. The problem is perceived to be the
adjective καινόν placed after the verb, picking up the Semitic
expression 'fruit of the vine' in a manner characteristic of Greek
rather than Hebrew or Aramaic. Consequently, Hampel, offering a
reconstruction, left several words out, so that Jesus merely said that
he would not drink of the fruit of the vine again until that day in
the kingdom of God.[26] These comments, however, repeat the error
of method which everyone commits though no one actually believes
in it, namely that of trying to translate Mark's Greek *literally into*
Aramaic. I have suggested instead an idiomatic piece of Aramaic
which would cause our translator to put what we have got: אשתינה
והוא חדת. It would be foolish to translate this literally: πινω αὐτον
και αὐτον καινον?? Mark's text is an excellent and straightforward
solution to this difficulty, but it does require of us some flexibility
in considering what translators really do. Looking at the sentence
as a whole, we should not describe it as a vow of abstinence, but
rather as a prediction. Jesus knew that this was to be his last meal
with his disciples, and he had spent his ministry recreating the
traditional hope for the forthcoming establishment of the kingdom
of God. At one level, the sentence merely says that they will not
drink together again until the kingdom comes. At another,
however, it presupposes that God will establish his kingdom soon,
having been enabled to do so by Jesus' redemptive death.

The eschatological orientation of this saying ought to be
obvious, but it has been denied, and Chilton has recently denied it
at the hand of an Aramaic reconstruction:[27]

לָא עוֹד אִשְׁתֵּי מִפְּרִי גֻפְנָא עַד דִי אִשְׁתֵיה חֲדָתָא בְּמַלְכְּתָא
אֱלָהָא

---

[26] Dalman, *Jesus-Jeshua*, p. 182; Black, *Aramaic Approach* (1946), p. 235, and
likewise Jeremias, *Eucharistic Words*, p. 184; Hampel, *Menschensohn*, p. 351.

[27] B. D. Chilton, *A Feast of Meanings: Eucharistic Theologies from Jesus through
Johannine Circles* (NT. S LXXII. 1994). The reconstruction is on pp. 44, 177.

The first problem is the missing introduction. Chilton comments, 'An introductory formula such as בְּקֻשְׁתָּא אָמְרְנָא לְכוֹן ("In truth, I say to you") may have been used at an Aramaic stage in the transmission of the saying, or ἀμὴν λέγω ὑμῖν may have been introduced at a latter stage.'[28] Neither suggestion is reasonable. אמן is a Hebrew word which occurs millions of times as a response, mostly to prayers, but also in other circumstances. In Aramaic texts extant after our period, it is used in the same way. As an asseverative opening to a saying, it is probably unique. While בקושט(א) is perfectly satisfactory Aramaic already before the time of Jesus, it simply means 'in truth', 'truly', 'truthfully' (for example 1QapGen II.5; II.10) and is not used as an asseverative opening. But the main problem is not the pointlessness of this change. What is quite beyond belief is that the translators of sayings for the Gospels would transliterate the Hebrew אמן, when they should have been translating the Aramaic בקושטא, for the benefit of Greek-speaking congregations. Luke, who retains only six examples of ἀμήν, occasionally replaces it with ἀληθῶς (Luke 9.27; 12.44; 21.3), which a Greek translator would surely think of as a rendering of בקושטא, together with the more literal ἐπ' ἀληθείας (used in the same way at Luke 4.25), even if he were not so literal as to put ἐν ἀληθείᾳ. Chilton notes that the Syriac translators of the Gospels do not invariably transliterate ἀμήν.[29] Although transliterating it is very common (in Mark, sin pesh hark transliterate it every time except 12.43 sin), it is possible that the exceptions are due to the fact that אמן at the beginning of sentences is not normal Aramaic. What this means, however, is that אמן is a probably unique usage from the ipsissima verba of Jesus, not that we are entitled to replace it with something more conventional.

Chilton also suggests that where the Syriac versions of the Bible have בקושתא rather than שְׁרִירָאִית, they do so as a reminiscence of the earlier בקשתא.[30] This possibility should be rejected, in the first place because the suggested בקשתא in place of אמן should not be accepted. We would also need very strong evidence that translators who invariably put ברה דאנשא or the like rather than בר (א)(א)נש(א) for ὁ υἱὸς τοῦ ἀνθρώπου knew other aspects of dominical tradition. Thirdly, Chilton's only reason for this extraordinary conjecture is

[28] *Ibid.*, pp. 44, 177.
[29] B. D. Chilton, ' "Amen": An Approach through Syriac Gospels', *ZNW* 69, 1978, 203–11, at 208–9.
[30] *Ibid.*, pp. 209–10.

the mere fact that the Syriac translators sometimes have בקושתא where he would expect שׁרירא, but his expectation that they should not have it is contradictory to their usage, and not properly grounded in anything else.

It should also be obvious that, since אמן is Hebrew, it did not originate in the Hellenistic church.[31] It is surely original at Mark 14.25, for it has such an excellent Sitz im Leben in the incident itself. Jesus has just predicted his betrayal and interpreted his death. He was soon to pray that this cup might be taken away from him, and to confess that his flesh was weak (Mark 14.34–8). For his own sake, therefore, as well as that of the disciples, he *must* make an authoritative declaration of his forthcoming vindication. What was the point of his asseverative אמן if he did not use it here? When therefore our oldest primary source tells us that he did so (unlike Matt. 26.29; Luke 22.18), we should believe it.

The next problem is עוד. This is perfectly satisfactory Aramaic, but Chilton does not offer an explanation of the readings of D Θ 565, on account of which the above reconstruction is to be preferred. Equally, the end of Chilton's reconstruction does not provide a solution to the problem of the viability of חדתא picking up פרי גפנא, and מלכותא should either be in the construct state or followed by ד or די. This leaves us with a central problem, Chilton's omission of any equivalent to τῆς ἡμέρας ἐκείνης. This is absolutely arbitrary and never properly justified. Chilton's generally supporting arguments show a remarkable combination of imagination and destructiveness. He suggests that the prediction is implausible because Jesus did not know how many more meals he would have, and that it is contradicted by the synoptic narrative, in which Jesus was given wine before the crucifixion (Matt. 27.34// Mark 15.23) and offered vinegar on the cross (Matt. 27.48//Mark 15.36//Luke 23.36).[32] This does not happen with the reconstruction which I have proposed, in which I have used the plural נוסף because this is sound Aramaic and the best explanation of the origin of the reading of Θ, προσθῶμεν, which Chilton does not discuss. In any case, Jesus intended to go to the Garden of Gethsemane and wait to be arrested, as the following narrative shows. He will not have expected wine from the chief priests. He

---

[31] For brief but clear demolition of this kind of view, see Meier, *Marginal Jew*, vol. II, pp. 367–9, n. 62.
[32] Chilton, *Feast of Meanings*, pp. 40–4.

refused the drugged wine offered him before the crucifixion (Mark 15.23), and if Mark 15.36 is literally true rather than a midrash on Ps. 69.22, it does not record that he drank the vinegar offered him when he was viciously mocked in contradiction to his view of Elijah. We should not invent contradictions in the perfectly coherent parts of Mark's narrative.

With the narrative outline of our primary source destroyed, Chilton imagines a new context for the saying in many of Jesus' meals. 'To join in his meals consciously was, in effect, to anticipate the kingdom in a certain manner, the manner delineated by Jesus. Each meal was a proleptic celebration of God's kingdom; the promise of the next was also an assurance of the kingdom.'[33] Where is the evidence of that? Not in the teaching of Jesus! Chilton proceeds to imagine many meals after Jesus' entry into Jerusalem, and declares that 'The focus on the *single* meal immediately prior to Jesus' death is a function of the ritual dramatization which characterizes the Gospels, and their theology of solidarity with the archetypical martyr.'[34] This does not explain the indirect features of a Passover meal, or the Jewish assumptions of Mark's source, or the fact that the Gospels do not overtly expound this view, which they surely must have done if they had needed to invent it. Of course Jesus will have eaten with his disciples many times, but Passover was a major Jewish feast, so it is intelligible that Jesus should have used this particular meal in the dramatic way which Mark reports.

Chilton proceeds to a detailed discussion which tries to establish that עד . . . לא need not have, or need not have primarily, a temporal sense.[35] Apart from doubts over the real comparability of the texts which he cites, this underlines the arbitrary nature of his omission of τῆς ἡμέρας ἐκείνης. We have seen that it is one of the worst features of Aramaic reconstructions that they can be used in accordance with a hidden agenda. This is the same hidden agenda as that of Dodd, removing the scandal of Jesus' false expectation of an early coming of the kingdom.[36] We must restore the whole text to interpret it accurately as an account of what Jesus really said and did. When we do so, we have a clear prediction that Jesus will not drink wine again, and a specific time when he will: 'that day . . . in

[33] *Ibid.*, p. 39.
[34] *Ibid.*, pp. 63–4.
[35] *Ibid.*, pp. 41–2, 169–71.
[36] P. 27 above.

the kingdom of God'. This can only have an eschatological reference. We have the same basic nexus of ideas which we encountered as the background to Mark 10.35–45. The death of Jesus, and the deaths of any disciples who would die with him, would enable God to redeem Israel. That would be the coming of the kingdom, with the resurrection of the dead and the judgement of the twelve tribes of Israel by Peter, Jacob, John and the other members of the twelve.

After Jesus' prediction, he and his disciples sang the Hallel psalms, which brought the Passover meal to a close. I have suggested that our source used the actual word הללו, even though הלל is usually rendered in the LXX with αἰνέω, αἴνεσις or ἐπαινέω. הלל is the obvious word for our source to have used of the singing of the Hallel psalms. It is rendered with ὑμνεῖν four times in the LXX, and with ὕμνος once or twice. At 2 Chr. 29.30, the two examples of הלל rendered with ὑμνεῖν have clear reference to psalms of David and Asaph. At the Passover of Hezekiah, the Hebrew מהללים is rendered καθυμνοῦντες (2 Chr. 30.21). The proposed rendering of הללו with ὑμνήσαντες is therefore perfectly in order. These were the second group of Hallel psalms, in which it is written that the son of man goes. We should infer that this is why they are mentioned, and the singing of the first group is not. We should also infer that the cultural assumptions made by the author of our source included the Jesus movement's interpretation of the scriptures according to which Jesus died and rose again, including the scriptures set for Passover. As they sang Ps. 116.15, they would be reminded of Jesus' intention to die, and this would help them to make their commitment to die with him (Mark 14.31). They also sang the pleas for resurrection. The following narrative shows that Jesus could have escaped if he had wished to, and makes it evident that he did not wish to. This coheres entirely with his prediction and interpretation of his death in the passages which we have considered in detail.

We are now in a position to consider briefly the later rewriting of these traditions. There is a small one at Matt. 26.28, εἰς ἄφεσιν ἁμαρτιῶν. This significantly increases the function of Jesus' death in accordance with trends normal in the early church and especially visible in Paul, as already in the old formula of 1 Cor. 15.3. While Matthew retained the expectation of the kingdom (26.29), he wrote after a successful Gentile mission: this development satisfied the needs of Gentiles to feel forgiven and to understand Jesus' death.

More comprehensive rewriting is found in Paul. Paul was faced with Corinthian Christians who gathered together as if they were at a Gentile banquet, so that, for example, some would be drunk when others were still hungry (1 Cor. 11.21). He roundly declared that when they gathered together, it was not to eat κυριακὸν δεῖπνον (11.20). Here we have the 'Lord's Supper', the cause of Paul's rewriting: there is no mention of Passover. Paul tried to control the Corinthians by getting them to eat the 'Lord's Supper', connecting it with 'the Lord Jesus' by means of his rewritten tradition. He begins by saying that he 'received' and 'handed on' to them the account, both words being normal terms for the transmission of traditions. He claims to have 'received' the tradition ἀπὸ τοῦ κυρίου, thereby naming the fountainhead of the tradition, in accordance with normal Jewish custom.[37] He locates the meal ἐν τῇ νυκτὶ ᾗ παρεδίδετο, so there is no doubt that he refers to the same meal as we have discussed.

The first discrepancy is Paul's omission of καὶ ἔδωκεν αὐτοῖς. This is part of Mark's narrative report, and Paul did not need it. The next discrepancy is in the interpretation of the bread. In Mark's account this must be unleavened bread, because the sacrifice was dated on the first day for unleavened bread (Mark 14.12), and because the meal has been declared a Passover meal. Paul mentions neither, which facilitates the application of Jesus' rewritten words to Corinthian meals, at which the bread will have been leavened. In the interpretation, Paul moves μού from its Aramaic position so as to add τὸ ὑπὲρ ὑμῶν. This facilitates the appropriation of the word of interpretation by the Corinthians. It does not have a proper Sitz im Leben in the original event, for Jesus was not dying especially for those present, and some of them were supposed to die with him. Paul adds τοῦτο ποιεῖτε εἰς τὴν ἐμὴν ἀνάμνησιν. This was essential, to coerce the Corinthians into treating regular meals as an imitation of Jesus' last meal. It is another reason why he should omit the Passover context, as this would inhibit the application to anything other than an annual celebration at Passover time. It has no Sitz im Leben at the original event, when Jesus expected God to establish the kingdom, not leave the disciples on earth celebrating memorial meals. The twelve

---

[37] I have gathered together the results of recent work on the authorship of Jewish documents: Casey, *Is John's Gospel True?*, ch. 8.

should have been judging the twelve tribes of Israel long before Paul got to Corinth!

The word over the cup has been equally rewritten. It is placed μετὰ τὸ δειπνῆσαι, so that the Corinthians will not start to drink before they have finished eating. They will then be less likely to get drunk, and certainly will not do so while some are still hungry (cf. 1 Cor. 11.21). There is no mention of all drinking the cup, another part of Mark's narrative report that Paul did not need, not least because the Corinthians will not have all drunk from the same cup. The interpretation of the cup has been completely altered. The identity statement Τοῦτό ἐστιν τὸ αἷμά μου has gone. With the Passover context gone, and the Eucharistic context not yet established, the identification of red wine with Jesus' blood could be very unpleasant, for Gentiles as well as for Jews. In place of דקימא הוא, translated τῆς διαθήκης, Paul has ἡ καινὴ διαθήκη. This is just what Paul wanted Gentile Christians to have. It does not have a proper Sitz im Leben in the original event, when Jesus' death took place within the framework of God's covenant with Israel. Consequently, Paul has removed τὸ ἐκχυννόμενον ὑπὲρ πολλῶν, which belongs in the original context of God's covenant with Israel. The command to repeat the rite is even more carefully focussed than before, since it has ὁσάκις ἐὰν πίνητε, pushing all fellowship meals into the Pauline frame of reference. This is pushed further in 11.26, which has these meals relate to Jesus' death ἄχρις οὗ ἔλθῃ. Here hope for the parousia replaces Jesus' expectation of the kingdom, a standard shift from the teaching of Jesus to a central concern of the early church.

There should therefore be no doubt that Paul's version of this meal has been completely rewritten in order to meet the situation which he tells us about. Luke's account is also a result of rewriting tradition. We have already seen that Luke 22.24–30 contains secondary rewriting.[38] The longer text of the words of interpretation, the originality of which is very difficult to determine, has been extensively influenced by the Pauline rewriting.

All this throws into relief the nature of Mark's source, and the literal and unelaborated translation of it which now stands in Mark's Gospel. It gives a literally accurate but abbreviated account of the original event, and shows no serious signs of rewriting in the

---

[38] Pp. 207–9 above.

interests of the early church in general, or of the community to which Mark belonged.

The following conclusions may therefore be suggested. It is possible to produce an Aramaic substratum of Mark 14.12–26, such that normal translators using conventional methods might produce the Greek text of Mark. When conventional Jewish assumptions are applied to this source, it makes excellent sense as an historical account of extracts from Jesus' final Passover with his disciples. This includes a coherent interpretation of Jesus' death which is necessary to understand his actions during the final days of his life. Indeed, the point of the account is to explain how and why Jesus died, and a fuller picture of the meal could be reconstructed by anyone who knew what normally happened at a Passover meal, knowledge assumed by the author of this account. It does not, however, include two of the main points that would be required if we were to regard it as in any serious sense a product of the early church. There is no mention of the effect of Jesus' death on Gentiles, and no mention of any institution of the Eucharist. Nor is there any significant smaller indication of secondary development. We must infer that the proposed Aramaic source is genuine and reliable.

We have also seen reasons for supposing that it was a single written source. The translation strategies uncovered at verse 21 require that it was a written Aramaic source: verse 21a also requires the references to Psalm 41 in verses 18 and 20, and the reference to the second group of Hallel psalms in verse 26, for the scriptures in which a/the son of man goes to be too obvious to need mentioning. This is supported by all the other Semitisms, particularly μήτι in verse 19, and also the specifically Aramaic form πάσχα (14.12, 14, 16), σοί (14.12), ἐκ (14.13, 20), ἀμήν (14.18, 25), εἷς κατὰ εἷς (14.19), τὸ ἕν (14.20), ὑπάγει (14.21), the succession of dependent genitives μου τῆς διαθήκης (14.24), οὐ μὴ προσθῶμεν πιεῖν (14.25), τοῦ γενήματος τῆς ἀμπέλου (14.25), ἐκείνης (14.25), extensive parataxis and the position of several verbs at or near the beginning of sentences. Those points not shared with Matthew provide an additional argument for the priority of Mark. At a cultural level, all parts of the narrative need all the other parts. The preparation of the Passover, with the sacrifice assumed to be in the Temple and the taking of the victim to a private house where it was prepared, these preparations require a following account of Passover. The account itself, from Jesus turning up when it was dark to remaining inside greater Jerusalem rather than going back to Bethany, this account requires the information that it was Passover to make complete sense. This has not generally been noticed because the account takes so much for granted. Who would write an Aramaic account which assumes that when we are told they were sacrificing the Passover we would know that they were in the Temple? that when we are told the victim was prepared, we would know that it was eaten and interpreted on traditional lines? that verse 21a would send us straight to Psalm 41 and the second group of Hallel psalms? We must once more infer that the Aramaic source was written by a Jewish Christian from Israel. He is not likely to have been one of the twelve, for we are told nothing about them that the others did not know, and it is not very likely that nothing memorable happened between verses 16 and 17. On the other hand, there is no sign of the editorial activity of the early church, and the selection of information suggests someone recounting what struck them at the time. There is therefore a strong probability that Mark's Aramaic source was written by one of the disciples who took part in Jesus' final Passover meal. This is more likely to have happened sooner rather than later, as part of the felt need to explain how and why Jesus died. We may reasonably infer a date c. 27–40 CE for this source, depending on when we date the events narrated.

It remains to reflect more generally on the significance of this episode in the life of Jesus. In *From Jewish Prophet to Gentile God*, I have put forward a general picture of him as the embodiment of Jewish identity from a prophetic perspective, and I suggest that this incident fits perfectly into this picture. If the disciples wanted to know how to be Jewish as God intended them to be, then from their perspective they needed to look no further than Jesus himself. At his final meal with them, he faithfully performed the ritual of a major feast, as laid down in the biblical text and amplified by Jewish custom. He did not, however, stop at doing exactly the same as everyone else. Rather, he recreated that tradition to say something new. In this case, the new material was dramatic indeed. He predicted his betrayal, and interpreted his forthcoming death. This was done within the context of the major feast, and it was seen to be foretold in scripture, including the Hallel psalms, the scriptures for this very feast. Moreover, the disciples did not merely witness this picture: they participated in it. Some were in the Temple for the public sacrifice, some prepared the meal, the twelve were with him for at least part of the day, and a number of disciples gathered together for the final Passover meal. There they participated with him in the shared experience of the redemption of Israel from Egypt, and there they ate the bread which he had blessed and drank from a common cup, a shared experience of the future redemption to be brought by God because of his death. They sang the Hallel psalms, in which they believed that they sang of his death and vindication by God. They each refused to betray him, knowing that he would insist on dying, for they knew the scriptures in which they saw his betrayal and hope of resurrection. Their own Jewish identity, already recreated in the historic ministry, was vigorously reinforced.

All this was done in the context of opposition from other Jewish leaders, scribes and Pharisees who had opposed the ministry for a long time, and chief priests in charge of the Temple, where he had controlled the halakhah in the outer court with sufficient effect to stop people from carrying vessels through it. The Passover victim was taken to the upper room with some difficulty, to ensure that Jesus was not arrested too early. After the meal, Jesus went to the Garden of Gethsemane, there to await his arrest by Jews who would have finished eating the Passover meal by midnight. His arrest and death had been predicted, and seen as the will of God written in scripture. It follows that, when he was executed, the only available option for the disciples was to believe that he had in fact been vindicated by God. They were then left to preach the good news, in which he was ever more central, and the theological significance of his death was necessarily further developed. The further development of this is another story. We should infer, however, that Jesus' final Passover with his disciples was not only a significant event at the time, but also important as a connecting link between the ministry of Jesus and the preaching of the earliest Christians, at a time when all followers of Jesus were faithful and observant Jews.

7

CONCLUSIONS

We saw in ch. 1 that the quest of the historical Jesus has made little use of Aramaic as an investigative tool. This is a remarkable fact. Most people have noticed that language is a significant part of culture, but the study of Jesus has proceeded as if this were not the case. It has been largely a Christian enterprise, and the sacred text is in Greek. Too much reconstruction of a Jewish man is liable to create problems for the doctrine of the Trinity. Hence a few specialised people have done all the existing work. Only two outstanding books have been written, those of Meyer and Black, in 1896 and 1946, before the discovery of the Dead Sea scrolls. As we consider the history of scholarship so long afterwards, no praise can be too high for these two brilliant and independent men.

The discovery of the scrolls puts us in a position to alter the nature of this work. Throughout the first century of critical scholarship, the use of Aramaic was beset with such severe problems that most scholars might well feel that it was a specialised area of dubious value. We saw this especially in considering the work of scholars such as Torrey and Burney, most of whose suggestions could not be accepted. The use of Aramaic of different times and places, the use of only one word at a time, the elevation of supposed puns to the level of a major tool when they could not be properly verified, all this was enough to keep Aramaic as a specialised area.

It still is, but the discovery of the scrolls means that we should bring this most unsatisfactory state of affairs to an end. We now have the majority of words that we need extant in Aramaic from the right period. In reconstructing Mark 9.11–13, 2.23–3.6, 10.35–45 and 14.12–26, we have found only two related words, βάπτισμα and βαπτίζομαι, where there is such serious doubt about the Aramaic underlay that we cannot use it to illuminate a main point. There have been very few words, such as κατάλυμα at Mark 14.14, where we have had to fill in something from later sources to ensure that we have a complete sentence to interpret. In general, it has been possible to reconstruct Mark's Aramaic sources with Aramaic of the right period, with careful use of earlier and later Aramaic when the Dead Sea scrolls do not have the appropriate words. The level of uncertainty has therefore been very limited. Moreover, the problem of dialect has been much less serious than it seemed previously. Previous attempts to use 'Galilean' Aramaic suffered badly from the late date and corrupt nature of the source material, and invariably used a high proportion of material which was not Galilean at all. Now, however, most of the words in the Dead Sea scrolls have turned out to be used in other dialects too. This means that they are not specific to the dialect of Judaea as opposed to anywhere else, and can reasonably be used to reconstruct the Galilean Aramaic of Jesus.

Throughout the unnecessarily long period during which the Dead Sea scrolls were published, knowledge went vigorously ahead in related fields of study, the results of which are essential for the kind of work done in this book. Three fields were especially important: Bilingualism, Translation Studies and the study of the early biblical versions. We now understand much better than anyone did a few years ago what it is like to be bilingual, and what a variety of phenomena are found among people who have a speaking or passive knowledge of more than one language. We also know a great deal more about the translation process in general. In particular, we know what a variety of possibilities are available to translators, and how certain phenomena repeat themselves in different places and over different languages. One of the most important is the concept of interference, which is more extreme among translators than among bilinguals speaking freely. The study of biblical versions is especially important because many of the phenomena known from Translation Studies are repeated among the translators from about our period. These gives us further insight into what problems the translators of Mark's Aramaic sources would encounter, and what range of possibilities are likely to have occurred to them.

All this would be to no avail if Mark's Gospel were really Greek fiction, or if all of it had been so heavily edited that Aramaic sources were irrecoverable. We have found substantial and decisive evidence that parts of Mark's Gospel are literal translations of written Aramaic sources. This follows from an argument of cumulative weight, which is dependent on evidence of several different kinds. First of all, we found clear evidence that Aramaic was the lingua franca of Jesus' environment, the language which he would have had to use in teaching normal Jews, and the natural language for his first followers to use when they reported on his life and teaching. Secondly, we found many reasons for supposing that the passages studied are generally accurate accounts of what Jesus said and did. They are therefore just the sorts of passage to be transmitted in Aramaic, quite different from the secondary narratives of the fourth Gospel, many of which originated in Greek. Thirdly, we found many details of the selected passages which are explicable only if they are part of translations of written Aramaic sources.

At this level the central piece of evidence is the most controversial and misunderstood term in the whole of the New Testament, ὁ υἱὸς τοῦ ἀνθρώπου. Though this is a title in the Greek New Testament as it stands, it is a translation of the Aramaic term (א)שנ(א) בר, which is an ordinary term for man. More than that, we found that the use of ὁ υἱὸς τοῦ ἀνθρώπου, together with its non-use with primary reference to anyone else and its virtual absence in the plural, means that it can only be understood as a result of the strategy of the translators and/or editors of the Gospels. Their strategy was to render (א)שנ(א) בר with ὁ υἱὸς τοῦ ἀνθρώπου when it referred to Jesus, and to render it otherwise when it referred to anyone else, and when it was in the plural. This strategy makes sense only if the synoptic authors had substantial written Aramaic sources.

This interpretation is confirmed by numerous small details which have nothing to do with the term ὁ υἱὸς τοῦ ἀνθρώπου. Mark 9.11–13 is the most remarkable passage of all. It does not make proper sense in the existing Greek text, and has consequently puzzled scholars for years. In Aramaic, however, it is an entirely lucid piece. We found it possible to account for the transition from lucid Aramaic to obscure Greek, not by a rotten translator or by the obtuse and destructive redactor who stalks the pages of NT scholarship, but precisely by means of a careful and accurate translator. This translator was landed with the translator's nightmare, a passage which, by the very nature of the two languages and the differences between the source and target cultures, simply will not go smoothly from the one language into the other. This pointed up a major facet of this kind of study of material moving from one language and culture to another, that there may be a massive difference between the understanding of a text by a bilingual translator moving from one language and culture towards another, and by monoglot speakers who belong entirely to the target culture. All the problems of interpreting this passage stem from treating it as if it were the work of a monoglot Greek-speaking Christian. The solution emerged from recovering the work of a bilingual translator who was suffering from interference as he attempted an impossible transfer.

Similar remarks apply to the other passages studied in detail. Again and again we found small pieces of evidence which entailed written source material in Aramaic, and small features of Markan Greek which should be accounted for as the work of a translator suffering from interference. Another consequence follows: a new and independent argument for the priority of Mark. Again, Mark 9.11–13 was the most straightforward piece of evidence: a whole passage, which makes excellent sense as the work of a bilingual translator suffering from interference while trying to render an impossible passage, does not make sense as the effort of Mark to revise the work of Matthew. We found many small pieces of evidence to the same effect. Our discussion of Mark 2.23–8 was in some ways the most remarkable, for this passage is generally treated as having so many 'minor agreements' as to cast doubt on the normal theory of Markan priority. Reminding ourselves that Matthew and Luke were both vigorous editors, we found that most of these agreements emerged at points where Mark's Greek had something about it that could be understood as a literal presentation of the original Aramaic source, that Matthew and Luke made independent changes, and that most of the ones they had in common consisted of interpretation with the needs of the same target language and culture in mind.

It is natural that the results of this research should have serious consequences for our picture of the historical Jesus. It clearly points towards a more Jewish Jesus than is conventional. This is well indicated by the most controversial and dramatic phrase: whereas ὁ υἱὸς τοῦ ἀνθρώπου has been a Christian Christological title for centuries, (א)בר (א)שׁנ is a normal term for a man. This basic difference between a Jewish Jesus and one overlaid by the cultural shift already underway in the translation process emerged from each of the passages studied. At Mark 9.11–13, the major problem at issue was that of understanding the death of John the Baptist. To do this, Jesus resorted to the study of scriptures which we were able to recover. These contained general statements about the death of man, not specific references to Elijah or John the Baptist, and consequently Jesus used a general statement containing the term (אנש)בר (א) to refer primarily to his understanding of the death of John the Baptist – his comments were not primarily about his own fate. At Mark 2.23–8 we found Jesus immersed in a vigorous debate about a detail of the halakhah, whether his poor and hungry disciples might take Peah on the sabbath. This interpretation was not available to monoglot Christian readers of the surface level of the Greek text, but emerges inevitably from studying Mark's Aramaic source against the background of the assumptions natural to first-century Jews from Israel. Jesus settled the matter from a prophetic perspective by means of vigorous interpretation of more scriptural passages.

Our study of Mark 3.1–6 showed another massive gap between Christian scholarship and the realities of first-century Jewish life. It has generally been treated as a miracle story. We found that it was another detailed halakhic argument about what was permissible on the sabbath. Jesus' most vigorous opponents did not doubt that he could perform a healing on the sabbath, nor were they amazed when he did so. We were able to use the cross-cultural study of healing and features of specifically Jewish culture to understand what Jesus was really doing. The Aramaic source was especially helpful in revealing the assumptions of his detailed halakhic argument.

Scholars have found it difficult to understand the connections between the different parts of Mark 10.35–45. We found that they follow more easily in Aramaic than from the surface level of Mark's Greek text. Of especial importance is the general level of the (אנש)בר (א) saying at Mark 10.45, which flows naturally from the context of a debate begun by Jacob and John's question. To understand this fully, we had to drop traditional Christian assumptions about the uniqueness of Jesus' death, and restore Jewish assumptions about the position of the twelve when Jesus was in glory following God's establishment of his kingdom. Jacob and John understood perfectly well that they might have to die before they could sit on Jesus' right and left in his glory, and they accepted this without hesitation. This was not, however, a position which they should have wanted, so Jesus taught all twelve about service. The final son of man statement includes service to the point of death. It is this which links up with Jacob and John's question. It presupposes that all twelve might die with him, and this would redeem Israel, not atone for sins as later Christianity understood the death of Jesus alone.

The reconstruction of the Aramaic source of Mark 14.12–26 provided an even more dramatic result. Christian scholarship has traditionally seen here the institution of the Eucharist. We found instead a dramatic story of Jesus celebrating his final Passover with his disciples. The conventional view is a classic case of the interpretation of details within a strong but alien frame of reference. Jesus' words over the bread and wine, in an altered form, are still used in the Christian Eucharist, as part of an aetiological narrative in which he used them to institute it. Christian scholars have deduced from this that part of Mark's account really is an account of the institution of the Eucharist. We found that Mark's Aramaic source did not mention the Eucharist. Instead, it openly and clearly described the preparations for a Passover meal, and proceeded on the assumption that this is what the meal was. Where Christian scholars have separated the explicit preparations for Passover from the account of the Eucharist as though Mark's account resulted from the transmission of fragments, we found a unified narrative which made excellent sense provided that we applied Jewish assumptions to it in a reasonably uniform way. Jesus' death was seen in this light. As God had redeemed Israel at the Exodus, so he would redeem Israel by establishing his kingdom. To recover the original meaning of Mark's source, we had to suppose that the narrative was originally written by a Jew from Israel. In the process, we found numerous signs of this, including evidence of the literal translation of a written Aramaic source.

The nature of these assumptions is another crucial finding. These sources were written by people who assumed that if we were told that disciples were walking on a path between fields plucking grain, we would know that they were taking Peah, because everybody knew that that was the only possible reason why they could be walking between other people's fields plucking grain; and that if we were told that two disciples prepared the Passover and Jesus came with the twelve when it was evening, we would know that this was so that they would begin to eat the Passover when it was dark, because everybody knew this. Assumptions of this type have run through all four of the passages studied in detail. They have been crucial to establishing the unity of these passages. One reason why these passages have been split into small pieces by Gentile Christian scholars is the Jewish nature of the assumptions made.

Who, then, can have written these sources, and at what date? The answer to these questions is another crucial finding. Only Jews from Israel, who could assume that their Jewish assumptions would be intelligible, would write in this way, without explaining things that they feared others would not understand. It follows that these sources were originally written by Jews, for people who were sufficiently Jewish to understand these assumptions. One of the twelve must have been the original source for Mark 10.35–45, because only the twelve are said to have been there, and we saw reason to believe that the passage is an authentic account of real conversations. Equally, one of the twelve need not have written it personally, and we saw on the other hand reason to believe that Mark 14.12–26 was written by an eyewitness who was not a member of the twelve. We noted also the implication of the very small quantity of information about the twelve that one of them is not likely to have been the author of much of the material.

The date of such material is likely to be very early indeed. There is no reason why the accounts from the ministry should not have been written down by eyewitnesses shortly after the events occurred. After a few years, however, they are likely to have needed more extensive editing. We can see the editing process already felt necessary by Mark in such places as the passion predictions and the declaring of all foods clean: the creation of new material to fit the early church's Christology, the delay of the parousia and so on. This process was carried through more extensively by Matthew and by Luke. Mark's sources, however, had no such need, and he felt sufficient confidence in them simply to transmit a literal translation. He did not alter mistakes, perhaps because he was translating as he went along. It is regrettable that these comments cannot lead us to a precise date. I do not see how such a source could have been written later than c. 40 CE, when the Gentile mission was such a great success that it would have to be taken note of. A date earlier than this is surely more probable.

We must therefore reopen the question of the date of Mark itself. A date of c. 65 CE was more or less conventional for some time, and American scholars have recently tended to go for an even later date. The basis for these late dates was, however, always slim, and the portrayal of this document as flimsy post-70 fiction is the unsatisfactory consequence of reading it in the light of literary theory which has emerged from the study of modern fiction. Very early dates have been proposed, but always by evangelical scholars whose arguments were barely critical. We now have a purely critical argument for an earlier date than is conventional. If Mark wrote as late as 65, he would surely have altered these passages as much as he edited some others. We have seen how Matthew and Luke felt a need to do so. Once again, this basic observation does not give us a precise date. It does, however, mean that a date c. 40 CE must be regarded as highly probable.

Finally, I have sought to demonstrate in this book the central importance of studying these very early traditions in their original language. We have seen that there should be no doubt that Jesus spoke Aramaic, or that Aramaic was the language in which the traditions about him were first transmitted. Scholars seeking to end the third quest of the historical Jesus by finding him should learn Aramaic as one of the essential tools for this work. We have seen repeatedly that many New Testament scholars have made many mistakes through their unwillingness to learn the language that Jesus spoke. It has made the son of man problem absolutely incomprehensible, and prevented the kind of work attempted in this book from being done at all. The use of Aramaic permits us for the first time to see past Mark's Gospel to its very early sources, to see glimpses of Jesus as he really was in first-century Judaism. The quest for the historical Jesus demands more work of this kind, so that we can see how extensive the evangelists' early sources were, and use them to reconstruct a more accurate picture of the Jesus of history. The results will not be convenient for everyone, but they should appeal to all those who have a genuine and serious concern for truth.

SELECT BIBLIOGRAPHY

1 Aramaic texts and tools of study

Beyer, K., *Die aramäischen Texte vom Toten Meer* (Göttingen, 1984).
Die aramäischen Texte vom Toten Meer – Ergänzungsband (Göttingen, 1994).
Boer, P. A. H. de et al., *The Old Testament in Syriac according to the Peshitta Version*, edited on behalf of the International Organization for the Study of the Old Testament by the Peshitta Institute, Leiden (many vols., Leiden, 1966–).
Bokser, B. M., 'An Annotated Bibliographical Guide to the Study of the Palestinian Talmud', *ANRW* II. 19.2 (1979), pp. 139–256.
Brock, S. P., 'A Syriac Verse Homily on Elijah and the Widow of Sarepta', *Le Muséon* 102, 1989, 93–113.
Brockelmann, C., *Lexicon Syriacum* (Berlin, 1894–5; Halis Saxonum, ²1928).
Brown, F., Driver, S. R. and Briggs, C. A., *A Hebrew and English Lexicon of the Old Testament* (Oxford, 1906).
Ceriani, A. M. (ed.), *Translatio Syra Pescitto Veteris Testamenti ex Codice Ambrosiano Sec. Fere VI Photolithographice Edita* (2 vols., Milan, 1876–83).
Clarke, E. G., with Aufrecht, W. E., Hurd, J. C. and Spitzer, F., *Targum Pseudo-Jonathan of the Pentateuch: Text and Concordance* (Hoboken, 1984).
Corpus Scriptorum Christianorum Orientalium – Series Syriaca (many vols., Leuven, 1903–).
Cowley, A., *Aramaic Papyri of the Fifth Century B.C.* (Oxford, 1923).
Dalman, G., *Grammatik des jüdisch-palästinischen Aramäisch nach den Idiomen des palästinischen Talmud, des Onkelostargum und Prophetentargum und der jerusalemischen Targume* (Leipzig, ²1905).
Díez Macho, A., *Neophyti 1: Targum Palastinense Ms de la Biblioteca Vaticana* (6 vols., Madrid, 1968–79).
Dirksen, P. B., *An Annotated Bibliography of the Peshitta of the Old Testament* (Leiden, 1989).
  'Appendix: Supplement to *An Annotated Bibliography, 1989*', in P. B. Dirksen and A. van der Kooij (eds.) *The Peshitta as a Translation* (MPIL 8. Leiden, 1995), pp. 221–36.

Donner, H., and Röllig, W., *Kanaanäische und Aramäische Inschriften* (Wiesbaden, 1962).

Epstein, I. (ed.), תלמוד בבלי Hebrew–English Edition of the Babylonian Talmud (32 vols., London, 1952–90).

Fitzmyer, J. A., *The Genesis Apocryphon of Qumran Cave I: A Commentary* (BibOr 18. Rome, 1966; BibOr 18A, ²1971).

The Aramaic Inscriptions of Sefire (BibOr 19. Rome, 1967. Rev. edn, BibOr 19A, 1995).

Fitzmyer, J. A. (ed.), 'A. Tobit', in M. Broshi, et al. (eds.), *Qumran Cave 4 XIV: Parabiblical Texts, Part 2* (DJD XIX. Oxford, 1995).

Fitzmyer, J. A., and Harrington, D. J. (eds.), *A Manual of Palestinian Aramaic Texts* (BibOr 34. Rome, 1978).

Fitzmyer, J. A., and Kaufman, S. A., *An Aramaic Bibliography. Part I: Old, Official, and Biblical Aramaic* (Baltimore/London, 1992).

Frishman, J., 'The Ways and Means of the Divine Economy: An Edition, Translation and Study of Six Biblical Homilies by Narsai', Ph.D. thesis, Rijksuniversiteit, Leiden (1992).

Graffin, R. (ed.), *Patrologia Syriaca: Pars Prima. Ab Initiis usque ad Annum 350* (3 vols., Paris, 1894–1926).

Grossfeld, B., *A Bibliography of Targum Literature* (3 vols., Cincinnati/ New York, 1972–90).

Hillers, D. R., and Cussini, E., *Palmyrene Aramaic Texts* (Baltimore, 1996).

Hoftijzer, J., and Jongeling, K., *Dictionary of the North-West Semitic Inscriptions* (2 vols., Leiden, 1995).

Jastrow, M., *A Dictionary of the Targumim, the Talmud Babli and Yerushalmi, and the Midrashic Literature* (2 vols., London, 1886–1903. Rep. New York, 1950).

Kasowsky, Ch. J. and B. (eds.), *Thesaurus Talmudis Concordantiae Verborum Quae in Talmude Babylonico Reperiuntur* (42 vols., Jerusalem, 1954–89).

Kiraz, G. A. (ed.), *Comparative Edition of the Syriac Gospels, Aligning the Sinaiticus, Curetonianus, Peshîṭtâ and Harklean Versions* (4 vols., NTTS XXI. Leiden, 1996).

Klein, M. L., *Genizah Manuscripts of the Palestinian Targum to the Pentateuch* (2 vols., Cincinnati, 1986).

Kosovsky, M. (ed.), *Concordance to the Talmud Yerushalmi* (many vols., Jerusalem, 1979–).

Lagarde, P. de (ed.), *Hagiographa Chaldaice* (Leipzig, 1873. Rep. Osnabrück, 1967).

Leloir, L. (ed.), *Saint Ephrem: Commentaire de L'Evangile concordant. Texte syriaque* (Ms Chester Beatty 709) (CBM 8. Dublin, 1963)

Levy, J., *Chaldäisches Wörterbuch über die Targumim und einem grossen Theil des rabbinischer Schriftthums* (2 vols., Leipzig, 1867–8; ³1881).

Neuhebräisches und chaldäisches Wörterbuch über die Talmudim und Midraschim (4 vols., Leipzig, 1876–89. 2nd ed., Berlin/Vienna, 1924).

Lewis, A. S. and Gibson, M. D. (eds.), *The Palestinian Syriac Lectionary of the Gospels, Re-edited from two Sinai MSS. and from P. de Lagarde's Edition of the 'Evangeliarium Hierosolymitanum'* (London, 1899).

Macuch, R., *Grammatik des Samaritanischen Aramäisch* (Berlin, 1982).

Mandelkern, S., קונקורדנציה לתנ"ך Concordance on the Bible (2 vols., Leipzig, 1896: rev. C. M. Brecher, New York, 1955).

Milik, J. T., *The Books of Enoch: Aramaic Fragments of Qumrân Cave 4* (Oxford, 1976).

Milik, J. T., and de Vaux, R. (eds.), *Qumrân Grotte 4.II. I. Archéologie II. Tefillin, Mezuzot et Targums (4Q128–4Q157)* (DJD VI. Oxford, 1977).

Müller-Kessler, Ch., *Grammatik des Christlich-Palästinisch-Aramäischen*, part I, *Schriftlehre, Lautlehre, Formenlehre* (Hildesheim, 1991).

Patrologia Orientalis (many vols., Paris/Turnhout, 1907–).

Payne-Smith, R. et al. (eds.), *Thesaurus Syriacus* (2 vols., Oxford, 1868–1901).

Ploeg, J. P. M. van der, and Woude, A. S. van der (eds.), *Le Targum de Job de la Grotte XI de Qumrân* (Leiden, 1971).

Porten, B., and Yardeni, A., *Textbook of Aramaic Documents from Ancient Egypt, Newly Copied, Edited and Translated into Hebrew and English* (4 vols., Jerusalem, 1986–).

Rosenthal, F., *A Grammar of Biblical Aramaic* (Wiesbaden, [2]1963).

Schäfer, P. and Becker, H.-J., with Reeg, G. et al. (eds.), *Synopse zum Talmud Yerushalmi.* סינופסיס לתלמוד הירושלמי (several vols., Tübingen, 1991–).

Schulthess, F., *Lexicon Syropalaestinum* (Berlin, 1903).

Grammatik des christlich-palästinischen Aramäisch (Tübingen, 1924).

Sokoloff, M., *The Targum to Job from Qumran Cave XI* (Ramat Gan, 1974).

A Dictionary of Jewish Palestinian Aramaic of the Byzantine Period (Ramat-Gan, 1990).

Sperber, A. (ed.), *The Bible in Aramaic* (5 vols., Leiden, 1959–73).

Strack, H. L., and Stemberger, L. *Introduction to the Talmud and Midrash* (1982. ET Edinburgh, [2]1996).

Strothmann, W. (ed.), *Jakob von Sarug: Drei Gedichte über den Apostel Thomas in Indien* (Göttinger Orientforschungen, 1 Reihe: Syriaca, vol. 12. Wiesbaden, 1976).

Stuckenbruck, L. T., 'Revision of Aramaic–Greek and Greek–Aramaic Glossaries in *The Books of Enoch: Aramaic Fragments of Qumrân Cave 4*, by J. T. Milik', *JJS* 41, 1990, 13–48.

Tal, A. (ed.), התרגום השומרוני לתורה *The Samaritan Targum of the Pentateuch* (3 vols., Tel-Aviv, 1980–3).

2 Secondary literature

Abrahams, I., 'The Sabbath', *Studies in Pharisaism and the Gospels* (First Series. Cambridge, 1917).

Aejmelaeus, A., 'OTI *causale* in Septuagintal Greek', in N. Fernández Marcos (ed.), *La Septuaginta en la investigación contemporanea (V Congreso de la IOSCS)* (Madrid, 1985), pp. 115–32 = A. Aejmelaeus, *On the Trail of the Septuagint Translators: Collected Essays* (Kampen, 1993), pp. 17–36.

Aichinger, H., 'Quellenkritische Untersuchung der Perikope vom Ähren-raufen am Sabbat Mk 2, 23–28 par', in A. Fuchs (ed.), *Jesus in der Verkündigung der Kirche* (SNTU 1. Linz, 1976), pp. 110–53.

Albrecht, J., et al. (eds.), *Translation und interkulturelle Kommunikation* (FAS A, 8. Frankfurt-on-Main, 1987).

Allison, D. C., 'Elijah Must Come First', *JBL* 103, 1984, 256–8.

Anderson, H., *The Gospel of Mark* (NCB. London, 1976).

Angerstorfer, A., 'Ist 4Q Tg Lev das Menetekel der neueren Targum-forschung?', *BN* 15, 1981, 55–75.

'Überlegungen zu Sprache und Sitz im Leben des Toratargums 4Q Tg Lev (4Q 156), sein Verhältnis zu Targum Onkelos', *BN* 55, 1990, 18–35.

Appel, P. and Muysken, P., *Language Contact and Bilingualism* (London, 1987).

Bacon, B. W., 'Pharisees and Herodians in Mark', *JBL* 39, 1920, 102–12.

Baker, M., *In Other Words: A Coursebook on Translation* (London, 1992).

Banks, R., *Jesus and the Law in the Synoptic Tradition* (MSSNTS 28. Cambridge, 1975).

Barr, J., *The Typology of Literalism in Ancient Bible Translation* (NAWG 11. Göttingen, 1979).

'Which Language Did Jesus Speak? – Some Remarks of a Semitist', *BJRL* 53, 1970–71, 9–29.

'The Hebrew/Aramaic Background of "Hypocrisy" in the Gospels', in P. R. Davies, and R. T. White (eds.), *A Tribute to Geza Vermes: Essays on Jewish and Christian Literature and History* (JSOT. SS 100. Shef-field, 1990), pp. 307–26.

Barrett, C. K., 'The Background of Mark 10.45', in A. J. B. Higgins (ed.), *New Testament Essays: Studies in Memory of T. W. Manson* (Manchester, 1959), pp. 1–18.

'Mark 10.45: A Ransom for Many', *New Testament Essays* (London, 1972), pp. 20–6.

Bass, C. (ed.), *Somatization: Physical Symptoms and Psychological Illness* (London, 1990).

Beare, F. W., 'The Sabbath was Made for Man?', *JBL* 79, 1960, 130–6.

Beattie, D. R. G. 'Boanerges: A Semiticist's Solution', *IBS* 5, 1983, 11–13.

Beattie, D. R. G. and McNamara, M. J. (eds.), *The Aramaic Bible: Targums in their Historical Context* (JSOT. SS 166. Sheffield, 1994).

Berger, P.-R., 'Zum Aramäischen der Evangelien und der Apostel-geschichte', *TRev* 82, 1986, 1–16.

Best, E., *Following Jesus: Discipleship in the Gospel of Mark* (JSNT. SS 4. Sheffield, 1981).

Birkeland, H., *The Language of Jesus* (Avhandlinger utgitt av Det Norske Videnskaps-Akademi i Oslo II. Hist. Filos. Klasse. 1954. No. I. Oslo, 1954).

Black, M., *An Aramaic Approach to the Gospels and Acts* (Oxford, 1946.[2]1954, [3]1967).

'The Recovery of the Language of Jesus', *NTS* 3, 1956–7, 305–13.

'Aramaic Studies and the Language of Jesus', in M. Black, and

G. Fohrer (eds.), *In Memoriam Paul Kahle* (BZAW 103. Berlin, 1968), pp. 17–28, rep. with corrections in Porter (ed.), *Language of the New Testament*, pp. 112–25.

Blum-Kulka, S., 'Shifts of Cohesion and Coherence in Translation', in House and Blum-Kulka (eds.), *Interlingual and Intercultural Communication*, pp. 17–35.

Bokser, B. M., *The Origins of the Seder: The Passover Rite and Early Rabbinic Judaism* (Berkeley, 1984).

Brock, S. P., 'Aspects of Translation Technique in Antiquity', *GRBS* 20, 1979, 69–87.

'Towards a History of Syriac Translation Technique', in R. Lavenant (ed.), *IIIe Symposium Syriacum* (OCA 221, 1983), pp. 1–14, rep. in S. P. Brock, *Studies in Syriac Christianity: History, Literature and Theology* (London, 1992).

'Translating the Old Testament', in D. A. Carson, and H. G. M. Williamson, *It is Written: Scripture Citing Scripture, Essays in Honour of Barnabas Lindars* (Cambridge, 1988), pp. 87–98.

Brown, R. E., *The Death of the Messiah* (2 vols., ABRL. London/New York 1994).

Bultmann, R. K., *Die Geschichte der synoptischen Tradition* (FRLANT 29, N. F. 12. Göttingen, 1921). ET *The History of the Synoptic Tradition* (Oxford, 1963).

Burkett, D., 'The Nontitular Son of Man: A History and Critique', *NTS* 40, 1994, 504–21.

Burney, C. F., *The Aramaic Origin of the Fourth Gospel* (Oxford, 1922).

The Poetry of Our Lord (Oxford, 1925).

Burridge, R. A., *What are the Gospels? A Comparison with Graeco-Roman Biography* (MSSNTS 70. Cambridge, 1992).

Cancik, H. (ed.), *Markus-Philologie: Historische, literargeschichtliche und stilistische Untersuchungen zum zweiten Evangelium* (WUNT 33. Tübingen, 1984).

Carmignac, J., *La Naissance des Evangiles synoptiques* (Paris, 1984).

Casey, P. M., *Son of Man: The Interpretation and Influence of Daniel 7* (London, 1980).

From Jewish Prophet to Gentile God: The Origins and Development of New Testament Christology (The Edward Cadbury Lectures at the University of Birmingham, 1985–6. Cambridge/Louisville, 1991).

Is John's Gospel True? (London, 1996).

'The Son of Man Problem', *ZNW* 67, 1976, 147–65.

'The Jackals and the Son of Man (Matthew 8.20//Luke 9.58)', *JSNT* 23, 1985, 3–22.

'General, Generic and Indefinite: The Use of the Term "Son of Man" in Aramaic Sources and in the Teaching of Jesus', *JSNT* 29, 1987, 21–56.

'Culture and Historicity: The Plucking of the Grain (Mark 2.23–28)', *NTS* 34, 1988, 1–23.

'The Original Aramaic Form of Jesus' Interpretation of the Cup', *JThS* NS 41, 1990, 1–12.

'Method in our Madness, and Madness in their Methods: Some

Approaches to the Son of Man Problem in Recent Scholarship', *JSNT* 42, 1991, 17–43.

'No Cannibals at Passover!', *Theology* 96, 1993, 199–205.

'The Use of the Term (א)שׁנ(א) בר in the Aramaic Translations of the Hebrew Bible' *JSNT* 54, 1994, 87–118.

'Idiom and Translation: Some Aspects of the Son of Man Problem', *NTS* 41, 1995, 164–82.

'Culture and Historicity: The Cleansing of the Temple', *CBQ* 59, 1997, 306–32.

'In Which Language Did Jesus Teach?', *ExpT* 108, 1997, 326–8.

Chilton, B. D., *A Feast of Meanings: Eucharistic Theologies from Jesus through Johannine Circles* (NT. S LXXII. 1994).

"Amen": An Approach through Syriac Gospels', *ZNW* 69, 1978, 203–11.

'Exorcism and History: Mark 1:21–28', in D. Wenham, and C. Blomberg (eds.), *Gospel Perspectives VI* (Sheffield, 1986), pp. 253–71.

Christie, M. J. and Mellett, P. G., *Foundations of Psychosomatics* (Chichester, 1981).

Clyne, M., *Perspectives on Language Contact, Based on a Study of German in Australia* (Melbourne, 1972).

Cohen, B., 'The Rabbinic Law presupposed by Matthew xii. 1 and Luke vi. 1', *HThR* 23, 1930, 91–2.

Cohn-Sherbok, D. M., 'An Analysis of Jesus' Arguments Concerning the Plucking of Grain on the Sabbath', *JSNT* 2, 1979, 31–41.

Colpe, C., 'ὁ υἱὸς τοῦ ἀνθρώπου', *TWNT* VIII (1969).

Dalman, G. H., *Die Worte Jesu*, vol. I, *Einleitung und wichtige Begriffe* (Leipzig, 1898. There was no second volume); ET *The Words of Jesus. I. Introduction and Fundamental Ideas* (Edinburgh, 1902; [2]1930).

Jesus-Jeschua: Die drei Sprachen Jesu (Leipzig, 1922); ET *Jesus-Jeshua: Studies in the Gospels* (London, 1929).

Daube, D., *The New Testament and Rabbinic Judaism* (London, 1956).

Davies, S. L., *Jesus the Healer: Possession, Trance and the Origins of Christianity* (London, 1995).

Davies, W. D., and Allison, D. C., *A Critical and Exegetical Commentary on the Gospel according to Saint Matthew* (3 vols., ICC. Edinburgh, 1988–97).

Delcor, M., 'Le Targum de Job et l'Araméen du temps de Jésus', *RevSR* 47, 1973, 232–61.

Doudna, J. C., *The Greek of the Gospel of Mark* (JBL. MS 12. Philadelphia, 1961).

Downing, J., 'Jesus and Martyrdom', *JThS* NS 14, 1963, 279–93.

Dunn, J. D. G., 'Mark 2.1–3.6: A Bridge between Jesus and Paul on the Question of the Law', *NTS* 30, 1984, 395–415; rev. edn *Jesus, Paul and the Law* (London, 1990), pp. 10–36.

Eck, E. van, and Aarde, A. G. van, 'Sickness and Healing in Mark: A Social Scientific Interpretation', *Neotestamentica* 27, 1993, 27–54.

Eisenberg, L., and Kleinman, A. (eds.), *The Relevance of Social Science for Medicine* (Dordrecht, 1981).

Embleton, S., 'Names and their Substitutes: Onomastic Observations on *Astérix* and its Translations', *Target* 3, 1991, 175–206.

Emerton, J. A., 'Did Jesus Speak Hebrew?', *JThS* NS 12, 1961, 189–202.

'The Problem of Vernacular Hebrew in the First Century A.D. and the Language of Jesus', *JThS* NS 24, 1973, 1–23.

Faierstein, M. M., 'Why Do the Scribes Say that Elijah Must Come First?', *JBL* 100, 1981, 75–86.

Fishman, J. A. (ed.), *The Sociology of Jewish Languages, IJSL* 30 (1981).

(ed.), *Readings in the Sociology of Jewish Languages* (Leiden, 1985).

(ed.), *The Sociology of Jewish Languages, IJSL* 67 (1987).

Fitzmyer, J. A., *Essays on the Semitic Background of the New Testament* (London, 1971, rep. Missoula, 1974).

A Wandering Aramean (SBLMS 25. Missoula, 1979).

The Gospel According to Luke (2 vols., AB 28–28A. New York, 1981–5).

'The Targum of Leviticus from Qumran Cave 4', *Maarav* 1, 1978, 5–23.

'Another View of the "Son of Man" Debate', *JSNT* 4, 1979, 58–68.

'More About Elijah Coming First', *JBL* 104, 1985, 295–6.

'4Q246: The "Son of God" Document from Qumran', *Bib* 74, 1993, 153–74.

'Problems of the Semitic Background of the New Testament', in J. M. O'Brien, and F. L. Horton (eds.), *The Yahweh/Baal Confrontation and Other Studies in Biblical Literature and Archaeology: Essays in Honour of E. W. Harrick* (New York, 1995), pp. 80–93.

'The Aramaic and Hebrew Fragments of Tobit from Qumran Cave 4', *CBQ* 57, 1995, 655–75.

France, R. T., *Jesus and the Old Testament* (London, 1971).

Frank, J. D. and Frank, J. B., *Persuasion and Healing: A Comparative Study of Psychotherapy* (Oxford, 1961. Baltimore, [3]1991).

Geller, M. J., Greenfield, J. C. and Weitzman, M. P., *Studia Aramaica: New Sources and New Approaches* (JSS. S 4. Oxford, 1995).

Glik, D. C., 'Psychosocial Wellness among Spiritual Healing Participants', *Social Science and Medicine* 22, 1986, 579–86.

Gnilka, J., *Das Evangelium nach Markus* (2 vols., EKK II/1–2. Solothurn/ Düsseldorf/Neukirchen, [4]1994).

Good, M.-J. D., Good, B. J. and Fischer, M. J. (eds.), *Emotion, Illness and Healing in Middle Eastern Societies* (*Culture, Medicine and Psychiatry* 12, 1, 1988).

Goulder, M. D., *Luke – A New Paradigm* (2 vols., JSNT. SS 20. Sheffield, 1989).

Greenhut, Z., 'The "Caiaphas" Tomb in North Talpiyot, Jerusalem', *'Atiqot*, 21, 1992, 63–71.

Grelot, P., *L'Origine des Evangiles – Controverse avec J. Carmignac* (Paris, 1986).

Grimm, W., *Die Verkündigung Jesus und Deuterojesaja* (Frankfurt-on-Main, [2]1981).

Gudykunst, W. B. (ed.), *Language and Ethnic Identity* (Philadelphia, 1988).

Gundry, R. H., *Mark – A Commentary on his Apology for the Cross* (Grand Rapids, 1993).

Haenchen, E., *Der Weg Jesu: Eine Erklärung des Markus-Evangeliums und der kanonischen Parallelen* (Berlin, [2]1968).
Halverson, J., 'Oral and Written Gospel: A Critique of Werner Kelber', *NTS* 40, 1994, 180–95.
Hampel, V., *Menschensohn und historischer Jesus – Ein Rätselwort als Schlüssel zum messianischen Selbstverständnis Jesu* (Neukirchen-Vluyn, 1990).
Hengel, R. and Hengel, M., 'Die Heilungen Jesu und medizinisches Denken', in P. Christian and D. Rössler (eds.), *Medicus Viator: Fragen und Gedanken am Wege Richard Siebecks. Eine Festgabe . . . zum 75. Geburtstag* (Tübingen/Stuttgart, 1959), rep. in E. Suhl (ed.), *Der Wunderbegriff im NT* (WdE CCXCV. Darmstadt, 1980), pp. 338–73.
Hoehner, H. W., *Herod Antipas* (MSSNTS 17. Cambridge, 1972).
Hoffmann, C., *An Introduction to Bilingualism* (London/New York, 1991).
Hogan, L. P., *Healing in the Second Temple Period* (NTOA 21. Göttingen/Freibourg, Switzerland, 1992).
Hollenbach, P. W., 'Jesus, Demoniacs, and Public Authorities: A Socio-Historical Study', *JAAR* 49, 1981, 567–88.
Hooker, M. D., *Jesus and the Servant* (London, 1959).
The Gospel According to St Mark (London, 1991).
Horbury, W., 'The Twelve and the Phylarchs', *NTS* 32, 1986, 503–27.
'The "Caiaphas" Ossuaries and Joseph Caiaphas', *PEQ* 126, 1994, 32–48.
Horsley, G. H. R., 'The Fiction of "Jewish Greek"', in G. H. R. Horsley, *New Documents Illustrating Early Christianity, vol. V, Linguistic Essays* (Marrickville, 1989), pp. 5–40.
House, J. and Blum-Kulka, S. (eds.), *Interlingual and Intercultural Communication: Discourse and Cognition in Translation and Second Language Acquisition Studies* (Tübinger Beiträge zur Linguistik 272. Tübingen, 1986).
Howard, G., *The Gospel of Matthew according to a Primitive Hebrew Text* (Macon, 1987); rev. edn, *Hebrew Gospel of Matthew* (Macon, 1995).
Hsu, L. K. and Folstein, M. F., 'Somatoform Disorders in Caucasian and Chinese Americans', *Journal of Nervous and Mental Disease* 185, 1997, 382–7.
Hurst, L. D., 'The Neglected Role of Semantics in the Search for the Aramaic Words of Jesus', *JSNT* 28, 1986, 63–80.
Hurtado, L. W., 'The Gospel of Mark: Evolutionary or Revolutionary Document?', *JSNT* 40, 1990, 15–32.
Jeremias, J., *The Parables of Jesus* (ET London, [2]1963).
The Eucharistic Words of Jesus (2nd ET London, 1966).
The Prayers of Jesus (ET London, 1967).
New Testament Theology, vol. I (London, 1971).
Jonge, M. de, 'The Use of the Word "Anointed" in the Time of Jesus', *NT* 8, 1966, 132–48.
'The Earliest Christian Use of *Christos*: Some Suggestions', *NTS* 32, 1986, 321–43.
'Jesus' Death for Others and the Death of the Maccabean Martyrs', in T. Baarda, et al. (eds.), *Text and Testimony: Essays on New Testament*

and Apocryphal Literature in Honour of A. F. J. Klijn (Kampen, 1988), pp. 142–51.

Joosten, J., *The Syriac Language of the Peshitta and Old Syriac Versions of Matthew: Syntactic Structure, Inner-Syriac Developments and Translation Technique* (Leiden, 1996).

Kaufman, S. A., *The Akkadian Influences on Aramaic* (Assyriological Studies, 19. Chicago, 1974).

'On Methodology in the Study of the Targums and their Chronology', *JSNT* 23, 1985, 117–24.

Kee, H. C., 'The Terminology of Mark's Exorcism Stories', *NTS* 14, 1967–8, 232–46.

Kelber, W. H., *The Oral and the Written Gospel* (Philadelphia, 1983).

Klein, M. L., 'Converse Translation: A Targumic Technique', *Bib* 57, 1976, 515–37.

Kleinman, A., *Patients and Healers in the Context of Culture* (Berkeley/Los Angeles/London, 1980).

Knox, W. L., *The Sources of the Synoptic Gospels. I. St Mark* (Cambridge, 1953).

Kutscher, E. Y., *Studies in Galilean Aramaic* (Hebrew, Jerusalem, 1952. ET Jerusalem, 1976).

'The Language of the Genesis Apocryphon: A Preliminary Study', *Scripta Hierosolymitana IV, Aspects of the Dead Sea Scrolls*, ed. Ch. Rabin and Y. Yadin (Jerusalem, 1957), pp. 1–35.

Labbé, G., 'Ponce Pilate et la munificence de Tibère', *Revue des Etudes Anciennes* 93, 1991, 277–97.

Landy, D., *Culture, Disease and Healing* (New York, 1977).

Lane, W. L., *The Gospel of Mark* (London, 1974).

Lapide, P., 'Insights from Qumran into the Languages of Jesus', *RQ* 8, 1975, 483–501.

Larsen, S. (ed.), *Translation: A Means to an End* (The Dolphin 18. Aarhus, 1990).

Le Déaut, R., 'Goûter le calice de la mort', *Bib* 43, 1962, 82–6.

Lehiste, I., *Lectures on Language Contact* (Cambridge, Mass., 1988).

Lenglet, A., 'La Structure littéraire de Daniel 2–7', *Bib* 53, 1972, 169–90.

Léon-Dufour, X., *Sharing the Eucharistic Bread: The Witness of the New Testament* (1982. ET New York/Mahwah, N.J., 1987).

Leuven-Zwart, K. M. van, and Naaijkens, T., *Translation Studies: The State of the Art*. Proceedings of the First James S. Holmes Symposium on Translation Studies (Amsterdam, 1991).

Lietzmann, H., *Der Menschensohn: Ein Beitrag zur neutestamentlichen Theologie* (Freiburg i. B. /Leipzig, 1896).

Lindars, B., *Jesus Son of Man* (London, 1983).

Lindsey, R. L., *A Hebrew Translation of the Gospel of Mark* (Jerusalem, 1969).

Lohse, E., 'Jesu Worte über den Sabbat', in W. Eltester (ed.), *Judentum-Urchristentum-Kirche*. Festschrift J. Jeremias (BZNW 26. Berlin, 1960), pp. 79–93.

Loisy, A., *Les Evangiles synoptiques* (2 vols., Ceffonds, 1907).

Loos, H. van der *The Miracles of Jesus* (NT. S VIIII. Leiden, 1965).

Lyon, J. P., *Syriac Gospel Translations: A Comparison of the Language and Translation Method used in the Old Syriac, the Diatessaron, and the Peshitta* (CSCO Subs. 88. Leuven, 1994).

Mack, B. L., *A Myth of Innocence: Mark and Christian Origins* (Philadelphia, 1988).

Maloney, E. C., *Semitic Interference in Markan Syntax* (SBLDS 51. Chico, 1981).

Manson, T. W., 'Mark II. 27f', *CNT* 11, 1947, 138–46.

Marcus, J., *The Way of the Lord: Christological Exegesis of the Old Testament in the Gospel of Mark* (Edinburgh, 1993).

'Mark 9, 11–13: "As it Has Been Written"', *ZNW* 80, 1989, 42–63.

Marsella, A. J., and White, G. M. (eds.), *Cultural Concepts of Mental Health and Therapy* (Dordrecht, 1982).

Meier, J. P., *A Marginal Jew: Rethinking the Historical Jesus* (2 vols so far, ABRL. New York, 1991–4).

Meye, R. P., *Jesus and the Twelve: Discipleship and Revelation in Mark's Gospel* (Grand Rapids, 1968).

Meyer, A., *Jesu Muttersprache: Das galiläische Aramäisch in seiner Bedeutung für die Erklärung der Reden Jesu und der Evangelien überhaupt* (Freiburg i. B. /Leipzig, 1896).

Mohr, T. A., *Markus- und Johannespassion* (AThANT 70. Zurich, 1982).

Muraoka, T., 'Notes on the Aramaic of the Genesis Apocryphon', *RQ* 8, 1972, 7–51.

'The Aramaic of the Old Targum of Job from Qumran Cave XI', *JJS* 25, 1974, 425–43.

'Notes on the Old Targum of Job from Qumran Cave XI', *RQ* 9, 1977, 117–25.

'A Study in Palestinian Jewish Aramaic', *Sefarad* 45, 1985, 3–21.

Murmelstein, B., 'Jesu Gang durch die Saatfelder', *Angelos* 3, 1930, 111–20.

Neirynck, F. et al., *The Gospel of Mark: A Cumulative Bibliography 1950–1990* (BEThL CII. Leuven, 1992).

Neubert, A., *Text and Translation* (Übersetzungswissenschaftliche Beiträge 8. Leipzig, 1985).

Neubert, A., and Shreve, G. M. *Translation as Text* (Translation Studies 1. Kent, Ohio, 1992).

Nineham, D. E., *Saint Mark* (Harmondsworth, 1963).

Nord, C., 'Scopos, Loyalty, and Translational Conventions', *Target* 3, 1991, 91–109.

Ogg, G., 'The Chronology of the Last Supper', in D. E. Nineham et al., *Historicity and Chronology in the New Testament* (London, 1965), pp. 75–96.

Ott, H., 'Um die Muttersprache Jesu: Forschungen seit Gustaf Dalman', *NT* 9, 1967, 1–25.

Owen, A. R. G., *Hysteria, Hypnosis and Healing: The Work of J.-M. Charcot* (London, 1971).

Parker, D. C., *Codex Bezae: An Early Christian Manuscript and its Text* (Cambridge, 1992).

Parker, D. C. and Amphoux, C.-B. (eds.), *Codex Bezae: Studies from the Lunel Colloquium June 1994* (NTTS XXII. Leiden, 1996).

Pattison, E. M., Lapins, N. A. and Doerr, H. A., 'Faith Healing: A Study of Personality and Function', *Journal of Nervous and Mental Disease* 157, 1973, 397–409.

Pesch, R., *Das Abendmahl und Jesu Todesverständnis* (QD 80. Freiburg/ Basle/Vienna, 1978).

Porter, S. E., 'Did Jesus Ever Teach in Greek?', *TynBull* 44, 1993, 199–235; revised as 'Jesus and the Use of Greek in Galilee', in B. Chilton and C. A. Evans (eds.), *Studying the Historical Jesus: Evaluations of the State of Current Research* (NTTS XIX. Leiden, 1994), pp. 123–54.

Porter, S. E. (ed.), *The Language of the New Testament: Classic Essays* (JSNT. SS 60. Sheffield, 1991).

Pryke, E. J., *Redactional Style in the Markan Gospel* (MSSNTS 33. Cambridge, 1978).

Reiser, M., *Syntax und Stil des Markusevangeliums* (WUNT II, 11. Tübingen, 1984).

Reiß, K. and Vermeer, H.-J., *Grundlegung einer allgemeinen Translationstheorie* (Linguistische Arbeiten 147. Tübingen, 1984).

Riley, H., *The Making of Mark: An Exploration* (Macon, 1989).

Rüger, H. P., 'Die lexikalischen Aramaismen im Markusevangelium', in Cancik (ed.), *Markus-Philologie*, pp. 73–84.

Sanders, E. P., *Jesus and Judaism* (London, 1985).

Jewish Law from Jesus to the Mishnah (London, 1990).

'Priorités et dépendances dans la tradition synoptique', *RSR* 60, 1972, 519–40.

Schiffman, L. H., *The Halakhah at Qumran* (SJLA XVI. Leiden, 1975).

Schmidt, H. (ed.), *Interferenz in der Translation* (Übersetzungswissenschaftliche Beiträge 12. Leipzig, 1989).

Schwarz, G., *'Und Jesus sprach'. Untersuchungen zur aramäischen Urgestalt der Worte Jesu* (BWANT 118 = VI, 18; Stuttgart, 1985, [2]1987).

Jesus 'der Menschensohn': Aramaistische Untersuchungen zu den synoptischen Menschensohnworten Jesu (BWANT 119 = VI, 19; Stuttgart, 1986).

Jesus und Judas: Aramaistische Untersuchungen zur Jesus-Judas-Überlieferung der Evangelien und der Apostelgeschichte (BWANT 123. Stuttgart, 1988).

Schweizer, E., *The Good News according to Mark* (London, 1971).

Seeley, D., 'Rulership and Service in Mark 10:41–45', *NT* 35, 1993, 234–51.

Séguinot, T. C., 'The Editing Function of Translation', *Bulletin of the Canadian Association of Applied Linguistics* 4, 1982, 151–61.

Selinker, L., 'Language Transfer', *General Linguistics* 9, 1969, 67–92.

'Interlanguage', *International Review of Applied Linguistics* 10, 1972, 209–31.

Snell-Hornby, M., Pöchhacker, F. and Kaindl, K. (eds.), *Translation Studies: An Interdiscipline. Selected papers from the Translation Studies Congress, Vienna, 9–12 Sept. 1992* (Amsterdam/Philadelphia, 1994).

Sokoloff, M., 'The Current State of Research on Galilean Aramaic', *JNES* 37, 1978, 161–7.

Stacey, M., *The Sociology of Health and Healing* (London, 1988).
Stuckenbruck, L. T., 'Revision of Aramaic–Greek and Greek–Aramaic Glossaries in *The Books of Enoch: Aramaic Fragments of Qumrân Cave 4*, by J. T. Milik', *JJS* 41, 1990, 13–48.
'An Approach to the New Testament through Aramaic Sources: The Recent Methodological Debate', *JSP* 8, 1994 (*sic!*), 3–29, esp. 17–28.
Švejcer, A. D., 'Literal Translation as a Product of Interference', in Schmidt (ed.), *Interferenz*, pp. 39–44.
Taylor, R. A., *The Peshiṭta of Daniel* (MPI. VII. Leiden, 1994).
Taylor, V., *The Gospel According to St. Mark* (London, 1952).
Torrey, C. C., *The Four Gospels: A New Translation* (London, 1933).
Our Translated Gospels (London, 1937).
Tov, E., 'Transliteration of Hebrew Words in the Greek Versions of the Old Testament', *Textus* 8, 1973, 78–92.
'Die griechischen Bibelübersetzungen', *ANRW* II. 20.1 (1987) pp. 121–89.
'The Septuagint', in *Mikra* (ed. M. J. Mulder and H. Sysling; CRINT II, 1. Assen/Maastricht/Philadelphia, 1988), pp. 161–88.
Turner, N., 'The Language of Jesus and his Disciples', in *Grammatical Insights into the New Testament* (Edinburgh, 1965), pp. 174–88, reprinted in Porter (ed.), *Language of the New Testament*, pp. 174–90.
Twelftree, G., *Jesus the Exorcist* (WUNT 2, 54. Tübingen, 1993).
Vermes, G., *Jesus the Jew* (London, 1973).
'The Use of בר נשא/בר נש in Jewish Aramaic', App. E in Black, *Aramaic Approach* ([3]1967), pp. 310–28; rep. in G. Vermes, *Post-Biblical Jewish Studies* (Leiden, 1975), pp. 147–65.
'The Present State of the "Son of Man" Debate', *JJS* 29, 1978, 123–34.
'The "Son of Man" Debate', *JSNT* 1, 1978, 19–32.
Vielhauer, P., 'Gottesreich und Menschensohn in der Verkündigung Jesu', in W. Schneemelcher (ed.), *Festschrift für Gunter Dehn* (Neukirchen, 1957), pp. 51–79.
Weinert, F. J., '4Q 159: Legislation for an Essene Community outside of Qumran?', *JSJ* 5, 1974, 179–207.
Weiss, W., *'Eine neue Lehre in Vollmacht': Die Streit- und Schulgespräche des Markusevangeliums* (BZNW 52. 1989).
Wellhausen, J., *Skizzen und Vorarbeiten* VI (Berlin, 1899).
Das Evangelium Marci (Berlin, 1903).
Einleitung in die drei ersten Evangelien (Berlin, [2]1911).
Wensinck, A. J., 'The Semitisms of Codex Bezae and their Relation to the non-Western Text of the Gospel of Saint Luke', *Bulletin of the Bezan Club* 12 (Leiden, 1937), pp. 11–48.
Wickramasekera, I. E., 'Somatization: Concepts, Data, and Predictions from the High Risk Model of Threat Perception', *Journal of Nervous and Mental Disease* 183, 1995, 15–23.
Wierzbicka, A., 'Different Cultures, Different Languages, Different Speech Acts: Polish vs. English', *Journal of Pragmatics* 9, 1985, 145–78.
Wilcox, M., 'Semitisms in the New Testament', *ANRW* II. 25.2 (1984), pp. 978–1029.

'The Aramaic Background of the New Testament', in Beattie and McNamara, *Aramaic Bible*, pp. 362–78.

Wilkinson, J., *Health and Healing: Studies in NT Principles and Practice* (Edinburgh, 1980).

Yardeni, A., 'New Jewish Aramaic Ostraca', *IEJ* 40, 1990, 130–52.

York, A. D., 'The Dating of Targumic Literature', *JSJ* 5, 1974, 49–62.

Zimmermann, F., *The Aramaic Origin of the Four Gospels* (New York, 1979).

INDEX OF PASSAGES DISCUSSED

INDEX OF NAMES AND SUBJECTS